Contingent Valuation of Environmental Goods

A Comprehensive Critique

Edited by

Daniel McFadden

*Department of Economics, University of C[...]
USA*

Kenneth Train

*Department of Economics, University of C[...]
USA*

Cheltenham, UK • Northampton, MA, USA

Contents

Contributing authors		vii
Acknowledgment		ix
Introduction		x
Daniel McFadden and Kenneth Train		

1	Response to cost prompts in stated preference valuation of environmental goods *James Burrows, Powell Dixon, and Hiu Man Chan*	1
2	Fat tails and truncated bids in contingent valuation: an application to an endangered shorebird species *George Parsons and Kelley Myers*	17
3	Inadequate response to frequency of payments in contingent valuation of environmental goods *Kelley Myers, George Parsons, and Kenneth Train*	43
4	An adding-up test on contingent valuations of river and lake quality *William Desvousges, Kristy Mathews, and Kenneth Train*	58
5	Do contingent valuation estimates of willingness to pay for non-use environmental goods pass the scope test with adequacy? A review of the evidence from empirical studies in the literature *James Burrows, Rebecca Newman, Jerry Genser, and Jeffrey Plewes*	82
6	Stated preference methods and their applicability to environmental use and non-use valuations *Daniel McFadden*	153
7	Some findings from further exploration of the "composite good" approach to contingent valuation *Michael Kemp, Edward Leamer, James Burrows, and Powell Dixon*	188

8	Inferences from stated preference surveys when some respondents do not compare costs and benefits *Edward Leamer and Josh Lustig*	224
9	Assessing the validity of stated preference data using follow-up questions *Kelley Myers, Doug MacNair, Ted Tomasi, and Jude Schneider*	252
10	Hypothetical bias: a new meta-analysis *Harry Foster and James Burrows*	270
11	Legal obstacles for contingent valuation methods in environmental litigation *Brian D. Israel, Jean Martin, Kelly Smith Fayne, and Lauren Daniel*	292

Index 307

Contributing authors

James Burrows, Vice Chairman, Charles River Associates, Boston, USA

Hiu Man Chan, Vice President, Analysis Group, Boston, USA

Lauren Daniel, Associate, Arnold & Porter Kaye Scholer, LLP

William Desvousges, W.H. Desvousges & Associates, Raleigh, NC, USA

Powell Dixon, Associate Principal, Charles River Associates, Boston, USA

Kelly Smith Fayne, Associate, Latham & Watkins, LLP

Harry Foster, Principal, Charles River Associates, Boston, USA

Jerry Genser, Associate, Charles River Associates, Boston, USA

Brian D. Israel, Partner, Arnold & Porter Kaye Scholer, LLP

Michael Kemp, Senior Consultant, Charles River Associates, Boston, USA

Edward Leamer, Chauncey J. Medberry Professor in Management and Professor in Economics & Statistics at UCLA

Josh Lustig, Principal, Charles River Associates, Boston, USA

Doug MacNair, Technical Director, Economics and Decision Sciences, ERM, Raleigh, NC, USA

Jean Martin, Senior Counsel, BP America Inc.

Kristy Mathews, Independent Consultant

Daniel McFadden, E. Morris Cox Professor of Economics, University of California, Berkeley, USA

Kelley Myers, Senior Economist, Cardno, Newark, DE, USA

Rebecca Newman, Associate, Charles River Associates, Boston, USA

George Parsons, Professor, School of Marine Science & Policy and Department of Economics, University of Delaware, USA

Jeffrey Plewes, Principal, Charles River Associates, Boston, USA

Jude Schneider, Senior Consultant, Cardno, Santa Barbara, CA, USA

Ted Tomasi, Vice President, Cardno, Newark, DE, USA

Kenneth Train, Adjunct Professor Emeritus of Economics, University of California, Berkeley, USA

Acknowledgment

The research presented in this book (with the exception of Chapter 6) was partially funded by BP Exploration & Production Inc. Dee Compson provided helpful editorial comments and corrections. The research conclusions and opinions contained in this volume are solely those of the authors.

Introduction
Daniel McFadden and Kenneth Train

Contingent valuation (CV) is a procedure that attempts to estimate the value to households of public goods. While CV can be used in many contexts, we consider its use for evaluating environmental goods. The method is implemented through a survey of households. Respondents are given a detailed description of a program that will improve the environment, such as protecting wilderness areas from development or repairing coral reefs. Each respondent is asked whether they would vote in favor or against a ballot measure to fund the project at a specified cost to each household. The cost is varied over respondents, and the share of respondents who say that they would vote in favor is tabulated for each cost level. These shares are then used to estimate the mean willingness to pay (WTP) for the program. The method is sometimes revised to ask each respondent to make choices among several different programs at different costs, instead of just one. For convenience, we use the term CV as encompassing the traditional referendum method as well as these variations.

This book is born of our concern about the reliability of CV. We have collected a series of papers, two previously published and nine new in this book, that tell a unified story about CV. We describe each of the studies briefly below, as a way of introducing them to the reader. Bringing the papers together in one volume allows a picture of CV to emerge that could not, we think, be obtained from any one paper alone. Our narrative is intended to bring out the connection among the papers.

INADEQUATE RESPONSE TO COST

CV studies ask respondents whether they are WTP a specified dollar amount for a program or improvement that has been described to them. Different dollar amounts – called cost prompts, or bids – are asked of different respondents to obtain the variation in cost that is needed to estimate mean WTP. The question arises: how sensitive are CV estimates to the researchers' choice of cost prompts? The answer seems to be: tremendously.

Burrows, Dixon, and Chan (Chapter 1) examined this issue for a prominent CV study conducted by NOAA[1] on WTP for the preservation of marine species, using the original study's data. The survey included several designs with cost prompts that were twice and half, respectively, the costs used in the main survey design. In these variants, one sample of respondents was presented with prompts that ranged from $5 to $50, and another sample of respondents was given prompts ranging from $20 to $200. The original study's report only presented results for the main design; it did not report how the estimates differed under the alternative sets of prompts. Burrows, Dixon, and Chan performed the relevant calculations and found that the estimated WTP was three times greater with the higher-cost prompts than with the lower prompts. That is, raising the cost prompts by a factor of four raised the estimated WTP for the program by a factor of three. This result is consistent with the view that respondents take the cost prompts as a suggestion of the amount that is reasonable to pay and adjust their concepts of their own WTP in relation to these prompts. As a result, CV is not actually estimating a true WTP, but rather is creating an estimated WTP through the researcher's choice of the cost prompts.

Parsons and Myers (Chapter 2) examine the issue of cost prompts from a different perspective. They review CV studies and find that the estimated WTP depends greatly on the highest cost prompt. They find that the share of "yes" votes – that is, the share of respondents who say they are WTP the specified cost prompt – stays relatively high no matter how large the cost prompt is. They call this the "fat tails" phenomenon. To investigate how far the fat tail extends, Parsons and Myers conducted a study about protecting the red knot, a migratory shorebird whose population has declined in recent years. In this study, they kept raising the highest cost prompt, asking new samples of respondents ever-higher prompts, and found that the yes share never approached zero. They raised the prompt as high as $10,000, and still 23% of the CV respondents said that, yes, they would be willing to pay $10,000. The estimated mean WTP ranged from $102 to $2,254, depending on the highest cost prompt that they used. Their study suggests that (essentially) any estimated WTP can be obtained through specification of the highest cost prompt.

---

[1] National Oceanic and Atmospheric Administration.

INADEQUATE RESPONSE TO THE NUMBER OF PAYMENTS

CV studies can specify the cost prompt as a one-time payment, annual payments over a period of time, or other payment schedules. The question arises: is the estimated present value willingness to pay (PV WTP), which is the relevant measure for resource allocation decisions, sensitive to the payment schedule that is specified in the CV study? The answer is: yes.

Myers, Parsons, and Train (Chapter 3) review studies that have examined this issue. All of the past studies find that results differ greatly depending on how the payment schedule is specified, with the estimated PV WTP being far greater when the researcher specifies a series of periodic payments rather than a one-time, lump-sum payment. The implicit discount rate that reconciles the CV responses under different payment schedules has been found in all studies to be implausibly high. In addition to their literature review, Myers, Parsons, and Train implemented a CV study to compare one-time and annual payments. They found that the estimated PV WTP is 32 times larger when the cost prompt is specified as annual payments than when the cost prompt is specified as a one-time payment.

INADEQUATE RESPONSE TO SCOPE

One of the most important issues in CV is whether CV estimates reflect the scope of the environmental good that is described to respondents. An early influential study (Boyle et al., 1994) found, for example, that CV estimates of WTP to protect birds were essentially the same whether respondents were told that 2,000 birds would be saved or 200,000 birds. Controversy about this issue led NOAA to convene an expert panel to provide guidelines for CV studies. The panel stated (Arrow et al., 1993, p. 38) that a CV study would be deemed unreliable if it exhibited "[i]nadequate responsiveness to the scope of the environmental insult." The panel stated that the burden of proof for demonstrating adequate response must rest with the researchers who conducted the CV study.

As discussed by Desvousges, Mathews, and Train (Chapter 4), out of the hundreds of CV studies that have been conducted, only one has tested for adequate response to scope – despite the expert panel's requirement. This one study concluded that its CV responses evidenced inadequate response. To extend this line of inquiry, Desvousges, Mathews, and Train implemented an "adding-up" test on a prominent and well-funded CV survey. The test examines whether the estimated WTP for each component of a multi-part program, when evaluated incrementally, sum up to the estimated WTP for the whole program – as required by the definition of WTP. They found that the test fails: the sum of the parts is estimated to be valued three times more than the whole. This finding suggests that respondents' answers to CV questions reflect their expression of interest in the *concept* of an improvement, rather than the scope of the actual improvement that is described to them.

A scope test has often been applied to determine whether there is *any* response to scope, as opposed to the response being adequate in magnitude. Burrows, Newman, Genser, and Plewes (Chapter 5) review the CV studies that have conducted external scope tests[2] and find that more studies fail the test than pass it. That is: more often than not, CV studies don't find *any* response to scope, much less an adequate response. The authors show that previous reviews that have found otherwise (i.e., that passing a scope test is more common than failing) have ignored many studies that failed, have inappropriately included internal tests, and have interpreted results as representing a pass when there is insufficient or contradictory evidence for this inference. Interestingly, the incidence of scope failures has risen over time as the quality of studies has presumably improved, which suggests that the failures cannot be attributed in general to faulty design of the studies but seem instead to be intrinsic to the CV procedure.

DIFFICULTY ANSWERING CV QUESTIONS

Why do CV studies evidence inadequate response to cost, the frequency of payments, and the scope of the program? McFadden (Chapter 6) reviews the history of stated preference (SP) elicitation in general and examines studies that have used these methods in various fields. He identifies the features of a study, and of the good being evaluated, that affect the reliability of the method. He concludes that CV studies of environmental goods possess the very features that make SP elicitation least reliable. The main problem is that respondents are unfamiliar with making choices about environmental goods. The respondent, struggling to provide meaningful answers to CV questions, is susceptible to suggestion by the survey instrument (especially the cost prompt) and to substituting general political concerns for the specific, but unanswerable, personal valuation question.

The difficulty that respondents have in answering CV questions about

---

[2] An external test uses a split-sample design, where one sample is asked about a program with a specified scope and another sample is asked about a program with a greater (or smaller) scope.

environmental goods seems to be evidenced neurologically. Khaw et al. (2015) measured brain activity of respondents in choice exercises for four classes of goods: snack food, market goods, daily activities, and environmental proposals. For the first three classes, activity was evidenced in the traditional valuational area of the brain, as expected. However, for the environmental proposals, activity was not evidenced in this valuational area. Instead neurological activity appeared in a region of the brain that is associated with cognitive control and shifting decision strategies. Neural measurement is fairly new in economics, and further research is required before conclusions can be drawn. But at face value, the results are consistent with McFadden's assessment that respondents do not know how to approach the CV questions about environmental goods and are struggling for ways to approach the task.

What makes the task so difficult? At least part of the problem is thinking about a budget constraint in the context of environmental goods. A respondent can think that paying $100 to clean up a polluted lake sounds reasonable but then might start to wonder about the thousands of other lakes that need cleaning up, and realize that paying $100 for each of them is impossible. The respondent might then remember all the birds and other species that need protection, and people dying of curable diseases who could be helped with some money for medicine. The respondent faces a quandary about allocation among public goods that the CV survey ignores by asking about only one public good.[3]

Kemp, Leamer, Burrows, and Dixon (Chapter 7) examine the issue of respondents' budget awareness by asking WTP in several ways, including the traditional CV single-focus referendum and by walking the respondent explicitly through a budget allocation task for components of a much larger environmental protection program. The authors found that the estimated mean WTP for a specified project is about $120 when asked in the traditional way but only $2 to $3 when the respondent budgets components of the composite good. And several findings of their study point to pervasive respondent difficulties in thinking about the costs of environmental goods in relation to one another and to other public goods.

But does a budget constraint even come into play when people answer CV questions? The fundamental assumption of CV is that respondents, in giving their response to the cost prompt, are trading off the costs of the program with the benefits. However, as explained above, respondents seem

---

[3] If the respondent gets so far as to think of the "ordering" problem for public good allocations, then the respondent will also realize that the socially optimal order is not reflected in what projects CV researchers happen to do surveys about.

to have a hard time answering the CV question about WTP for environmental goods. The problem of how to think about the budget constraint in this context, and respondents' sense that the survey is an opportunity to send messages (about, say, culpability or politics) can lead the respondent to answer in ways that do not represent a trade-off of the benefits of the specified program with the cost prompt that they are offered. To examine this issue, Leamer and Lustig (Chapter 8) estimated a latent class model in which each class represents a decision-making process that the respondent might use. The traditional compensatory utility model with a trade-off between costs and benefits is represented by one class, and other decision heuristics are represented by other classes. The shares of respondents using each decision process were estimated as parameters. The authors found that fewer than 25% of respondents seem to be trading off benefits and costs; the other 75% are using decision rules that do not incorporate trade-offs and for which there is no WTP.

THE SEARCH FOR APPROPRIATE CORRECTIONS

It has been suggested that CV samples can be restricted, through the use of follow-up questions, to the "core" of respondents who seem to be answering the CV question appropriately. Past studies have considered eliminating respondents who say they are unsure of their answer, or say that they think the survey is inconsequential, or say that they considered the impact of the program on jobs or other non-environmental outcomes. Each of these studies has generally looked at one issue only, determining the effect of eliminating respondents who do not adhere correctly with respect to that one issue. Myers, MacNair, Tomasi, and Schneider (Chapter 9) apply the procedure to all the issues in combination. They use follow-up questions to address the various issues that past articles have examined only one by one. They find that, out of a sample of 1,224, only two respondents are not eliminated. That is, the "core" group of respondents that seem to be answering the CV question appropriately consists of only two people. And both of these people voted against the specified program.

Similarly, it has been suggested that CV estimates can perhaps be adjusted to account for hypothetical bias, that is, for the bias that arises because the data are for hypothetical programs and payments rather than real ones. The idea behind this suggestion is that, for some kinds of goods, estimates of value can be obtained in both hypothetical and actual settings, and the ratio of these estimates (called the "bias ratio") can perhaps be used to adjust CV estimates for their inherent hypothetical nature. Foster and Burrows (Chapter 10) examine this possibility, using 432 comparisons between paired estimates in hypothetical and real settings drawn from previous studies. They find that the bias ratios vary greatly, with no ratio being "typical" or common. Using regression analysis, they find that only a small portion of the variation can be explained by attributes of the study or product. The bias ratios in past studies vary so greatly and with so little explainable pattern that they provide no reliable guidance for adjusting CV estimates.

LEGAL ISSUES

Given these issues about the reliability of CV to estimate WTP, how have CV results actually been used in decision-making processes, especially litigation? Lawyers Israel, Martin, Fayne, and Daniel (Chapter 11) review the history of CV in litigation and find that CV results have not been relied upon by any court and have been explicitly rejected in a few cases. The authors describe the legal requirements for reliability of damage estimates in court cases. They conclude that it is doubtful that CV estimates of environmental damages can, or could, meet these requirements. On the regulatory front, the authors point out that natural resource damage (NRD) regulations strongly disfavor CV, allowing it as a last resort to be used only when other methods are not possible. The authors show that the other, more favored methods can practically always be applied. They describe the *Deepwater Horizon* oil spill as a case in point, where the trustees were able to (and did) use non-CV methods of valuation despite the extent and variety of resources affected by the spill.

A CONCLUDING THOUGHT

One additional issue needs to be discussed, because it seems to get to the heart of the CV debate. There seems to be a view that supporting CV is pro-environmental and criticizing CV is anti-environmental. This is a deeply dangerous view. Importantly, results-driven science has an uncanny tendency to circumvent the instigators' intentions. CV can indeed be used to claim large damages against responsible parties (RPs), which seems, in itself, to be a pro-environmental outcome. But CV is used for restoration programs as well as environmental injury, and it gives large benefits for restoration programs. This side of CV provides an incredible boon to RPs, by allowing them to pay off their debts to society at pennies on the dollar. RPs are legally allowed, and in fact expected, to implement restoration projects to compensate for the environmental damage that they inflicted. CV studies estimate large benefits for environmental projects that cost very little.

Consider, for example, NOAA's study of reef protection (Bishop et al., 2011). This CV study estimated that a program to repair five acres of reefs a year provides a social benefit of $7.3 billion per year. The cost of repairing five acres of reefs has been estimated to be $13.2 million dollars or less (Edwards and Gomez, 2007) – giving a benefit–cost ratio of 553. If CV is actually considered to be reliable, then an RP can rightfully claim $7.3 billion in compensatory restoration by spending $13.2 million on reef repair.

Let's put this into the context of the *Deepwater Horizon* oil spill. A CV study of the spill (Bishop et al., 2016) estimated that households' WTP to avoid a future spill was $15.3 billion or $17.2 billion, depending on how the harm from the spill was described to respondents.[4] Assuming the restoration benefits derived in the study by Bishop et al. (2011), a responsible party could repair five acres of reef per year for three years, creating compensatory benefits of $21.9 billion. So, if CV estimates are believed to be reliable, a responsible party would be able to more than fully compensate the public for the entirety of the *Deepwater Horizon* natural resource damages by paying just $13.2 million per year for three years – less than $40 million in total.

Anti-environmental outcomes like this are the inevitable consequence of CV's inadequate response to scope. The ramifications are wider than the issue of assessing compensation by responsible parties. In benefit–cost analysis, CV tilts the calculations against large environmental improvements. Small measures with relatively little environmental impact (e.g., repairing 15 acres of reef) obtain higher benefit–cost ratios than larger projects with substantial impact (preventing another Gulf spill) because, by CV, the former have about the same benefit as the latter but cost far less. Recognizing CV's unreliability – especially the form it takes – is not just scientifically responsible: it is ecologically responsible.

---

[4] As we stated above, the trustees did not use CV results in their valuation; see the discussion in Israel, Martin, Fayne, and Daniel in Chapter 11 this volume. Nevertheless, the trustees funded a CV study that obtained these numbers, which were then not used in the NRD valuation.

REFERENCES

Arrow, K., R. Solow, P. Portney, E. Leamer, R. Radner, and H. Schuman (1993), *Report of the NOAA Panel on Contingent Valuation*, accessed November 25, 2016 at http://www.economia.unimib.it/DATA/moduli/7_6067/materiale/noaa%20report.pdf.

Bishop, R. and the Total Value Team (2016), "Technical Memo TM-11: Aggregate estimate of total loss value" (Revised Draft), dated January 25, 2016, to Katherine Pease, NOAA, accessed November 25, 2016 at https://www.fws.gov/doiddata/dwh-ar-documents/980/DWH-AR0302133.pdf.

Bishop, R., D. Chapman, B. Kanninen, J. Krosnick, B. Leeworthy, and N. Meade (2011), *Total Economics Value for Protecting and Restoring Hawaiian Coral Reef Ecosystems (Final Report)*, accessed November 28, 2016 at http://docs.lib.noaa.gov/noaa_documents/NOS/CRCP/TM_CRCP/TM_CRCP_16.pdf.

Boyle, K., W. Desvousges, F. Johnson, R. Dunford, and S. Hudson (1994), "An investigation of part-whole biases in contingent valuation studies," *Journal of Environmental Economics and Management*, **27**(1), 64–83.

Edwards, A. and E. Gomez (2007), *Reef Restoration Concepts and Guidelines: Making Sensible Management Choices in the Face of Uncertainty*, St Lucia, Australia: Coral Reef Targeted Research & Capacity Building for Management Programme.

Khaw, M., D. Grab, M. Livermore, C. Vossler, and P. Glimcher (2015), "The measurement of subjective value and its relation to contingent valuation and environmental public goods," *PLOS ONE*, **10**(7), e0132842, DOI:10.1371/journal.pone.0132842.

1. Response to cost prompts in stated preference valuation of environmental goods[1]

James Burrows, Powell Dixon, and Hiu Man Chan[2]

INTRODUCTION

The stated preference discrete choice experiment, also known as conjoint analysis, is now a standard method for estimating non-use values of natural resources from respondents' answers to survey questions.[3] A choice experiment (CE) consists of a sequence of choices among several options, each offering various combinations of features together with costs (often expressed as taxes imposed on each household over some number of years). Through their choices respondents are presumed to reveal whether they would accept a given cost in exchange for a better level of a natural resource. These hypothetical "votes" are then fed into econometric models to produce willingness-to-pay (WTP) estimates, both individual and aggregate, which are the ultimate objects of interest in most applications.[4] In the standard random utility model (RUM) widely used for inferring WTP from data from choice experiments, the underlying utility functions are

---

[1] The authors gratefully acknowledge the essential contributions to this chapter by Drazen Prelec, Ed Leamer, Renee Miller-Mizia, Jerome Genser, and Stamatia Kostakis.

[2] Respectively, Vice Chairman, Charles River Associates; Associate Principal, Charles River Associates; Vice President, Analysis Group.

[3] Boxall et al. (1996) commented: "For approximately 30 years contingent valuation (CVM) methods have been employed by economists to value environmental goods and services... Other types of [stated preference] approaches capable of eliciting environmental preferences have not been widely used in environmental valuation." According to Hanley et al. (1998), the choice experiment ("CE") technique had not been applied to environmental management problems until 1994 by Adamowicz et al., and the first application of the technique to estimating non-use or passive use values was as late as 1998 by Adamowicz et al. By 2008, however, Bateman et al. indicated that CE "has become the most popular approach for valuing a range of multi-attribute public goods."

[4] See Train (2009) and Hensher et al. (2015), commonly used reference texts for discrete choice modeling.

assumed to be logit and uniform throughout the cost distribution. Under these assumptions, the estimated WTPs should be independent of the cost scale, as long as the cost scale is in a range in which some respondents select a do-nothing option and some select a do-something option.

Because of the unfamiliar nature of many environmental improvements, and the unfamiliar task of evaluating a non-market good, survey respondents may not know their WTP for environmental amenities or even how to think about their WTP. To perform the choice tasks, the respondents may look for clues in the survey to assist in determining what they think is an appropriate or reasonable WTP. In particular, the costs that are offered in the survey might affect what respondents think they are, or should be, willing to pay. If the effect is small, then it can perhaps be ignored, but if two studies that present different costs but are otherwise identical lead to large differences in willingness-to-pay estimates, it would be inappropriate to assume – without additional analysis – that either set reveals respondents' prior valuations of the natural resource.

A number of studies have documented cost-anchoring effects (or starting-point bias) in double-bounded or multiple-bounded dichotomous choice CV surveys, in which respondents are presented with follow-up valuation questions after the first valuation question – examples include Silverman and Klock (1989), Herriges and Shogren (1996), Green et al. (1998), Fryklbom and Shogren (2000), and Flachaire et al. (2007). Other studies, including most notably Ariely et al. (2003), have shown anchoring effects of costs that respondents see outside of the survey itself (for example, costs seen in a different context in advance of the survey or in test questions for the survey).

Several studies have examined the influence of cost scales on WTPs estimated from CV surveys; these differences generally arise not from the effects of cost anchoring but on the effects of truncating responses in the tails of the distribution, which can affect estimated WTPs if the missing observations do not accord with the functional form of the assumed distribution function. Cameron and Huppert (1989) examine the impact of truncating higher tails of the cost vector and find that this can change the estimated WTPs. They conclude that:

> [. . .]it seems that an unscrupulous researcher could readily influence the estimated total value of the resource by appropriately tailoring the upper intervals of the payment card, making a judicious choice of the arbitrary "midpoint" for that interval, and then selecting either the medians or the means in order to achieve the desired effect. (Cameron and Huppert, 1989, p. 241)

Duffield and Patterson (1991) focus on the selection of the measure of central tendency and the question of sample allocation. They find through simulation that the optimal sample allocation is sensitive to the measure chosen by the analyst. Cooper and Loomis (1992) evaluate the sensitivity of WTP estimates to the bid range and the size of the bid intervals. They report fluctuations in their WTP measures with respect to both the range of bids and coarseness of bid intervals ranging from a 63% decrease in WTP to a 37% increase in WTP. Cooper and Loomis (1992) find their preferred WTP measure is particularly sensitive to the higher bid levels. With respect to the bid intervals, Cooper and Loomis (1992) find that while the effect on WTP can be large in magnitude, its affect is generally unpredictable.

Only a handful of studies have examined the effects of cost scales on estimated WTPs in CE surveys (see Table 1). With respect to use amenities, Ryan and Wordsworth (2000) assess the sensitivity of estimates of WTP for different attributes of cervical screening, including the cost attribute. The two split samples vary both the cost scale and the scales of two of the attributes (time to receive results and chance of dying from cervical cancer), considerably complicating the interpretation of their results. They find that the WTPs for four of the five attributes they measured are different between the low-cost sample and the high-cost sample, but two of these are not in the expected direction. They also find that when "the overall estimated WTP for a hypothetical policy change was considered, WTP estimates were shown not to differ substantially across the two estimates." Carlsson and Martinsson (2008) analyze the WTP for reducing power outages, using a base cost scale of 150, 200, 275, and 375 kroner and a high-cost scale that is 200 kroner higher at each point (an average increase in cost of 80%), and report an average WTP increase of 105%. Mørkbak et al. (2010) analyze the effects of increasing just the maximum price (from 65 kroner to 80 or 120 kroner) in a cost scale on the WTP for minced pork, and find increases in WTPs of 21.7–68.31%. They observe that at the higher maximum prices fewer respondents say yes.

With respect to non-use amenities, in a study of WTP to protect nature areas from motorized roadway development, Ladenburg and Olsen (2008) find that an increase in the cost vector from 100 and 200 kroner to 400 and 1,100 kroner in an instructional pre-test question has a significant effect on their WTP measure. However, their finding of a significant effect is limited to females only. In a split sample survey valuing river health improvements in which the cost attribute varies by a factor of 3 (£0.67, 1.67, 3.67, 5, 8 vs 2, 5, 11, 15, 24), Hanley et al. (2005) estimate mean WTP to be 73–113% greater for all attributes in the high-cost survey version. However, the WTP differences are not statistically significant. The authors report that a larger fraction of respondents (25% vs 17%) reject any option but the status quo

Table 1 Summary of cost scale studies

Author	Year	Amenity	Fielded Surveys	Completed Surveys	Cost Scales (High) (Low)	Use/ Non-use	Effects
Ryan and Wordsworth	2000	Cervical screening	2,000	641	(2, 8, 29, 35) (7, 29, 40, 60)	Use	Mixed results
Carlsson and Martinsson	2008	Power outages	2,000	791	(150, 200, 275, 375) (350, 400, 475, 575)	Use	Avg. increase in WTP of 105% for 82% increase in cost
Morkbak et al.	2010	Minced pork		3,345	Vary max price (65 | 80 | 120)	Use	Cost scales the same except for maximum price; avg. increase in WTPs 22–68%; fewer say yes at maximum price
Hanley et al.	2005	Water quality		330	(0.67, 1.67, 3.67, 5, 8) (2, 5, 11, 15, 24)	Non-use	WTPs lower in low scale, but not significantly different In high-cost sample 25% reject any option but the status quo; this drops to 17% in low-cost sample, with the difference significant at $p = 0.05$
Kragt	2013	Catchment area	772	523	(30, 60, 200, 400) (50, 100, 300, 600)	Non-use	WTPs higher in high cost, but not significantly different No significant differences in proportions of choices at any of the cost scales

in the high cost scale vs the low cost scale. In a study analyzing the valuation of improved river catchment areas, Kragt (2013) finds that WTPs using a high-cost scale of A$50, 100, 300, and 600 are higher than WTPs estimated using a low-cost scale of A$30, 60, 200, and 400, but that the differences in WTPs are not significant. She reports that there are no significant differences in the proportions of choices at any of the cost levels.

One would expect that cost scales would have a larger anchoring effect for non-use amenities than for use amenities. In the case of use amenities, where respondents have more experience valuing the amenities, respondents may enter the choice situation with more information and thus be less reliant on the survey to supply missing information. However, two of the three studies that examined the effects of cost scales in CEs for use amenities found substantial and significant cost scale effects, while the two studies of the effects of cost scales in CEs for non-use amenities found substantial directional effects that had the right sign but were not significant. The study of the effects of cost scale in an instructional choice set found a significant effect, but only for females.

The study reported here contributes to the literature on cost scale effect in CEs by examining the effects of cost scale on an important non-use amenity (threatened and endangered species status) using a data set larger than any of the prior CE studies of the effects of cost scale on CE estimates of WTPs for non-use amenities. We extend the literature by examining the pattern of choices for the status quo, the do-something options, and the choices made at the highest costs seen by respondents and find evidence that supports the conclusion that respondents are making choices based on relative, not absolute costs. We also extend the literature by analyzing responses by choice set and show that absolute costs seem to have some effect on choices in the first choice set, while choices in the second and third choice sets seem to be based on relative costs.

NOAA SURVEY DATA

The data used for this study come from Phase I of the Protected Species Valuation Survey undertaken by the National Marine Fisheries Service of the National Oceanic and Atmospheric Administration ("NOAA Survey").[5] The survey objective was to value potential improvements in the Endangered Species Act ("ESA") status of eight threatened and endangered ("T&E") marine species under the stewardship of NOAA – the

---

[5] The data and related documents were obtained through a Freedom of Information Act request.

North Pacific right whale, the North Atlantic right whale, the loggerhead sea turtle, the leatherback sea turtle, the Hawaiian monk seal, the wild Upper Willamette River Chinook salmon, the wild Puget Sound Chinook salmon, and the smalltooth sawfish.[6] Each version of the survey presented only three of these eight species.

Before answering choice questions, respondents are provided information about the ESA and the three species in their version, as well as information on what is currently being done to protect the species and what additional protection actions could be undertaken. They are then asked to select the most preferred option in each of a sequence of three choice questions. In each choice set respondents are queried on the same three (of the eight) T&E species; both species improvements and costs are varied across options and across questions. Figure 1 presents a sample choice screen. Within each question, respondents compare the status quo with two alternative options, each of which offers additional protection actions for at least one of the three T&E species, and select the option that they would most prefer. Each option is described by the ESA status of each species (endangered, threatened, or recovered) before and after the option is implemented and the amount of added household cost per year over a period of ten years. The three options are labeled A, B, and C from left to right, with Option A always being the status quo option, with no added household cost.

Knowledge Networks conducted the survey with a random sample of their Internet panel of US households. The main survey was fielded in June and July of 2009, yielding 13,684 completed surveys with a completion rate of 70.8%. There are 44 versions of the main survey, differing by species combination, species order, cost scale, and "cheap talk" treatment. Each version is further divided into 16 sub-versions with different levels of ESA status and costs.[7] Two version pairs (four of the 44 survey designs) are identical except that the cost scales differ by a factor of 4.[8] In our analyses

---

[6] Wallmo and Lew (2012) use a substantial portion of these survey data as the basis for their analysis, and their paper describes the portion of the data set upon which they relied.

[7] According to Wallmo and Lew (2012, p. 833), "Attribute levels were determined with an experimental design that accounted for main effects and maximized a D-efficiency criterion (i.e., a measure of the goodness of a design relative to an optimal orthogonal design that may be impossible to attain) (Louviere et al. 2000)."

[8] The following "cheap talk" script is used in all but three of the 44 survey versions, and in the four versions used in this study: "For hypothetical questions like these, studies have shown that many people say they are willing to pay more for protecting threatened and endangered species than they actually would pay out of their pockets. We believe this happens because people do not really consider how big an impact an extra cost actually has to their family's budget when answering these types of questions. It is easy to be generous when you do not really need to open your wallet. To avoid this, as you consider each question, please imagine your household actually paying the cost of the choice you select out of your household's budget."

As in the previous question, please compare Options A, B, and C in this table and select the option you most prefer.

Remember that any money you spend on these options is money that could be spent on other things.

Expected result in 50 years for each option

	Option A *No additional protection actions*	Option B *Additional protection actions*	Option C *Additional protection actions*
Loggerhead sea turtle ESA status	Threatened	Recovered	Recovered
North Pacific right whale ESA status	Endangered	Threatened	Endangered
Leatherback sea turtle ESA status	Endangered	Threatened	Recovered
Cost per year Added cost to your household each year for 10 years	$0	$100	$60
Which option do you prefer?	○	○	○

Figure 1   Sample choice question screen

we follow the common practice of excluding so-called "protesters."[9] In addition to the Wallmo and Lew exclusions, we also eliminate data for respondents who failed to respond to all three choice problems.

---

[9] We use the same exclusion criteria used by Wallmo and Lew (2012). Protesters are (a) respondents who indicated that they were not confident at all about their answers, or (b) who chose status quo Option A in all three choice questions, and indicated any of the following as the reason for choosing Option A in the first choice questions: "Protecting threatened and endangered species places too many restrictions on industries or private landowners"; "I did not feel it is my responsibility to pay for protecting these species"; "I don't trust the government to run the program"; "I should not have to pay more taxes for any reason"; "I need more information to make a choice"; "I am too unsure about how I feel about threatened and

The Impact of a Fourfold Increase in Costs on Willingness to Pay

The four survey versions (two version pairs) testing cost scale are identical except that the dollar amounts in one pair (high-cost versions, with costs ranging from $20 to $200) are exactly four times the dollar amounts in the other pair (low-cost versions, with costs ranging from $5 to $50). Three of the species are endangered with two possible steps of improvements. Two are threatened species with one possible step of improvement. Hence, the two split-sample experiments evaluate a total of eight possible status improvements. A total of 916 completed questionnaires (completion rate of 74.7%) were obtained for the four split-sample versions, resulting in 2,572 completed choice responses.[10]

If respondent utility functions are rational and well behaved, the RUM estimation methodology should yield the same expected WTPs regardless of cost scale, as long as the cost scale includes costs that result in some respondents making trade-offs between the status quo option (A) and the do-something options (B and C). A RUM model assumes that each respondent chooses the option that maximizes utility, and that the measured utility from each option is a function only of the attributes or cost of the good in each choice option and not a function of the attributes or costs of other options seen by the respondent (either in the current question or in earlier questions). An implication of these assumptions is that respondents' choices in the higher-cost scale should result in more status quo choices and fewer do-something choices at each point in the two cost scales. For example, if the low-cost scale has costs ranging from $5 to $50 and the high-cost scale has costs ranging from $20 to $200, the percentage of status quo choices at $20 in the high-cost scale should be higher than at $5 in the low-cost scale. As shown in Table 2, the proportion of choice sets in which an improvement option is chosen at corresponding costs does not differ significantly between respondents facing different cost scales in any of the data sets (the entire sample, the sample after excluding non-responses, and the sample after excluding both non-responses and protestors). In fact, contrary to expectation, the incidence of choosing an

---

endangered species"; "I do not think the programs will be effective"; and "More research to understand one or more species needs to be done before I would pay for additional protection options."

[10] The Group A version includes the North Atlantic right whale, the Upper Willamette River Chinook salmon, and the smalltooth sawfish (survey versions 41 and 43 in the original NOAA survey, respectively; each version includes all three species, with version 41 having the low-cost scale and version 43 having the high-cost scale). The Group B version includes the North Pacific right whale, the loggerhead sea turtle, and the smalltooth sawfish (survey versions 42 and 44, respectively; each version uses all three species, with version 42 using the low-cost scale and version 44 the high-cost scale).

Table 2 Frequency of choosing an improvement option by survey cost scale and average cost

Average Cost in Low-cost/ High-cost versions	# Choice Sets Low-cost Versions	# Choice Sets High-cost Versions	% B/C Chosen Low-cost Versions	% B/C Chosen High-cost Versions	(%) Difference in Proportion (Low−High)	P-value for Test of Difference in Proportion
No data exclusions						
<$15/<$60	232	227	61.2	58.1	3.1	0.504
$15–17.5/$60–70	386	382	58.5	59.2	−0.6	0.863
$17.5–20/$70–80	269	269	63.2	57.2	5.9	0.159
$20–27.5/$80–110	309	306	53.1	65.0	−12.0	0.003
$27.5–30/$110–120	348	343	56.3	60.3	−4.0	0.283
≥$30/≥$120	307	303	58.6	58.4	0.2	0.957
Total	1,851	1,830	58.2	59.8	−1.6	0.324
Exclude non-responses[a]						
<$15/<$60	214	208	66.4	63.5	2.9	0.533
$15–17.5/$60–70	354	350	63.8	64.6	−0.7	0.840
$17.5–20/$70–80	245	234	69.4	65.8	3.6	0.403
$20–27.5/$80–110	286	281	57.3	70.8	−13.5	0.001
$27.5–30/$110–120	315	322	62.2	64.3	−2.1	0.589
≥$30/≥$120	272	282	66.2	62.8	3.4	0.402
Total	1,686	1,677	63.9	65.3	−1.4	0.411
Exclude non-responses & protesters[b]						
<$15/<$60	171	152	81.9	86.2	−4.3	0.292
$15–17.5/$60–70	270	272	83.0	81.6	1.3	0.682
$17.5–20/$70–80	199	180	83.4	83.9	−0.5	0.901
$20–27.5/$80–110	208	212	77.9	90.1	−12.2	0.001
$27.5–30/$110–120	241	241	80.1	84.6	−4.6	0.189
≥$30/≥$120	212	214	84.0	80.8	3.1	0.398
Total	1,301	1,271	81.7	84.3	−2.6	0.075

Notes:
a. "Non-responses" are choice sets for which the respondent did not select any of the three options.
b. "Protesters" are defined as respondents who always chose the status quo (Option A), and indicated their protest in the debriefing questions. See footnote 9.

improvement option is slightly (but not statistically significantly) higher among respondents receiving the high-cost versions. The difference is statistically significant only for one of the six subgroups, and the direction is unexpected, with the frequency of choosing an improvement option significantly higher for respondents receiving high-cost surveys. These results are similar to those reported by Kragt (2013), but are at variance with those reported by Hanley et al. (2005) (status quo rejection higher in high-cost scale).

Table 3 presents a similar analysis by choice set. We find that in the first choice set a higher percentage of respondents in the high-cost scale choose the status quo and a lower percentage choose a do-something option, but that these relationships are reversed in the second and third choice sets. The differences in the choice percentages are small across all choice sets. These results are consistent with an interpretation that some respondents are responsive to absolute costs in the first choice set but that as a result of anchoring, more respondents are making choices in the second and third choice sets on the basis of relative costs. Using the same data, a related paper (Prelec et al., forthcoming) develops and tests formal utility models to explain the results reported here.

We also review evidence that respondents are constrained by the smaller scale by looking at the proportion of respondents that choose the improvement option with the highest cost seen. If respondents are considering only absolute costs, a higher fraction of respondents in the low-cost scale

Table 3 Status quo and corner choices by cost scale

	Status Quo (%)		
	Low scale	High scale	Difference
All choice sets	18.3	15.7	2.6
Choice set 1	12.9	20.0	−7.1
Choice set 2	19.4	11.8	7.6
Choice set 3	22.2	15.5	6.7
	At Corner (%)		
	Low scale	High scale	Difference
All choice sets	44.2	44.9	−0.7
Choice set 1	38.2	28.3	9.9
Choice set 2	48.1	50.8	−2.7
Choice set 3	45.9	54.6	−8.7

Note: Protesters are excluded as described above. "At Corner" describes respondents who choose the improvement option with the highest cost seen.

versions should choose the maximum cost. As shown in Table 3, this relationship is found only in the first choice set. In the second and third choice sets, fewer respondents appear to be "at the corner" in the low-cost scale. Mørkbak et al. (2010) test the effects of increasing the highest cost in the cost scale; they find fewer respondents say yes at the maximum price in the cost scales with higher maximum prices, but they do not examine this effect across choice sets. If the responses to all three choice sets are pooled, there is virtually no difference between the two cost scales. These results indicate that the choices of most respondents depend on the cost of the option relative to other costs seen in the survey, rather than on the absolute cost of the option itself.

Table 4 presents estimates of the conditional logit models for the low-cost and high-cost data samples.[11] WTPs based on these models are summarized in Table 5, which shows that mean WTP estimates from the high-cost versions vary from 1.60 to 5.22 times higher than the WTP estimates from the low-cost versions, and average 2.97 times higher. The differences in WTPs between the two versions are statistically significant for seven of the eight species' improvements.

Our hypothesis, explored in detail in Prelec et al. (forthcoming), is that our results with respect to cost scale effects are driven by respondents making choices based on relative, not absolute, costs. It is possible that our results could be explained by preference learning, in which respondents "discover" their preferences through completing multiple choices. If the impact of earlier costs on later choices disappeared over the course of the survey, that finding would constitute evidence in favor of the learning hypothesis. We do not see this pattern in our data. However, the three choices presented in the NOAA design may not be a sufficiently long series to give the learning hypothesis a fair test (Dekker et al., 2014).

CONCLUSION

It is implicitly assumed in choice experiments that the choice of cost scale has no effect on the utility function that is revealed by the survey. We find that this is not true in the case of the NOAA endangered and threatened species survey: a fourfold increase in the cost scale leads to about a

---

[11] The models presented here are estimated using conditional logit. This modeling choice derives from the small samples utilized in the cost scale designs. Using all survey versions, models estimated with mixed logit estimation methods are very similar to models estimated with the conditional logit methodology.

Table 4 Estimation results for conditional logit model by cost scale

	Low-cost Scale ($5–50)			High-cost Scale ($20–200)		
	Estimate	Std. Err.	Z-value	Estimate	Std. Err.	Z-value
One-step improvement from endangered to threatened						
Sawfish = T	0.3453	0.0865	3.99	0.4734	0.0906	5.22
N. Atl. right whale = T	0.3166	0.1165	2.72	0.2831	0.1199	2.36
N. Pac. right whale = T	0.2728	0.1132	2.41	0.7963	0.1224	6.51
One-step improvement from threatened to recovered						
UWR Chinook salmon = R	0.6746	0.1020	6.62	0.9242	0.1074	8.61
Loggerhead = R	0.6452	0.0999	6.46	0.8588	0.1075	7.99
Two-step improvement from endangered to recovered						
Sawfish = R	0.6523	0.1030	6.33	1.0851	0.1086	10.00
N. Atl. right whale = R	0.8544	0.1385	6.17	1.2049	0.1414	8.52
N. Pac. right whale = R	0.6448	0.1247	5.17	1.5103	0.1376	10.98
Cost	−0.0160	0.0034	−4.69	−0.0090	0.0009	−9.58
Log likelihood	−1,337			−1,225		
Observations	1,301			1,271		

Table 5 Effect of quadrupling costs on mean willingness-to-pay estimates derived from the conditional logit model

Species Improvements	Low-cost Scale Estimate	95% C.I. Lower	95% C.I. Upper	High-cost Scale Estimate	95% C.I. Lower	95% C.I. Upper	Ratio
N. Pac. right whale (E) = T	$17.01	$4.96	$35.04	$88.82	$62.91	$121.54	5.22
N. Pac. right whale (E) = R	$40.20	$25.01	$64.64	$168.46	$137.52	$209.56	4.19
Sawfish (E) = R	$40.67	$29.25	$62.23	$121.04	$101.38	$147.68	2.98
N. Atl. right whale (E) = R	$53.27	$35.80	$83.75	$134.40	$106.89	$169.56	2.52
Sawfish (E) = T	$21.53	$12.20	$35.41	$52.81	$35.35	$73.89	2.45
UWR Chinook salmon (T) = R	$42.06	$28.49	$67.61	$103.09	$81.32	$129.49	2.45
Loggerhead (T) = R	$40.23	$27.87	$64.98	$95.80	$73.96	$124.30	2.38
N. Atl. right whale (E) = T	$19.74	$6.07	$38.05	$31.58	$5.23	$57.21	1.60

Note: The initial ESA status for each improvement is indicated in parentheses: E denotes endangered, T denotes threatened. The distribution of WTP is simulated using the Krinsky-Robb method. The difference in WTP distributions, evaluated through the method of convolutions, is significant at the 5% level for all improvements, except N. Atl. right whale improving to the threatened ESA status.

threefold increase in the average estimated WTPs of the species surveyed in the study. Our analysis of the data also reveals that the high-cost scale results in fewer, not more, choices of the status quo option and in about the same number of responses in which the highest cost offered is chosen. It appears from our results that after the first choice set, respondents base their choices on relative, not absolute costs.

The cost scale lift we have found is for certain non-use environmental goods (marine species status). While the cost scale effect we document here may be present in many stated preference experiments, such effects are likely to be more pronounced in stated preference studies involving non-use environmental goods because respondents have no experience valuing such goods and may be more receptive to contextual information (such as cost prompts) to assist in deriving values.

The type of cost scale effect we observe may also occur in consumer goods, as occurs in the minced pork study we review (Mørkbak et al., 2010). With consumer products in stable markets, the selection task by respondents is more straightforward than for non-use environmental goods, in that the prices displayed in the study would not generally be dramatically different from the prices that the consumer has experienced in the marketplace. If these prices determine what will be regarded as expensive or cheap relative to other products in the market, then that fact is precisely what a preference measurement method should uncover. When no market exists, as is the case with public goods, the realism criterion is replaced by fidelity to a thought experiment in which public goods are secured through an imaginary private transaction. Whether the individualistic model of consumer preferences does justice to the issues raised by this thought experiment is a separate question – one arguably more critical for the CV method of public good valuation than the contextual anomalies discussed here.

Our results raise two important issues with respect to both use and non-use studies and to our understanding of actual choice behavior. First, since the effect of cost scale is found in both use and non-use studies, it is important that the influence of cost scale be measured. Even in the case of use amenities, if the respondent interprets the prices presented as suggesting options as cheap or expensive relative to the alternatives, this effect should be separated from other aspects of preferences. Second, we note that the effects measured in this chapter and elsewhere may not be a result of the measurement technique, but may reflect the realities of the psychology of choice. On both fronts, the evidence suggests that survey design is an important determinant of measured values, and therefore survey design must be considered in analyzing and interpreting survey results. Further research into the effect of survey design on measurement is warranted.

REFERENCES

Adamowicz, W., J. Louviere, and M. Williams (1994), "Combining revealed and stated preference methods for valuing environmental amenities," *Journal of Environmental Economics and Management*, **26**(3), 271–92.

Adamowicz, W., P. Boxall, M. Williams, and J. Louviere (1998), "Stated preference approaches for measuring passive use values: Choice experiments and contingent valuation," *American Journal of Agricultural Economics*, **80**(1), 64–75.

Ariely, D., G. Lowenstein, and D. Prelec (2003), "Coherent arbitrariness: Stable demand curves without stable preferences," *The Quarterly Journal of Economics*, **18**(1), 73–105.

Bateman, I.J., R.T. Carson, B. Day, D. Dupont, J.J. Louviere, S. Morimoto, R. Scarpa, and P. Wang (2008), "Choice set awareness and ordering effects in discrete choice experiments," *CSERGE Working Paper: EDM*, No. 08-01.

Boxall, P.C., W.L. Adamowicz, J. Swait, M. Williams, and J. Louviere (1996), "A comparison of stated preference methods for environmental valuation," *Ecological Economics*, **18**(3), 243–53.

Cameron, T.A. and D.D. Huppert (1989), "OLS versus ML estimation of non-market resource values with payment card interval data," *Journal of Environmental Economics and Management*, **17**(3), 230–46.

Carlsson, F. and P. Martinsson (2008), "How much is too much? An investigation of the effect of the number of choice sets, context dependence and the choice of bid vectors in choice experiments," *Environmental and Resource Economics*, **40**(2), 165–76.

Cooper, J. and J. Loomis (1992), "Sensitivity of willingness to pay to bid design in dichotomous choice contingent valuation models," *Land Economics*, **68**(2), 211–22.

Dekker, T., P. Koster, and R. Brouwer (2014), "Changing with the tide: Semiparametric estimation of preference dynamics," *Land Economics*, **90**(4), 717–45.

Duffield, J.W. and D.A. Patterson (1991), "Inference and optimal design for a welfare measure in dichotomous choice contingent valuation," *Land Economics*, **67**(2), 225–39.

Flachaire, E., G. Hollard, and S. Luchini (2007), "Heterogeneous anchoring in dichotomous choice valuation framework," *Louvain Economic Review*, **73**(4), 369–85.

Frykblom, P. and J.F. Shogren (2000), "An experimental testing of anchoring effects in discrete choice questions," *Environmental and Resource Economics*, **16**(3), 329–41.

Green, D., K.E. Jacowitz, D. Kahneman, and D. McFadden (1998), "Referendum contingent valuation, anchoring, and willingness to pay for public goods," *Resource and Energy Economics*, **20**(2), 85–116.

Hanley, N., W. Adamowicz, and R.E. Wright (2005), "Price vector effects in choice experiments: An empirical test," *Resource and Energy Economics*, **27**(3), 227–34.

Hanley, N., R.E. Wright, and V. Adamowicz (1998), "Using choice experiments to value the environment," *Environmental and Resource Economics*, **11**(3–4), 413–28.

Hensher, D.A., J.M. Rose, and W.H. Greene (2015), *Applied Choice Modeling*, Cambridge, UK: Cambridge University Press.

Herriges, J.A. and J.F. Shogren (1996), "Starting point bias in dichotomous choice valuation with follow-up questioning," *Journal of Environmental Economics and Management*, **30**(1), 121–31.

Kragt, M.E. (2013), "The effects of changing cost vectors on choices and scale heterogeneity," *Environmental and Resource Economics*, **54**(2), 201–21.

Ladenburg, J. and S.B. Olsen (2008), "Gender-specific starting point bias in choice experiments: Evidence from an empirical study," *Journal of Environmental Economics and Management*, **56**(3), 275–85.

Louviere, J.J., D.A. Hensher, and J.D. Swait (2000), *Stated Choice Methods: Analysis and Applications*, Cambridge, UK: Cambridge University Press.

Mørkbak, M.R., T. Christensen, and D. Gyrd-Hansen (2010), "Choke price bias in choice experiments," *Environmental and Resource Economics*, **45**(4), 537–51.

Prelec, D., J. Burrows, and P. Dixon (forthcoming), "Context sensitivity in stated preference experiments," available from the authors on request.

Ryan, M. and S. Wordsworth (2000), "Sensitivity of willingness to pay estimates to the level of attributes in discrete choice experiments," *Scottish Journal of Political Economy*, **47**(5), 504–24.

Silverman, J. and M. Klock (1989), "The behavior of respondents in contingent valuation: Evidence on starting bids," *Journal of Behavioral Economics*, **18**(1), 51–60.

Train, K. (2009), *Discrete Choice Methods with Simulation*, Cambridge, UK: Cambridge University Press.

Wallmo, K. and D.K. Lew (2012), "Public willingness to pay for recovering and downlisting threatened and endangered marine species," *Conservation Biology*, **26**(5), 830–39.

2. Fat tails and truncated bids in contingent valuation: an application to an endangered shorebird species[1]

George Parsons and Kelley Myers[2]

INTRODUCTION

Fat tails in contingent valuation (CV) refers to the phenomenon of a yes-response function having a high and slowly declining yes-response rate at high bid levels offered in a CV survey. So, for example, a yes-response rate might hold at 20% or greater over the three or four highest bids offered in a survey. The "tails" of the yes-response function are said to be "fat" in this case. A truncated bid refers to a circumstance where high bids are not offered over a range where it appears as though the survey instrument would produce a non-zero percentage of yes responses – essentially ignoring the behavioral response to high bids or "truncating" the yes-response function.

Fat tails has been recognized and discussed in the CV literature for more than two decades (Desvousges et al., 1993). Analysts have also recognized that fat tails can create problems for parametric estimators (e.g., logit and probit), wherein the estimators are sensitive to the highest bids offered in a survey (Cooper and Loomis, 1992; Desvousges et al., 1993). In part because of this problem and in part because of the problem of negative willingness-to-pay (WTP) estimates from parametric estimators, the field has turned toward non-parametric estimators, especially the Turnbull lower bound (Kriström, 1990; Carson et al., 1994; Haab and McConnell, 1997). This chapter shows that fat tails also create problems for non-parametric estimators. The real issues presented in the data do not go away by simply changing estimators.

---

[1] Reprinted from *Ecological Economics*, Vol. 129, George Parsons and Kelley Myers, "Fat tails and truncated bids in contingent valuation: an application to an endangered shorebird species," pp. 210–19, copyright 2016, with permission from Elsevier.
[2] Respectively, Professor, School of Marine Science & Policy and Department of Economics, University of Delaware; Senior Economist, Cardno, Newark, DE.

The tail of a yes-response function is equivalent to the portion of a conventional demand curve nearest the choke price, which is where much of consumer surplus for valuation lies. For this reason, it is important to have a good measure of the yes-response function over the high-bid range; the accuracy of willingness-to-pay estimates hinges upon it. Yet, it seems common to truncate bids, forcing analysts to either ignore or to infer the yes-responses over the high-bid range from response data over low-range bids. Whether this is intentional to avoid the complications of fat tails is uncertain, but it is common.

A search over the recent CV literature shows that many studies have truncated yes-response functions. Table 1 is a list of 86 CV studies along with their yes-response rate at the highest bid. This list includes studies published in eight of the leading environmental economics journals from 1990 to 2015 for which there were sufficient data to make the calculation.[3] Approximately 60% of the studies have at least one scenario in their analysis where the yes-response rate at the highest bid is 20% or greater. Nearly 50% have at least one scenario above 30%.

In this chapter, we explore the implication of fats tails in the context of a CV survey designed to value the protection of a relatively unknown migratory bird species whose population has declined in recent years. Our analysis is in three steps. First, we provide a review of the relevant literature. Second, we document the extent of fat tails in the response data. To do this we purposefully seek to pin down the tail of the yes-response function by offering high, what seem like unusually high, bid levels to find the choke price and explore behavioral response to high bids. We do this using an Internet-based survey and follow the standard protocol for state-of-the-art CV studies – a clear and balanced description of the good, budget reminders, follow-up certainty questions, referendum format, reinforcing consequentiality, and so forth. Third, we analyze the implications of including high bids on mean willingness to pay. We simulate this impact by calculating willingness to pay assuming different maximum bid offers and use non-parametric measures of willingness to pay throughout our analysis.

---

[3] *American Journal of Agricultural Economics* (*AJAE*), *Agricultural and Resource Economics Review* (*ARER*), *Environmental and Resource Economics* (*ERE*), *Land Economics* (*LE*), *Marine Resource Economics* (*MRE*), *Journal of the Association of Environmental and Resource Economists* (*JAERE*), *Journal of Agriculture and Resource Economics* (*JARE*), *Journal of Environmental Economics and Management* (*JEEM*).

Table 1   Yes-response rates to highest bid in referendum-style CV studies published in eight environmental economics journals from 1990 to 2015

Author (Journal Publication Year)[a]	Resource Valued	% Yes at Highest Bid Amount[c]
Adamowicz et al. (2014)	Heart disease risk reduction for self and children	18–32
Alberini et al. (1997)	Wetland and wildlife protection, wilderness area protection, oil spill prevention	34–46 (14–43)
Andersson et al. (2013)	Car safety	3–24
Balistreri et al. (2001)	Insurance game	11[b]
Banzhaf et al. (2006)	Ecological condition of Adirondack Lakes	34–52
Berrens et al. (1996)	Endangered species	8–22
Berrens et al. (1997)	Expansion of cultural center programs	13–23
Blamey et al. (1999)	Salinity in soil	17–69
Blomquist et al. (2009)	Health management programs	0–19[b]
Boman et al. (1999)	Wolf preservation and forest protection	6–11
Brown et al. (1996)	Unpaved road removal	33
Brown et al. (2003)	Scholarship fund	25–69[b]
Cameron and Quiggin (1994)	Wilderness area protection	54 (41)
Carson et al. (2003)	Prevent oil spill	34 (14)
Champ and Bishop (2001)	Wind-generated electricity	31[b]
Champ and Bishop (2006)	Wind-generated electricity	7
Champ et al. (1997)	Unpaved road removal	28
Champ et al. (2002)	Open space	28–30
Champ et al. (2009)	Whooping crane	15–36
Chien et al. (2005)	Air quality	51–63 (17–42)
Cook et al. (2012)	Cholera and typhoid vaccines	7–20
Cooper and Loomis (1992)	Hunting, wildlife viewing and risk reduction	6–42
Corrigan et al. (2008)	Water quality	32–35
Desvousges et al. (2015)	Water quality	15–45
Egan et al. (2015)	Water quality	40–42
Farmer and Lipscomb (2008)	Emissions test waiver	21
Frykblom (1997)	Environmental education book	17[b]
Frykblom and Shogren (2000)	Environmental education book	5–8[b]
Gerking et al. (2014)	Leukemia vaccine	21–67
Giraud et al. (2001)	Endangered species	39
Giraud et al. (2005)	Local food product	10–33

Table 1 (continued)

Author (Journal Publication Year)[a]	Resource Valued	% Yes at Highest Bid Amount[c]
Guria et al. (2005)	Risk reduction	7–13
Haab and McConnell (1997)	Wolf recovery, beach cleaning	15–53
Haab and McConnell (1998)	Beach cleaning	15
Hammitt and Zhou (2006)	Treatment of illnesses caused by air pollutants	8–33
Harrison and Lesley (1996)	Oil spill prevention	35
Herriges et al. (2010)	Water quality	35
Hite et al. (2002)	Water quality	13–14
Holmes and Kramer (1995)	Forest protection	5
Huth and Morgan (2011)	Cave diving	16–19
Ivehammar (2009)	Urban scenic view	5–36
Johnston (2006)	Public water supply	33[b]
Koford et al. (2012)	Curbside recycling	17
Kovacs and Larson (2008)	Open space	12–25 (6–17)
Kramer and Evan Mercer (1997)	Rain forest protection	0(0)
Kriström (1990)	Forest protection	11
Labao et al. (2008)	Endangered species	9–13
Landry and List (2007)	Sports memorabilia	20–75[b]
Langford et al. (1998)	Flood prevention and wetland protection	18
Leiter and Pruckner (2009)	Prevention of death in avalanche	24–25 (5–6)
Leon and Arena (2012)	Reconstructing natural feature	6–19
Lindberg et al. (1997)	Traffic/noise reduction	24
Longo et al. (2012)	Climate change mitigation	45–49
Longo et al. (2015)	Cutting greenhouse gas emissions	24–58
Loureiro et al. (2009)	Oil spill prevention	15
Lunander (1998)	Movie preview	11–91[b]
Lusk (2003)	Genetically engineered rice	62–72
Michael and Reiling (1997)	Outdoor recreation and congestion	0
Moore et al. (2011)	Water quality	25
Morrison and Brown (2009)	Meal for disadvantaged children	27–53[b]
Murphy et al. (2005)	Sign placement and endangered species	0[b]
Myers et al. (2010)	Recreational bird watching	8–13
Nahuelhual et al. (2004)	Open space	28–47

Table 1 (continued)

Author (Journal Publication Year)[a]	Resource Valued	% Yes at Highest Bid Amount[c]
Nunes and Van den Bergh (2004)	Algal bloom and water quality	13 (4)
Petrolia and Kim (2009)	Barrier island restoration	18–65
Polome et al. (2006)	Natural mudflat for birds	32–50 (22–39)
Poor (1999)	Wetland preservation	11–14 (1–6)
Popp (2001)	Air and water quality	42
Ready and Hu (1995)	Preservation of horse farms	29
Ready et al. (1996)	Food-borne risk	13–18
Reaves et al. (1999)	Red-cockaded woodpecker	0
Richardson et al. (2013)	Reduce symptom days caused by wildfires	13
Riddel and Loomis (1998)	Spotted owl protection	9–60
Roach et al. (2002)	Recreational moose hunting	5–11
Ropicki et al. (2010)	Eco-label for seafood	4–13[d]
Saz-Salazar and Garcia-Menendez (2001)	Improved waterfront area	24
Scarpa et al. (2001)	Speed reduction	8–14
Smith (1996)	Tire recycling and wildflower enhancement programs	44
Tuan and Navrud (2007)	Visitation to cultural heritage price	12–13
Wang (1997)	Environmental quality	12
Weldesilassie et al. (2009)	Improved wastewater irrigation	49 (31)
Welsh and Poe (1998)	Dam releases	19[b]
Whitehead et al. (2001)	Saltwater fishing	13–50
Whitehead (2002)	Water quality, agriculture	36–53[b]
Whittington (2002)	Water services	23–38
Zhang et al. (2010)	Anjou pears with ethylene treatment	21–76 (6–47)

Notes:
a. The table includes all CV studies with sufficient information to calculate yes-response rate at the highest bid from the following journals: *AJAE, ARER, ERE, LE, MRE, JAERE, JARE, JEEM*. See footnote 3.
b. The study was done all or in part in an experimental setting but we only include hypothetical payment responses from the study.
c. For studies reporting more than one result, the range of outcomes is shown. For studies that use double-bounded dichotomous choice, we use percentage yes at initial highest bid. The numbers in parentheses are the percentage yes at the highest second bid amount and when the initial bid was the highest bid possible – or percentage responding yes – yes beginning at the highest initial bid.
d. Four percent of respondents would always pay the highest bid and 13% of respondents would sometimes pay the highest bid.

RELATED LITERATURE

As mentioned in our introduction, several authors have called attention to the issue of fat tails in the context of estimation with a parametric model. Cooper and Loomis (1992), for example, asked, "How does bid design affect parameter estimates in a binary choice model and, in turn, mean willingness to pay?" They analyzed ten discrete-choice CV questions from three surveys (covering valuation of wildlife and hazardous waste clean up). When the top four bid levels and associated data were removed and the models re-estimated, mean willingness to pay declined on average to about 75% of its initial level. Most of the underlying data exhibited yes-response rates above 20% at the maximum bid.

Desvousges et al. (1993) have a similar, but more dramatic, finding. In a study of migratory bird valuation, they tested the effect of dropping the highest bid on mean willingness to pay. The highest bid was $1,000; the next highest was $250. Both bids had yes-response rates close to 30%. Estimated mean willingness to pay declined to 48% of the initial value in one case and to 34% of its initial value in another.

McFadden and Leonard (1993) found the same. In a study valuing the preservation of wilderness areas, they drop respondents who received a bid of $2,000 (where the next highest is $200) and mean willingness to pay declined to 54% of its initial value.

Brown et al. (1996) conducted a survey to value the removal of abandoned roads in the Grand Canyon to provide more wilderness area. In the course of their analysis they write, "33% of the respondents to highest bid level ($50) chose 'yes', providing a less-than-ideal bid distribution for the purpose of estimating WTP." In an ensuing footnote they write:

> [i]n order to provide a more accurate estimate of hypothetical WTP, in the fall of 1994 we sent the hypothetical dichotomous choice survey to a comparable sample at higher bid levels (up to $200). However, there was no large drop in percent "yes" at these higher bid levels. Including the additional data tended to *increase* mean WTP compared with the estimate based only on the 1993 data. (Brown et al., 1996, p. 159; original emphasis)

Their effort to pin down the tail of the distribution fell short and their recognition that having limited response data around the highest bids as "less than ideal" is consistent with our own concern.

Haab and McConnell (2002) present a nice discussion of how binary choice models (in many forms) fit and don't fit yes-response data with truncation at high-end and low-end bids. They show the extreme sensitivity of willingness to pay to the choice of functional form and the nature of the yes-response data. In one case, the same data are shown to generate mean willingness-to-pay estimates of less than zero or greater than $1,000 depending on the chosen functional form. A low yes-response rate at low bids (falling well below 100%) and a high yes-response rate at high bids (falling well above 0%) seem to cause a breakdown in binary choice models. In a concluding section they write, "[t]he set of offered bids should be designed to ensure that the tails of the distribution are well defined. Undefined tails can lead to unreliable measures of central tendency of WTP."

One of Haab and McConnell's criteria for a valid measure of willingness to pay is that "[e]stimation and calculation are accomplished with no arbitrary truncation." This would seem to apply whether one is using parametric or non-parametric methods for estimating value.

The sensitivity of functional form and, in turn willingness to pay, to response data with fat tails discussed by Haab and McConnell (2002) is, no doubt, one reason we see *intentional* bid truncation in much of the literature. Kanninen (1993) and Kanninen and Kriström (1993) found that binary response models fit yes-response data better if the bid design concentrates bids around the expected mean and drops bids in the tails. There is no doubting their statistical finding. However, it does involve ignoring or truncating real response data over high bids in favor of predicting responses for high bids based on how people responded to lower or closer to "average" bids. If response data to high bids are truncated, binary choice models smooth out the tails in a statistically satisfying way but do so by censoring response data over the very range where we would like to know more about true behavioral response.

Herriges et al. (2010) conducted a contingent valuation survey for valuing water quality improvements on lakes in Iowa. Their focus was on exploring the implications of policy consequentiality on the results of dichotomous-choice contingent valuation surveys. In the course of their analysis they write:

> [. . .]34.5% of individuals are willing to pay the maximum bid value of $600. As such, the posterior predictives *must* place considerable mass to the right of this largest bid point. The problem here is that we do not observe any outcomes to the right of the maximum bid of $600 to inform the shape of this distribution over that region; instead, its shape is determined by estimating a mean, a variance and other statistics to purely form a sequence of binary responses, which are then used (together with our parametric assumptions) to characterize the entire WTP predictive.

This is a nice explanation of the extrapolation required to predict the shape of the yes-response surface over the truncated range.

SURVEY

Our inquiry centers around a CV survey designed to value the protection of the red knot – a migratory bird species whose population has declined in recent years. The red knot is one of many species of shorebirds that makes a stop on the Delaware Bay during its annual 10,000-mile migration from South to North America. The stopover in May/June is timed during the horseshoe crab spawning season. The red knot relies on the horseshoe crab eggs to regain weight lost during their long-distance flight before proceeding north to breed. Over the past decade, annual counts of the red knot indicate a decline in numbers, which scientists have attributed to the overharvesting of horseshoe crabs and habitat loss. This has triggered an interest in regulations to protect the red knot such as beach/habitat preservation measures, horseshoe crab harvest limitations, and listing as an endangered species.

In our application we attempt to value the protection of the red knot via a hypothetical resource conservation program. We used an Internet-based survey and sampled households in New Jersey and Delaware. We followed standard guidelines for conducting a CV survey.[4] We began with a series of introductory warm-up questions about the environment and migratory birds in the region. Then, we described the historic and current condition of the red knot using maps, pictures, and graphs. Next, we laid out a hypothetical resource conservation program to be conducted jointly by the states of New Jersey and Delaware to protect the red knot. People were then asked to vote for or against the program at some cost to their household in a referendum-style CV question (Figure 1[5]). We used a one-time tax as the payment vehicle. Each person was asked to vote once. Our survey included a budget reminder, a statement to encourage respondents to treat the survey as consequential, and a clear description of the voting mechanism. Again, see footnote 4 for a link to the entire survey. Various versions of the survey and the valuation question in particular were pre-tested and discussed in focus groups until we felt confident that respondents understood the resource and the vote.

The bid design used in our survey was motivated by an interest in pinning down the tails of our yes-response function. As noted earlier, this is a region of the distribution that captures those with the highest willingness to pay and, no doubt, will figure importantly in any calculation

---

[4] See the Delaware Bay Shorebird Survey, accessed November 27, 2016 at https://delaware.qualtrics.com/SE/?SID=SV_cvXTegW9jXmVD5r.

[5] Figure 1 is slightly different from the graph shown to respondents because the original figure included color that cannot be shown in this black-and-white book.

Now, suppose the *Red Knot Protection Agreement* was on the ballot and that the actions in the Agreement were expected to improve the projected status of the **Atlantic Red Knot** in ten years from *endangered* to *stabilized* as shown below

Expected Improvement in the Status of the Atlantic Red Knot in ten Years

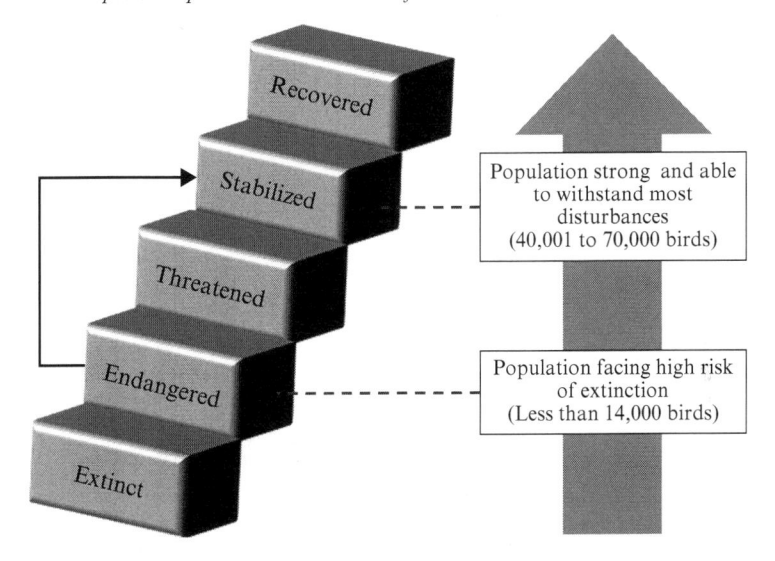

- Recovered
- Stabilized — Population strong and able to withstand most disturbances (40,001 to 70,000 birds)
- Threatened
- Endangered — Population facing high risk of extinction (Less than 14,000 birds)
- Extinct

3. If the total cost to your household to finance the Agreement was a one-time payment of $5,000, how would you vote if the Agreement were on the ballot in the next election?

Please consider your income, expenses and other possible uses of this money before you vote. Also, please remember that the results of this survey will be provided to policy makers.

○ I would vote for the Agreement
○ I would vote against the Agreement

Figure 1   Example voting question

of mean willingness to pay for use in a benefit–cost or natural resource damage assessment. We are also interested in the implications of truncating bids at the higher end of the distribution. For these reasons, our bid design is heavy on bids at the higher end and uses sample sizes that are sufficient to accurately capture the yes-response rate to high bids. Our bids included the following one-time state tax in dollars: 25, 50, 100, 150, 200, 300, 500, 1,000, 2,000, 3,000, 5,000, and 10,000.

We drew our sample from two sources: Qualtrics and Knowledge Networks (now GfK). The Qualtrics sample is an opt-in Internet sample

Table 2 Respondent characteristics

Variable (n = 1,382)	Mean
Age	49.8
Gender (1 = Male)	0.47
Income (2010)	$82,033
Education (1 = College degree or higher)	0.54
Heard of red knot (1 = Yes)	0.12
Knowledge about shorebirds (1 = Somewhat knowledgeable or Very knowledgeable)	0.28
Made a trip in past five years for primary purpose of bird watching (1 = Yes)	0.17
Belongs to a bird watching group	<1%
Distance from the Delaware Bay	220.52
Number of years lived in DE or NJ	35.2

that matches the New Jersey and Delaware populations along the lines of income, age, and gender. The Knowledge Networks (KN) sample is probability based and comes with probability weighting needed to adjust the sample to be representative of the underlying population. We apply these throughout our analysis. Our sample size is 1,382 and is split 775 opt-in and 607 probability-based.[6] Table 2 shows some descriptive statistics for our sample.

RESULTS

In this section we present our results including the yes-response function, willingness-to-pay estimates, and some tests of the robustness of our results.

Yes-response Function

Our yes-response function is shown in Figure 2. The box-line in the figure plots the raw response data. Please note that the scale on the x-axis is inconsistent – the same increment represents significantly more money as you move to the right. The actual shape of the curve is much longer and flatter than shown. We have a downward slope but there are some instances of non-monotonicity at bids $150, $500, $3,000, and $10,000.

---

[6] The sample was split this way to test for differences in willingness to pay in the two samples. Since the effects of splitting the sample have no effect on our basic finding, we focus on the combined results.

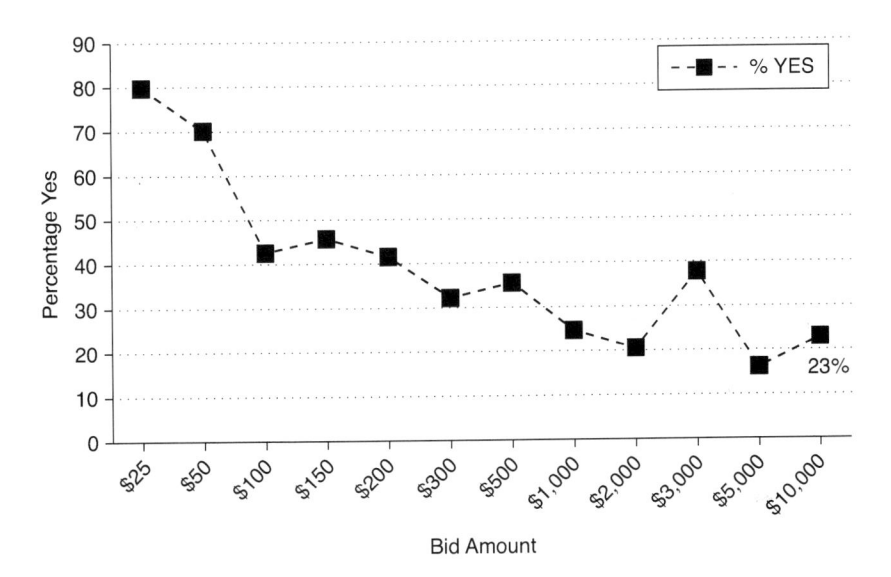

Figure 2   Percentage of yes responses by bid amount

Table 3   Non-parametric estimates by bid amount

High-end Bid Amounts ($)	% of Yes Responses	Sample Size	Lower-bound Mean WTP ($)	% of Mean Accounted for by Highest Bid
200	41	80	102	91
300	32	90	134	76
500	35	148	204	81
1,000	25	132	327	84
2,000	21	148	533	78
3,000	38	144	897	91
5,000	16	143	1,220	69
10,000	23	136	2,254	84

Table 3 shows the yes-response rates for bids $200 to $10,000 along with other data. At bids between $200 and $500, about 30–40% of the sample are voting yes for red knot protection. At bids over $1,000, about 20–25% vote yes. At $10,000, our highest bid, we still have 23% of the sample voting yes.[7] Obviously, our response data exhibit fat tails.

---

[7] Every yes-response percentage is statistically significantly different from zero at the 99% level of confidence.

Willingness to Pay Estimates

Table 3 also presents our non-parametric mean estimates of willingness to pay assuming different maximum bids. For example, if we had used $2,000 as our maximum bid, mean willingness to pay would have been $533 per household using a lower-bound non-parametric estimate. We used Vaughn and Rodriguez's (2001) lower-bound measure for this calculation. The estimate applies the yes-response probability over a given interval to the lower bound of that interval in each instance (e.g., if our smoothed function places 5% of the sample between $200 and $300, all 5% are assumed to have a willingness to pay of $200, even though some may be as high as $299). The formula for the lower bound (see Vaughn and Rodriguez, 2001, Table 1) is:

$$WTP_{LB} = \sum_{j=1}^{M+1} b_{j-1} \cdot p_j, \qquad (1)$$

where p_j is the probability density in bid group j; b_j is one of M bid offers; $p_j = F_j - F_{j-1}$, where $F_j = N_j/(N_j + Y_j)$ is the cumulative density for bid group j; N_j is the number of no votes in bid group j, and Y_j is the number of yes votes in bid group j.[8] (Note: $b_0 = 0$, $F_0 = 0$, $F_{M+1} = 100$.)

Table 3 shows the dramatic effect of bid truncation on willingness to pay. If we had used $200 as a maximum bid instead of $10,000, our lower-bound mean willingness to pay would have been $102 per household. This ignores the density under the yes-response function in Figure 2 for bids greater than $200 or what is essentially the demand curve over the high price range. Lower-bound mean willingness to pay doubles (versus $200) if $500 is used as the maximum bid, triples if $1,000 is used, increases ninefold if $3,000 is used, and finally jumps as high as 20 times if $10,000 is used.[9,10]

To further appreciate the importance of the maximum bid selection, we have calculated the percentage of the lower-bound mean willingness to pay accounted for by the highest bid, which is also reported in Table 3. Think

---

[8] This computation assumes no folding back of probabilities due to non-monotonicity. See Vaughn and Rodriguez (2001) or Haab and McConnell (2002) for folding back.

[9] We also calculated intermediate values of willingness to pay following Vaughn and Rodriguez (2001). As expected, these gave us even larger willingness-to-pay estimates. At $200, willingness to pay is $331 and at $10,000 it is $2,706. The computed choke price in these cases played a large role in the final values.

[10] It is interesting to note that the median value ($89) does not change with the maximum bid. This may have implications for voting outcomes but it is not useful in a benefit–cost or damage assessment setting where means are needed.

of adding up the bid increments in the non-parametric calculation in equation (1). The increment over the final bid is the share attributed to the highest bid offer. For our lower-bound measure of willingness to pay, that share is $HB_{share} = b_{MpM+1}/\text{WTPLB}$, where b_M is the highest bid. As shown the share ranges from about 69 to 91% of the total value. In effect, a high yes-response rate at the highest bid places enormous weight on that bid and hence accounts for a large share of the value. This result emphasizes the importance of good resolution on the upper end of the distribution. If one believes the estimates, this result also suggests that concentrating bids near the upper end of the tail where most of the willingness to pay is located is a sensible research strategy, contrary to the current practice of truncating this range. Concentrating bids at the high end of the tail also helps detect hypothetical bias in willingness to pay.

Finally, consider the sheer size of the mean bids when high bid levels are introduced. The mean (lower-bound) willingness to pay is $2,254 when the highest bid is used. Keep in mind that only 12% of the population was aware of the red knot before taking the survey. One would expect a greater awareness of a resource worth thousands of dollars per household. These estimates give an aggregate value for the states of New Jersey and Delaware over $15 billion. Since the contingent valuation question has the bird population increasing by 16,000 to 36,000 birds, the values translate to about $400,000–900,000 per "sustained" bird. For more perspective, the average household contributes about $4 to wildlife conservation programs. Although suffering from free-riding effects (and hence understating full value), these include all wildlife, well beyond our single bird species. For all environmental causes this value is about $18 per household.[11] We made a similar calculation for environmental outlays per household in the United States and estimate that the average household implicitly pays about $2,600. Again, this is for all federal and state environmental protection, fish and wildlife management, forest management, and several other "environmental" categories.[12] Viewed next to these numbers, our estimates are difficult to accept as true resource values.

We see fat tails as a manifestation of hypothetical bias, which has been an issue with contingent valuation response data since its inception – people not taking the survey seriously and not treating the willingness-to-pay question as a real trade-off (with money) as intended. Seeing fat tails this way implies that it is a symptom of a larger problem present in

---

[11] These calculations were made using aggregate data from Charity Navigator (charitynavigator.org).

[12] These calculations were made using budgets from environmental-related agencies and include a Resources for the Future estimate of regulatory compliance cost (2% of GDP), which is the highest component of the value (Morgenstern et al., 1998).

contingent valuation data and not a separate, isolated issue to be dealt with on its own. Fat tails is consistent with many of the issues surrounding CV: yea-saying, treating the survey as hypothetical, anchoring, voting simply to show support for a program, treating the good as some broader environmental purpose, and so on. All of these it would seem could generate fat-tailed response data. Boyle (2003), for example, sees the issue of fat tails as a manifestation of yea-saying:

> Another problem has been termed "yea saying," which is the propensity of some respondents to answer yes to any bid amount presented to them. Here it seems that bid amounts are not acting as a quality or price cue. The manifestation of this problem has been the so-called "fat-tails" problem, with as much as 30% of a sample answering yes to any bid amount. When the inverse of the empirical cumulative distribution function (CDF) asymptotically approaches 0.30, rather than 0.00, the result is an extremely large estimate of central tendency with a large standard error. (Boyle, 2003, p. 140) [Citations within the quote have been removed.]

Responses to extreme (high) bid offers in a CV survey are in a sense a test of the method itself – a way of revealing the reasonableness of responses that cannot be seen as easily over lower bid offers. If a survey is valid, one would expect a reasonable yes-response rate over the higher-end bids and an ability to pin down the tail of the distribution with plausible mean willingness-to-pay estimates. If not, something must be amiss and explanations are needed.

Adjusting for Hypothetical Bias

We adjusted our yes-response function using a follow-up certainty question. This is one of several approaches commonly used to account for hypothetical bias (Champ et al., 2009). Immediately following our CV referendum question we asked respondents:

On a scale of 1 to 10, where 1 means "very uncertain" and 10 means "very certain," how certain are you that this is how you would vote if the Red Knot Protection Agreement were actually on the ballot?

Please recall that you voted for/against the Agreement at a one-time cost to your household of [respondent's bid offer].

We used this variable to weight our response data. A person reporting a certainty level of 10 (very certain of their response) was assigned a weight of 1.0; a person with a certainty level of 9 was assigned a weight of 0.9 and

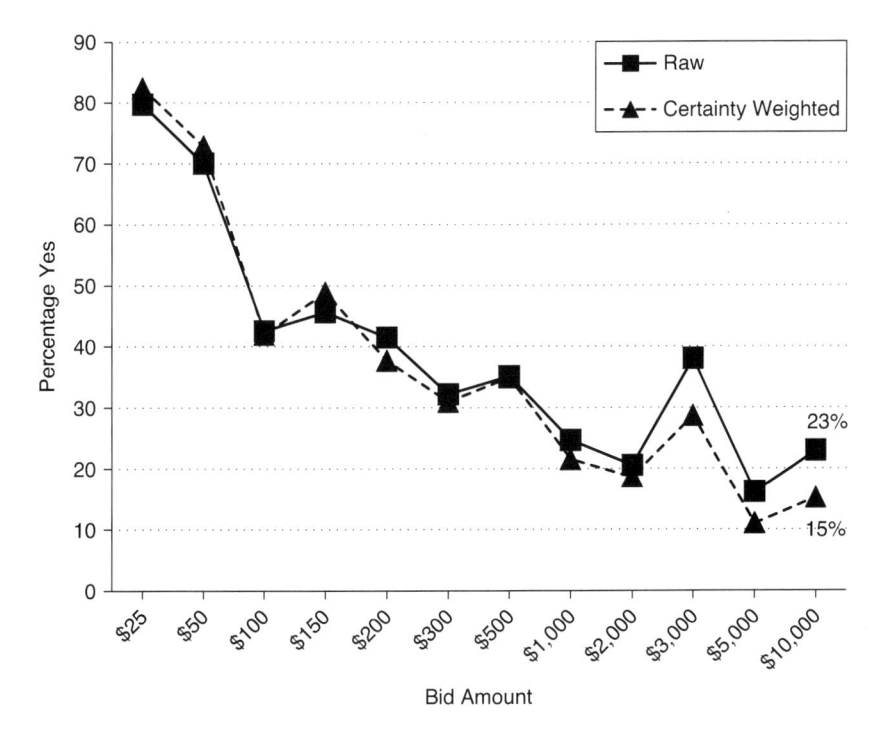

Figure 3 Comparison of percentage of yes responses vs responses adjusted for certainty

so forth. In this way, responses with greater certainty were given a higher weight.

Figure 3 shows the weighted and unweighted yes-response functions. The weighted function is about the same as the unweighted function until the bid reaches $2,000. From there and up the weighted function has a lower tail. Yes responders tend to have a lower certainty level over the higher bids and this pulls the tail down. At $10,000, for example, the percentage voting yes declines from 23% to 15% of the sample.

Table 4 shows the adjusted willingness-to-pay estimates. In line with the yes-response functions, there is little change in the lower-bound willingness-to-pay estimates for the weighted response data until the bid levels of $2,000 and above are reached. At $10,000 mean willingness to pay using the lower-bound data is reduced from $2,254 to $1,030. Still, the levels of willingness to pay, even after certainty adjustment, are high.

Table 4   Non-parametric estimates by bid amount and adjusted for hypothetical bias

High-end Bid Amounts ($)	% of Yes Responses	Sample Size	Lower-bound Mean WTP ($)	% of Mean Accounted for by Highest Bid
200	38	58	103	81
300	31	65	134	75
500	35	117	204	84
1,000	22	105	311	71
2,000	19	113	497	84
3,000	29	102	774	83
5,000	11	126	993	56
10,000	15	98	1,030	71

Belief in Bid Values

Respondents are told that if more than half of the population votes in favor of the Red Knot Protection Agreement their household will pay a tax of $X into a Red Knot Protection Fund and the program described will be implemented. Respondents may or may not believe the $X presented in the survey. People may use another amount they find more believable. For example, people may make a mental calculation of what a reasonable per household cost for the program is and adjust the amount given in the survey up or down accordingly. Or, people may look for some historical context of what a realistic tax in their state might be for the program and use that expected level. In our case, particularly with regard to the high bid levels shown, people may not believe that a tax for a bird protection program would ever reach such heights. Similarly, people may be skeptical of a low tax on the valuation question, thinking in the real world that the cost the government will incur to achieve success will actually be higher. Whether respondents accept the bid they are told and then vote based on that bid is simply unknown. To explore this issue, we asked the following follow-up question:

When you voted, did you think that your household would actually end up paying the tax amount stated, or did you think you would pay more or less than that amount?

Table 5 shows the response frequencies for this question. About 17% of all voters thought they would have to pay less than the amount stated in the survey and about 21% thought they would pay more. Figure 4 shows how the sample responded by bid levels. As the bid level increases more people

Table 5   Responses to follow-up question about the tax amount in vote

When you voted, did you think that your household would actually end up paying the tax amount stated, or did you think that your household would pay more or less than that amount?	Percentage of Total		
	Yes voters N = 493	No voters N = 879	Entire sample N = 1,372
The amount stated	32	42	39
More than the amount stated	24	19	21
Less than the amount stated	21	15	17
Unsure	23	24	24

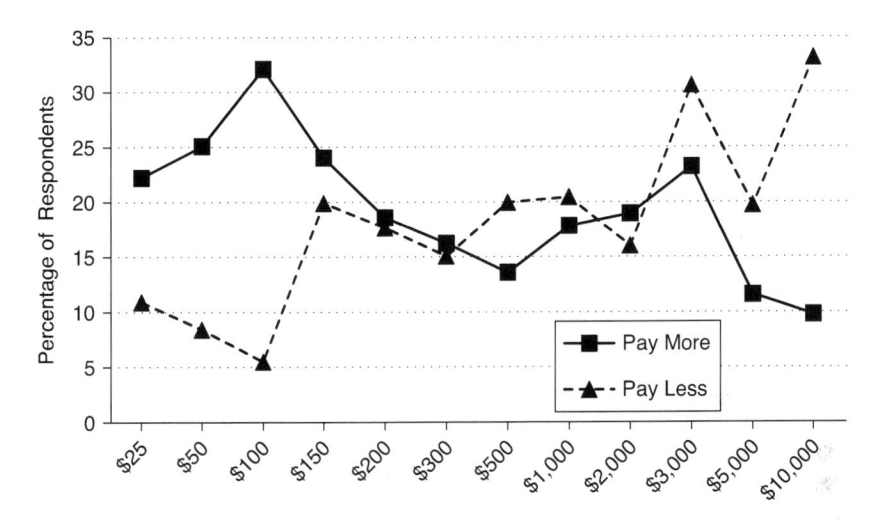

Figure 4   Percentage of respondents who believed they would pay more or pay less than offered bid amount

believe that they would pay less than the stated amount. This suggests that people who received high bids may simply reject the plausibility of the bid and insert one of their own. At $10,000, for example, about 33% of the sample believed that they would actually pay less than the amount stated. At $25 only 11% believe they would pay less. In contrast, as the bid increases the share of people saying they would pay more declines. Surprisingly, even at the highest bid levels 10% believed they would pay more and most believed the stated amount.

Following this question, we asked the respondents who believed that they would pay something other than the stated amount in the survey

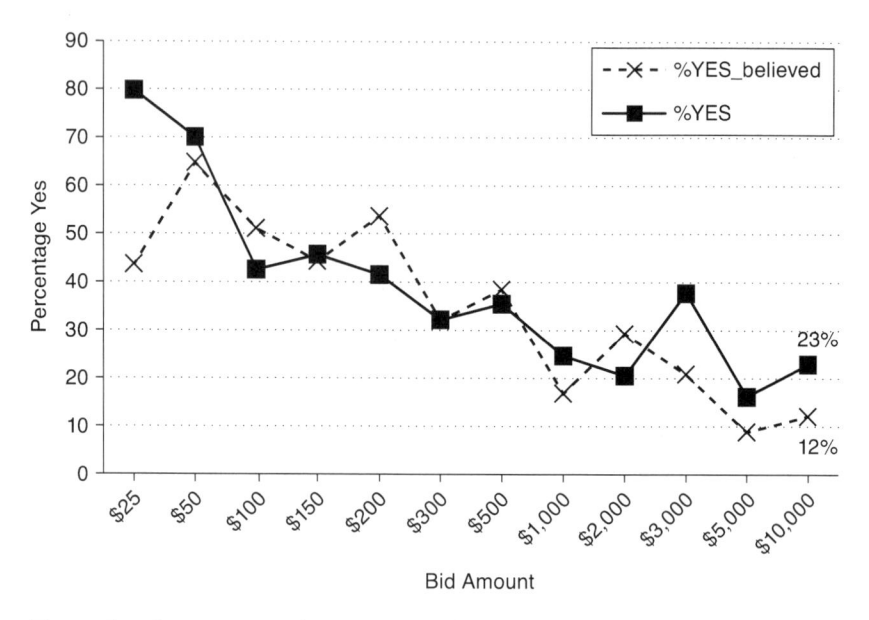

Figure 5   Comparison of percentage of yes responses vs responses adjusted for "believed" bid amount

(about 38% of the sample) to report the amount they actually thought they would pay. We used this amount to recode the data and reconfigure the yes-response function. For example, if someone was asked if they would vote yes at $5,000 but believed they would actually pay only $100, we recoded this respondent as a yes at $100. This presumes that the person voted using $100 as the tax. It is entirely possible that a person may have voted using the amount stated even if they found the amount implausible. Our adjusted yes-response curve is shown in Figure 5. Our mean willingness-to-pay estimates using the same non-parametric procedure reported earlier are shown in Table 6. Again, we report the values assuming truncation at each bid shown. The estimates fall versus the raw data as expected. The decline over the higher-end bids is largest. At $10,000, for example, the mean lower-bound WTP declines from $2,254 using the raw data to $1,508 using the newly configured data. But again, the values after adjusting are still high.

Follow-up Questions

Finally, we included a number of other follow-up questions to explore respondent behavior at high bids. The results are mixed on explaining why the tail of the yes-response function is fat. On one hand, we found

Table 6   Non-parametric estimates by bid amount and adjusted for believed bid

High-end Bid Amounts ($)	% of Yes Responses	Sample Size	Lower-bound Mean WTP ($)	% of Mean Accounted for by Highest Bid
200	54	104	103	98
300	32	93	135	75
500	38	153	211	85
1,000	17	120	295	59
2,000	29	131	560	78
3,000	21	87	779	80
5,000	9	138	955	46
10,000	12	124	1,508	60

a tendency of respondents to mentally scale down high bids and to vote simply to show support (so dollars may be largely ignored), which may explain why the yes-response rate stays high at higher bids. On the other hand, we found people to be more neoclassical (think in terms of money trade-offs) at the high bid levels and more likely to think that the red knot funds would not be used solely for protecting the red knot. Both of these effects work to decrease yes responses at high bids. In short, we cannot say we found anything in the follow-up-question responses to "explain away" the presence of fat tails and the response to high bids.

DISCUSSION

Consider Table 1 again. Based on our findings, we are left wondering what would have happened if higher bids had been considered in many of these studies where the yes-response function is truncated. While we cannot say for sure, we suspect they may have had findings similar to ours: a difficulty pinning down the tail of the yes-response function and a mean willingness-to-pay estimate that is highly sensitive to choice of maximum bid and perhaps implausibly high at extreme bids. It would be interesting to test their surveys.

Consequentiality has become an important issue in contingent valuation (Herriges et al., 2010). In order for respondents to provide meaningful data, they need to believe that the survey is consequential and that their responses matter for policy purposes. At least two recent studies are designed to address consequentiality (Herriges et al. 2010; Petrolia et al., 2014). Both appear to have fat tails, suggesting that a lack of consequentiality may not be the issue. Obviously, more is needed here to draw definitive conclusions.

Again, we see fat tails as a manifestation of hypothetical bias (the tendency of people to report a value other than their true value due to the hypothetical nature of a survey) and not an isolated contingent valuation issue. Fat tails are, after all, consistent with most contingent valuation phenomena believed to cause hypothetical bias: yea-saying, anchoring, using valuation questions to express emotive instead of trade-off values, using valuation questions to show support for a program, and so on. Viewed in this way, fixing fat tails amounts to fixing the fundamental hypothetical bias presence in contingent valuation.

Truncating high-end bids is a tempting response to fat tails. If the tail of the yes-response surface is ignored over its high end, the analyst may offer truncated values using a lower-bound non-parametric estimator as a conservative value. But, this is not a real fix to the underlying problem of hypothetical bias, nor is the resulting willingness to pay truly conservative. Indeed, it "hides" the effects of fat tails. One may falsely believe that he or she has a reasonable estimate of value when in fact the survey instrument could produce vastly different values with only modest changes in the bid levels offered. Truncating offers nothing new for understanding underlying preferences, explaining why contingent valuation data yield fat tails, or dealing with hypothetical bias.

Perhaps our most startling finding is the sensitivity of mean willingness to pay to the largest bid. This is because so much of the willingness to pay is captured in the high-end tail of the yes-response function (or demand function over high prices). One can easily double or triple a mean willingness to pay by simply picking a larger bid. This lack of robustness is troubling.

We encourage more exploration into the causes and consequences of fat tails in contingent valuation response data. Follow-up questions similar to ours but perhaps more probative might shed some light on underlying behavior and intentions of respondents facing high bids. It should be kept in mind, however, that the behavioral anomalies present for people facing high bids are likely to exist for all respondents, since bids are assigned randomly. We are also interested in knowing whether there is a fat tails equivalent for choice experiments. This would manifest through sensitivity of willingness-to-pay estimates to the maximum bid level used for the payment attribute in the choice experiment. Finally, alternative behavioral models, along with tests, to better explain choice by respondents in a survey setting may lead to a better understanding of the unexpected responses we see to high bids.

REFERENCES

Adamowicz, V., M. Dickie, S. Gerking, M. Veronesi, and D. Zinner (2014), "Household decision making and valuation of environmental health risks to parents and their children," *Journal of the Association of Environmental and Resource Economists*, **1**(4), 481–519.

Alberini, A., B. Kanninen, and R.T. Carson (1997), "Modeling response incentive effects in dichotomous choice contingent valuation data," *Land Economics*, **73**(3), 309–24.

Andersson, H., J. Hammitt, G. Lindberg, and K. Sundström (2013), "Willingness to pay and sensitivity to time framing: A theoretical analysis and application on car safety," *Environmental and Resource Economics*, **56**(3), 437–56.

Balistreri, E., G. McClelland, G. Poe, and W. Schulze (2001), "Can hypothetical questions reveal true values? A laboratory comparison of dichotomous choice and open-ended contingent values with auction values," *Environmental and Resource Economics*, **18**(3), 275–92.

Banzhaf, H.S., D. Burtraw, D. Evans, and A. Krupnick (2006), "Valuation of natural resource improvements in the Adirondacks," *Land Economics*, **82**(3), 445–64.

Berrens, R.P., A.K. Bohara, and J. Kerkvliet (1997), "A randomized response approach to dichotomous choice contingent valuation," *American Journal of Agricultural Economics*, **79**(1), 252–66.

Berrens, R.P., P. Ganderton, and C.L. Silva (1996), "Valuing the protection of minimum instream flows in New Mexico," *Journal of Agricultural and Resource Economics*, **21**(2), 294–308.

Blamey, R.K., J.W. Bennett, and M.D. Morrison (1999), "Yea-saying in contingent valuation surveys," *Land Economics*, **75**(1), 126–41.

Blomquist, G.C., K. Blumenschein, and M. Johannesson (2009), "Eliciting willingness to pay without bias using follow-up certainty statements: Comparisons between probably/definitely and a 10-point certainty scale," *Environmental and Resource Economics*, **43**(4), 473–502.

Boman, M., G. Bostedt, and B. Kriström (1999), "Obtaining welfare bounds in discrete-response valuation studies: A non-parametric approach," *Land Economics*, **75**(2), 284–94.

Boyle, K.J. (2003), "Contingent valuation in practice," in P.A. Champ, K.J. Boyle, and T.C. Brown (eds), *A Primer on Nonmarket Valuation*, Dordrecht: Kluwer Academic Publishers, pp. 111–69.

Brown, T.C., I. Ajzen, and D. Hrubes (2003), "Further tests of entreaties to avoid hypothetical bias in referendum contingent valuation," *Journal of Environmental Economics and Management*, **46**(2), 353–61.

Brown, T.C., P.A. Champ, R.C. Bishop, and D.W. McCollum (1996), "Which response format reveals the truth about donations to a public good?," *Land Economics*, **72**(2), 152–66.

Cameron, T.A. and J. Quiggin (1994), "Estimation using contingent valuation data from a 'dichotomous choice with follow-up' questionnaire," *Journal of Environmental Economics and Management*, **27**(3), 218–34.

Carson, R.T., R.C. Mitchell, M. Hanemann, R.J. Kopp, S. Presser, and P.A. Ruud (2003), "Contingent valuation and lost passive use: Damages from the Exxon Valdez oil spill," *Environmental and Resource Economics*, **25**(3), 257–86.

Carson, R.T., W.M. Hanemann, R.J. Kopp, J.A. Krosnick, R.C. Mitchell, S. Presser, P.A. Ruud, and V.K. Smith (1994), *Prospective Interim Lost Use Value Due to DDT and PCB Contamination in the Southern California Bight*, report prepared for the National Oceanic and Atmospheric Administration, La Jolla, CA: Natural Resource Damage Assessment, Inc.

Champ, P.A. and R.C. Bishop (2001), "Donation payment mechanisms and contingent valuation: An empirical study of hypothetical bias," *Environmental and Resource Economics*, **19**(4), 383–402.

Champ, P.A. and R.C. Bishop (2006), "Is willingness to pay for a public good sensitive to the elicitation format?," *Land Economics*, **82**(2), 162–73.

Champ, P.A., R. Moore, and R.C. Bishop (2009), "A comparison of approaches to mitigate hypothetical bias," *Agricultural and Resource Economics Review*, **38**(2), 166–80.

Champ, P.A., R.C. Bishop, T.C. Brown, and D.W. McCollum (1997), "Using donation mechanisms to value nonuse benefits from public good," *Journal of Environmental Economics and Management*, **33**(2), 151–62.

Champ, P.A., N. Flores, T. Brown, and J. Chivers (2002), "Contingent valuation and incentives," *Land Economics*, **78**(4), 591–604.

Chien, Y., C. Huang, and D. Shaw (2005), "A general model of starting point bias in double-bounded dichotomous contingent valuation surveys," *Journal of Environmental Economics and Management*, **52**(2), 362–77.

Cook, J., M. Jeuland, B. Maskery, and D. Whittington (2012), "Giving stated preference respondents 'time to think': Results from four countries," *Environmental and Resource Economics*, **51**(4), 473–96.

Cooper, J. and J. Loomis (1992), "Sensitivity of willingness-to-pay estimates to bid design in dichotomous choice contingent valuation models," *Land Economics*, **68**(2), 211–24.

Corrigan, J., C. Kling, and J. Zhao (2008), "Willingness to pay and the cost of commitment: An empirical specification and test," *Environmental and Resource Economics*, **40**(2), 285–98.

Desvousges, W.H., K. Mathews, and K. Train (2015), "An adding-up test on contingent valuations of river and lake quality," *Land Economics*, **91**(3), 556–71.

Desvousges, W.H., F.W. Johnson, R.W. Dunford, S.P. Hudson, K.N. Wilson, and K.J. Boyle (1993), 'Measuring natural resource damages with contingent valuation: Tests of validity and reliability', in J.A. Hausman (ed.), *Contingent Valuation: A Critical Assessment*, Amsterdam: Elsevier Science, pp. 91–164.

Egan, K., J. Corrigan, and D. Dwyer (2015), "Three reasons to use annual payments in contingent valuation surveys: Convergent validity, discount rates, and mental accounting," *Journal of Environmental Economics and Management*, **75**, 123–36.

Farmer, M. and C. Lipscomb (2008), "Conservative dichotomous choice responses in the active policy setting: DC rejections below WTP," *Environmental and Resource Economics*, **39**(3), 223–46.

Frykblom, P. (1997), "Hypothetical question modes and real willingness to pay," *Journal of Environmental Economics and Management*, **34**(3), 275–87.

Frykblom, P. and J.F. Shogren (2000), "An experimental testing of anchoring effects in discrete choice questions," *Environmental and Resource Economics*, **16**(3), 329–41.

Gerking, S., M. Dickie, and M. Veronesi (2014), "Valuation of human health: An integrated model of willingness to pay for mortality and morbidity reductions," *Journal of Environmental Economics and Management*, **68**(1), 20–45.

Giraud, K.L., C.A. Bond, and J.J. Bond (2005), "Consumer preferences for locally made specialty food products across northern New England," *Agricultural and Resource Economics Review*, **34**(2), 204–16.

Giraud, K.L., J.B. Loomis, and J.C. Cooper (2001), "A comparison of willingness-to-pay estimation techniques from referendum questions," *Environmental and Resource Economics*, **20**(4), 331–46.

Guria, J., J. Leung, M. Jones-Lee, and G. Loomes (2005), "The willingness to accept value of statistical life relative to the willingness to pay value: Evidence and policy implications," *Environmental and Resource Economics*, **32**(1), 113–27.

Haab, T.C. and K.E. McConnell (1997), "Referendum models and negative willingness to pay: Alternative solutions," *Journal of Environmental Economics and Management*, **32**(2), 251–70.

Haab, T.C. and K.E. McConnell (1998), "Referendum models and economic values: Theoretical, intuitive, and practical bounds on willingness to pay," *Land Economics*, **74**(2), 216–29.

Haab, T.C. and K.E. McConnell (2002), *Valuing Environmental and Natural Resources*, Cheltenham, UK and Northampton, MA, USA: Edward Elgar Publishing.

Hammitt, J.K. and Y. Zhou (2006), "The economic value of air-pollution-related health risks in China: A contingent valuation study," *Environmental and Resource Economics*, **33**(3), 399–423.

Harrison, G.W. and J.C. Lesley (1996), "Must contingent valuation surveys cost so much?," *Journal of Environmental Economics and Management*, **31**(1), 79–95.

Herriges, J., C. Kling, C. Liu, and J. Tobias (2010), "What are the consequences of consequentiality?," *Journal of Environmental Economics and Management*, **59**(1), 67–81.

Hite, D., D. Hudson, and W. Intarapapong (2002), "Willingness to pay for water quality improvements: The case of precision application technology," *Journal of Agricultural and Resource Economics*, **27**(2), 433–49.

Holmes, T.P. and R.A. Kramer (1995), "An independent sample test of yea-saying and starting point bias in dichotomous-choice contingent valuation," *Journal of Environmental Economics and Management*, **29**(1), 121–32.

Huth, W.L. and O.A. Morgan (2011), "Measuring the willingness to pay for cave diving," *Marine Resource Economics*, **26**(2), 151–66.

Ivehammar, P. (2009), "The payment vehicle used in CV studies of environmental goods does matter," *Journal of Agricultural and Resource Economics*, **34**(3), 450–63.

Johnston, R.J. (2006), "Is hypothetical bias universal? Validating contingent valuation responses using a binding public referendum," *Journal of Environmental Economics and Management*, **52**(1), 469–81.

Kanninen, B.J. (1993), "Bias in discrete response contingent valuation," *Journal of Environmental Economics and Management*, **28**(1), 114–25.

Kanninen, B. and B. Kriström (1993), "Sensitivity of willingness to pay estimates to bid design in dichotomous choice valuation models: Comment," *Land Economics*, **69**(2), 199–202.

Koford, B., G. Blomquist, D. Hardesty, and D. Troske (2012), "Estimating consumer willingness to supply and willingness-to-pay for curbside recycling," *Land Economics*, **88**(4), 745–63.

Kovacs, K.F. and D.M. Larson (2008), "Identifying individual discount rates and valuing public open space with stated-preference models," *Land Economics*, **84**(2), 209–24.

Kramer, A. and D. Evan Mercer (1997), "Valuing a global environmental good: U.S. residents' willingness to pay to protect tropical rain forests," *Land Economics*, **73**(2), 196–210.

Kriström, B. (1990), "A non-parametric approach to the estimation of welfare measures in discrete response valuation studies," *Land Economics*, **66**(2), 135–9.

Labao, R., H. Francisco, D. Harder, and F.I. Santos (2008), "Do colored photographs affect willingness-to-pay responses for endangered species conservation?," *Environmental and Resource Economics*, **40**(2), 251–64.

Landry, C.E. and J.A. List (2007), "Using ex ante approaches to obtain credible signals for value in contingent markets: Evidence from the field," *American Journal of Agricultural Economics*, **89**(2), 420–29.

Langford, I., I. Bateman, A. Jones, H. Langford, and S. Georgiou (1998), "Improved estimation of willingness-to-pay in dichotomous choice contingent valuation studies," *Land Economics*, **74**(1), 65–75.

Leiter, A.M. and G.J. Pruckner (2009), "Proportionality of willingness-to-pay to small changes in risk: The impact of attitudinal factors in scope tests," *Environmental and Resource Economics*, **42**(2), 169–86.

Leon, C. and J. Arana (2012), "The dynamics of preference elicitation after an environmental disaster: Stability and emotional load," *Land Economics*, **88**(2), 362–81.

Lindberg, K., R.L. Johnson, and R.P. Berrens (1997), "Contingent valuation of rural tourism development with tests of scope and mode stability," *Journal of Agricultural and Resource Economics*, **22**(1), 44–60.

Longo, A., D. Hoyos, and A. Markandya (2012), "Willingness to pay for ancillary benefits of climate change mitigation," *Environmental and Resource Economics*, **51**(1), 119–40.

Longo, A., D. Hoyos, and A. Markandya (2015), "Sequence effects in the valuation of multiple environmental programs using the contingent valuation method," *Land Economics*, **91**(1), 20–35.

Loureiro, M.L., J.B. Loomis, and M.X. Vázquez (2009), "Economic valuation of environmental damages due to the Prestige oil spill in Spain," *Environmental and Resource Economics*, **44**(4), 537–53.

Lunander, A. (1998), "Inducing incentives to understate and to overstate willingness-to-pay within the open-ended and the dichotomous-choice elicitation formats: An experimental study," *Journal of Environmental Economics and Management*, **35**(1), 88–102.

Lusk, J.L. (2003), "Effects of cheap talk on consumer willingness-to-pay for golden rice," *American Journal of Agricultural Economics*, **85**(4), 840–56.

McFadden, D. and G.K. Leonard (1993), "Issues in the contingent valuation of environmental goods: Methodologies for data collection and analysis," in J.A. Hausman (ed.), *Contingent Valuation: A Critical Assessment*, Amsterdam: Elsevier Science, pp. 165–216.

Michael, J.A. and S.D. Reiling (1997), "The role of expectations and heterogeneous preferences for congestion in the valuation of recreation benefits," *Agricultural and Resource Economics Review*, **26**(2), 166–73.

Moore, R., B. Provencher, and R.C. Bishop (2011), "Valuing a spatially variable environmental resource: Reducing non-point-source pollution in Green Bay, Wisconsin," *Land Economics*, **87**(1), 45–59.

Morgenstern, R., W. Pizer, and J. Shih (1998), "The cost of environmental protection," *Resources for the Future Discussion Paper No. 98-36.*

Morrison, M. and T. Brown (2009), "Testing the effectiveness of certainty scales, cheap talk, and dissonance-minimization in reducing hypothetical bias in contingent valuation studies," *Environmental and Resource Economics*, **44**(3), 307–26.

Murphy, J.J., T.H. Stevens, and D. Weatherhead (2005), "Is cheap talk effective at eliminating hypothetical bias in a provision point mechanism?," *Environmental and Resource Economics*, **30**(3), 327–43.

Myers, K.H., G.R. Parsons, and P.E. Edwards (2010), "Measuring the recreational use value of migratory shorebirds on the Delaware Bay," *Marine Resource Economics*, **25**(3), 247–64.

Nahuelhual, L., M.L. Loureiro, and J. Loomis (2004), "Using random parameters to account for heterogeneous preference in contingent valuation of public open space," *Journal of Agricultural and Resource Economics*, **29**(3), 537–52.

Nunes, P. and J. van den Bergh (2004), "Can people value protection against invasive marine species? Evidence from a joint TC–CV survey in the Netherlands," *Environmental and Resource Economics*, **28**(4), 517–32.

Petrolia, D. and T. Kim (2009), "What are Barrier Islands worth? Estimated of willingness to pay for restoration," *Marine Resource Economics*, **24**(2), 131–46.

Petrolia, D., M. Interis, and J. Hwang (2014), "America's wetland? A national survey of willingness-to-pay for restoration of Louisiana's coastal wetlands," *Marine Resource Economics*, **29**(1), 17–37.

Polome, P., A. Veen, and P. Geurts (2006), "Is referendum the same as dichotomous choice contingent valuation?," *Land Economics*, **82**(2), 174–88.

Poor, P.J. (1999), "The value of additional central flyway wetlands: The case of Nebraska's rainwater basin wetlands," *Journal of Agricultural and Resource Economics*, **24**(1), 253–65.

Popp, D. (2001), "Altruism and the demand for environmental quality," *Land Economics*, **77**(3), 339–49.

Ready, R.C. and D. Hu (1995), "Statistical approaches to the fat tail problem for dichotomous choice contingent valuation," *Land Economics*, **71**(4), 491–9.

Ready, R.C., J.C. Buzby, and D. Hu (1996), "Difference between continuous and discrete contingent value estimates," *Land Economics*, **72**(3), 397–411.

Reaves, D.W., R.A. Kramer, and T.P. Holmes (1999), "Does question format matter? Valuing an endangered species," *Environmental and Resource Economics*, **14**(3), 365–83.

Richardson, L., J. Loomis, and P. Champ (2013), "Valuing morbidity from wildfire smoke exposure: A comparison of revealed and stated preference techniques," *Land Economics*, **89**(1), 76–100.

Riddel, M. and J. Loomis (1998), "Joint estimation of multiple CVM scenarios under a double bounded questioning format," *Environmental and Resource Economics*, **12**(1), 77–98.

Roach, B., K.J. Boyle, and M. Welsh (2002), "Testing bid design effects in multiple-bounded, contingent-valuation questions," *Land Economics*, **78**(1), 121–31.

Ropicki, A.J., S.L. Larkin, and C.M. Adams (2010), "Seafood substitution and mislabeling: WTP for a locally caught grouper labeling program in Florida," *Marine Resource Economics*, **25**(1), 77–92.

Saz-Salazar, S. and L. Garcia-Menendez (2001), "Willingness to pay for environmental improvements in a large city," *Environmental and Resource Economics*, **20**(2), 103–12.

Scarpa, R., K. Willis, and G. Garrod (2001), "Estimating benefits for effective enforcement of speed reduction from dichotomous-choice CV," *Environmental and Resource Economics*, **20**(4), 281–304.

Smith, V.K. (1996), "Can contingent valuation distinguish economic values for different public goods?," *Land Economics*, **72**(2), 139–51.

Tuan, T.R. and S. Navrud (2007), "Valuing cultural heritage in developing countries: Comparing and pooling contingent valuation and choice modeling estimates," *Environmental and Resource Economics*, **38**(1), 51–69.

Vaughan, W.J. and D.J. Rodriguez (2001), "Obtaining welfare bounds in discrete-response valuation studies: Comment," *Land Economics*, **77**(3), 457–65.

Wang, H. (1997), "Treatment of 'don't-know' responses in contingent valuation surveys: A random valuation model," *Journal of Environmental Economics and Management*, **32**(2), 219–32.

Weldesilassie, A.B., O. Frör, E. Boelee, and S. Dabbert (2009), "The economic value of improved wastewater irrigation: A contingent valuation study in Addis Ababa, Ethiopia," *Journal of Agricultural and Resource Economics*, **34**(3), 428–49.

Welsh, M.P. and G.L. Poe (1998), "Elicitation effects in contingent valuation: Comparisons to a multiple bounded discrete choice approach," *Journal of Environmental Economics and Management*, **36**(2), 170–85.

Whitehead, J. (2002), "Incentive compatibility and starting-point bias in iterative valuation questions," *Land Economics*, **78**(2), 285–97.

Whitehead, J., W.B. Clifford, and T.J. Hoban (2001), "Willingness to pay for a saltwater recreational fishing license: A comparison of angler groups," *Marine Resource Economics*, **16**(3), 177–94.

Whittington, D. (2002), "Improving the performance of contingent valuation studies in developing countries," *Environmental and Resource Economics*, **22**(2), 323–67.

Zhang, H., K. Gallardo, J. McCluskey, and E. Kupferman (2010), "Consumers' willingness-to-pay for treatment-induced quality attributes in Anjou pears," *Journal of Agricultural and Resource Economics*, **35**(1), 105–17.

3. Inadequate response to frequency of payments in contingent valuation of environmental goods

Kelley Myers, George Parsons, and Kenneth Train[1]

INTRODUCTION

The purpose of this chapter is to test the sensitivity of a willingness to pay (WTP) derived from a referendum-style contingent valuation (CV) survey to the frequency of payments specified in the valuation question. Using a split-sample survey we consider a one-time payment versus an annual reoccurring payment under the null hypothesis that the present values from the two payment frequencies will be the same. We offer this as a simple test of the validity of the CV method. In principle, one would hope that values are invariant with respect to frequency of payment. Boyle (forthcoming) notes that "[t]his is another area where there is scant research" and cites some evidence that suggests respondents may fail to seriously consider the time frame of payments in the valuation question.

The setting for our analysis is the valuation of a conservation program designed to protect a migratory shorebird that has recently been in decline. We redesigned a survey previously used by Myers (2013) and Parsons and Myers (2016) to conduct our test. The split-sample surveys are identical but for the frequency of payment required – one uses one-time payment, the other uses annual reoccurring payment. With response data from both surveys, we estimate willingness to pay using a non-parametric Turnbull estimator and a parametric probit estimator and test for differences in willingness to pay between our treatments. We also consider sensitivity tests – weighting to align data with the census, adjustments for certainty of response, and adjustment for disbelief in bid amount.

---

[1] Respectively: Senior Economist, Cardno, Newark, DE; Professor, School of Marine Science & Policy and Department of Economics, University of Delaware; Adjunct Professor Emeritus, University of California, Berkeley.

For the non-parametric and parametric measures, and across all our sensitivity analyses, we reject the null hypothesis that the present value of the willingness to pay from the one-time payment and reoccurring annual payment are equal. Indeed, respondents more or less treat the one-time payment and reoccurring annual payments as the same, which implies a present value for the annual payments that is about 30 times larger than for one-time payment. The implied discount rates, depending on the estimation method, range from 300 to 900%.

Our results contribute to a small but growing literature that shows that CV estimates of willingness to pay are highly sensitive to the time frame of payment that is specified to respondents. The next section examines that literature before we present a discussion of our survey and results.

LITERATURE REVIEW

To our knowledge, six studies have compared CV estimates under annual versus one-time payments using a split-sample design (Table 1). In all six, the present value of respondents' willingness to pay (PV WTP) was estimated to be far higher when the cost prompts were stated as annual payments over a period of time than when the cost prompts were a one-time payment. Stated equivalently, the implicit discount rate that reconciles the responses under the two types of cost prompts was found to be implausibly high in all six studies.

Table 1   Implicit discount rates comparing one-time versus annual payments

Authors	Resource	Duration of Payments	Discount Rate (%)
Kahneman and Knetsch (1992)	Toxic waste treatment facility	Five years	130+
Echeverria et al. (1995)	Forest preservation	In perpetuity	559
Stevens et al. (1997)	Atlantic salmon restoration	Five years	270
Bond et al. (2009)	Sea lion protection	Five years	1,315
		Fifteen	61
Kim and Haab (2009)	Oyster reef restoration	Duration of project	98–131
		In perpetuity	45
Egan et al. (2015)	Wetlands protection for beachgoers	Ten years	104
		In perpetuity	62

Kahneman and Knetsch (1992) compared respondents' stated WTP for a toxic waste treatment facility by a one-time payment versus annual payments for five years. The mean WTP was estimated to be $141 when respondents were asked about a one-time payment, and $81 annually when asked about annual payments for five years, which implies a discount rate of 130%. When seven respondents (out of 206) with unreasonably large stated WTPs were eliminated, the results became even more extreme. The authors concluded that "[t]he results provide no reliable indication that the respondents discriminated between payment schedules that differed greatly in total present value."

Echeverria et al. (1995) examined WTP to prevent a forest preserve from being converted to agricultural use and stated that "no plausible discount rate equates [their finding of] a recurring annual annuity of $110.64 to a single lump sum net present value of $130.43." The implicit discount rate is 559%.[2]

Stevens et al. (1997) examined restoration of Atlantic salmon and found that respondents have a mean WTP of $21.20 annually for five years, which has a present value (PV) of $96.37 at a 5% discount rate, versus a lump-sum mean WTP of $29.00.[3] That is, the mean PV WTP is estimated to be more than three times greater when the cost prompt is stated as annual payments for five years rather than a lump-sum payment. The implicit discount rate is 270%.[4] The authors state that, "[i]nsensitivity to payment schedule may therefore be an important, but often overlooked factor in the design, interpretation, and use of contingent valuation studies."

Bond et al. (2009) examined WTP for measures that protect the Western stock of the Stellar sea lion in Alaska using three payment mechanisms that differed in duration. Some respondents considered the protection measures hurtful (negative WTP) and others as helpful (positive WTP), and to account for this difference, the authors segmented the sample on the basis of exogenous factors that partially differentiated the two groups. For the group that tended to have a positive WTP, the authors report a PV WTP of $208.78 based on a one-time payment, $874.38 based on

---

[2] The present value of annuity that starts immediately is $X(1 + r)/r$ where X is the annual payment and r the discount rate. The value of r that equates $130.43 = 110.64(1 + r)/r$ is $r = 5.59$. The same r is obtained when the payments are assumed to start at the end of the current year.

[3] The PV calculation assumes that the payments begin immediately. If the lump-sum and first annual payment are made at the end of the year, then each PV is lower by $1/(1.05)$, but the ratio of PVs and the implicit discount rate are the same.

[4] 2.7 is the value of r that equates $29 = 21.2*(1 + (1 + r)^{-1} + (1 + r)^{-2} + (1 + r)^{-3} + (1 + r)^{-4})$. In parametric models with different specifications, the authors report that the estimated discount rate "ranged from 50 to 270%."

annual payments for five years, and $886.72 based on annual payments for 15 years, using a discount rate of 5.49%.[5] That is: changing the payment plan in the survey from a one-time payment to annual payments raised the estimated PV WTP by a factor of over four. The implicit discount rate is 1,315% (no, that is not a typo) for the five-year plan compared to the one-year plan, 61% for the 15-year plan compared to the one-year plan, and 5.85% for the 15-year plan compared to the five-year plan.[6] The high implicit discount rates arose in this study when comparing the one-time payment with a stream of payments over time, and not when comparing streams of different lengths.[7]

Kim and Haab (2009) study oyster reef restoration using a variety of project lengths (five and ten years) and different payment schemes: one-time payment, annual payment over the life of the project, and annual payment in perpetuity. For the comparison of one-time versus annual payments for the duration of the project, discount rates were estimated to be 98–131%. A relatively low rate of 45% was obtained in the comparison of one-time payments against annual payments in perpetuity.[8]

Egan et al. (2015) estimated WTP by beachgoers on beaches on Lake Erie to preserve a nearby wetland that would, in turn, improve water quality and other environmental conditions where people swim and enjoy the park. They considered one-time, ten-year annual and perpetual payments. They compared their results to a travel cost model. Their PV WTP

---

[5] The authors reported that 5.49% was the 30-year bond yield at the time.

[6] With payments that start immediately and $r = 0.0549$, 194.05 is the value of X that equates $874.38 = X*(1 + (1 + r)^{-1} + (1 + r)^{-2} + (1 + r)^{-3} + (1 + r)^{-4})$. Then the implicit discount rate at which the PV of the one-year payment of 208.78 equals that of five-year payments of 194.05 apiece is the r at which $208.78 = 194.05*(1 + (1 + r)^{-1} + (1 + r)^{-2} + (1 + r)^{-3} + (1 + r)^{-4})$, which is $r = 13.15$. Similar calculations provide the implicit discount rates for the other plan comparisons. Note that the same value of r is obtained if payments are assumed to start at the end of the current year.

[7] Using parametric models, the authors estimated a discount rate of 23% when all payment plans were pooled and 80% when the one- and 15-year plans were pooled. The 80% corresponds to the 61% given above from direct estimation. The lower discount rate for all three plans combined is apparently due to the comparatively low discount rate implicit in the five- and 15-year comparison. The authors did not report a parametric estimate of discount rate for the one- and five-year plans combined.

[8] The abstract to the Kim and Haab (2009) study says that "the temporal willingness to pay for the project is the same across different payment schemes," which can be confusing to people who have not read the full article. The authors tested whether the non-cost coefficients of a probit model were the same under different payment schemes, allowing the cost coefficient to differ by payment scheme. The hypothesis of no difference in non-cost coefficients was accepted, with the estimated cost coefficient differing over payment schedules. The non-cost terms in utility capture the benefits of the program, which is the basis of the authors' statement in the abstract. The PV WTP, which is the utility benefits divided by the coefficient of PV costs, differed considerably over payment schemes, as the authors show by their calculation of the discount rates that we give in the text above.

estimates are $45, $185, and $360 for one-time, ten-year annual, and perpetual annual payments using a 5% discount rate. The implied discount rates for the one-time payment is 104% when compared to the ten-year annual payments and 62% when compared to the perpetual annual payments. The implied rate for ten-year annual payments when compared with perpetual payments is 15%. Egan et al. (2015) go on to argue that perpetual annual payments are preferred because their estimated values (at least in their application) are closest to the travel cost estimates and in their judgment people are unlikely to be able to do the discounting implicitly required in a one-time payment option.

In addition to these six studies, five other studies have conducted analyses that shed light on CV estimates under different payment horizons, but were not comparing annual versus lump-sum payments. All of these studies found that CV estimates differ greatly depending on how the payment question is formulated. The five studies are the following.

Rowe et al. (1992) compared two ways of describing a five-year payment schedule. The authors asked one group of respondents how much they were WTP annually for five years, and asked another group of respondents how much they were WTP in total over five years. If the latter group considered the payments to be evenly spaced over the five years, then the two groups were considering the same payment schedule. However, if the latter group thought that the payments would not be evenly spaced (e.g., occurring more up front, or more later), then the two schedules differ. In any case, the authors found that total WTP over the five years was considerably higher for the first group (who were asked WTP annually for five years) than for the second group (who were asked total WTP over five years).

Solino et al. (2009) conducted a similar comparison of two different ways of paying the same total amount: "In one [version of the survey] we considered an annual payment and in the other a bimonthly payment, with equivalent aggregated monetary amounts." Their cost prompts were €5–20 bimonthly in one survey and €60–120 annually in the other. The total amount paid in each year was the same under both sets of prompts, with just the periodicity differing. Consistent with Rowe et al. (1992), Solino et al. (2009) found more favorable response for smaller but more frequent payments even when the total amount of payment was the same: "[W]e observe that 76.87% [of respondents] replied affirmatively to the valuation question in the bimonthly version, while in the annual version this percentage drops to 67.27%."

Stumberg et al. (2001) compared three-year and ten-year annual payment schedules. Using a split-sample design, they found that "payment time horizon has a significant effect on valuation statements," with the PV WTP being far greater when based on the ten-year scheme than the three-year scheme.[9]

Kovacs and Larson (2008) examined monthly payments for one, four, seven, and ten years. They report estimated discount rates of "around 30%." However, the authors' estimates were obtained from models that included responses to follow-up questions (double-bounded data) and a variety of adjustments for potential behavioral issues. Direct examination of their data indicates that the discount rate implied by their study is actually over 85%. In particular: the one-year and four-year plans were designed to have the same present value at a discount rate of 85%. However, more respondents said "yes" to the four-year plan than the one-year plan, which means that the implicit discount rate exceeds 85%. Similarly, high discount rates arise for the seven- and ten-year plans compared to the one-year plan.

Chen et al. (2014) employed an internal comparison of one-time versus annual payments (as opposed to using split samples) by asking each respondent their WTP under both schedules and allowing them to go back and change their answer for one schedule after considering the other schedule. This procedure tests the internal consistency of respondents' answers to both schedules. The authors report that "the LBM [lower bound mean] estimated was €49.99 per year...using the recurrent payment model; and a lump-sum amount of €99.83...using the single payment model. The implicit discount rate was 100.3%."

The past studies raise a methodological issue in addition to their substantive findings. While most studies kept the cost prompts constant while varying the payment schedules, Kovacs and Larson (2008) and Kim and Haab (2009) adjusted the cost prompts for each payment schedule, using smaller cost prompts with longer payment schedules. That is, the payment schedules were designed, in these two studies, so that a rational individual, using a specified discount rate, would be indifferent between the schedules. This design, while it might seem reasonable intuitively, means that the schedules cannot be used to detect irrational behavior. As an extreme example, consider a survey that compares a $100 lump-sum payment versus annual payments of $23 for five years, where the $23 annual payment was set because it provides the same present value at 8% as the single $100. If the same share of respondents vote yes in each case, the results could mean that (1) respondents are responding rationally to both the bid amount and

---

[9] The authors report (p. 127) that mean WTP is $57 per year for respondents offered the ten-year scheme and $87 per year for those offered the three-year scheme. At the 4% discount rate that the authors use and payments starting immediately, PV WTP is $480 under the ten-year scheme and $251 under the three-year scheme. The implicit discount rate is 39.5% for this comparison of three-year and ten-year plans.

the number of payments, using a discount rate of 8%, or (2) respondents are not responding to either the bid amount or the number of payments.[10] By specifying the bid amounts to reflect rational response, the design makes non-response look the same as rational response.[11]

SURVEY

We conduct our test using a survey instrument previously used by Myers (2013) and Parsons and Myers (2016). We launched essentially the same survey, but amended the willingness-to-pay questions to test for sensitivity to payment frequency. We used their one-time payment schedule for one of our treatments, and specified an annually recurring payment for our second treatment.

The valuation scenario in our survey is a conservation program designed to protect the Atlantic red knot, a migratory shorebird, which has been in decline for decades. We use an Internet-based survey and sample households in New Jersey and Delaware, a primary stopping point on the red knot's annual migration path. We use Survey Sampling International's opt-in respondent panel and gather data to mimic the New Jersey-Delaware (NJ-DE) population along the lines of income, age, and gender. In the final analysis we needed to do some additional weighting of the data to bring the sample in line with actual population characteristics (more on that later).

The survey design follows a common format. We begin with a series of introductory warm-up questions about the environment and migratory birds in the region. Then, we describe the historic and current condition of the red knot using maps, pictures, and graphs. Next, we lay out a hypothetical resource conservation program to be conducted jointly by the states of New Jersey and Delaware to protect the red knot. People were then asked to vote for or against the program at some cost to their

---

[10] Burrows et al. (2016) and Parsons and Myers (2016) provide evidence, in their own and others' studies, of small response to the bid amounts in CV. This chapter suggests that there also exists a small response to the number of payments.

[11] Solino et al. (2009) also adjusted their costs prompts. However, their purpose was different, namely, to examine response to payment periodicity when the total amount of payment is the same. They varied the feature in question (periodicity) while holding another feature (total payment) constant, which prevents collinearity. The purpose of the studies by Kovac and Larson (2008) and Kim and Haab (2009) was to examine whether different lengths of payment streams affect the CV estimate of PV WTP under standard discount rates and, equivalently, to estimate the implicit discount rate that reconciles the differences in responses. For this purpose, varying together the number of payments over time and the size of each payment creates collinearity that operates against the goal of estimation.

household in a referendum-style CV question. Here we use a split-sample survey wherein half of the population sees the program cost as a one-time payment (Version A) and the other sees the program cost as a reoccurring annual payment (Version B). In both surveys respondents are shown one of the following bids in a random draw: $25, $50, $100, $150, $200, or $300. Our null hypothesis is that mean willingness to pay in present value terms is the same in the two samples.

The actual CV referendum question is shown in Figure 1. The wording variation in the one-time versus annual-payment versions of the survey is in square brackets. In addition, in the preamble to the CV question respondents were told that the upcoming payment frequency would be either one-time or annual. The survey finishes with some auxiliary follow-up questions and the usual set of demographic data. Our sample size is n = 963 for the one-time payment groups and n = 964 for the annual recurring group. Table 2 gives demographic information for the two groups.

ANALYSIS

In Version A of the survey instrument, respondents were asked whether they would be willing to make a one-time payment that would be paid as part of their taxes in 2017. The present value of this payment, at the time that the respondent answered the question, is $PV_A = XA/(1 + r)$ where XA is the dollar amount of the payment and r is the discount rate, since the taxes will not be paid until a year hence. In Version B, respondents were asked to pay a given amount annually starting in 2017. The present value is $PVB = XB/r$. The discount rate that equates the present values is $r = XB/(XA - XB)$.[12]

Table 3 gives the share of "yes" votes at each bid level for both versions of the survey. For each bid, the share is lower for the annual payments than the one-time payment, which indicates a response to the difference in the number of payments. The differences in shares are not statistically significant, but the pattern is uniform.

Table 4 gives (1) the lower-bound (Turnbull) estimate of the mean WTP per payment of each payment frequency, calculated in the usual way (Haab and McConnell, 2002, Ch. 3) with folding back to account for

---

[12] Here is the derivation. Find the r that solves $XA/(1 + r) = XB/r$. Rearranging gives $r/(1 + r) = XB/XA$. Let $Z = XB/XA$. Rearranging again gives $r = (1 + r)Z$ and then $r = Z/(1 - Z)$. Substituting XB/XA back into the equation for Z and simplifying gives $r = XB/(XA - XB)$.

> Now, suppose the *Red Knot Protection Agreement* was on the ballot and that the actions in the Agreement were expected to improve the projected status of the **Atlantic red knot** in ten years from *endangered* to *stabilized* as shown below, and then maintain its stabilized status after ten years
>
> *Expected Improvement in the Status of the Atlantic red knot in ten years*
>
> [Diagram: Steps labeled Extinct, Endangered, Threatened, Stabilized, Recovered, with arrow indicating movement from Endangered to Stabilized]
>
> Population strong and able to withstand most disturbances (40,001 to 70,000 birds)
>
> Population facing high risk of extinction (Less than 14,000 birds)
>
> If the total cost to your household to finance the Agreement was [a one-time, or, an annual] payment of $[25, 50, 100, 150, 200, or 300] [in 2017, or, starting in 2017], how would you vote if the Agreement were on the ballot in the next election?
>
> Please consider your income, expenses and other possible uses of this money before you vote. Also, please remember that the results of this survey will be provided to policy makers.
>
> ○ I would vote for the Agreement
> ○ I would vote against the Agreement

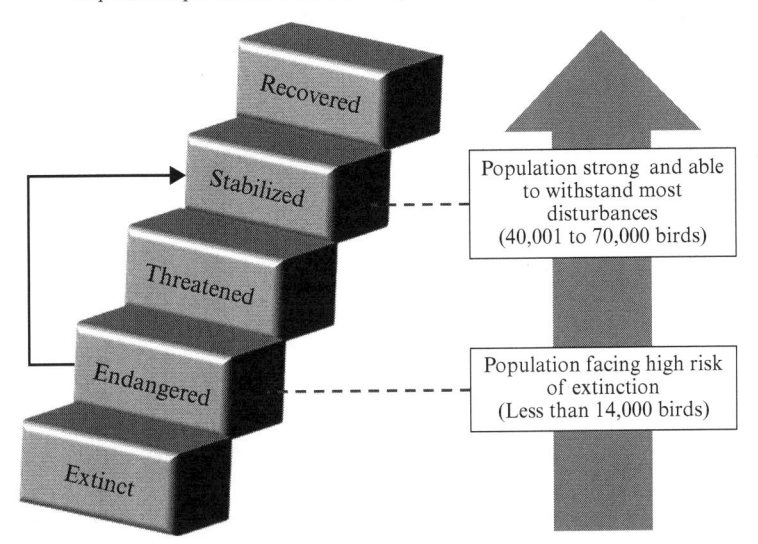

Figure 1   Referendum question in survey: terms in square brackets varied over respondents

non-monotonicities; (2) the lower-bound estimate of the mean present value WTP, based on the yield on 30-year Treasury securities of 2.84% in 2015[13] (which is the yield that Bond et al., 2009 used for their present value calculations, though the yield was 5.49% in 2009); (3) the implicit discount

---

[13] Accessed November 29, 2016 at http://www.federalreserve.gov/releases/H15/data.htm.

Table 2   Comparison of split samples

	One-time Payment	Annual Payments
Number of respondents	964	963
Income group shares		
<$30,000	19.61	19.42
30,000–50,000	19.29	19.31
50,000–100,000	37.34	37.38
100,000+	23.76	23.88
Age group shares		
18–34	23.86	23.88
35–54	36.31	36.14
55+	39.83	39.98
Percentage male	40.46	41.02
Education-level shares		
Some high school or less	1.45	1.14
High school degree	17.32	16.61
Technical school or some college	21.78	25.03
College degree	34.65	35.93
Some graduate work	5.08	5.30
Graduate degree	19.71	15.99

Table 3   Share of yes vote by bid amount

Bid	One-time Payment		Annual Payments	
	Number of respondents	Percentage yes	Number of respondents	Percentage yes
25	161	77.64	161	70.81
50	161	71.43	160	69.38
100	158	70.25	160	58.13
150	162	55.56	161	52.17
200	160	60.63	161	50.93
300	162	49.38	160	45.00

rate that equates the present values of the mean WTP per payment for the one-time and annual payments; and (4) 95% confidence intervals for each of these statistics. The confidence intervals were calculated by the bootstrap method, which explicitly accounts for the random nature of non-monotonicities in the shares. Confidence intervals are reported instead of standard errors because the bootstrap method does not utilize asymptotic normality.

Table 4 Turnbull lower-bound estimates (95% confidence intervals in parentheses)

	One-time Payment	Annual Payments
WTP per payment	$179.85	$160.66
	(170.09–189.85)	(150.09–171.15)
Present value of WTP (discount rate = 2.84%)	$174.88	$5,657.04
	(165.39–184.61)	(5,284.86–6,026.41)
Implicit discount rate	837%	
	(434–3,570%)	

With a one-time payment to be made a year after the survey, the lower-bound estimate of the mean WTP is $180, which has a present value of $175 based on the Treasury yield. With annual payments in perpetuity, the mean WTP for each payment has a lower bound of $161, giving a present value of $5,657. By asking WTP in terms of annual payments instead of a one-time payment, the estimated social value of protecting the red knot rises by a factor of 32. The implicit discount rate is 837%, under which each passing year reduces the value of a payment by 89%.[14] This implicit discount rate is at the higher end of the range found in other studies, but below that in Bond et al. (2009). In any case, it is implausible as a measure of the actual time-value of money to consumers. We also estimated a probit model of the yes/no vote to obtain a parametric estimate of the mean WTP, as opposed to the lower-bound estimate. The results are given in Table 5, with asymptotic standard errors for each statistic. The estimated mean WTP is $279 for a one-time payment at the end of the year, which translates into a present value of $271 at the Treasury yield. As expected, the parametric estimate is higher than the lower-bound estimate. For annual payments, the estimated mean WTP per payment is $217, which translates into a present value of $7,649 – higher by a factor of 28. The discount rate implied by the parametric estimates is 351%.

To investigate whether the results are sensitive to various issues, we recalculated the above statistics in the following ways:

---

[14] As discussed above, we define the discount rate in the standard way, under which each year reduces the present value of a payment by $1/(1 + r)$. The discount rate is sometimes defined such that each year reduces the present value of a payment by $(1 - d)$. The implicit r of 837% is equivalent to $d = 89\%$.

Table 5 Probit estimates (standard errors in parentheses)

	One-time Payment	Annual Payments
Constant	0.7337	0.5445
	(0.0764)	(0.0743)
Cost	−0.002629	−0.002507
	(0.000447)	(0.000442)
WTP per payment	$279.04	$217.23
	(28.02)	(21.30)
Present value WTP	$271.33	$7,648.94
	(27.26)	(750.00)
Implicit discount rate		351%
		(222%)

- *Census weights:* Using weights for respondents such that the weighted sample reflects the US census shares by age, income group, and gender.[15]
- *Certainty weights:* Using weights that account for each respondent's level of certainty about their yes/no vote. In a follow-up question, each respondent was asked to give, on a slider-scale between 1 and 10, their level of certainty in their vote. We created weights that are proportional to level of certainty and sum to sample size.
- *Uncertainty elimination:* Using only those respondents whose level of certainty was 7 or higher. This requirement eliminated 402 respondents, with the analysis performed on the remaining 1,525, of whom 984 voted yes.
- *Elimination based on disbelief of cost:* In a follow-up question, respondents were asked whether they believed, if the measure passed, they would actually be charged the amount that they had been told. The 737 respondents who indicated that they thought that they would pay a different amount (either higher or lower) were omitted, and the analysis was conducted on the remaining 1,190 respondents, of whom 760 voted yes.

Table 6 gives the point estimates for each statistic; confidence intervals and standard errors are available on request from the authors. The findings are essentially the same as those shown in Tables 4 and 5: the estimated

---

[15] As noted above, Survey Sampling International (SSI) generated a sample as close as possible to the population along these lines. However, due to limits in their pool of respondents in certain cells, their outcomes missed the population proportions. This correction brings the sample in line with the population.

Table 6 Sensitivity results

	Baseline	Census Weights	Certainty Weights	Uncertainty Elimination	Cost Disbelief Elimination
Lower-bound estimates					
One-time payment ($):					
WTP	179.85	191.06	182.45	188.76	183.64
PV WTP	174.88	185.78	177.41	183.55	178.57
Annual payments ($):					
WTP per payment	160.66	167.00	162.67	169.24	165.19
PV WTP	5,657.04	5,880.28	5,727.82	5,959.16	5,816.55
Implicit discount rate (%)	837	694	822	867	895
Parametric estimates					
One-time payment ($):					
WTP	279.04	331.41	279.15	298.67	270.51
PV WTP	271.33	322.26	271.44	290.42	263.04
Annual payments ($):					
WTP per payment	217.23	249.29	217.09	230.25	217.89
PV WTP	7,648.94	8,777.82	7,644.01	8,107.39	7,672.18
Implicit discount rate (%)	351	304	350	337	414

present value at the Treasury yield is far greater when the survey asks about annual payments than a one-time payment, and the implicit discount rate is implausibly large.

CONCLUSIONS

One would expect and certainly hope for validity purposes that WTP response data would be sensitive to the frequency of payment in a referendum-style CV question. In our application, we found little sensitivity to payment frequency when comparing one-time with annual reoccurring payments. Our finding is consistent with the literature investigating such effects. Given respondents' inattention to the detail of payment frequency (essentially treating them as the same), the implied PV WTP is substantially larger with annual reoccurring payments versus one-time payments in all cases. Indeed, in other studies, as the payment frequency increases, so does the implied WTP. It is not possible to discern from our study or the other studies whether one of the payment frequencies leads to a "truer" WTP. More likely, in our judgment, respondents are either or both using the referendum as a means to convey support for the shorebird and not treating the tax as an actual payment or they have little idea of what their actual WTP is and are anchoring on the values offered. Whatever the cause, care must be taken in using CV response data as it pertains to payment frequency. Using one-time versus annual reoccurring payments can swing benefit estimates by as much as a factor of 30 and for reasons at this time we really do not understand. Further research documenting and exploring the effect of payment frequency and perhaps follow-up questions on the issue would be useful given the limited evidence we have to date.

REFERENCES

Bond, C., K. Cullen, and D. Larson (2009), "Joint estimation of discount rates and willingness to pay for public goods," *Ecological Economics*, **68**(11), 2,751–59.

Boyle, K. (forthcoming), "Contingent valuation in practice," in P. Champ, K. Boyle, and T. Brown (eds), *A Primer on Nonmarket Valuation*, New York: Springer.

Burrows, J., H.-M. Chan, and P. Dixon (2016), "Response to cost prompts in stated preference valuation of environmental goods," in D. McFadden and K. Train (eds), *Contingent Valuation of Environmental Goods: A Comprehensive Critique*, Cheltenham, UK and Northampton, MA, USA: Edward Elgar Publishing.

Chen, W., J. Aertsens, I. Liekens, S. Broekx, and L. Nocker (2014), "Impact of perceived importance of ecosystem services and stated financial constraints on willingness to pay for riparian meadow restoration in Flanders (Belgium)," *Environmental Management*, **54**(2), 346–59.

Echeverria, J., M. Hanrahan, and R. Solorzano (1995), "Valuation of non-priced amenities provided by the biological resources within the Monteverde Cloud Forest Preserve, Costa Rica," *Ecological Economics*, **13**(1), 43–52.

Egan, K., J. Corrigan, and D. Dwyer (2015), "Three reasons to use annual payments in contingent valuation surveys: Convergent validity, discount rates, and mental accounting," *Journal of Environmental Economics and Management*, **72**, 123–36.

Haab, T. and K. McConnell (2002), *Valuing Environmental and Natural Resources: The Econometrics of Non-Market Valuation*, Cheltenham, UK and Northampton, MA, USA: Edward Elgar Publishing.

Kahneman, D. and J. Knetsch (1992), "Valuing public goods: The purchase of moral satisfaction," *Journal of Environmental Economics and Management*, **22**(1), 57–70.

Kim, S.I. and T. Haab (2009), "Temporal insensitivity of willingness to pay and implied discount rates," *Resource and Energy Economics*, **31**(2), 89–102.

Kovacs, K. and D. Larson (2008), "Identifying individual discount rates and valuing public open space with stated-preference models," *Land Economics*, **84**(2), 209–24.

Myers, K. (2013), 'The effect of substitutes on willingness to pay for endangered species: The case of the Atlantic red knot', PhD thesis, School of Marine Science & Policy, University of Delaware, Publication No. 3613043 at ProQuest Dissertations and Theses.

Parsons, G. and K. Myers (2016), "Fat tails and truncated bids in contingent valuation: An application to an endangered shorebird species," *Ecological Economics*, **129**, 201–19.

Rowe, R., W. Shaw, and W. Schulze (1992), "Nestucca oil spill," in K. Ward and J. Duffield (eds), *Natural Resource Damages: Law and Economics*, New York: John Wiley, pp. 527–54.

Solino, M., M. Vazquez, and A. Prada (2009), "Social demand for electricity from forest biomass in Spain: Does payment periodicity affect the willingness to pay?," *Energy Policy*, **37**(2), 531–40.

Stevens, T., N. DeCoteau, and C. Willis (1997), "Sensitivity of contingent valuation to alternative payment schedules," *Land Economics*, **73**(1), 140–48.

Strumberg, B., K. Barenklau, and R. Bishop (2001), "Nonpoint source pollution and present values: A contingent valuation study of Lake Mendota," *Review of Agricultural Economics*, **23**(1), 120–32.

4. An adding-up test on contingent valuations of river and lake quality[1]

William Desvousges, Kristy Mathews, and Kenneth Train[2]

INTRODUCTION

Contingent valuation (CV) is a survey procedure designed to estimate respondents' willingness to pay (WTP) for natural resource services. See Carson and Hanemann (2005) for a review. One of the most prominent concerns about CV is whether the estimated WTP from CV studies varies adequately with the amount, extent, or, more generally, "scope" of the environmental good.[3] This concern was emphasized by a panel of experts that the National Oceanic and Atmospheric Administration (NOAA) convened with the purpose of making recommendations about the reliability of CV. The panel concluded that they would judge the findings of a CV study to be unreliable if it evidenced "[i]nadequate responsiveness to the scope of the environmental insult," and said that the burden of proof "must rest" with the researchers who designed and implemented the study (Arrow et al., 1993).

Researchers have implemented scope tests that examine whether the estimated WTP in CV studies increases (or at least does not decrease) when the scope of environmental benefits is expanded. See Carson (1997) and Desvousges et al. (2012) for reviews. However, passing the scope test (i.e., finding that estimated WTP increases with scope) does not imply that the

---

[1] Desvousges, W., K. Mathews, and K. Train (2015), "An adding-up test on contingent valuations of river and lake quality," *Land Economics*, **91**(3), 556–71. Copyright 2015 by the Board of Regents of the University of Wisconsin System. Reproduced courtesy of the University of Wisconsin Press.

[2] Respectively, W.H. Desvousges & Associates, P.O. Box 99203, Raleigh, NC; Independent Consultant, 104 McWaine Lane, Cary, NC; Adjunct Professor Emeritus of Economics, University of California, Berkeley.

[3] Boyle et al. (1994) were among the first to provide empirical evidence about the relevance of scope and its implications for the reliability of CV estimates, especially for non-use, or passive use, values.

estimated response is adequate in magnitude. Members of the expert panel (Arrow et al., 1994) explicitly stated that the scope test does not address their concern about adequacy of response to scope.[4]

In this chapter, we discuss and implement Diamond et al.'s (1993) adding-up test, which has important implications for the issue of adequate response. Diamond et al. point out that standard utility theory implies a relation called the "adding-up condition," namely, that the WTP for one good, plus the WTP for a second good once the consumer has paid for and obtained the first one, is necessarily equal to the consumer's WTP for both goods combined. A more precise definition is given in the second section below; colloquially, the condition is often expressed as "the whole equals the sum of the incremental parts," with "incremental" meaning that the second good is evaluated after having paid for and received the first good.

Diamond et al.'s (1993) test of the adding-up condition is implemented as follows: one group of respondents is asked their WTP for one good; a second group is told that this good has already been provided to them and asked their WTP for a second good; then a third group is asked their WTP for both goods. If the WTP from the first group plus the WTP from the second group equals the WTP from the third group, then the adding-up test is passed: the WTPs are consistent with the adding-up condition.

The adding-up test can address the NOAA panel's concern about adequate response to differences in scope. If the sum of WTPs for individual benefits, evaluated incrementally, equals the WTP for all of them combined (i.e., the adding-up test is passed), then the response to differences in scope is clearly adequate. However, if the sum of the estimated WTPs for the incremental benefits exceeds the estimated WTP for all of them combined (i.e., the adding-up test is failed), then questions arise about the adequacy of the CV responses to changes in scope.

Despite the potential value of the test, no studies since Diamond et al. (1993) have applied an adding-up test to incremental parts of public goods.[5] Several studies have examined adding-up for non-incremental

---

[4] "We believe that there is a very sharp contrast between the basic character of the proposed scope test and the sense of the NOAA panel. Because of this difference, we do not think that this test is a proper response to the Panel report... The report of the NOAA panel calls for survey results that are '*adequately*' responsive to the scope of the environment insult. The proposed scope test is built to assure that there is a *statistically detectable* sensitivity to scope. This is, in our opinion, an improper interpretation of the word 'adequately.' Had the panel thought that something as straightforward as statistical measurability were the proper way to define sensitivity, then we would (or should) have opted for language to that effect" [emphasis in the original].

[5] One study, Bateman et al. (1997), applied the adding-up test to private goods with a bidding-based elicitation procedure in a laboratory setting. We discuss this study and its implications in the fourth section.

benefits.[6] In particular, they elicited consumers' WTP for one good, the WTP for a second good, and the WTP for the two goods combined; however, the WTP for the second good was evaluated without the consumer having obtained the first good. The adding-up condition applies only for goods that are obtained incrementally. As noted by the authors of these studies, as well as others, failure of adding-up on non-incremental parts can arise because of diminishing marginal utility or substitution, both of which are consistent with standard utility theory. Diamond and colleagues specified the test for incremental benefits, such that diminishing marginal utility and substitution, to the extent they exist, are incorporated into the valuations.

The previous CV studies on adding-up are potentially problematic for another reason as well. Carson and Groves (2007) identified features of the CV scenario that are designed to induce truthful answers from respondents. Except for De Zoysa (1995),[7] all of the previous studies that examined the adding-up condition have used CV methods that differ from those designed to induce truthfulness. Failures of the adding-up test in these studies could therefore be attributed to the design of their CV scenarios.

In this chapter, we test the adding-up condition using incremental parts on CV scenarios that are designed to induce truthful answers. To our knowledge, this is the first investigation that satisfies both these criteria. We implement the test on a study by Chapman et al. (2009) that evaluated a restoration program for a specified river system and lake in Oklahoma. "Chicken litter," which caused an overgrowth of algae, had polluted the lake and river system; the study estimated the WTP for a program to put alum on the water to reduce the algae. We chose this study because it represents the current state-of-the-art for CV and its scenarios were designed

---

[6] The studies that examine adding-up on non-incremental parts include Wu (1993), De Zoysa (1995), Stevens et al. (1995), White et al. (1997), Macmillan and Duff (1998), Alvarez-Farizo et al. (1999), Christie (2001), Nunes and Schokkaert (2003), Powe and Bateman (2004), Veisten et al. (2004), and Bateman et al. (2008). The test is failed in all of these studies except Nunes and Schokkaert, who pass their adding-up test when they use a factor analysis to account for warm glow, and not otherwise. Other studies have designs that support an adding-up test on non-incremental parts, but the authors do not report the results (Hoevengal, 1996; Loomis and Gonzalez-Caban, 1998; Riddel and Loomis, 1998; Rollins and Lyke, 1998; Streever et al., 1998).

[7] De Zoysa's survey asked a referendum-style question, which is consistent with Carson and Groves's recommendations, but followed up with an open-ended question asking respondents to state their maximum WTP, which violates Carson and Groves's concepts. If respondents did not anticipate that the follow-up was going to be asked when answering the referendum question (or did not read ahead before answering the referendum question in the mail survey), then the answers to the referendum question can be considered to be consistent with Carson and Groves's recommendations.

to meet the conditions identified by Carson and Groves (2007) for truthful answers. Also, the study had already described its program in incremental parts for the purposes of a scope test and had developed the survey instrument for one of these increments (in addition to the instrument for the program as a whole), with wording that described to respondents how the first increment had already been funded and provided. This feature allowed us to implement an adding-up test with minimal changes in the questionnaires.

We find that the adding-up condition does not hold in this study, with the sum of the WTP for the incremental parts being three times greater than that for the whole. This result implies that either (1) the CV procedure, with incremental parts and procedures designed for truthfulness, did not elicit the true preferences of consumers, or (2) consumers' true preferences are not consistent with standard utility theory.

The remainder of the chapter is organized as follows. The next section describes the adding-up condition more formally, with the third section enumerating practical issues that need to be considered in implementing the adding-up test. The fourth section describes past studies whose designs allowed an adding-up test on incremental parts, even if the test were not performed. The fifth discusses the study by Chapman et al. (2009) as it relates to the adding-up test, and in the sixth section we describe the increments that we specified for the test and the way that the original surveys were revised for the additional increments. Results are given in the seventh section. Income effects are investigated in the eighth. The chapter concludes with a discussion of the interpretation and implications of the results.

THE ADDING-UP TEST

Diamond et al. (1993, p. 48) explain the adding-up test through analogy:

> For instance, consider asking one group of people how much they are willing to pay for a cup of coffee. Ask a second group how much they would be willing to pay just for a doughnut if they already had been given a cup of coffee. Ask a third group how much they would be willing to pay for a cup of coffee and a doughnut. The value obtained from the third group should equal the sum of the values obtained from the first two groups if the answers people give reflect underlying economic preferences.

More formally, let $e(x, y, p, u)$ be the consumer's expenditure function at prices p for private goods, utility level u, and levels x and y of two public goods. Consider a program that increases the quantity of the public goods from x_0 to x_1 and y_0 to y_1. WTP for this improvement is defined as $WTP(x_1, y_1|x_0, y_0) \equiv e(x_0, y_0, p, u) - e(x_1, y_1, p, u)$. Adding and subtracting terms gives:

$$WTP(x_1, y_1|x_0, y_0) = e(x_0, y_0, p, u) - e(x_1, y_0, p, u) + e(x_1, y_0, p, u) - e(x_1, y_1, p, u) \equiv WTP(x_1, y_0|x_0, y_0) + WTP(x_1, y_1|x_1, y_0),$$

which is the adding-up condition. The same relation occurs for a program that increases x_0 to x_1 without changing y, with the increments defined by an intermediate level x_1' with $x_0 < x_1' < x_1$. Note that the only assumptions that are required for the adding-up condition are those required for the existence of the expenditure function.

The adding-up test extends the scope test in an informative way. For the standard scope test, one group of respondents is asked about their WTP for a specified set of benefits, $WTP(x_1, y_1|x_0, y_0)$, and a second group is asked about their WTP for a subset of these benefits, for example, $WTP(x_1, y_0|x_0, y_0)$. The adding-up test is implemented by also asking another group of respondents about their WTP for the benefits included in the first set but excluded from the second set, with the benefits defined incrementally, for example, $WTP(x_1, y_1|x_1, y_0)$.

This extension resolves the uncertainties that arise in interpreting scope test results. Suppose, for example, that the scope test is passed when comparing $WTP(x_1, y_1|x_0, y_0)$, with $WTP(x_1, y_0|x_0, y_0)$. As stated above, this result does not imply that the magnitude of the estimated difference is adequate. The adding-up test provides a means to evaluate the magnitude of this difference, by testing whether it equals the directly estimated $WTP(x_1, y_1|x_1, y_0)$. Suppose instead that the scope test fails. As stated above, diminishing marginal utility and substitution can cause little or no response, which can lead to failure of the scope test. The adding-up test assesses whether the failure reflects these kinds of preferences, by determining whether $WTP(x_1, y_1|x_1, y_0)$ is sufficiently small.[8]

---

[8] The adding-up condition does not contradict the fact that goods are often priced with bundled discounts, under which buying each good individually costs more in total than buying the goods as a bundle. The adding-up condition describes the amount that consumers are *willing* to pay, while the pricing mechanism describes the amount that consumers are *required* to pay. In fact, marketers exploit consumers' adding-up condition when offering bundled prices. For example, suppose a consumer is willing to pay $7 for one unit of a good, and $5 for a second unit once the first unit is obtained. By the adding-up condition, the consumer is willing to pay $12 for two units. With non-bundled pricing, the seller can price at $7, sell one unit to this customer, and make $7 in revenue; or price at $5, sell two units, and make revenue of $10. However, by offering a bundled price of two units for $12, the seller sells two units and obtains revenue of $12. If the consumer's WTP for the two units

Haab et al. (2013, p. 10) state that the adding-up test imposes additional structure on preferences beyond that imposed by the scope test and that the additional structure is unnecessary. For the scope test, they say that "[a] simple theoretical model of WTP, a difference in expenditure functions with changes in quality or quantity, can be used to show that WTP is nondecreasing in quality or quantity". The same theoretical model, with differences in expenditure functions (as described above), is all that is needed to show the adding-up condition. The assumptions that Whitehead and colleagues (1998) use to show non-negative scope effects for the scope test are sufficient to show the adding-up condition for the adding-up test. No additional assumptions or structure is required.[9]

The adding-up test examines a different implication of utility theory than the scope test, which might explain Haab et al.'s concern. However, the difference constitutes one of the potential values of the test: the adding-up test can address the issue that NOAA's expert panel enumerated, while the scope test does not. Given that the panel said that the burden of proof "must rest" on the researcher, the adding-up test seems particularly useful.

More generally, the adding-up test can be considered similar to the research on the WTP and willingness to accept (WTA) discrepancy. Haab et al. (2013) note that evidence of a WTP/WTA disparity is "a call for the curious researcher to more closely examine the assumptions and structures leading to these seemingly anomalous results." The adding-up test can be seen as a similar call to researchers to identify when and why these seemingly anomalous results arise and to expand our traditional theory and/or elicitation methods to include them.

---

incrementally exceeded the amount the consumer is willing to pay for both units together (in violation of the adding-up condition), then the seller could not make as much, or any, extra revenue through bundling.

[9] Using their notation, Whitehead et al. (1998) define $\Delta WTP = WTP_{1,2} - WTP_2$ and show that $\Delta WTP = e(p_1, p_2, q_1, q_2^*, u) - e(p_1, p_2, q_1^*, q_2^*, u)$ and then $\Delta WTP \geq 0$ under the standard assumptions of utility theory. By the definition of WTP, this second equation shows that ΔWTP is the WTP for 1 given 2, which can be denoted $WTP_{1|2}$. Their first equation then becomes $WTP_{1|2} = WTP_{1|2} - WTP_2$, which is the adding-up condition. No new assumptions have been introduced.

POTENTIAL DIFFICULTIES IN IMPLEMENTING THE ADDING-UP TEST

There are several potential difficulties that must be addressed in implementing an adding-up test. Haab et al. (2013) describe these issues and seem to suggest that the potential problems are so great that they outweigh the potential benefits of the test. We believe that these issues need to be considered on a case-by-case basis. In the paragraphs below, we describe these potential difficulties and how they are addressed in our application.

Cognitive Burden

The test requires that one part of the package of benefits be valued by respondents who are told that they already received another part. In many situations, this type of conditioning can be difficult for respondents to understand. In our application, we have been able to avoid this potential difficulty. One of the reasons we chose the Chapman et al. (2009) study is that its design is amenable to descriptions of incremental parts. As discussed below, the surveys for the incremental parts are the same from the respondents' perspective as the survey for the whole. No additional cognitive burden is imposed. In the original study for the base program (the whole), the years in which recovery will occur with and without the proposed intervention were stated to respondents. We simply changed these stated years for each of the incremental parts. In fact, this change in stated years was used in the original study for differentiating its scope and base versions, which gave us the idea that other increments could be defined similarly. In other applications, describing increments might be more difficult. But it can be useful to identify studies, like Chapman et al. (2009), in which the increments can be described without undue additional burden, and to apply adding-up tests in these applications.

Income Effects

Ideally, respondents who are asked to evaluate the remaining part of the benefit bundle would have already paid for and received the first part of the bundle. The income effect is the recognition that if the respondent has already paid for the first part, then the available income on which they will state their WTP for the second part is reduced by the amount paid for the first part. Implementing such a payment is difficult and perhaps impossible in a survey setting. However, empirical methods can be applied to address the issue. We apply these methods in our application, as did Bateman et al. (1997) in theirs. Note that if there are no income effects on

WTP, then not conditioning on the payment does not affect the results of the analysis. In many situations, respondents' WTP for the goods in question are sufficiently small relative to their income such that income effects can reasonably be assumed to be negligible within that range (Diamond, 1996). If potential income effects are a concern, the relation of respondents' incomes to their survey responses can be estimated. If income effects are found to exist, then the adding-up test can be implemented twice: once with the original responses and once with responses that are predicted at lower income levels to represent the WTP for the parts that are conditioned upon. In our application, we predict the votes at a lower income for each respondent. Since the estimated income effects are sufficiently small in our application, the predicted and actual votes are the same, such that the prediction under lower income did not change the results of the adding-up test.

Provision Mechanism

Respondents might value a prospective good differently based on the way that a prior good is provided. For example, a prior good provided by nature can be viewed differently than the same good provided through human intervention, and this difference might affect the respondents' WTP for a prospective good.[10] In our application, government programs (though different kinds of programs) provide both the prior and prospective goods, and so there is less difference in the provision mechanism than between nature and human intervention. Also, in the original survey, the base program (the whole) was conditioned on government programs that provided prior benefits, with this conditioning described to respondents; the conditioning for the increments in our study takes the same form.

As Diamond (1996) originally pointed out, if respondents did indeed value a prospective good differently based on the provision method for a prior good, then their preferences would not be consistent with standard utility theory. In contrast, Hanemann (1994), for example, argues that any factor may be a permissible element of consumers' utility. He does not, however, describe how normative allocation procedures can be derived in such an economic system.

---

[10] It is not clear what the direction of effect would be: does valuing the prior good differently because of its provision method raise or lower the respondent's WTP for the prospective good? The different valuation of the prior good would need to raise the respondents' WTP of the prospective good in order to induce false failures of the adding-up test. The opposite would cause false acceptances of the adding-up test.

Cost

The adding-up test is usually more expensive to apply than a scope test because it requires at least one more subsample. Fielding the survey is only one element of the overall cost of a project, and so a study with, for example, three subsamples is not 50% more expensive than a study with two subsamples. In our application, the cost of fielding one additional subsample increased the overall cost by less than 5%. Given that the adding-up test potentially addresses the expert panel's concern about adequate response while the scope test does not, and that the burden of meeting the panel's concern "must rest" with the researcher, the extra cost seems justified, at least in some studies.

REVIEW OF PAST STUDIES OF ADDING-UP ON INCREMENTAL PARTS

We searched the natural resource valuation literature and could find only four studies whose designs permit an adding-up test on incremental parts: Samples and Hollyer (1990), Binger et al. (1995a, 1995b), Diamond et al. (1993), and Bateman et al. (1997). In the first two of these, the authors did not test for statistical significance or present results that allow readers to perform it. The first three studies are for public goods using CV, and the fourth is for private goods using an experimental setting for elicitation of WTP. We describe all four below.

Samples and Hollyer (1990) investigated whether the presence of substitutes or complements affected WTP values. In their design, respondents are first asked their WTP to save one type of marine mammal from a fatal disease and subsequently asked the additional amount they would pay to save a second type of mammal from the same disease, assuming that the first mammal is saved. A separate sample is asked their WTP to save both types of marine mammals simultaneously. They found that the sum of the WTPs for each mammal when asked incrementally greatly exceeded the WTP for the two mammals when asked about them together. Samples and Hollyer (1990) do not report the necessary statistical information to determine whether the difference is statistically significant.

Binger et al. (1995a, 1995b) also utilized a design that is amenable to an adding-up test. Their questionnaire first tells respondents about 57 different wilderness areas in four western states. In split samples, one group of respondents is first asked for their willingness to protect a specified wilderness area from timber harvests. Subsequently, that same group of respondents is asked for their WTP to protect the additional 56 wilderness areas, assuming that the first area is already protected. A separate sample of respondents is asked for their WTP to protect all 57 wilderness areas. They find that the sum of the average WTPs obtained from the first sample exceeds the average WTP from the second sample. However, like Samples and Hollyer (1990), these authors do not provide the necessary information that would reveal whether the difference is statistically significant.

Diamond et al. (1993) administered CV questionnaires to split samples of respondents that elicited their WTP to preserve specific wilderness areas, controlling for incremental parts by offering the various split samples different numbers of wilderness areas that are already being developed. Their design allowed for two different adding-up tests, one with two parts and one with three parts. The results of the tests are mixed. The two-part test passes (the incremental parts add up to the total) while the three-part test fails (the incremental parts do not add up to the total).

In summary, of the three studies using CV on public goods, all three found that the sum of WTP for the incremental parts exceeded the WTP for the whole. Only one of the three studies (Diamond et al., 1993) tested whether the difference was statistically significant, finding that the adding-up test failed in their three-part test and passed in their two-part test.

In addition to the three studies of public goods, there has been one study of adding-up of incremental parts with private goods. Bateman et al. (1997) used bidding in an experimental laboratory setting to measure respondents' WTP or WTA for vouchers for two components of a meal (the main course and dessert). Respondents were given an endowment of money and vouchers (one, two, or none). To elicit WTP for a voucher, respondents who had not been given that voucher were told that they would need to state their WTP and then a random number would be drawn as the price of the voucher; if their stated WTP exceeded the randomly drawn price, then they would obtain the voucher at that price. WTP for both vouchers and WTA were elicited similarly. Four adding-up tests were applied based on WTP and WTA in each direction of conditioning. In all four comparisons they found that the sum of the WTP/WTA for the vouchers individually, when treated incrementally, exceeded the WTP/WTA for the two vouchers together. The difference was statistically significant for three of the comparisons (rejecting adding-up) and not significant for the fourth (one of the WTP comparisons).[11]

As is the case for CV, the failures of adding-up found by Bateman et al. (1997) can be attributed to the elicitation method or because consumers'

---

[11] The authors recently corrected the t-statistics in their Table 3 (personal communication). The corrected t-statistics, in order of the rows in Table 3, are 2.55, 0.96, 2.98, and 2.23.

preferences do not adhere to the adding-up condition. Regarding the elicitation method, their experimental design might have introduced an effect that is similar to the "warm glow" that can arise in CV.[12] In particular, respondents may obtain some enjoyment from winning vouchers in each bid, independent of the value of the vouchers themselves.[13] The small amount of money being bid, the fact that each respondent was given money by the experimenter to spend in bidding, and the use of random draws to determine whether the respondent wins, contribute to a gamelike quality of the exercise.[14] This warm glow of winning vouchers would cause the adding-up test to fail even if the true values of the vouchers themselves adhere to the adding-up condition. Alternatively, their results, as the authors say, "may be a symptom of some fundamental property of individuals' preferences which conventional consumer theory does not allow for" (p. 331).

The amount by which the sum of the parts exceeds the whole is substantially smaller in Bateman et al. (1997) than in the studies, including ours, of CV for public goods. Bateman et al. (1997) find that the sum of the parts exceeded the whole by 5.3–16% in their experimental bidding for private goods, while we find that the sum of the parts in our CV study of a public good exceeds the whole by more than 200%. This comparison suggests that deviations from the adding-up condition – whether they arise from the elicitation method or from true preferences – are less severe with experimental bidding for private goods than with CV methods for public goods. More research is needed on adding-up, for both private and public goods and (if possible) with different elicitation methods, to assess the reasons and magnitudes of deviations from the adding-up condition.

THE ORIGINAL STUDY

The study by Chapman et al. (2009) (hereafter, "the Study") provides the basis for implementing the adding-up test. It was conducted by some of the most experienced researchers in the field and was funded at a sufficient level (over $2 million) to allow extensive design and revision of the various

---

[12] "Warm glow" refers to the idea that respondents obtain satisfaction from expressing support for an environmental improvement, independent of their value of the improvement itself.

[13] Where winning vouchers means getting or keeping the vouchers in each potential trade.

[14] As the authors describe, "each subject faced a screen, rather like a roulette wheel, around which were located a range of prices at which the trade might conceivably be carried out... A 'ball' then circled around the wheel and alighted at one sum at random" (p. 326).

aspects of the Study, including focus groups and pretesting of the instruments. It followed the procedures suggested by Carson and Groves (2007) that are intended to induce truthfulness; indeed, it is one of only three CV studies (that test for sensitivity to scope) to date to do so.[15] Its results served as the basis of expert testimony about damages in a court case, which is one of the most prominent purposes for which natural resource damages are calculated.

The goal of the Study was "to measure natural resource damages associated with excess phosphorus from poultry waste and other sources entering the Illinois River system [within Oklahoma] and Tenkiller Lake." The phosphorus creates excess algae that deplete the oxygen in the water, which is needed by aquatic species to survive. Respondents were informed that the state was taking measures to stop the spreading of poultry litter but that this action would not restore the lake and river[16] for a considerable period of time. Respondents were told that restoration could be hastened by putting alum (described as a naturally occurring mineral that is safe for humans) on the land and in the water, which binds to the phosphorus, rendering it harmless. In a referendum-type question, respondents were asked about their WTP for a program of alum treatment.

Two scenarios were specified and administered to two separate sets of respondents. For the "base" scenario, respondents were told that the ongoing actions of the state to reduce further pollution would restore the river to a natural state in 50 years and restore the lake in 60 years. With alum treatments in addition to these actions, the river would be restored in 10 years instead of 50, which is 40 years earlier, and the lake would be restored in 20 years instead of 60, which is also 40 years earlier.

A "scope" scenario with reduced benefits was specified for the purposes of a standard scope test. Under the scope scenario, the impact of the state's current actions and the alum program were both specified differently than in the base scenario. Respondents were told that the state's current actions would restore the river in 10 years and the lake in 60 years. The alum treatment was for the lake, making its recovery "somewhat faster." In particular, respondents were told that, with alum treatment of the lake, the lake would be restored in 50 years instead of 60, which is 10 years earlier. Note that the accelerated river restoration, which in the base scenario occurred

---

[15] The others are Carson et al. (1994) and (possibly) De Zoysa (1995). Desvousges et al. (2012) identify several other papers that nearly adhere to the Carson and Groves procedures.
[16] For linguistic convenience, we refer to "Illinois River system within Oklahoma" as "the river."

as a result of the proposed alum treatments, occurs in the scope scenario as part of the state's current actions.

Given the base and scope scenarios, the Study's design represents three incremental parts:

A. Restoration of the river in 10 years instead of 50.
B. Restoration of the lake in 50 years instead of 60, given A.
C. Restoration of the lake in 20 years instead of 50, given A and B.

The base scenario is A, B, and C combined, and the scope scenario is B with its conditioning on A described to respondents.

ADAPTATION FOR ADDING-UP TEST

We expanded the number of increments from three to four for the following reason. Note that the Study's scope scenario provides only 10 years of faster restoration starting 50 years in the future. We were interested in whether respondents can differentiate distant times in their valuations. To address this question, we created another increment of lake restoration that provides only 10 years of faster restoration (like the scope scenario) but starts in 40 years instead of 50 years. Table 1 describes the resulting set of scenarios, and Figure 1 depicts them graphically.

For the "whole" and 2nd increment, we used the Study's survey instruments. For the 1st, 3rd, and 4th increments, we modified its instruments as little as possible to represent these situations.[17] As discussed above, an important issue in adding-up tests is how to describe to respondents the conditioning on prior parts. We used the procedure that the Study utilized for the 2nd increment (its scope scenario). In particular, the conditioning for each increment is straightforward with this Study because respondents are already told that the state's current actions to prevent further pollution will restore the river and lake in some stated number of years for each. The numbers of years are changed for each version of the instrument to represent the conditioning. For the "whole" and the 1st increment, respondents are told 50 years for the river and 60 years for the lake. For the 2nd increment, the years are 10 and 60, respectively. For

---

[17] The Study provided considerable background information to respondents to allow them to place the alum program in context. We provided the same background information to respondents of the increment versions. For interested readers, the survey used in the Study is described in the citation for Chapman et al. (2009) in the References section below. The instruments that we used are available from the authors on request.

Table 1   Questionnaire versions

Version	Description
Whole: River + Lake	WTP for accelerating the restoration of the lake from 60 years to 20 years (40 years sooner) *and* accelerating the restoration of the river from 50 years to 10 years (40 years sooner), given that the state's current actions will induce the river to be restored in 50 years and the lake to be restored in 60 years
1st increment: River	WTP for accelerating the restoration of the river from 50 years to 10 years (40 years sooner), given that the state's current actions will induce the river to be restored in 50 years and the lake to be restored in 60 years
2nd increment: Lake 10 years	WTP for accelerating the restoration of the lake from 60 years to 50 years (10 years sooner), given that the state's current actions will induce the river to be restored in 10 years and the lake to be restored in 60 years
3rd increment: Lake 10 more years	WTP for accelerating the restoration of the lake from 50 years to 40 years (10 years sooner), given that the state's current actions will induce the river to be restored in 10 years and the lake to be restored in 50 years
4th increment: Lake 20 more years	WTP for accelerating the restoration of the lake from 40 years to 20 years (20 years sooner), given that the state's current actions will induce the river to be restored in 10 years and the lake to be restored in 40 years

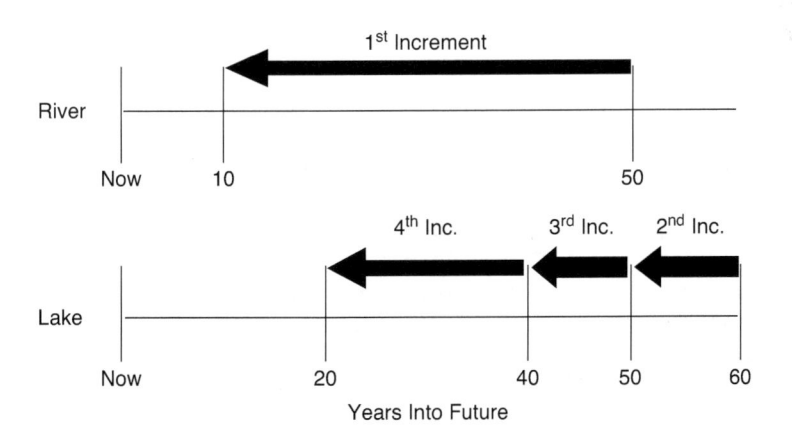

Figure 1   Incremental parts for accelerated restoration

the 3rd increment, 10 and 50 years. And for the 4th increment, 10 and 40 years.

Note that the conditioning in each increment provides the same service as in the "whole" (accelerated river and/or lake restoration), but not through exactly the same form of provision as in the "whole" (the state's actions to prevent pollution rather than alum treatments). Both forms of provision are through actions by the state, but the prior increments are obtained through current government actions while the prospective ones are obtained through the new alum program.

We administered the questionnaires through the Internet, a procedure that is increasingly common in non-market valuation surveys (Berrens et al., 2004; Banzhaf et al., 2006; Fleming and Bowden, 2009; Windle and Rolfe, 2011). In addition to the lower cost relative to in-person interviews, Internet surveys have the advantage of seamless incorporation of diagrams, photos, and other visual aids. Our practice differs from the Study, which conducted in-person interviews. The difference largely reflects a difference in purpose. The Study was estimating damages for litigation purposes, for which the sample needs to be representative of the target population. Our purpose is to assess whether CV responses are adequately sensitive to differences in scope, and our findings are relevant at least to our experimental samples.

We took several steps to adapt the Study's in-person questionnaire to an Internet survey. First, we conducted 105 cognitive, in-person interviews, using several versions of the questionnaire, to better appreciate how people answered the questions, which informed our structuring of the online versions. Second, we pre-tested two online versions of the questionnaire with 79 respondents, all of whom were able to complete the survey without the aid of an interviewer. Third, we added an opportunity for the online respondents to provide open-ended comments at the end of the questionnaire, and nearly all of these open-ended responses indicated that the respondents considered the questionnaire to be understandable and enjoyable.

To implement the adding-up test, we fielded five versions of the questionnaire, which are described in Table 1. We randomly assigned to each respondent one of the six bids ($10, $45, $80, $125, $205, and $405) used in the Study, as well as one of the five versions.

The surveys were fielded between November 2011 and March 2012. For our primary analysis, we excluded some responses. First, we excluded respondents who spent less than 15 minutes or more than 120 minutes completing the survey. In the first case, we did not believe that respondents could carefully consider the full content of the questionnaire in such a short amount of time. When respondents took more than 120 minutes

Table 2   Demographic variables by subsample

Demographics	Whole	1st increment	2nd increment	3rd increment	4th increment
Percentage male	33	27	33	34	29
Percentage college graduate	28	28	30	27	34
Percentage strong environmentalist	14	15	8	12	13
Average age	46	49	47	48	48
Average income ($)	42,900	44,300	43,700	40,400	43,800
Sample size	172	293	159	174	182

to complete the questionnaire, we believed that they likely walked away from their computer during the course of the survey, such that we could not know whether they had actually spent at least 15 minutes on the task. We also eliminated the 14 respondents who did not answer the open-ended question about why they voted for or against the proposed program to accelerate restoration because we were concerned that including respondents who gave no reasons could bias the results against a finding of adequate, or reasonable, response to scope. After these eliminations, the primary analysis contained 980 responses across the five versions.

We compared the subsamples to determine whether there were significant differences among them. The demographic characteristics of each subsample are given in Table 2. On visual inspection, the subsamples seem to be similar, as would be expected from the fact that respondents were selected randomly for the subsamples. We performed one-way ANOVA tests of equality of the demographic means across subsamples. In all cases, the hypothesis of no difference could not be rejected at usual confidence levels.

RESULTS

We first report on the traditional scope tests for each of the four increments (separately) relative to the whole. We use the same non-parametric approach used by the Study. Specifically, we compare the percentage of respondents who voted for the program at each bid and use a Wald test to test jointly whether the differences are statistically significant. Table 3 shows the details. The hypothesis of no difference is rejected twice (for the

Table 3 Percentage of respondents voting for the alum treatments

Bid	Whole: River + Lake	1st Increment: River	2nd Increment: Lake 10 years	3rd Increment: Lake 10 more years	4th Increment: Lake 20 more years
10	68.0	74.5	50.0	82.8	72.7
45	60.6	58.3	37.5	48.1	44.0
80	69.2	64.6	29.2	32.3	64.9
125	50.0	57.4	42.9	23.1	62.5
205	44.8	38.9	24.0	40.7	35.7
405	45.2	40.0	15.4	35.3	40.7
Wald test f-statistic		0.23	3.98	2.71	0.56
P-value		0.9674	0.0007	0.0139	0.7634

2nd and 3rd increments, which pass the scope test)[18] and accepted twice (for the 1st and 4th increments, which fail the scope test).

To estimate WTP associated with each of the versions, we used the ABERS non-parametric estimator (Ayer et al., 1955), the same as the Study. Table 4 shows the summary statistics for each of the versions.[19] Given the interval nature of the data, we used bootstrapping techniques (Efron, 1982; Davison and Hinkley, 1997) to determine whether these WTP values are statistically different from each other. The WTP differences are consistent with the test of proportions in Table 3 above. Specifically, WTP for the whole is statistically different from the WTP for the 2nd and 3rd increments and is not statistically different from the WTP for the 1st and 4th increments.

The adding-up test is based on the mean WTP values displayed in Table 4. The sum of the four increments totals $609 (=187 + 97 + 144 + 181), which is about three times as large as the value of the whole ($200). We applied the bootstrap method to simulate the sampling distribution of the difference between the mean WTP for the whole and the sum of the mean WTP from the four increments. The 99% confidence interval

---

[18] The Study's scope test is equivalent to our 2nd increment relative to the whole, which was passed, as we also find.

[19] For the whole, the Study's mean is $184. For the 2nd increment, the Study's mean is $138. Our and the Study's confidence intervals overlap. The similarity of results suggests that our application of the survey in Internet form, and the passage of time since the original Study, did not materially affect the responses. It does not suggest that either set of responses is reliable as a measure of WTP, just that similar surveys induce similar responses.

Table 4 WTP estimates

Version	Mean WTP ($)	Standard Error	95% Confidence Interval ($)
Whole: River + Lake	200	17.71	165–235
1st increment: River	187	12.31	163–211
2nd increment: Lake 10 years	97	13.73	70–124
3rd increment: Lake 10 more years	144	15.34	114–174
4th increment: Lake 20 more years	181	18.69	144–218

does not contain zero, such that the hypothesis of equality is rejected: the responses fail the adding-up test.

We conducted several types of sensitivity analyses. To investigate whether our results would change if sample sizes were larger, we re-fielded the 2nd increment version, which was the Study's scope version, with a larger sample size: nearly 500 respondents after exclusions. The mean WTP for this re-fielded version is $103, which is not statistically different from the $97 in Table 4. We also included respondents who took 10–14 minutes to complete the survey, which increased the sample size across the five versions from 980 to 1,106. With these higher sample sizes, our results do not change. Finally, we also applied post-stratification weights to our respondents' answers to reflect the population in terms of gender, age, and education. This weighting does not change the results of the adding-up test. With the weighted data, the ratio of the sum of the parts to the whole is still larger than 3:1.

As discussed above, the 2nd and 3rd increments both provide 10 years of faster lake restoration, but starting at different times in the future. If consumers discount appropriately, the 3rd increment should be valued more than the 2nd increment, since the benefits in the 3rd increment start sooner than those in the 2nd increment. The estimates in Table 4 conform to this expectation. These values are not statistically different from each other at the 95% level but are different at the 90% level.

INCOME EFFECTS

As discussed above, in an ideal adding-up test, the incremental specification of benefits would reduce respondents' income by their WTP for prior parts before they evaluate a prospective part. If there were no income

Table 5 Logit model of yes/no vote

	Estimated Coefficient	Standard Error
Cost, in dollars	−0.0031	0.0005
Income, in thousands of dollars	0.0022	0.0023
Age	−0.0025	0.0046
Male	−0.1039	0.1506
College graduate	−0.3278	0.1636
Concerned about environment	1.0609	0.2205
Whole	0.6744	0.2870
1st increment	0.6680	0.2763
2nd increment	−0.3791	0.2969
3rd increment	0.1582	0.2908
4th increment	0.6654	0.2875
Log-likelihood	−608.502	
Sample size	950	

effects in the relevant range, then not reducing respondents' incomes does not affect their valuations. We tested for the existence of income effects. In particular, we estimated binary logit models of whether the respondent answered "yes" or "no" to the referendum question (i.e., voted for or against the program at the specified cost). We included the cost that the respondent faced, as well as income and other demographics. The results are given in Table 5 for the entire sample. Income enters with a *t*-statistic of 0.95, such that the hypothesis of no income effects cannot be rejected. The point estimate of the impact of income on response is exceedingly small. We also estimated the model for each subsample separately. In all models (not shown), the income coefficient was insignificant. The point estimate was positive in four of the subsamples and negative in one, and very small in magnitude in all subsamples.

We used the estimated model in Table 5 to simulate the impact of a decrease in income for the respondents who faced an increment that conditioned on a prior increment, that is, who faced the 2nd, 3rd, and 4th increments. (Respondents who faced the whole and the 1st increment had no prior benefits upon which to condition.) The simulation was performed as follows.

Let $U_n(y_n)$ be person n's utility from the benefits that were described to the person, net of the cost that was specified, given an income of y_n.[20] As usual for derivation of choice models, utility is decomposed into a part

---

[20] The utility function might take the form $U_n(y_n) = \alpha(WTPn(y_n) - c_n)$ where c_n is the program costs that the person faced and WTP is random from the researcher's perspective.

observed by the researcher and an unobserved part: $U_n(y_n) = V_n(y_n) + \varepsilon_n$. Assuming that ε_n is distributed logistic, the probability that the person votes "yes" is:

$$P_n(y_n) = Prob(U_n(y_n) > 0) = Prob(\varepsilon_n > -V_n(y_n)) = \frac{1}{1 + e^{-V_n(y_n)}}.$$

This probability was used for the model in Table 5, which gives the estimate of $V_n(y_n)$.

Consider now the person's choice if the original income is lower by deduction d. Utility is $U_n(Y_n - d) = V_n(y_n - d) + \varepsilon_n$ and the probability of voting "yes" is $P_n(y_n - d) = \frac{1}{1 + e^{-V_n(y_n - d)}}$. This is the unconditional probability; however, we observe whether respondents voted "yes" or "no" at their original income, and this information can be used to provide a better estimate of the probability of voting "yes" at the lower income. For respondents who voted "no" at their original income, the conditional probability of voting "yes" at a lower income is zero (assuming income effects are non-negative). For respondents who voted "yes" at their original income, the conditional probability of voting "yes" at a lower income is:

$$Prob(U_n(y_n - d) > 0 | U_n(y_n) > 0) = \frac{Prob(U_n(y_n - d) > 0) * Prob(U_n(y_n) > 0 | U_n(y_n - d) > 0)}{Prob(U_n(y_n) > 0)}$$

$$= \frac{Prob(U_n(y_n - d) > 0)}{Prob(U_n(y_n) > 0)} = \frac{1 + e^{-V_n(y_n)}}{1 + e^{-V_n(y_n - d)}}$$

We calculated the conditional probabilities of voting "yes" if d were deducted from the income for all respondents who voted "yes" at their original income. We then simulated each of these respondents' votes by taking a draw from a uniform distribution and changing the "yes" vote to "no" if the draw for that respondent exceeded the conditional probability. We set $d = \$1,000$, which is far greater than the largest cost that was presented to anyone.

Among respondents who voted "yes" at their original income, the conditional probability of voting "yes" at the lower income is, on average, 99.89%. With such a high probability, no respondents were simulated to change their vote from "yes" to "no" at the lower income. This result, of course, is due to the fact that the estimated income effect is so small. If there had been a difference between the simulated and original votes, then the adding-up test could be applied to the simulated votes and the results compared to those, described above, for the original votes.

DISCUSSION AND CONCLUSIONS

The scope test has been applied as a means to ascertain whether CV results reflect economic preferences. However, passing the scope test does not imply that the magnitude of the estimated response is adequate, and scope test failures can be explained by certain conditions that are consistent with economic theory. As an additional step to resolve these uncertainties, and to address the NOAA expert panel's concern about adequate response to scope changes, we recommend Diamond et al.'s (1993) adding-up test.

Building on a CV study by Chapman et al. (2009) that already contained incremental parts, we expanded the study to contain a full set of incremental parts and then applied an adding-up test. We found that the adding-up condition does not hold for the CV results: the sum of the estimated WTPs for the incremental parts greatly exceeds the estimated WTP for the whole. Our results mirror the conclusions of Diamond et al. (1993) using CV on public goods and Bateman et al. (1997) using a laboratory setting on private goods.

As discussed above, failure of the adding-up test in our study can indicate that the CV procedure is not obtaining truthful answers from respondents, and/or that consumers' preferences are not consistent with standard utility theory. In regard to truthfulness, unlike previous studies of adding-up for public goods, we used CV scenarios that adhere to Carson and Groves's (2007) recommendations to induce truthful answers from respondents. So either the Carson and Groves procedures do not actually induce truthfulness, or respondents' truthful answers are not consistent with the adding-up condition.

Behavioral theories may be useful in understanding the sources and patterns of responses and might provide a behavioral explanation for failures of the adding-up test. Bateman et al. (2004), Powe and Bateman (2004), and Heberlein et al. (2005), provide explanations for scope test failures that might also be applicable to the adding-up test. As well as developing the explanations, steps are needed to derive an expanded theory of welfare that incorporates these explanations, or elicitation methods that avoid the behaviors.

Bateman (2011) suggests tests that complement the adding-up test and could be explored. Diamond (1996) proposed methods based on properties of the second derivatives of utility, which, to our knowledge, have not been implemented in empirical work. We endorse more research along these lines to develop and apply other tests of the consistency of responses with standard utility theory and, insofar as inconsistencies are found, to develop methods that account for them and theories that explain them.

REFERENCES

Alvarez-Farizo, B., N. Hanley, R.E. Wright, and D. Macmillan (1999), "Estimating the benefits of agri-environmental policy: Econometric issues in open-ended contingent valuation studies," *Journal of Environmental Planning and Management*, **42**(1), 23–43.

Arrow, K., E.E. Leamer, H. Schuman, and R. Solow (1994), "Comments of proposed NOAA scope test," Appendix D of *Comments on Proposed NOAA/ DOI Regulations on Natural Resource Damage Assessment*, U.S. Environmental Protection Agency.

Arrow, K., R. Solow, P.R. Portney, E.E. Leamer, R. Radner, and H. Schuman (1993), *Report of the NOAA Panel on Contingent Valuation*, Federal Register, January 15, **58**(10), 4,601–14.

Ayer, M., H.D. Brunk, G.M. Ewing, W.T. Reid, and E. Silverman (1955), "An empirical distribution function for sampling with incomplete information," *The Annals of Mathematical Statistics*, **26**(4), 641–7.

Banzhaf, H.S., D. Burtraw, D. Evans, and A. Krupnick (2006), "Valuation of natural resource improvements in the Adirondacks," *Land Economics*, **82**(3), 445–64.

Bateman, I.J. (2011), "Valid value estimates and value estimate validation: Better methods and better testing for stated preference research," in J. Bennett (ed.), *The International Handbook on Non-Market Environmental Valuation*, Cheltenham, UK and Northampton, MA, USA: Edward Elgar Publishing.

Bateman, I.J., M.P. Cameron, and A. Tsoumas (2008), "Investigating the characteristics of stated preferences for reducing the impacts of air pollution: A contingent valuation experiment," in T.L. Cherry, S. Kroll, and J.F. Shogren (eds), *Environmental Economics, Experimental Methods*, London: Routledge.

Bateman, I.J., A. Munro, B. Rhodes, C. Starmer, and R. Sugden (1997), "Does part whole bias exist? An experimental investigation," *Economic Journal*, **107**(441), 322–32.

Bateman, I.J., M. Cole, P. Cooper, S. Georgiou, D. Hadley, and G.L. Poe (2004), "On visible choice sets and scope sensitivity," *Journal of Environmental Economics and Management*, **47**(1), 71–93.

Berrens, R.P., A.K. Bohara, H.C. Jenkins-Smith, C.L. Silva, and D.L. Weimer (2004), "Information and effort in contingent valuation surveys: Application to global climate change using national internet samples," *Journal of Environmental Economics and Management*, **47**(2), 331–63.

Binger, B., R. Copple, and E. Hoffman (1995a), "Contingent valuation methodology in the natural resource damage regulatory process: Choice theory and the embedding phenomenon," *Natural Resources Journal*, **35**(3), 443–59.

Binger, B.R., R.F. Copple, and E. Hoffman (1995b), "The use of contingent valuation methodology in natural resource damage assessments: Legal fact and economic fiction," *Northwestern University Law Review*, **89**(3), 1029–53.

Boyle, K.J., W.H. Desvousges, F. Reed Johnson, R.W. Dunford, and S.P. Hudson (1994), "An investigation of part-whole biases in contingent valuation studies," *Journal of Environmental Economics and Management*, **27**(1), 64–83.

Carson, R.T. (1997), "Contingent valuation and tests of insensitivity to scope," in R.J. Kopp, W. Pommerhene, and N. Schwartz (eds), *Determining the Value of Non-Marketed Goods: Economic, Psychological, and Policy Relevant Aspects of Contingent Valuation Methods*, Boston, MA: Kluwer.

Carson, R.T. and T. Groves (2007), "Incentive and informational properties of preference questions," *Environmental and Resource Economics*, **37**(1), 181–210.

Carson, R. and W.M. Hanemann (2005), "Contingent valuation," in K.-G. Mäler and J.R. Vincent (eds), *Handbook of Environmental Economics, Vol. 2*, Amsterdam: Elsevier, pp. 822–935.

Carson, R.T., W.M. Hanemann, R.J. Kopp, J.A. Krosnick, R.C. Mitchell, S. Presser, P.A. Ruud, and V.K. Smith (1994), *Prospective Interim Lost Use Value Due to DDT and PCB Contamination in the Southern California Bight*, report prepared for the National Oceanic and Atmospheric Administration, La Jolla, CA: Natural Resource Damage Assessment, Inc.

Chapman, D.J., R.C. Bishop, W.M. Hanemann, B.J. Kanninen, J.A. Krosnick, E.R. Morey, and R. Tourangeau (2009), *Natural Resource Damages Associated with Aesthetic and Ecosystem Injuries to Oklahoma's Illinois River System and Tenkiller Lake, Expert Report for State of Oklahoma, Volume I*, accessed November 30, 2016 at http://elsa.berkeley.edu/~train/chapman.pdf.

Christie, M. (2001), "A comparison of alternative contingent valuation elicitation treatments for the evaluation of complex environmental policy," *Journal of Environmental Management*, **62**(3), 255–69.

Davison, A.C. and D.V. Hinkley (1997), *Bootstrap Methods and Their Application*, Cambridge Series in Statistical and Probabilistic Mathematics, Cambridge, UK: Cambridge University Press.

Desvousges, W., K. Mathews, and K. Train (2012), "Adequate response to scope in contingent valuation," *Ecological Economics*, **84**, 121–8.

De Zoysa, A.D.N. (1995), "A benefit valuation of programs to enhance groundwater quality, surface water quality, and wetland habitat in Northwest Ohio," PhD dissertation, Ohio State University.

Diamond, P.A. (1996), "Testing the internal consistency of contingent valuation surveys," *Journal of Environmental Economics and Management*, **30**(3), 337–47.

Diamond, P.A., J.A. Hausman, G.K. Leonard, and M.A. Denning (1993), "Does contingent valuation measure preferences? Experimental evidence," in J.A. Hausman (ed.), *Contingent Valuation: A Critical Assessment*, Amsterdam: Elsevier, pp. 41–89.

Efron, B. (1982), *The Jackknife, the Bootstrap, and Other Resampling Plans*, Society of Industrial and Applied Mathematics CBMS-NSF Monographs.

Fleming, C.M. and M. Bowden (2009), "Web-based surveys as an alternative to traditional mail methods," *Journal of Environmental Management*, **90**(1), 284–92.

Haab, T.C., M.G. Interis, D. Petrolia, and J.C. Whitehead (2013), "From hopeless to curious? Thoughts on Hausman's 'dubious to hopeless' critique of contingent valuation," *Applied Economic Perspectives and Policy*, **35**(4), 593–612.

Hanemann, W.M. (1994), "Valuing the environment through contingent valuation," *The Journal of Economic Perspectives*, **8**(4), 19–43.

Heberlein, T.A., M.A. Wilson, R.C. Bishop, and N.C. Schaeffer (2005), "Rethinking the scope test as a criterion for validity in contingent valuation," *Journal of Environmental Economics and Management*, **50**(1), 1–22.

Hoevengel, R. (1996), "The validity of the contingent valuation method: Perfect and regular embedding," *Environmental and Resource Economics*, **7**(1), 57–78.

Loomis, J. and A. Gonzalez-Caban (1998), "A willingness-to-pay function for protecting acres of spotted owl habitat from fire," *Ecological Economics*, **25**(3), 315–22.

Macmillan, D.C. and E.I. Duff (1998), "Estimating the non-market costs and benefits of native woodland restoration using the contingent valuation method," *Forestry*, **71**(3), 247–59.

Nunes, P.A.L.D. and E. Schokkaert (2003), "Identifying the warm glow effect in contingent valuation," *Journal of Environmental Economics and Management*, **45**(2), 231–45.

Powe, N.A. and I.J. Bateman (2004), "Investigating insensitivity to scope: A split-sample test of perceived scheme realism," *Land Economics*, **80**(2), 258–71.

Riddel, M. and J. Loomis (1998), "Joint estimation of multiple CVM scenarios under a double bounded questioning format," *Environmental and Resource Economics*, **12**(1), 77–98.

Rollins, K. and A. Lyke (1998), "The case for diminishing marginal existence values," *Journal of Environmental Economics and Management*, **36**(3), 324–66.

Samples, K.C. and J.R. Hollyer (1990), "Contingent valuation of wildlife resources in the presence of substitutes and complements," in R.L. Johnson and G.V. Johnson (eds), *Economic Valuation of Natural Resources: Issues, Theory, and Applications*, Boulder, CO: Westview Press, pp. 177–92.

Stevens, T.H., S. Benin, and J.S. Larson (1995), "Public attitudes and values for wetland conservation in New England," *Wetlands*, **15**(3), 226–31.

Streever, W.J., M. Callaghan-Perry, A. Searles, T. Stevens, and P. Svoboda (1998), "Public attitudes and values for wetland conservation in New South Wales, Australia," *Journal of Environmental Management*, **54**(1), 1–14.

Veisten, K., H. Fredrik Hoen, and J. Strand (2004), "Sequencing and the adding up property in contingent valuation of endangered species: Are contingent non-use values economic values?," *Environmental and Resource Economics*, **29**(4), 419–23.

White, P.C.L., K.W. Gregory, P.J. Lindley, and G. Richards (1997), "Economic values of threatened mammals in Britain: A case study of the otter *Lutra lutra* and the water vole *Arvicola terrestris*," *Biological Conservation*, **82**(3), 345–54.

Whitehead, J.C., T.C. Haab, and J.-C. Huang (1998), "Part-whole bias in contingent valuation: Will scope effects be detected with inexpensive survey methods?," *Southern Economic Journal*, **65**(1), 160–68.

Windle, J. and J. Rolfe (2011), "Comparing responses from internet and paper-based collection methods in more complex stated preference environmental valuation surveys," *Economic Analysis and Policy*, **41**(1), 83–97.

Wu, P.-I. (1993), "Substitution and complementarity in commodity space: Benefit evaluation of multidimensional environmental policy," *Academia Economic Papers*, **21**(1), 151–82.

5. Do contingent valuation estimates of willingness to pay for non-use environmental goods pass the scope test with adequacy? A review of the evidence from empirical studies in the literature[1]

James Burrows, Rebecca Newman, Jerry Genser, and Jeffrey Plewes[2]

INTRODUCTION

Contingent valuation (CV) is commonly used in environmental economics to estimate non-use values of environmental goods and services.[3] Use values are amenable to direct analysis based on revealed preference data, either from direct approaches such as reviewing evidence of actual

---

[1] The authors gratefully acknowledge the essential contributions made to this chapter by Ed Leamer, Ken Train, Renée Miller-Mizia, Stamatia Kostakis, Hasat Cakkalkurt, Hiu Man Chan, and Connor Tobin.

[2] Respectively, Vice Chairman, Charles River Associates, Boston; Associate, Charles River Associates, Boston; Associate, Charles River Associates, Boston; Principal, Charles River Associates, Boston.

[3] Contingent valuation (CV) is a survey-based methodology often used to estimate values of non-market resources, such as environmental amenities. The survey may directly ask respondents how much they would be willing to pay (or willing to accept) for an environmental amenity (or to avoid the loss of an environmental amenity). A choice experiment (CE) is an application of the CV method in which respondents are presented with multiple questions with two or more choices in each question and are asked to select the preferred alternative in each choice question. The choice data are then econometrically analyzed to infer WTPs. CV can employ a variety of elicitation techniques, including open ended (in which respondents are asked to specify their WTP without a prompted amount), dichotomous choice (DC), in which respondents are asked whether their willingness to pay is at least an offered cost, double-bounded and multiple-bounded dichotomous choice (in which respondents are asked follow-up valuation questions to narrow the range of their WTPs), payment cards (in which respondents are shown a payment card with suggested values), and bidding games, among others.

purchases, or indirect approaches such as travel cost and hedonic price analysis. CV is likely to be much less accurate for non-use amenities than for use amenities, as respondents asked about non-use amenities have no market experience to guide their thinking, and are unlikely to have ever given thought to assigning monetary values for this type of good.

From its earliest days, the CV method has been scrutinized with respect to whether its results are consistent with the assumptions of rational choice. In this chapter we focus on one of the key tests of rational choice: do estimates of willingness to pay (WTP) derived from CV studies increase as the amount of the good (or the number of goods) increases (i.e., as scope increases), and, if so, are the WTP estimates "adequately" responsive to scope?[4]

A fundamental tenet of consumer utility theory is that utility increases as consumption of most goods increases (i.e., as the scope of consumption increases). For most goods and services, marginal utility generally declines as consumption increases; accordingly, some decline in WTP per unit as scope increases is to be expected for most goods over a reasonable range of costs or prices. A finding in a study that demand for an environmental amenity is not scope sensitive (i.e., the WTP for the amenity does not increase with scope, or increases by an amount that is too small to be credible) can occur for a number of reasons: respondents in fact do not experience increasing utility from increased scope of the amenity,[5] the methodology may be flawed, or respondents receive a "warm glow" from indicating (to themselves and/or the survey administrator) that they are willing to contribute to a worthy cause. If a flawed methodology or warm glow are the cause of scope non-responsiveness, the WTP results from the study are not usable for applications of CV,

---

[4] We define scope that is in terms of a single argument (e.g., acres of clean beaches) as quantitative scope, and scope that is in terms of multiple arguments (e.g., miles of clean beaches and number of lakes) as categorical scope. In the environmental literature the term "embedding" is often used to refer to instances of low or no scope sensitivity (with perfect embedding indicating that the value of a larger quantity is equal to the value of a smaller quantity).

[5] For example, it is quite possible that there is a positive WTP for wolves up to some minimum population size, but that the respondents on average may have no WTP (or even negative WTP) for additional numbers of wolves above this minimum population size. It is also possible that respondents may experience negative utility from any number of wolves. Boman and Bostedy (1999) and Wilson (2000) find no scope sensitivity for wolves. These wolf results are excluded from our tabulations because it is possible the respondents have no underlying positive marginal utility for wolves. As another example, there may be scope insensitivity for protecting land that gives access to a scenic body of water – WTP for preserving enough land for access may be high, but WTP for additional land above this threshold may be small.

including the allocation of public funds or the determination of damages in a litigation matter.

It would not be surprising to find a few studies in a large sample showing low or no scope effects. However, a finding that a large percentage of CV studies report no or very low scope effects would suggest that most environmental goods are subject to highly diminishing marginal utility, which, prima facie, seems improbable – for example, in the case of *quantitative* scope insensitivity is it really believable that respondents consistently place a high value on preserving one species, one pristine lake, or one pristine forest, and little or no value on additional species, pristine lakes, or pristine forests? In the case of *categorical* scope insensitivity, is it believable that respondents place a high value on preserving one species and little or no value in preserving one species and restoring one lake in addition? While previous reviews of the literature addressed how many studies pass or fail scope tests, none, to our knowledge, also attempted to quantify the adequacy or plausibility of these results over multiple studies.

We seek to review scope tests based on split-sample results ("external" scope tests in which responses of separate, independent groups are used to infer WTP for one scope of the environmental amenity) in CV studies of environmental amenities to determine the proportion that pass or fail. We also quantify the marginal utility implied by scope tests that pass, where applicable. We do not include within-respondent ("internal") scope tests because respondents who are presented with more than one choice task may attempt to appear internally consistent (either to themselves or to the survey administrator) and may also be affected by anchoring effects (to costs or prices that they have already seen in the survey) and/or by other context effects. We do not include scope tests derived from choice experiment (CE) surveys because scope tests using this methodology are, by their nature, internal tests in which the same respondents are making choices involving multiple scopes of environmental amenities. We focus in particular on scope tests involving non-use environmental goods, but we also include scope tests involving use environmental goods. Our review of 111 papers disproves the widely held conclusion that scope tests typically pass, as the majority of tests surveyed here fail. Those that do pass tend to do so with an implausibly low marginal WTP for additional units of the environmental amenity.

Scope insensitivity is often attributed to diminishing marginal utility and satiation. Amiran and Hagen (2010) argue that sharply diminishing marginal utility leading to low scope responsiveness can be explained by "bounded substitution" between environmental goods and market goods, in which survey respondents are willing to make few trades between money and environmental goods. Respondents may be willing to trade money for the first increment of an environmental amenity, but not additional increments.

Sharply diminishing marginal utility may well be true for particular goods over a particular range of prices. However, the instances in which this can be invoked are likely to be limited. Sharply diminishing marginal utility explains findings of limited scope only if respondents' preferences take a particular form: marginal utility from additional environmental goods must begin to diminish immediately after obtaining the smaller increment of the environmental good. Consider, for example, Araña and León (2008). For respondents with average emotional intensity scales, the authors find a WTP of €15.29 to increase the current length of walking paths from 300 to 330 kilometers (€0.50 for each additional kilometer). However, respondents are willing to pay only slightly more (€16.64) for a larger environmental good that would increase the length of the walking paths from 300 to 400 kilometers (€0.02 per kilometer, for the additional 70 kilometers). These results imply respondents are willing to pay nearly 30 times as much money per kilometer for the first 30 kilometers that are restored than they are for the remaining 70. Diminishing marginal utility rationalizes this finding only if survey respondents become satiated with kilometers soon after restoring the first 30 kilometers. Furthermore, if diminishing marginal utility does explain this result, it must be the case that Araña and León (2008) would have found increased sensitivity to scope if their large environmental good were smaller in size. If, for example, the larger environmental good increased the trail length from 300 to 350 kilometers (instead of 400), the empirical results indicate that the authors would necessarily have found WTPs per kilometer that were more similar across the smaller and larger environmental goods. In other words, findings similar to those of Araña and León (2008) can be rationalized by diminishing marginal utility only if we agree that the survey was accidentally designed not to find evidence of scope. Such accidents should be uncommon. However, as we show later, WTPs that imply sharply diminishing marginal utility are the rule and not the exception for those studies that find some scope responsiveness.

Carson and Mitchell (1989) identified a number of other factors that could also lead to apparent scope insensitivity: (1) part-whole bias, in which respondents confuse the good being offered with a much larger or smaller good;[6] (2) symbolic bias, in which respondents might perceive a

---

[6] Carson states: "Another problem...occurs when the researcher believes one good encompasses another, but respondents find the two goods offered indistinguishable. For example, suppose an ecosystem that provides habitat for five species is at risk. As a scope test, the researcher informs one sample that the habitat will be purchased to protect the five spe-

good as symbolic of a larger good; (3) metric bias, in which a respondent might be defining a good in a different metric than the survey designer; and (4) probability of provision bias, in which the respondent might believe that the larger good has a lower probability of being provided than the smaller good, and therefore bids less for the larger good than he or she otherwise would.

Biases of the types identified by Carson and Mitchell may well exist, and some may be curable by improved survey design. However, these types of biases considerably complicate, if not make impossible, the interpretation of a CV study. If a CV study subject to considerable part-whole bias finds that average WTP of respondents to clean up a mile of soiled beaches is, say, $10, how is the decision maker to know whether respondents are really valuing a much bigger good, such as all the beaches in a broad region? If the answer is that well-designed studies avoid the biases identified by Carson and Mitchell, what objective criteria can the decision maker use to determine whether a particular CV study is sufficiently well designed to be credible?

An alternative explanation of scope insensitivity is "warm glow" (see Andreoni, 1990 and Kahneman and Knetsch, 1992) – that is, respondents purchase "moral satisfaction" when they bid on a good (hypothetically or in actuality). If warm glow is fixed in size (scope insensitive) and large relative to the underlying marginal utility of the good being valued, then the WTP for that good will not increase very much as the quantity of the good increases. If scope insensitivity is caused by warm glow, estimates of WTP from CV surveys may not be informative about underlying WTP, as much of the estimated WTP may be for warm glow rather than for the amenity in question.

The *Exxon Valdez* spill in 1990 spawned a number of articles questioning or defending the CV methodology. In response to the controversy surrounding CV, the National Oceanic and Atmospheric Administration (NOAA) convened a panel of distinguished experts to review whether "the CV technique is capable of providing reliable information about lost existence or other passive-use values."[7]

The Panel examined various criteria of reliability of CVM, including whether CV estimates of WTP exhibit rationality:

---

cies and then informs another sample that the habitat will be purchased to protect only two species. Respondents in the second sample may reason that protecting the habitat will provide protection for all five species and are therefore paying for the same good as that offered to the first sample" (Carson, 1997, pp. 128–9).

[7] Arrow et al. (1993), p. 5.

Rationality in its weakest form requires certain kinds of consistency among choices made by individuals. For instance, if an individual chooses some purchases at a given set of prices and income, then if some prices fall and there are no other changes, the goods that the individual would now buy would make him or her better off. . . . Usually, though not always, it is reasonable to suppose that more of something regarded as good is better so long as an individual is not satiated. This is in general translated into a willingness to pay somewhat more for more of a good, as judged by the individual. Also, if marginal or incremental willingness to pay for additional amounts does decline with the amount already available, it is usually not reasonable to assume that it declines very abruptly.[8]

In its review of the literature the Panel identified a number of "maladies" that would render a CV study "unreliable." In particular, citing articles by Kahneman and Knetsch (1992), Desvousges et al. (1992), and Diamond et al. (1993), it observed that evidence supporting embedding had "multiplied" since Kahneman published a well-known Ontario study.[9] The Panel stated that:

[. . .]average willingness to pay is often substantial for the smallest scenario presented but is then substantially independent of the size of the damage averted. [This is] potentially a very damaging criticism of the method. . . If reported willingness to pay accurately reflected actual willingness to pay, then, under the "warm glow" interpretation, willingness to pay might well exceed compensation required because the former contains an element of self-approbation. It might be real but not properly compensable.[10]

---

[8] Ibid., pp. 10–11.
[9] Kahneman (1986) presents a chart from a split-sample telephone survey showing expressed WTP for three different scopes of lake clean-up (Muskoka only, Haliburton only, and all of Ontario). Kahneman states that "[t]he demand functions for the three cleanup operations are strikingly similar" and that "[t]he results indicate that people seem to be willing to pay almost as much to clean up one region or any other, and almost as much for any one region as for all Ontario together. We know from other surveys that these responses do not reflect expectations of personal enjoyment from the cleanup, since Toronto residents are willing to pay substantial amounts to clean up the lakes of British Columbia!. . . Because the questions all elicit symbolic expressions of the same attitude, there is not much difference between the numbers that are attached to a single region and to all of Ontario" (pp. 191–2). Carson (1997) observes that the Kahneman results demonstrate some limited scope sensitivity, as the WTP for clean-up of all Ontario lakes appears from the graph to exceed the WTPs for the smaller goods by about 50%. Desvousges et al. (1992) conduct a survey of WTP to prevent 2,000, 20,000, or 200,000 migratory waterfowl from dying in waste-oil holding ponds and report that they do not find scope sensitivity. Diamond et al. (1993) report on a survey of WTP to prevent various wilderness areas from being developed in which they generally do not find scope sensitivity.
[10] Arrow et al. (1993), pp. 26–7.

The Panel concluded that the findings of a survey would be "unreliable" if the survey exhibited "Inadequate responsiveness to the scope of the environmental insult."[11,12]

In a later document, four of the authors of the NOAA report clarified what they meant by the use of the word "inadequate":

> Had the panel thought that something as straightforward as statistical measurability were the proper way to define sensitivity, then we would (or should) have opted for language to that effect. A better word than "adequate" would have been "plausible": A survey instrument is judged unreliable if it yields estimates which are implausibly unresponsive to the scope of the insult. This, of course, is a judgment call, and cannot be tested in a context-free manner.[13]

We review the evidence on both the extent to which CV studies demonstrate significant sensitivity to scope and the plausibility of scope results that are measured. In accordance with the NOAA Panel's recommendation, any judgment about whether CV inferences about WTP are reliable needs to consider both statistical significance and plausibility of reported scope effects.

Diamond et al. (1993) proposed an "adding-up" test for the reliability of CV that does not rely on untestable assumptions about the structure of respondents' preferences with respect to diminishing marginal utility and bounded substitution.[14] Underlying the adding-up test is the following idea: if stated preference survey responses reflect well-formed stable preferences, then alternative measures of these preferences should yield similar effects. If alternative measures of the same preferences do not yield similar results, then the measures must be measuring something other than preferences.

Specifically, suppose we are interested in measuring willingness to pay for two environmental goods, A and B, and for the combination of the two goods, A + B = C. While a conventional scope analysis tests whether WTP (C) is ≥ WTP (A) or WTP (C) ≥ WTP (B), in an adding-up test the analyst

---

[11] Ibid., p. 37.

[12] Carson (1994) states: "As used by the Ohio court and in the NOAA Panel report, the reliability of a measure is the degree to which it measures the theoretical construct under investigation. However, in the empirical social sciences, this preceding definition pertains to *validity*, whereas reliability is defined as the extent to which the variance of the measure is not due to random sources and systematic sources of error...we...use the term *reliability* to refer to the degree to which CV surveys measure the theoretical construct under investigation" (footnote 11, p. 8; emphasis in original). Note that Carson, as is typical of the CV literature, is in effect focusing exclusively on statistical significance without regard to adequacy of scope.

[13] Arrow et al. (1994).

[14] See also Diamond (1996).

tests whether WTP (A) + WTP (B|A) = WTP (C). If respondents' answers reflect well-formed stable preferences over the costs and benefits associated with A and B, then it must be true that the sum of WTP (A) and WTP (B|A) approximately equals WTP (A + B). This equality must hold even if diminishing marginal utility or bounded substitution cause WTP (A + B) to be only slightly larger than WTP (A). However, if measures of WTP are contaminated by phenomena such as "warm glow," this equality will not hold. Upward bias in WTP caused by "warm glow" will cause the sum of WTP (A) and WTP (B|A) to exceed WTP (A + B). Thus, if WTP (A + B) is statistically different from the sum of WTP (A) and WTP (B|A), we can reject the hypothesis that survey responses are a measure of well-formed stable preferences.

The adding-up test and the scope test are related but are not the same. A survey can have zero or implausibly low scope and still pass an adding-up test. On the other hand, if warm glow is an important element of measured WTP (and if warm glow is substantially exhausted after the first "purchase"), a survey will fail both an adding-up test and a scope test.

Critics of the adding-up test object that the scenario presented to the respondents is implausible and difficult to describe: "[I]t is an ex-post counterfactual scenario. Respondents must be convinced that a currently nonexistent government program has been funded and implemented and that their budget has been reduced by the cost."[15] Although this is true, some published CV studies posit hypothetical scenarios in which the government has already completed some environmental investments and the respondent is now being asked to state WTP for more improvements (or ask the respondent to assume some base scenario of environmental characteristics about which the respondent has no prior knowledge).[16] The only manner in which the scenario in an adding-up test is different from CV studies like those of Rollins and Lyke (1998) and Whitehead et al. (2009) is asking the respondent to assume that he or she has already made a payment for A and that A has already been provided when he or she is asked to value B. However, even if the respondent does not take the cost of having paid for A into account in valuing B, the effect on estimated WTP for B is likely to be trivial – in most cases, the cost of B will be a tiny

---

[15] Whitehead (2016), p. 19.
[16] For example, Rollins and Lyke (1998) inform respondents that the government has set aside 29 of 39 natural regions as national parks and is now considering creating additional national parks; Whitehead et al. (2009) inform respondents that the government has set aside 9,000 acres of Saginaw Bay to be protected and is considering purchasing and protecting additional acreages.

percentage of wealth or income, so the effect of the cost of A on WTP for B should be similarly insignificant.[17]

The adding-up test has also been criticized because it increases survey costs.[18] An adding-up test requires at least three split samples, while a traditional scope test can be performed with as few as two split samples. However, many studies with scope tests contain more than two split samples, so cost can scarcely be the reason for avoiding an adding-up test. For example, a number of studies testing part-whole biases use multiple split samples that survey WTP for various goods separately and combined.[19]

In spite of the rigor of the Diamond et al. (1993) adding-up test, it has only been implemented in a handful of studies: Samples and Hollyer (1990) report adding-up tests that fail; Diamond et al. (1993) report adding-up tests that fail; Chapman et al. (2009) conduct a survey that would permit an adding-up test, but they do not perform an adding-up test (although they report a traditional scope test that exhibits scope sensitivity);[20] Desvousges and Matthews (2012) use the Chapman data to perform an adding-up test that fails; and Desvousges et al. (2016) conduct a new survey similar to the Chapman survey with additional scope variations and report adding-up tests that fail. Other studies that have examined part-whole and sequencing biases have used approaches that have most but not all of the elements of an adding-up test.[21]

---

[17] Hausman and Newey (2016) develop bounds that take account of the share of income spent on a good and its income derivative. Their results demonstrate that for the typical cost of contingent valuation goods, which are typically in the range of $10 to $200, the bounds are almost identical for consumer surplus.

[18] Whitehead (2016), p. 9.

[19] Furthermore, there is hardly any feature of a properly conducted CV study that is not subject to a cost–quality trade-off.

[20] Because these data fail the adding-up test, we report this paper as a fail in our tabulations.

[21] For example, Stevens et al. (1995) perform split-sample surveys that are close to a full adding-up test: they ask respondents in three split samples to value two rare plants, flood protection, and two rare plants plus flood protection. Respondents for the rare plants alone and flood protection alone scenarios are not told to assume that they have already purchased the other amenity, so in this respect the Stevens et al. study does not satisfy all the conditions of the adding-up test (but this should not have a substantial effect on the results). The WTPs for the two rare plants alone plus flood protection alone are more than two rare plants and flood protection combined, indicating that this modified adding up test fails. Warm glow is a possible explanation for this result. Substitution between rare plants and food protection could also explain the result, but it seems unlikely that rare plants and food protection are partial substitutes in any other sense than that contributing to them provides warm glow. Samples and Hollyer (1990) derive WTPs from three split samples for humpback whales alone, monk seals alone, and whales and seals directly. They report that the WTPs of whales alone + seals alone is greater than whales and seals combined. In this example, it is possible that whales and seals are partial substitutes for each other, although it still seems more likely is that the substitution effect is derived from warm glow even here.

Carson (1997) presents the first systematic review of scope studies.[22,23] This review focuses on the extent to which CV studies find statistically significant scope effects, but does not address the issue of whether reported scope results are plausible or adequate – the criterion stressed by the NOAA Panel. Carson presents a table enumerating 31 studies appearing between 1986 and 1997 that he states: "contain a rejection of the scope insensitivity hypothesis at $p < 0.10$. Most of the studies contain a rejection at $p < 0.05$ and many contain rejections at less than $p < 0.001$."[24] A casual reading of this statement would suggest that the 31 studies in the list all pass scope, but the precise reading is that each paper in the list includes at least one test passing a scope test even if other tests reported in the paper fail. For example, the Carson list includes the Diamond et al. (1993) paper, which reports two scope tests that pass and 43 scope tests that fail.

We differ from Carson with respect to nine of the studies he includes in his table: four studies do not include an external scope test,[25] three studies report mixed results,[26] and in two studies the scope tests fail.[27] In addition, we identify 34 additional scope studies published prior to 1997 involving environmental amenities studies that are not included in the Carson study; as shown in Table 1, seven of these additional studies pass (P) scope, 21 fail (F) scope, and six have mixed (M) results. With fractional allocations for studies reporting multiple scope tests, 9.7 pass scope and 24.3 fail scope. Carson also ignores the key issue of reliability of CV highlighted by the NOAA Panel – namely, whether CV studies have scope results that are adequate. This omission is not unique to Carson; CV researchers often ignore this issue entirely.

The only other systematic review of scope tests in CV studies besides Carson (1997) is Desvousges et al. (2012) (DMT). DMT include a table identifying 109 CV studies in which scope tests are reported (or contain information that permits a scope test even if not reported in the study). They report that more of these 109 studies pass scope than fail: 40 pass (P)

---

[22] Brown and Duffield (1995) present a table summarizing 14 CV studies with scope results, but this table includes both internal and external scope tests and omitted numerous other studies.

[23] Carson (1997) also includes a version of the Schkade and Payne (1993) bird study data without outliers. Because the standard errors overlap for the outlier removal across each size threshold and model, we tabulate this paper as a fail in our database. This is weighted as 0.5 with the original Schkade and Payne (1993) paper, which we list as 0.5 pass, 0.5 fail.

[24] Carson (1997), Table VI, pp. 143–6.

[25] Duffield and Neher (1991), Whitehead (1992), Wu (1993), and Boyle et al. (1993).

[26] Magnussen (1992), Loomis et al. (1993), Schkade and Payne (1994). These articles are not technically misrepresented in Table VI, as each contains at least one test that passes scope in addition to scope tests that fail.

[27] Navrud (1989); Diamond et al. (1993).

Table 1 Carson (1997) comparison

Authors	Pub Year	Commodity	External Test Pass/Fail/Mixed	Included in Carson (1997)?	Match Carson's Assessment?
[1] Brookshire et al.	1983	Benefit of hunting big horn sheep or grizzly bears in five or 15 years	F	No	
[2] Rahmatian	1985	Visibility in Grand Canyon National Park	F	No	
[3] Kahneman	1986	Clean-up to preserve fishing in Muskoka, Haliburton, and all Ontario	M	No	
[4] Bergstrom and Stoll	1987	Farmland protection in Greenville County, South Carolina	F	No	
[5] Navrud	1989	Reduced sulfur depositions to protect freshwater fish populations	F	Yes	No
[6] Carson et al.	1990	Air quality in Cincinnati	P	No	
[7] Samples and Hollyer	1990	Preserving Humpback whales and Hawaiian monk seals in Hawaii	F	No	
[8] Duffield and Neher	1991		N/A	Yes	No
[9] Gilbert et al.	1991	Lye Brook Wilderness Area in southwestern Vermont	F	No	
[10] Desvousges et al.	1992	Preventing waterfowl deaths in the Central Flyway	F	No	
[11] Desvousges et al.	1992	Preventing environmental damage from oil spills	F	No	
[12] Jakus	1992	Gypsy moth protection	P	Yes	Yes

[13]	Kahneman and Knetsch	1992	Preserving wilderness, protecting wildlife, providing parks, preparing for disasters, controlling air pollution, insuring water quality, routine treatment of industrial wastes; 12 embedding pairs	M	No
[14]	Magnussen	1992	Reduce Norwegian nutrient leaching to the North Sea	M	Yes
[15]	Rowe et al.	1992	Oil spill clean-up and prevention programs	P	Yes	Yes
[16]	Whitehead	1992		N/A	Yes	No
[17]	Boyle et al.	1993		N/A	Yes	No
[18]	Carson	1993	National versus regional water quality	P	Yes	Yes
[19]	Diamond et al.	1993	Marshall wilderness areas	M	Yes	No
[20]	Fischhoff et al.	1993	River clean-up in Pittsburgh area	F	No	
[21]	Loomis et al.	1993	Protections of forests in Southeast Australia	M	Yes	No
[22]	Greg	1993	Preservation of the Selway-Bitterroot Wilderness	F	No	
[23]	Tanguay et al.	1993	Maintaining woodland caribou population in northwestern Saskatchewan	F	No	
[24]	Wu	1993		N/A	Yes	No
[25]	Bowker and Didychuk	1994	Preserve units of Moncton area farmland	P	Yes	Yes
[26]	Boyle et al.	1994	Preventing waterfowl deaths in the Central Flyway	F	No	
[27]	Carson et al.	1994a	Preservation of Australia's Kakadu conservation zone from mining activity	P	Yes	Yes
[28]	Carson et al.	1994b	Program to accelerate natural restoration of injured resources due to PCB and DDT contamination in Southern California Bight	P	Yes	Yes
[29]	Gerrans	1994	Preservation of the Jandakot wetlands	F	No	

93

Table 1 (continued)

Authors	Pub Year	Commodity	External Test Pass/Fail/Mixed	Included in Carson (1997)?	Match Carson's Assessment?
[30] Welsh et al.	1994	Glen Canyon Dam downstream recreation, hydropower, and passive-use values	P	Yes	Yes
[31] Kahneman and Ritov	1994	Headline method – multiple	F	No	
[32] Krieger	1994	Anglers' WTP for changes in Michigan's public health advisory	P	Yes	Yes
[33] McFadden	1994	Preservation of the Selway-Bitterroot Wilderness in northern Idaho	F	No	
[34] Schkade and Payne	1994	Preserving migratory waterfowl in the Central Flyway of the USA (the bird study)	M	Yes	No
[35] Binger et al.	1995	Preservation of the Selway-Bitterroot Wilderness and 57 federal wilderness areas	P	No	
[36] Brown and Duffield	1995	Protect instream flow in either one or five Montana rivers	M	No	
[37] Brown et al.	1995	Preservation of natural areas in Fort Collins	F	No	
[38] Carson and Mitchell	1995	Preventing injuries from large open pit mine in Kakadu Conservation Zone	P	No	
[39] Fredman	1995	Protecting the white-backed woodpecker in Sweden	F	No	
[40] Schultze et al.	1995	Upper Clark Fork River, Montana, River Basin Restoration	F	No	
[41] Stevens et al.	1995	Preserving wetlands in New England	P	No	
[42] Welsh et al.	1995	Preserving resources of Colorado River downstream of Glen Canyon Dam	M	No	

[43]	Berrens et al.	1996	Protecting minimum instream flows in New Mexico: silvery minnow versus 11 threatened species	P	No
[44]	Choe et al.	1996	Improving water quality of rivers and sea in Davao, Philippines	M	No
[45]	Hoevenagel	1996	Greenhouse effect, depletion of ozone layer, deforestation, acid rain, surface water pollution, animal manure problem	P	Yes
[46]	Macmillan et al.	1996	Recovery/damage scenarios from reduced acid rain deposition	F	No
[47]	Carson	1997	Preventing birds from being killed	F	No
[48]	Huang et al.	1997	Quality improvement of Pamlico and Albemarle sounds (recreation areas) in North Carolina	M	No
[49]	Loomis and Ekstrand	1997	Preserving MSO or 62 endangered species	F	No
[50]	Mullarkey	1997	Wisconsin wetlands	P	No
[51]	Ready et al.	1997	Preventing a decrease in the number of horse farms in Kentucky	P	Yes
[52]	Smith et al.	1997	Controlling marine debris on beaches and coastal areas in New Jersey and North Carolina	P	Yes
[53]	Stevens et al.	1997	Movie passes and restoration of Atlantic salmon	P	No
[54]	White et al.	1997	Conservation of two otter species	F	No

	Yes
	Yes
	Yes

Table 1   (continued)

Notes:

[5]   Navrud (1989) reports the WTP results for two split samples in which respondents are asked WTP for 30, 50, and 70% reductions in sulfur emissions related to corresponding increments in fish populations, with subsamples for payment cards vs bidding game elicitation techniques. Navrud states "When looking at the mean of subsamples using bidding games the WTP appears to increase (but at a decreasing rate) with increasing improvements in the fish populations and for all affected goods... However, the observed tendency is not statistically significant, and the same tendency cannot be observed for the subsamples using payment cards. This indicates that the respondents have difficulties in perceiving the differences between the environmental improvements" (p. 81). We report this study as failing scope – with bidding games the results are not significant and for payment cards no scope sensitivity is found.

[8]   Duffield and Neher's (1991) study of economic value of waterfowl hunting reports split samples in which respondents are asked for WTP (in trip costs) for waterfowl hunting assuming they saw twice as many (or half as many) waterfowl in their prior trip, but this question occurs after they are asked for their WTP for their last trip – so the results reported are an internal scope test. We record this study as not providing an external scope test.

[14]   Magnussen (1992) reports WTP results for four split samples. The first questions are different for each sample (WTP's in parentheses); from largest good to smallest they are: (1) a package of four broad environmental goods (3,054 kroner), (2) a package of four pollution abatement methods (3,366 kroner), (3) a North Sea program (1943 kroner), and (4) improvement in local water quality from class 3 to class 2 (1,125 kroner). WTP for good 2 is higher than for good 1, but this difference is not significant. WTP for good 2 is significantly higher than for good 3. WTP for good 3 is higher than for good 4, but it is only significant at the 10% level. Respondents are also asked subsequent questions (for goods 2 and 3 for the respondents to good 1, for good 3 for respondents to good 2, and for good 5 [improvement from level 2] for respondents to good 2). These are all internal tests and are excluded from our survey (three of these internal tests pass and one fails). The author concludes that "the study did not support that people state the same value in CV surveys whatever amenity is valued. But for very inclusive packages of environmental improvements and 'loose' descriptions of the payment vehicle, this seemed to be the case... The small differences in WTP for different marginal water quality improvements question whether people are able to value different marginal changes" (p. 218). We classify this study as providing mixed results with respect to scope sensitivity.

[16]   Whitehead's (1992) study of WTP to preserve loggerhead sea turtle species. The respondents are asked to provide their assessments of the probability that the loggerhead sea turtle will become extinct in the next 25 years and then are asked for their WTP for a policy under which the loggerhead sea turtle will definitely not become extinct within the next 25 years. There is no split sample, so there is no external scope test in this study. Nor is there an internal scope test. However, the variable "extinction risk probability change" is significant in both a linear and a non-linear regression of WTP on a number of explanatory variables. This may appear to be a scope test, but the "extinction risk probability" is supplied by the respondents, not the survey administrator. We classify this study as not containing either an internal or external scope test.

[19] Diamond et al. (1993). Carson is correct that this study includes "a rejection of the scope insensitivity hypothesis"; the study reports two scope tests that pass and 43 that fail. Carson does additional analysis on Hypothesis 1 of the Diamond article and reports that the acreage variable is significant in a regression of WTP on acres. We therefore report this is as a pass with a 50% weight, offsetting the Diamond et al. (1993) test of fail with a 50% weight for this particular hypothesis. This changes the pass/fail count to 2.5/42.5. Diamond et al. report a scope test failure derived from Binger et al. (1995) using a similar survey comparing WTP for one part to WTP for 57 parks. We do not include this scope test failure in the Diamond et al. study because it is reported separately in our tabulations as a Binger et al. study. We report the Diamond et al. study as reporting mixed results with respect to scope sensitivity.

[21] Loomis et al.'s (1993) study of WTP for protection of forests in all of southeastern Australia and two smaller portions of that area. The answers to the first questions of each sample allow two scope tests (for East Gippsland vs all Southeast Australia and for the Errinundra Plateau of East Gippsland vs East Gippsland). The first scope test fails and the second passes. The second and third questions for the first sample and the second question for the second sample permit internal scope tests (which pass), but these are not included in our review of external scope tests. We record this study as reporting mixed effects with respect to scope sensitivity.

[24] Wu's (1993) study of value of three different environmental amenities relating to Ohio's Big Darby Creek. Three split samples were asked to value one policy first and then combinations of two and three policies. Only the first questions would permit an external scope test. The WTPs found are $42.80 for enhanced biological diversity, $35.18 for improved streambed visibility, and $19.18 for increasing hiking trails mileage. As these amenities are not nested, this study does not report an external scope test.

[26] Boyle et al.'s (1993) study of the economic value of Grand Canyon white-water boating. Two split samples were asked to value seven water flow scenarios; one sample was asked values for flows from low to high and the other was asked values for flows from high to low (i.e., each group was asked the same questions but in reverse sequence from the other). The authors found a question-ordering for commercial passengers (at the 10% level) but not for private passengers. This study collected data that could have been used for an external scope test as defined here, but no results of any such test are reported in the article. We categorize this study as N/A.

[34] Schkade and Payne's (1994) study of economic value of migratory waterfowl, reports results for three split samples for 2,000, 20,000, and 200,000 bird deaths. The raw WTPs appear mixed (mean WTP for 200,000 birds is greater than for 20,000, but mean WTP for 20,000 is less than mean WTP for 2,000 birds). Carson states that as a result of Schkade and Payne's "small sample sizes, they lack almost any statistical power because the models estimated do not incorporate information that the treatments... are monotonically ordered. It is possible to show that simply regressing the log of willingness to pay on the number of birds results in a rejection of the null hypothesis that WTP is not monotonically increasing in the number of birds valued at $p < 0.05$ using a one-sided t-test. The other problem with the data is that much of the value is driven by a small number of very large outliers... dropping out just the two highest observations eliminates the apparent violation of the economic restriction that WTPs increase monotonically with increases in the level of the good... dropping the next four largest observations does not change the relative rankings of WTP for the three treatments" (p. 136). We record Schkade and Payne as mixed but also report Carson's re-analysis of the data as a separate study showing a fail. Each of these studies is assigned a 50% weight in our tabulations, as they use the same underlying data.

a scope test, 17 fail (F) a scope test, 47 have mixed (M) results (i.e., report multiple tests, some of which are passes and some of which are fails), and five are listed as "NR" or not reported. However, the DMT tabulation includes both internal and external scope tests. Although not reported in the published article, these results are largely consistent after exclusion of internal tests in the DMT tabulation. Of 71 studies containing external, non-use or mixed non-use and use environmental scope tests, 25 pass, 13 fail, and 33 report mixed results. As in the case in the Carson paper, the DMT paper focuses only on whether CV studies report statistically significant scope effects, not on whether any scope effects reported found are adequate.

Our results differ from the 2012 DMT results, although not by the same extent as our differences with respect to the 1997 Carson results. For the same studies that are included in the DMT survey, as Table 2 shows we report 29 passes (39%), 18 mixed results (24%), and 27 fails (36%) out of a total count of 74 (including results for three studies that DMT include in their table but for which they do not report scope tests). After assigning fractional passes and fails for the mixed scope tests, our count is 37.25 pass; 36.75 fail. The principal difference between the DMT results and the results we present later in this chapter relates to the classification of scope tests as mixed – we report many of these tests as fails or fractionally allocate them.

In addition to the Carson and DMT surveys of scope tests in individual studies, a number of meta-studies have been published that draw inferences about scope effects from WTPs reported across different studies in particular applied areas. Ojea and Loureiro (2011) present a table summarizing the results of 14 meta-studies with respect to scope. They conclude that eight of the studies find positive sensitivity to scope and that six find no or negative scope sensitivity (three studies find insensitivity to scope, and three studies find negative sensitivity to scope). None of the scope meta-studies deals with the issue of adequacy of scope, although a few report data on the quantitative extent of scope.

Table 3 presents an updated version of the Ojea and Loureiro survey. We have included several additional studies that focus on environmental non-use or mixed non-use and use amenities.[28] Similarly to Ojea and Loureiro we excluded meta-studies that focus exclusively on recreational

---

[28] We have not included Loomis and White (1996) in Table 3, as Richardson and Loomis (2009) present an updated version of the earlier paper, using a very similar methodology and many of the same studies as in the earlier study. We have also replaced Boyle et al. (1994) with Poe et al. (2001), which is an update of Boyle et al. (1994).

Table 2 DMT (2012) comparison (external tests only)

DMT #	Author	Pub Year	Commodity	Results (Pass/Fail/Mixed)	DMT Results (Pass/Fail/Mixed)
DMT_1	Ahearn et al.	2006	Protecting grassland birds in the Central Plains region	M	M
DMT_2	Alvarez-Farzio et al.	1999	Preserving two environmentally sensitive areas in Scotland	P	P
DMT_3	Araña and León	2008	Rehabilitating walking paths in Gran Canaria, Spain	M	M
DMT_5	Banzhaf et al.	2006	Acid rain: quality of water and fish populations, bird species, and tree species (600 lakes versus 900 lakes)	F	P
DMT_8	Bateman et al.	2004	Open access lake improvements located in grounds of University of East Anglia	M	M
DMT_10	Bennett et al.	1998	Dryland salinity in Upper South East region of South Australia	P	M
DMT_12	Berrens et al.	2000	Protecting minimum instream flows in New Mexico: silvery minnow versus 11 threatened species	P	P
DMT_13	Berrens et al.	1996	Protecting minimum instream flows in New Mexico: silvery minnow versus 11 threatened species	P	P
DMT_14	Binger et al.	1995	Preservation of the Selway-Bitterroot Wilderness and 57 federal wilderness areas	P	P
DMT_15	Bliem and Getzner	2008	Ecological restoration in Danube river basin	F	F
DMT_16	Blomquist and Whitehead	1998	Preserving wetland areas in Kentucky	P	M

Table 2 (continued)

DMT #	Author	Pub Year	Commodity	Results (Pass/Fail/Mixed)	DMT Results (Pass/Fail/Mixed)
DMT_17	Bowker and Didychuk	1994	Preserve units of Moncton area farmland	P	P
DMT_18	Boyle et al.	1994	Preventing waterfowl deaths in the Central Flyway	F	F
DMT_20	Brookshire et al.	1983	Benefit of hunting big horn sheep or grizzly bears in five or 15 years	F	M
DMT_21	Brown and Duffield	1995	Protect instream flow in either one or five Montana rivers	M	M
DMT_22	Brown et al.	1995	Preservation of natural areas in Fort Collins	F	M
DMT_23	Carson	1997	Preventing birds from being killed	F	P
DMT_25	Carson et al.	1994b	Program to accelerate natural restoration of injured resources due to PCB and DDT contamination in Southern California Bight	P	P
DMT_26	Carson et al.	1994a	Preservation of Australia's Kakadu conservation zone from mining activity	P	M
DMT_27	Carson et al.	1990	Air quality in Cincinnati	P	NR
DMT_28	Chapman et al.	2009	Alum treatments to prevent algae growth in the Illinois River system and Tenkiller Lake	F	P
DMT_31	Choe et al.	1996	Improving water quality of rivers and sea in Davao, Philippines	M	M
DMT_32	Christie	2001	Recreation opportunities, Grampian region, Scotland	M	M
DMT_35	Day and Mourato	1998	Maintaining river water quality in Beijing	P	P
DMT_36	Desvousges et al.	1992	Preventing waterfowl deaths in the Central Flyway	F	F

DMT_37	Diamond et al.	1993	Preservation of Selway, Washakie, and Bob Marshall wilderness areas	F	M
DMT_40	Dupont	2003	Improvements to three recreational activities (swimming, fishing, and boating in Hamilton Harbor, Ontario, Canada)	M	M
DMT_41	Eom and Larson	2006	Water quality improvement in the Man Kyoung River in South Korea	P	P
DMT_42	Fischhoff et al.	1993	River clean-up in Pittsburgh area	F	F
DMT_43	Gerrans	1994	Preservation of the Jandakot wetlands	F	F
DMT_44	Giraud et al.	1999	Mexican spotted owl and 62 regional threatened & endangered species	P	M
DMT_45	Goodman et al.	1998	Non-use value of natural coastal environment in England	F	M
DMT_47	Hanemann	2005	Saving at-risk birds (the bird study revisited)	P	P
DMT_51	Heberlein et al.	2005	(1) Water quality, (2) Wisconsin's wild wolf population, (3) Indian spearfishing, (4) biodiversity	P	M
DMT_52	Hite et al.	2002	Subsidizing variable-rate technology to reduce polluted river runoff for the Mississippi River basin (in Mississippi)	P	P
DMT_53	Hoevenagel	1996	Greenhouse effect, depletion of ozone layer, deforestation, acid rain, surface water pollution, animal manure problem	P	P
DMT_55	Huang et al.	1997	Quality improvement of Pamlico and Albemarle sounds (recreation areas) in North Carolina	M	P
DMT_56	Kahneman	1986	Clean-up to preserve fishing in Muskoka, Haliburton, and all Ontario	M	NR
DMT_57	Kahneman and Ritov	1994	Headline method – multiple	F	M

Table 2 (continued)

DMT #	Author	Pub Year	Commodity	Results (Pass/Fail/Mixed)	DMT Results (Pass/Fail/Mixed)
DMT_58	Kahneman and Knetsch	1992	Preserving wilderness, protecting wildlife, providing parks, preparing for disasters, controlling air pollution, insuring water quality, routine treatment of industrial wastes; 12 embedding pairs	M	M
DMT_60	Krieger	1994	Angler's WTP for changes in Michigan's public health advisory	P	P
DMT_62	Loomis and Ekstrand	1997	Preserving MSO or 62 endangered species	F	P
DMT_66	Loomis et al.	1993	Protections of forests in Southeast Australia	M	M
DMT_67	Macmillan and Duff	1998	Native woodland restoration in the UK	P	P
DMT_68	Macmillan et al.	1996	Recovery/damage scenarios from reduced acid rain deposition	F	M
DMT_69	Magnussen	1992	Reduce Norwegian nutrient leaching to the North Sea	M	M
DMT_71	McDaniels et al.	2003	Benefits of fisheries enhancement on rivers in British Columbia	P	P
DMT_72	McFadden	1994	Preservation of the Selway-Bitterroot Wilderness in Northern Idaho	F	F
DMT_73	Navrud	1989	Reduced sulfur depositions to protect freshwater fish populations	F	M
DMT_75	Nunes and Schokkaert	2003	Protection of wilderness and recreation areas in Alentejo Natural Park, Portugal	M	M
DMT_77	Poe et al.	2005	Mexican spotted owl and 62 regional threatened and endangered species	M	P

ID	Author	Year	Description		
DMT_79	Pouta	2005	Forest regeneration cutting policy in Finland	F	M
DMT_80	Powe and Bateman	2004	Protect wetlands (nested area versus total) in Broadland, Eastern England	P	M
DMT_81	Ready et al.	1997	Preventing a decrease in the number of horse farms in Kentucky	P	P
DMT_84	Rollins and Lyke	1998	Creating parks in Canada's Northwest Territories	F	M
DMT_86	Rowe et al.	1992	Oil spill clean-up and prevention programs	P	M
DMT_87	Samples and Hollyer	1990	Preserving humpback whales and Hawaiian monk seals in Hawaii	F	F
DMT_88	Schkade and Payne	1994	Preserving migratory waterfowl in the Central Flyway of the USA (the bird study)	M	F
DMT_90	Smith et al.	2005	Improvements of eastern regional haze	F	M
DMT_91	Smith et al.	1997	Controlling marine debris on beaches and coastal areas in New Jersey and North Carolina	P	P
DMT_92	Stanley	2005	Riverside fairy shrimp versus all local endangered species	P	P
DMT_93	Stevens et al.	1997	Movie passes and restoration of Atlantic salmon	P	F
DMT_94	Stevens et al.	1995	Preserving wetlands in New England	P	P
DMT_95	Streever et al.	1998	Wetland conservation in New South Wales, Australia	F	F
DMT_96	Svedsäter	2000	Rain forests in South America, endangered wild animals, air pollution in central London, global warming	F	F
DMT_97	Tanguay et al.	1993	Maintaining woodland caribou population in Northwestern Saskatchewan	F	NR

103

Table 2 (continued)

DMT #	Author	Pub Year	Commodity	Results (Pass/Fail/Mixed)	DMT Results (Pass/Fail/Mixed)
DMT_98	Veisten et al.	2004a	Endangered species preservation in Norwegian forests	M	M
DMT_100	Welsh et al.	1995	Preserving resources of Colorado River downstream of Glen Canyon Dam	M	M
DMT_101	White et al.	1997	Conservation of two otter species	F	M
DMT_103	Whitehead and Cherry	2007	Green energy program in North Carolina (yielding improved air quality in western North Carolina mountains)	M	M
DMT_104	Whitehead and Finney	2003	Preserving submerged marine cultural resources (historic shipwrecks)	F	F
DMT_105	Whitehead et al.	2009	Purchase and managing additional acres of coastal marshes in Saginaw Bay	F	F
DMT_106	Whitehead et al.	1998	Quality improvement of Pamlico and Albemarle sounds (recreation areas) in North Carolina	P	P
DMT_108	Wilson	2000	Wolves, Chippewa Indian spearfishing, biological diversity, and water quality in Wisconsin	P	M

Table 3 Ojea and Loureiro (2011) comparison

Study	Year	Commodity	Region	Method	Studies	Obs.	Size Measure	Scope
Non-use								
Barrio and Loureiro	2010	Forests	Worldwide	CV	35	101	Hectares	Insensitive
Brouwer et al.	1999	Wetlands	North America, Europe	CV	30	92	% size of wetland with respect to all country wetlands	Insensitive
Ghermandi et al.	2008	Wetlands	Worldwide	CV, HP, TC, RC, PF, MP, CE	167	385	Hectares	Positive
Hjerpi et al.	2015	Forests and freshwater	Europe, USA, Canada	CV, CR, CE	22	127	Low, High	Positive
Johnston and Duke	2009	Farmland preservation	USA	CE	18	1,688	Acres	NA
Lindhjem	2007	Forests	Scandinavia	CV, CE	50	72	Hectares	Insensitive
Ojea et al.	2010	Forests	Worldwide	TC, RC, CV, others	65	172	ln(ha)	Negative
Ojea and Loureiro	2011	Ecosystems and diversity	USA, UK, some worldwide	CV	100	355	Absolute and relative changes in measurements in study	Insensitive (0.5) and Positive (0.5)
Richardson and Loomis[a]	2009	Threatened and endangered species	Worldwide	CV	31	67	% change	Positive
Smith and Osborne	1996	Visibility in national parks	USA	CV	5	115	% change in visibility	Positive

105

Table 3 (continued)

Study	Year	Commodity	Region	Method	Studies	Obs.	Size Measure	Scope
Woodward and Wui	2001	Wetlands	Worldwide	NFI, TC, RC, CV	39	65	ln(acres)	Negative
Zandersen and Tol	2009	Forests	Europe	TC	26	189	Hectares	Insensitive
Use								
Brander et al.[b]	2007	Coral reef ecosystems	Worldwide	TC, PF, NFI, CV	33	73	ln(km squared)	Positive
Johnston et al.	2005	Aquatic resources	USA	CV, others	34	81	Change in water quality	Positive
Van Houtven et al.	2007	Water quality	USA	CV, CE, TC, others	90	1,014	Water quality index	Positive
Poe et al.[c]	2001	Groundwater	USA	CV	14	208	% change in supply of water	Positive

Notes:
a. Richardson and Loomis (2009) is an update of Loomis and White (1996).
b. Brander et al. (2007) (coral reef ecosystems) is categorized as use because the studies examined WTP for entrance fees, not non-use values.
c. Poe et al. (2001) is an update of Boyle et al. (1994).

Key: CE choice experiment; CR contingent ranking; CV contingent valuation; HP hedonic prices; MP market prices; NFI net factor income; OC opportunity cost; PF production function; RC replacement cost; TC travel cost.

benefits, as these are entirely use in nature.[29] We have divided the updated Ojea and Loureiro table into meta-studies of largely or entirely non-use amenities and mixed use/non-use studies in one group and meta-studies of primarily or entirely use amenities in a second group.[30] For meta-studies of non-use and mixed non-use/use amenities, 5.5 studies find positive scope sensitivity and 6.5 find no or negative scope sensitivity.[31] The very mixed results of these scope meta-studies certainly do not support the view in the literature that most CV studies find scope sensitivity.

With respect to the primarily use category, the four meta-studies that focus largely or entirely on use amenities are Brander et al. (2007), which reviews studies estimating WTP for entry fees for coral reef ecosystems; Johnston et al. (2005), which reviews studies of water bodies that provide recreational benefits; Van Houten et al. (2007), which also reviews studies of the recreational benefits of water bodies; and Poe et al. (2001), which reviews studies of drinking water. All four of the meta-studies of amenities that are primarily use in nature find positive scope responsiveness. It is not surprising that studies of primarily use amenities find scope more frequently than studies of primarily non-use amenities, as respondents are much more likely to have well-formed utility functions for use amenities, particularly for amenities with which they have some experience purchasing or incurring costs (such as travel costs) to consume.

There are a number of flaws in the meta-studies that render their results unreliable for the purpose of evaluating whether CV studies pass scope. First, all the meta-studies in Table 3 include multiple data points from the same studies, including in some instances multiple data points from responses by the same respondent. Multiple WTPs elicited from the same respondent are "internal" WTPs.[32] As observations of this type are likely

---

[29] Meta-studies of recreational benefits include Walsh et al. (1984, 1992). Smith and Kaoru (1990), Sturtevant et al. (1998), Rosenberger and Loomis (2000a), Markowski et al. (2001), Bateman et al. (2003), Shrestha and Loomis (2003), and Van Houtven et al. (2007).

[30] We have not attempted to disentangle non-use from use WTP in studies of amenities that have both non-use and use values (estimates of WTP in such cases are commonly referred to as total use WTP).

[31] Ojea and Loureiro (2011) classify Johnston and Duke (2009) as finding negative scope sensitivity. However, while the coefficient of the scope variable is negative, the dependent variable is WTP/acre, so the sensitivity is negative only if total WTP declines with scope. The article does not provide data to determine if this is the case, so we change the classification of this study from negative sensitivity to N/A. Ojea and Loureiro conclude that Brouwer et al. (1999) find scope responsiveness. However, the relative size variable in the Brouwer et al. (1999) study is statistically not significant (p. 54) and the authors do not report whether the coefficient was positive or negative, so we report this study as scope insensitive.

[32] Some of the multiple estimates of WTP may be from split samples, and thus not subject to this criticism that they are internal.

to exhibit at least some scope sensitivity, including these contaminated observations in the meta-analysis will bias the overall results towards a finding of scope sensitivity.[33] A number of the studies included in the meta-scope reviews use choice experiments (CEs) as the elicitation methodology. Including observations from CE studies biases the results towards finding scope. WTPs inferred from these studies are based on choices of respondents who answer a series of questions with multiple choices. These responses are inherently "internal" in nature.

Second, the meta-studies conflate studies using a variety of non-CV methodologies for measuring WTP in addition to CV, including CE (as discussed above), the travel cost method, replacement cost, and hedonic analysis, among others. The only methodologies that are designed to infer WTP for non-use values are CV and CE – the others are either inappropriate or irrelevant for estimating non-use values. Only a handful of meta-studies are focused exclusively on CV.

Third, the studies do not correct for different cost scales across different studies. Cost scale has been found to have a strong positive correlation with WTP – see Cameron and Huppert (1989), Duffield and Patterson (1991), Cooper and Loomis (1992), Ryan and Wordsworth (2000), Hanley et al. (2005), Carlsson and Martinsson (2008), Mørkbak (2010), Kragt (2013), Prelec et al. (forthcoming) and Burrows, Dixon and Chan, Chapter 1 in this volume. For example, Carlsson and Martinsson (2008) find that an approximate doubling of the baseline cost range increase estimated WTP by two to three times; Burrows et al. find that increasing the cost scale by a factor of four increases estimated WTP by about three. As studies of "large" goods will tend to use cost scales that are larger than for studies of "small goods," not taking into account cost scale will bias a meta-study towards finding scope.

To illustrate the effect of cost scale on estimated WTPs, we examined the studies Ojea and Loureiro (2011) reviewed in their meta-analysis. Their analysis of scope effects is restricted to studies using area (measured in hectares) as the scope variable. We were unable to obtain the underlying database from the authors. We therefore reviewed the 109 studies they cited to identify all studies reporting hectares (or other measures convertible into hectares) as size variables. At least 70 of the 109 studies were not focused on environmental amenities measurable by area. For each of the studies involving benefits measured in areas, we collected information on

---

[33] Ojea and Loureiro (2011) is the only meta-scope study that recognizes this problem. The authors include a binary variable for split-sample observations vs within-subject observations. However, they do not interact this variable with the scope variable, so their approach does not test (and correct) for whether split-sample observations are more likely to exhibit scope than within-subject observations.

the area measurement (converted to hectares), reported WTPs and, where available, the cost scale. The reported WTPs were converted to 2016 US dollars. Many studies either did not report the cost scale or did not have a cost scale because they used an elicitation technique other than dichotomous choice. In addition, many of the studies did not provide area measurements and were focused on the number of land areas (such as forests, parks, and wetlands), as opposed to size.

We identified seven usable studies that reported areas, WTPs, and cost scale. One study (Petrolia and Kim, 2009) reports results for two hectare amounts and two separate cost scales for each.[34] A second study (McFadden, 1994) reports WTPs for 526,091 hectares, compared to size ranges of 100 hectares to 20,000 hectares for the other studies. McFadden (1994) also reported 26 WTP estimates using different elicitation and estimation methodologies. If authors reported multiple WTPs for the same amenity, we used the WTP that the authors indicated was preferred. As McFadden (1994) and Mill et al. (2007) do not indicate a preference, we used the average WTP reported in those studies. Table 4 summarizes the data for each study, ranked in order of size of affected amenity being valued. The range of hectares is huge, ranging from 100 hectares to 526,091 hectares. The range in cost scales is also huge, ranging from $1.04–12.45 to $3.65–3,653.89 (for the largest amenity measured in hectares). The range in WTPs is correspondingly large. In general, hectares, cost scale, and WTP seem to be broadly correlated, although the presence of an extremely large outlier would tend to drive the results of any econometric analysis, as is the case here.

Without the underlying data set and with only seven observations, we could not replicate the Ojea and Loureiro (2011) model including cost scale as an additional variable. Instead, we regressed WTP on hectares and the upper end of the cost scale, with and without a constant term and with and without the high hectare outlier (see Table 5). If the outlier is included and cost scale is excluded, hectares is highly significant, with or without a constant term. These equations viewed in isolation would suggest a highly significant scope effect. Cost scale is also highly significant if it is included without hectares, with or without a constant term. If both cost scale and hectares are included, the cost scale is significant and the hectares coefficient is insignificant in all of the estimated equations, with or without a constant term.

These results are suggestive, although there is a limit to how much can be inferred from seven studies. In these regressions, the cost scale seems to

---

[34] We also relied upon the average of the WTP estimates using the Turnbull, RE probit, income-bound RE probit, and high-bound RE probit methods for the two hectare amounts, per the authors' methodology on p. 144.

Table 4 *Key metrics from CV articles with total cost scale (2016 $US) and amenity measured in area (hectares)*

Authors	Year	Environmental Amenity	Hectares	Cost Scale Low ($)	Cost Scale High ($)	WTP ($)
Mill et al.[a]	2007	Forest preservation	100	15.79	236.85	215.23
Hammitt et al.	2001	Wetlands preservation	153	3.10	434.19	106.75
Kwak et al.	2003	Forest preservation	871	1.04	12.45	1.62
Petrolia and Kim	2009	Barrier island restoration	946	85.40	424.77	196.58
Petrolia and Kim	2009	Barrier island restoration	2,415	216.26	1,083.54	258.69
Loomis et al.	1994	Forest and animal preservation	2,833	3.22	483.36	145.15
Kniivila et al.	2002	Forest reservation	20,000	10.54	189.98	60.98
McFadden[b]	1994	Wilderness area preservation	526,091	3.65	3,653.89	1,217.50

Notes:

a. The WTP estimate in Mill et al. (2007) is an average of the means for the personal mixed, natural, and pine forests.
b. The WTP estimate in McFadden (1994) is an average of the 26 WTP estimates he gives for the 526,091-hectare Selway-Bitterroot Wilderness. WTP estimates range between $28.46 and $3,256.23.

Table 5 Regressions examining the relationship between WTP, hectares, and cost scale high

Variables	(1) WTP	(2) WTP	(3) WTP	(4) WTP	(5) WTP	(6) WTP	(7) WTP	(8) WTP	(9) WTP	(10) WTP	(11) WTP	(12) WTP
Hectares	0.0021**	0.002***	−0.0039	0.0060					0.0007	0.0003	0.0021	0.0003
	(0.00)	(0.00)	(0.01)	(0.01)					(0.00)	(0.00)	(0.00)	(0.00)
Cost Scale High					0.3249***	0.3274***	0.2102**	0.2856**	0.2202*	0.2842**	0.2016**	0.2843**
					(0.02)	(0.02)	(0.06)	(0.04)	(0.06)	(0.04)	(0.07)	(0.05)
Constant	127.6858**		150.6140**		5.7740		49.2112		42.5905		60.7100	
	(35.24)		(39.32)		(27.78)		(33.07)		(32.52)		(39.89)	
Observations	8	8	7	7	8	8	7	7	8	8	7	7
R-squared	0.9520	0.9011	0.1066	0.0853	0.9775	0.9853	0.6833	0.8811	0.9857	0.9876	0.7110	0.8813
RMSE	92.53	153	89.69	162.4	63.40	58.90	53.40	58.56	55.31	58.51	57.03	64.10

Notes:
Standard errors in parentheses; *** $p < 0.01$, ** $p < 0.05$, * $p < 0.1$.

Key (column no.):
1. WTP regressed on hectares with both the outlier and a constant in the model.
2. WTP regressed on hectares with outlier, but no constant in the model.
3. WTP regressed on hectares without the outlier, but with the constant in the model.
4. WTP regressed on hectares with no outlier and no constant in the model.
5. WTP regressed on CostScaleHigh with both the outlier and a constant in the model.
6. WTP regressed on CostScaleHigh with outlier, but no constant in the model.
7. WTP regressed on CostScaleHigh without the outlier, but with a constant in the model.
8. WTP regressed on CostScaleHigh with no outlier and no constant in the model.
9. WTP regressed on hectares and CostScaleHigh with both the outlier and a constant in the model.
10. WTP regressed on hectares and CostScaleHigh with outlier, but no constant in the model.
11. WTP regressed on hectares and CostScaleHigh without the outlier, but with the constant in the model.
12. WTP regressed on hectares and CostScaleHigh with no outlier and no constant in the model.

affect the WTP estimates in all versions of the estimations, while the size variable (hectares) is only significant when the cost scale or the cost scale and the outlier are omitted. These results support the hypothesis that cost scale variations could be an important explanatory variable in the analysis of scope effects in meta-studies. At a minimum, the effect of cost scales needs to be taken into account in future meta-studies.

SUMMARY OF THE STATE OF THE SCOPE LITERATURE

Based mostly on the 1997 Carson article and the (inconclusive) results of meta-studies, the currently prevailing conventional wisdom in the environmental literature is that most CV studies exhibit scope sensitivity, although the literature is largely silent with respect to the issue of the adequacy of scope (aside from arguing that low scope elasticity can be explained by sharply declining marginal utility). Heberlein et al. (2005) state that "[t]he scope test...is a fairly sure way of enhancing the credibility of one's study, since most CV studies pass scope tests."[35] Carson and Hanemann (2005) state that: "[t]he empirical evidence is that there is some sensitivity to scope for a wide range of goods." Kling et al. (2012), citing the 1997 Carson survey paper and three meta-studies,[36] conclude that "scope effects are typically present in well-executed studies."[37] Haab et al. (2013) cite the 2012 DMT paper and several meta-studies[38] and conclude that "CVM studies do, in fact, tend to pass a scope test."[39]

Whitehead (2016) goes further and concludes that "CVM studies that pass the scope test produce results that are most useful for policy analysis. CVM studies that do not pass the scope test should be critically examined for behavioral anomalies...before the CVM is determined to be a valuation method that cannot measure preferences."[40] In other words, the author implies that the burden of proof with respect to the use of CVM falls on those questioning CVM, as the accumulated evidence supports the conclusion that CVM studies "tend to pass the scope test."[41] As the brief

[35] Heberlein et al. (2005), p. 20. Ironically, for the four different amenities that are analyzed in the Heberlein study, most of the internal scope tests reported fail and one of the four external scope tests fails.
[36] Smith and Osborne (1996), Brouwer et al. (1999), and Ojea and Loureiro (2011).
[37] Kling et al. (2012), p. 19.
[38] Smith and Osborne (1996), Richardson and Loomis (2009), and Ojea and Loureiro (2011).
[39] Haab et al. (2013), p. 608.
[40] Whitehead (2016), p. 21.
[41] Ibid., p. 18.

history above has shown, the accumulated evidence consists only of the 1997 Carson survey (which was incomplete, error-prone, and now dated), the 2012 DMT paper (which includes internal scope tests and hardly supports the conclusion that most external CV tests pass scope), and a potpourri of meta-studies with mixed results and that use designs that are biased towards finding scope (e.g., by not accounting for the effects of cost scale and by including "internal" WTPs).

REVIEW OF SCOPE RESULTS REPORTED IN CV STUDIES

In this chapter, we focus on the frequency with which CV estimates of WTP for non-use environmental goods and services demonstrate sensitivity to scope and on whether scope effects that are found are adequate (or plausible). We have compiled a comprehensive and up-to-date survey of all CV studies of environmental goods and services that contain an external scope test. Our analysis of these studies focuses on those that include estimates of WTP for non-use environmental goods and services. As many environmental goods have elements of both use value and non-use value (for example, some respondents may have a positive WTP for a clean lake because the knowledge that the lake is clean provides non-use utility, while other respondents may derive use utility from a clean lake because they like to swim in it, and yet other respondents may derive both use value and non-use value), we also include CV studies that derive WTP for goods and services that have both significant non-use utility as well as use utility (classification of utilities as use or non-use obviously requires some subjective judgment).[42] In addition to the searches of the literature, we also cross-referenced citations in all the articles we identified and included studies that also tested for scope.

For reasons discussed earlier, we include in our survey only studies that perform external scope tests. Carson's 1997 paper includes a table that nicely highlights the interaction between external and internal scope tests (reproduced in Table 6). This table shows three goods, A, B, and C, whose values are nested (A > B > C). The valuation sequences are denoted by I, II, and III. The order in which the goods are offered is indicated by

---

[42] To assemble our database of studies related to testing scope in CV surveys, we searched the EVRI (Environmental Valuation Reference Inventory) and NOEP (National Ocean Economics Program – Middlebury College) databases, government websites and publication sources (including NOAA, EPA, and the US Fisheries and Wildlife Agency, among others), academic websites (including Richard Carson's invaluable website for collected studies RePEc. org, the mammoth bibliography in Carson, 2012, EBSCO, Econlit, and Google Scholar).

Table 6 Reproduction of Carson (1997) Table I

Subsample I	Subsample II	Subsample III
A_I^1		
B_I^2	B_{II}^1	
C_I^3	C_{II}^2	C_{III}^1

Note: Goods A, B, and C are nested, with good A being the "largest" good.

a subscript 1, 2, or 3. It is assumed that all of the goods are normal and that all are substitutes of each other. The above taxonomy lends itself to a number of sequencing and scope tests. However, the only tests that are purely external are those along the diagonal: $A_I^1 \geq B_{II}^1 \geq C_{III}^1$. The other tests ($A_I^1 \geq B_I^2 \geq C_I^3$ and $B_{II}^2 \geq C_{II}^3$) are internal tests in that in one or more of the estimates respondents are being asked to state a value of a good after already having given a value of another good that is senior or junior to the good in question in a normal valuation sequence.

We focus exclusively on split-sample tests along the diagonal. By analyzing only responses to the first choice question posed to respondents, we minimize the influence of context and anchoring effects. The other tests in Carson's taxonomy would be valid tests of scope if human beings were robots impervious to suggestion and ignored signals from the survey, but in the real world any answers by human respondents are affected by what they have already seen. Context and anchoring effects of prior questions (or cues in the current question) undermine the usefulness of survey responses. Sequencing effects have been widely reported in the literature in which WTP for an item is higher if it is placed first in a list than later: see, among many examples, Randall et al. (1981), Boyce et al. (1989), Boyle et al. (1990), Samples and Hollyer (1990), Boyle et al. (1993), Hoehn and Loomis (1993), Halvorsen (1996), DuPont (2003), and Bateman et al. (2004, 2006). DuPont (2003) reports that her "review of the literature on question order indicates that its effect may be more strongly felt in cases where passive use WTP values are being sought as opposed to active use values."[43]

Our focus is consistent with the NOAA panel's conclusion that "We must reject one possible approach, that of asking each respondent to express willingness to pay to avert incidents of varying sizes; the danger is that embedding will be forcibly avoided, still without realism."[44] As Bateman et al. (2004) also observe, "it is widely recognized that passage

---

[43] Dupont (2003), p. 325.
[44] Arrow et al. (1993), p. 27.

of internal tests is relatively facile and possibly related to the observation that respondents may simply be trying to be 'internally consistent' in their reported values."[45]

We identified 111 studies published between 1983 and 2016 that include external scope tests of environmental goods; 104 of these studies present scope tests of non-use or mixed non-use/use environmental goods and services. We excluded a small number of studies that asked for WTP for reducing the probability of health effects from environmental and other risks, as it has been reported that human beings have difficulty with assessing small probabilities; these studies are also use oriented, which was not the focus of our analysis. Table 7 presents summary information on the 111 studies in our database, including information on the environmental amenity, whether the goods surveyed are use, non-use, or non-use mixed with some use, and our conclusions about whether each study passes or fails a scope test or has mixed results. The classifications of studies into use, non-use, and mixed non-use/use were based on subjective judgment. Most, but not all, papers report test statistics that allow significance tests on the pass/fail results. We use $p < 0.05$ as the threshold for significance; for cases in which no test statistics are provided we accept the conclusions of the authors about significance. Of course, a finding in a study of statistically significant scope responsiveness is not enough to establish validity – there must also be an assessment of whether the size of the scope test is adequate or plausible. If scope is low it is possible that there is a large element of warm glow in the measured WTP for the amenity.

Several studies report both internal and external scope tests. For studies that report both external and internal scope tests, we focus only on the results of the external scope tests: for example, if the external scope test fails, but the internal scope tests passes, we report the study as failing an external scope test (as passing an internal scope test may simply be the result of respondents attempting to appear internally consistent). A number of studies have a perverse finding that an internal test fails but an external test passes. For example, in the Giraud et al. (1999) study of Mexican spotted owls the internal scope test fails and the external scope test passes. Heberlein et al. (2005) report that the majority of his internal scope tests fail, but spearfishing passes an external scope test. Day and Mourato (1998) report that the pilot survey in their study fails an internal scope test but that the full field survey passes an external scope test. We report all these studies as passing scope. This is a very conservative method, as failing an internal scope test is either a symptom of a failure of the survey design or an indication that respondents are inconsistent in their answers.

---

[45] Bateman et al. (2004), p. 83.

Table 7 Scope test summary

Author	Date	Result Pass/Fail (Mixed: % Pass)	Commodity	Use
Ahearn et al.	2006	M (25%)	Protecting grassland birds in the Central Plains region	Non-use
Ahlheim et al.	2014	F	Plant species and rainforest in Yunnan, China	Non-use
Alvarez-Farzio et al.*	1999	P	Preserving two environmentally sensitive areas in Scotland	Both
Araña and León*	2008	M (33%)	Rehabilitating walking paths in Gran Canaria, Spain	Both
Banzhaf et al.	2011	P	Southern Appalachian Mountains ecosystem services	Non-use
Banzhaf et al.	2006	F	Acid rain: quality of water and fish populations, bird species, and tree species (600 lakes versus 900 lakes)	Both
Bateman et al.	2004	M (83%)	Open access lake improvements located in grounds of University of East Anglia	Both
Bennett et al.*	1998	P	Dryland salinity in Upper South East region of South Australia	Non-use
Bergstrom and Stoll	1987	F	Farmland protection in Greenville County, South Carolina	Both
Berrens et al.	1996	P	Protecting minimum instream flows in New Mexico: silvery minnow versus 11 threatened species	Non-use
Berrens et al.	2000	P	Protecting minimum instream flows in New Mexico: silvery minnow versus 11 threatened species	Non-use
Binger et al.	1995	P	Preservation of the Selway-Bitterroot Wilderness and 57 federal wilderness areas	Non-use
Bliem and Getzner	2008	F	Ecological restoration in Danube river basin	Non-use
Bliem and Getzner	2012	F	River restoration along the Austrian Danube	Non-use
Blomquist and Whitehead	1998	P	Preserving wetland areas in Kentucky	Non-use
Bowker and Didychuk	1994	P	Preserve units of Moncton area farmland	Non-use
Boxall et al.	2012	M (83%)	Marine mammal species in St. Lawrence Estuary	Non-use

Author	Year	Type	Description	Use
Boyle et al.	1994	F	Preventing waterfowl deaths in the Central Flyway	Non-use
Brookshire et al.	1983	F	Benefit of hunting big horn sheep or grizzly bears in five or 15 years	Use
Brown and Duffield	1995	M (50%)	Protect instream flow in either one or five Montana rivers	Non-use
Brown et al.	1995	F	Preservation of natural areas in Fort Collins	Both
Carson	1997	F	Preventing birds from being killed	Non-use
Carson and Mitchell*	1993	P	National versus regional water quality	Both
Carson et al.	1994a	P	Preservation of Australia's Kakadu conservation zone from mining activity	Non-use
Carson et al.	1994b	P	Program to accelerate natural restoration of injured resources due to PCB and DDT contamination in Southern California Bight	Both
Carson et al.*	1990	P	Air quality in Cincinnati	Both
Carson and Mitchell	1995	P	Preventing injuries from large open pit mine in Kakadu Conservation Zone	Non-use
Caudill et al.	2011	F	Saginaw bay in Michigan	Non-use
Chapman et al.	2009	F	Alum treatments to prevent algae growth in the Illinois River system and Tenkiller Lake	Both
Choe et al.	1996	M (33%)	Improving water quality of rivers and sea in Davao, Philippines	Both
Christie	2001	M (17%)	Recreation opportunities, Grampian region, Scotland	Use
Day and Mourato	1998	P	Maintaining river water quality in Beijing	Both
Desvousges et al.	1992	F	Preventing waterfowl deaths in the Central Flyway	Non-use
Desvousges et al.	1993	F	Preventing waterfowl deaths in the Central Flyway	Non-use
Desvousges et al.	2016	F	Alum treatments to prevent algae growth in Oklahoma River and lake water clarity in Oklahoma	Both
Desvousges et al.	2012	F	Both
Diamond et al.	1993	F	Preservation Selway, Washakie, and Bob Marshall wilderness areas	Non-use

Table 7 (continued)

Author	Date	Result Pass/Fail (Mixed: % Pass)	Commodity	Use
DuPont	2003	M (17%)	Improvements to three recreational activities (swimming, fishing, and boating in Hamilton Harbor, Ontario, Canada)	Use
DuPont	2013	F	Reclaimed wastewater in Canada	Use
Eom and Larson	2006	P	Water quality improvement in the Man Kyoung River in South Korea	Both
Fischhoff et al.*	1993	F	River clean-up in Pittsburgh area	Both
Fredman*	1995	F	Protecting the white-backed woodpecker in Sweden	Non-use
Gerrans*	1994	F	Preservation of the Jandakot wetlands	Non-use
Gilbert et al.*	1991	F	Lye Brook Wilderness Area in Southwestern Vermont	Both
Gillespie and Bennett	2011	F	Marine Protected Areas in South-West Marine Region, Australia	Non-use
Giraud et al.	1999	P	Mexican spotted owl and 62 regional threatened and endangered species	Non-use
Gong and Baron	2011	P	Four endangered species, four health risks	Both
Goodman et al.*	1998	F	Non-use value of natural coastal environment in England	Non-use
Hanemann*	2005	P	Saving at-risk birds (the bird study revisited)	Non-use
Heberlein et al.	2005	P	(1) Water quality, (2) Wisconsin's wild wolf population, (3) Indian spearfishing, (4) biodiversity	Both
Hicks et al.*	2004	M (47%)	Oyster reef restoration in Chesapeake Bay (asked to general public and fishermen)	Both
Hite et al.	2002	P	Subsidizing variable-rate technology to reduce polluted river runoff for the Mississippi River Basin (in Mississippi)	Non-use
Hoevenagel	1996	P	Greenhouse effect, depletion of ozone layer, deforestation, acid rain, surface water pollution, animal manure problem	Both

Hsee and Rottenstreich	2004	M (50%)	Saving pandas	Non-use
Huang et al.	1997	M (50%)	Quality improvement of Pamlico and Albemarle sounds (recreation areas) in North Carolina	Both
Jakobsson and Dragun*	2001	P	Conserving endangered species and the Leadbeater's possum in Victoria, Australia	Non-use
Jakus*	1992	P	Gypsy moth protection	Both
Jin et al.	2010	M (25%)	Marine turtle conservation in multiple Asian cities	Non-use
Kahneman*	1986	M (50%)	Clean-up to preserve fishing in Muskoka, Haliburton, and all Ontario	Use
Kahneman and Knetsch	1992	M (50%)	Preserving wilderness, protecting wildlife, providing parks, preparing for disasters, controlling air pollution, insuring water quality, routine treatment of industrial wastes; 12 embedding pairs	Both
Kahneman and Ritov*	1994	F	Headline method – multiple	Both
Krieger*	1994	P	Anglers' WTP for changes in Michigan's public health advisory	Use
Longo et al.	2012	F	Climate change mitigation	Non-use
Loomis and Ekstrand	1997	F	Preserving Mexican spotted owl and 62 endangered and threatened species	Non-use
Loomis et al.	1993	M (50%)	Protections of forests in Southeast Australia	Non-use
Macmillan et al.	1996	F	Recovery/damage scenarios from reduced acid rain deposition	Non-use
Macmillan and Duff*	1998	P	Native woodland restoration in the UK	Non-use
Magnussen	1992	M (50%)	Reduce Norwegian nutrient leaching to the North Sea	Both
McDaniels et al.	2003	P	Benefits of fisheries enhancement on rivers in British Columbia	Both
McFadden	1994	F	Preservation of the Selway-Bitterroot Wilderness in Northern Idaho	Non-use

Table 7 (continued)

Author	Date	Result Pass/Fail (Mixed: % Pass)	Commodity	Use
McFadden and Leonard	1993	F	Preservation of the Selway-Bitterroot Wilderness	Non-use
Metcalfe	2012	P	Improvement of water quality in England and Wales	Use
Mullarkey and Bishop	1999	P	Wisconsin wetlands	Non-use
Mullarkey	1997	P	Wisconsin wetlands	Non-use
Navrud	1989	F	Reduced sulfur depositions to protect freshwater fish populations	Both
Nunes and Schokkaert	2003	M (50%)	Protection of wilderness and recreation areas in Alentejo Natural Park, Portugal	Both
Pattison et al.	2011	M (50%)	Wetland retention and restoration in Manitoba	Non-use
Poe et al.	2005	M (43%)	Mexican spotted owl and 62 regional threatened and endangered species	Non-use
Pouta	2005	F	Forest regeneration cutting policy in Finland	Both
Pouta*	2003	F	Preservation of nature conservation areas and environmentally oriented forest management in Finland	Both
Powe and Bateman	2004	P	Protect wetlands (nested area versus total) in Broadland, Eastern England	Non-use
Rahmatian	1986	F	Visibility in Grand Canyon National Park	Both
Rathnayake*	2016	P	Ecotourism in Kawdulla National Park, Sri Lanka	Use
Ready et al.	1997	P	Preventing a decrease in the number of horse farms in Kentucky	Non-use
Ressurreição et al.	2011	M (50%)	Marine taxa in Azores archipelago	Non-use
Rollins and Lyke	1998	F	Creating parks in Canada's Northwest Territories	Non-use
Rowe et al.	1992	P	Oil spill clean-up and prevention programs	Both

Author	Year	Method	Study	Value type
Samples and Hollyer*	1990	F	Preserving humpback whales and Hawaiian monk seals in Hawaii	Non-use
Schkade and Payne	1994	M (50%)	Preserving migratory waterfowl in the Central Flyway of the USA (the bird study)	Non-use
Schulze et al.	1995	F	Upper Clark Fork River, Montana, River Basin Restoration	Both
Smith et al.	1997	P	Controlling marine debris on beaches and coastal areas in New Jersey and North Carolina	Both
Smith et al.	2005	F	Improvements of Eastern regional haze	Both
Stanley	2005	P	Riverside fairy shrimp versus all local endangered species	Non-use
Stevens et al.	1997	P	Movie passes and restoration of Atlantic salmon	Both
Stevens et al.*	1995	P	Preserving wetlands in New England	Non-use
Streever et al.	1998	F	Wetland conservation in New South Wales, Australia	Non-use
Svedsäter	2000	F	Rain forests in South America, endangered wild animals, air pollution in central London, global warming	Both
Tanguay et al.*	1993	F	Maintaining woodland caribou population in Northwestern Saskatchewan	Non-use
Total Value Team	2015, 2015b	P	*Deepwater Horizon recovery*	Non-use
Veisten et al.	2004a	M (71%)	Endangered species preservation in Norwegian forests	Non-use
Veisten et al.	2004b	F	Norwegian forests endangered species preservation	Non-use
Vo and Huynh	2014	F	Groundwater protection program	Both
Welsh et al.*	1994	P	Glen Canyon Dam downstream recreation, hydropower, and passive-use values	Use
Welsh et al.*	1995	M (30%)	Preserving resources of Colorado River downstream of Glen Canyon Dam	Both

Table 7 (continued)

Author	Date	Result Pass/Fail (Mixed: % Pass)	Commodity	Use
White et al.*	1997	F	Conservation of two otter species	Non-use
Whitehead and Cherry*	2007	M (67%)	Green energy program in North Carolina (yielding improved air quality in western North Carolina mountains)	Both
Whitehead and Finney*	2003	F	Preserving submerged marine cultural resources (historic shipwrecks)	Non-use
Whitehead et al.	1998	P	Quality improvement of Pamlico and Albemarle sounds (recreation areas) in North Carolina	Both
Whitehead et al.	2007	F	Purchase and managing additional acres of coastal marshes in Saginaw Bay	Non-use
Whitehead et al.*	2009	F	Purchase and managing additional acres of coastal marshes in Saginaw Bay	Non-use
Wilson	2000	P	Wolves, Chippewa Indian spearfishing, biological diversity, and water quality in Wisconsin	Both

Note: * = excludes relevant test statistics.

To accommodate the different adaptations and interpretations of the same survey by various authors, we also track the occurrence of multiple authors using the same dataset. There are 11 instances in which one underlying survey provides the basis for two papers (i.e., both papers used the same underlying data) and one instance in which one survey has been the basis of three papers. To avoid over-weighting of the underlying survey, in our tabulations we assign partial weights to studies based on identical data sets (0.5 each for cases in which two papers rely on the same underlying survey and 0.33 each for the case in which three papers rely on the same underlying survey). These surveys include the following:

- Boyle et al. (1994) present survey results on WTP for preventing waterfowl deaths in the Central Flyway that fail scope. Hanemann (2005) administers a survey that is nearly identical to the Boyle et al. survey and finds scope sensitivity.
- Schkade and Payne (1994) also present survey results on WTP for preventing waterfowl deaths in the Central Flyway that fails scope in the 2,000 to 20,000 increment, and appears to pass (although no test statistics are explicitly provided) in the 20,000 to 200,000 increment. We consider this paper to be half-pass, half-fail. Carson (1997) shows that removal of certain data outliers results in a directional passage in both increments, but a statistical failure in both as well. This paper is a fail, weighted as 0.5 with the Schkade and Payne (1994) result.
- Giraud et al. (1999) on the Mexican spotted owl and 62 regional endangered and threatened species report a scope test as passing; using the same data and different statistical procedures, Poe et al. (2005) report mixed scope effects.
- Wilson (2000) presents survey results and external scope tests on WTP for wolves (N/A) and water quality (pass) in Wisconsin.[46] Using the same data, Heberlein et al. (2005) report external scope tests for wolves and for water quality that pass. As we state earlier, we treat the results for wolves as N/As because we cannot rule out that respondents' true underlying marginal WTP for more wolves might in fact be zero (or negative).
- Whitehead et al. (2007, 2009) and Caudill et al. (2011) all use the same survey data set with respect to protection of marshland and report that the scope tests fail.

[46] Wilson also reports internal scope tests for Chippewa spearfishing and biological diversity.

CV studies differ widely across many dimensions, including the data that are included in the analysis, the elicitation technique (such as dichotomous choice [DC], double-bounded [DB], payment card [PC], open ended [OE], and bidding), the payment vehicle (such as taxes, higher prices, and voluntary contributions), features of the survey designs and the survey design itself, and the analytical models and statistical procedures used to estimate WTPs. It is not feasible to deconstruct each of the studies to determine the preferred method in each context. If the authors report multiple scope tests and indicate which methods and results are preferred, in our tabulations we report the scope results that are favored by the authors; if the authors do not indicate which they feel are preferred, we report all the external scope tests and include them in our tabulations with fractional allocation.[47] This is the case for the factors described below.

VARIATIONS IN THE DATA INCLUDED IN THE ANALYSIS

One of the shortcomings of the CV literature is that different authors vary with respect to what data are included or excluded in their analyses. Some authors include all the data in a survey, although this is more the exception than the rule. It is common for authors to exclude so-called "protest" votes – some exclude all zeros, and some exclude zero answers if the respondents provide certain answers to debriefing questions. In some cases (but much less commonly than for protest votes), authors exclude WTP answers that are too high to be credible (for example, Rowe et al., 1992 exclude WTPs that are over 1% of a respondent's income and Smith et al., 2005 exclude the highest 5% of WTPs) or answers by respondents

---

[47] In one case, we report the conclusions of the authors even though we disagree with their methodology. Whitehead et al. (1998, water quality improvement in Albermarle [A] and Pamlico [P] sounds in North Carolina), report split-sample estimates of WTPs for A only and for A + P that pass scope; however, both samples included both A and P residents; P residents valuing A may have WTPs for A that are low or zero, which would lead to the result that WTP (A) is less than WTP (A + P) even if the respondents are not sensitive to scope. We report this study as passing scope. Loomis et al. (2009, reductions in acres burned by wildfires in California, Florida, and Montana) report three split-sample estimates for residents in each state. The authors report a logistic regression model in which acreage is significant. However, the acreage variable is fixed in size for each state, so this variable is equivalent to a dummy variable for each state. If California residents place a higher value than Montana residents and Montana residents place a higher value than Florida residents on reducing wildfires for reasons unrelated to acreages involved, the study would have found the same effects. We tabulate this study as N/A, as it does not appear to include a true external scope test.

that are judged to be yea-sayers as a result of follow-up questions. Authors sometimes exclude answers that the respondents indicate are uncertain. MacMillan and Duff (1998) include only respondents who say they are willing to pay taxes. Some studies interview local and non-local respondents separately. There is no accepted practice with respect to what data to include and what to include. As WTP estimates can be greatly influenced by what data are included or excluded, this gives analysts enormous latitude to vary which data to include (subsequently contributing to a wide variation in their possible results). Some examples of studies with idiosyncratic approaches to the data include the following:

- Powe and Bateman (2004) report a CV study of wetlands that fails scope, but after removing respondents who, based on debriefing questions, do not consider the program realistic, find scope. We report this study as passing scope in our tabulations.
- Nunes and Schokkaert (2003), in a study of wilderness and recreation areas in national parks in Portugal, report results that fail the scope test in their base case but that pass the scope test after removal of respondents who they conclude from econometric analysis of attitudinal questions gain utility from warm glow. We report this study as half-pass, half-fail.
- Christie (2001) reports scope tests using the full survey data set and 5% truncated samples (removing high bid outliers). As the author infers that the truncated sample is preferred, we include the results from only the truncated sample in our summary results.
- Welsh et al. (1995) report results for a national sample and a local sample for alternative flows for Glen Canyon. They conclude scope passes for the national sample, but the local marketing area results generally fail scope. The authors conclude that "combined with the lack of demonstrated sensitivity to scope for the marketing area in the pilot survey, the case for stating that the marketing area has passed advanced tests is somewhat weaker than for the national sample." We report mixed results and allocate passes and fails fractionally.

VARIATIONS IN SURVEY DESIGN

Survey designs also vary widely, and some surveys have unusual or one-off designs that generate results that are different from "standard" surveys. Examples include the following:

- Hanemann (2005) conducts a survey with a similar design as the Desvousges et al. (1993) bird study, with the only difference being that the amenity is prevention of bird deaths expressed in percentages instead of absolute amounts, and reports finding scope sensitivity. We record this study as passing scope, and include this study in our tabulations with a 50% weight (so that this result offsets the Desvousges et al. finding of scope failure, which also has a 50% weighting factor).
- Huang et al. (1997) report single-bounded dichotomous choice results that fail scope and double-bounded dichotomous choice results that pass scope. We weigh each result with a 50% weight.[48]
- Fischhoff et al.'s (1993) evidence for scope insensitivity with direct estimates and scope sensitivity when respondents make paired comparisons.[49] We report this study as failing scope.
- Veisten et al. (2004a, 2004b) report results from models based on both OE and PC approaches, without indicating which is preferred. These all fail scope.

VARIATIONS IN ANALYTICAL MODELS AND STATISTICAL PROCEDURES

The analytical models and statistical procedures used to derive WTPs vary significantly across studies, and include both parametric and non-parametric techniques. There is no accepted practice for which techniques to use and no science for which are preferable other than measuring which provide the best statistical fits to the data. Some studies use parametric models that include covariates and others do not. Some studies correct for heteroscedasticity and others do not. Some studies use a Box-Cox transformation to correct for skewed bids. The parametric functions used differ across studies and within studies. For cases in which authors report multiple models and statistical procedures, in our tabulation of scope conclusions we accept the versions that the authors favor; in cases in which authors present alternative versions without indicating which are

---

[48] This paper is weighted as 0.5 with the other Pamlico and Albemarle text (Whitehead et al., 1998), so overall it yields 0.25 pass, 0.25 fail in our fractional tabulations.

[49] Fischhoff et al. state that "The effects of task simplification are studied by contrasting the performance of subjects using two response modes: 1) *direct estimates*, i.e., assigning dollar values to individual goods; and 2) *paired comparisons*, i.e., choosing the better of two competing goods... Our results revealed a very high degree of embedding with the direct estimates, but only a moderate degree with the paired comparisons" (p. 212; original emphasis).

preferred, we accept all the results reported, with fractional weighting for our tabulations. Examples include the following:

- Poe et al. (2005) present results based on a linear logit model and also a non-parametric truncated Kriström model, some of which pass and some of which fail. We report these results fractionally.
- Choe (1996) presents alternative results for two scope scenarios based on an OLS model (pass at $p < 0.05$), a hazard/Weibull model (pass at $p < 0.10$), and a probit model (insignificant). We report these results as one-third pass, two-thirds fail.

INCONSISTENT STATISTICAL SIGNIFICANCE RESULTS

A number of studies report scope variables that are significant or tests that indicate that the coefficients of the estimating equations are significantly different for different scopes, even though the reported confidence intervals for the WTPs overlap. We report results such as these as passes even if the reported WTPs fail scope.[50] Examples include the following:

- Ready et al. (1997) report a logistic regression in which scope dummies are significant, but some of the confidence intervals for the reported WTPs overlap. We report this study as passing scope.
- Bowker and Didychuk (1994) report that the acreage variable is significant in an OLS regression of factors explaining WTP, but report mixed scope results with respect to WTPs for different acreage amounts. We record this study as passing scope.
- Smith et al. (1997) report that the 95% confidence intervals for WTPs for different levels of beach clean-up overlap, but that "using a likelihood ratio test to test whether the parameters of the hazard functions describing respondents' stated choices for each of the four default beach scenes were equal, we reject the null hypothesis with a

---

[50] The one exception is the case of Banzhaf et al. (2006). This paper includes a statistically significant and positive coefficient for the scope variable presented in Table 4; however, the 90% confidence intervals overlap using the Weibull model for their preferred symmetric all-econometric-controls option, indicating a fail, but pass at the 10% level using the lognormal model for the same option (the 95% test statistics, our threshold, are not provided). Last, the authors present their "cautious, best defensible estimates of the mean WTP" after adjusting for discount factors at $48–107 per year, per household in the base scenario, and $54–159 for the scope scenario. We report this paper as a fail.

p-value = 0.05."[51] We record this study as passing scope, even though the reported WTPs do not pass scope.

How Frequently do CV Studies Pass a Scope Test?

For the 111 studies of environmental goods in our study, 41 (37%) report scope tests that pass scope tests, 46 (41%) report scope tests that fail, and 24 (22%) report mixed results (see Table 7). After fractional allocation of the mixed tests to the pass and fail categories, 52.3 (47%) of the scope tests pass and 58.7 (53%) fail.[52] After appropriately weighting the studies that are based on common underlying data, 45.1 (46%) pass and 52.9 (54%) fail.

Table 7 also reports scope pass/fail results for environmental non-use and mixed use/non-use goods. Focusing on the latter category, after correction for weighting factors and fractional allocations, 40.3 (45%) of the studies pass scope and 48.7 (55%) fail scope. Excluding studies that do not report statistical tests to allow determination of significance of the scope tests, 31 (47%) pass and 35.2 (53%) fail the scope tests.

If the ability to detect scope effects in CV studies is a function of the quality of the survey, one would expect to find a positive relationship between survey quality and the percentage of studies passing a scope test. One way to test this is to determine if the percentage of CV studies that pass scope has increased over time, as presumably the quality of CV surveys has increased over time (see Figure 1). Over the 15-year period 1987–2001, 51% of the studies reported scope tests that pass (based on a fractional allocation) and 49% reported scope tests that failed. For the 15-year period from 2002 to the present, the pass percentage declined to 41% and the fail percentage increased to 59%. As applications of CVM have become increasingly sophisticated over time, with most studies following the guidelines developed over the history of CVM for meeting acceptable standards of quality, the percentage of reported scope tests that pass scope has actually dropped sharply over the past 15 years relative to the prior 15-year period. Presumably, the sharp decline in the pass rate is not the result of a decline in the quality of the studies reported, nor can it be the result of deteriorating human cognitive facilities.

Another indicator of quality of a study might be whether it is published in a peer-reviewed academic journal. The results for published studies are

---

[51] Smith et al. (1997), p. 239.
[52] If a study reports mixed results, we weight each result reported fractionally, with the weights adding up to one. For example, if a study reports three tests that pass and two that fail, in our tabulations the study is reported as 0.6 pass and 0.4 fail.

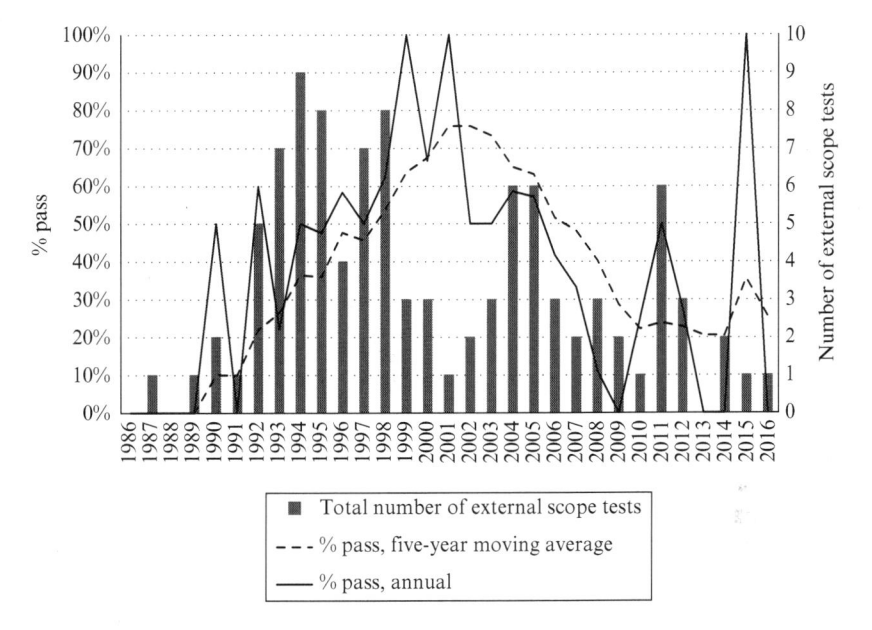

Figure 1 Passes as a percentage of total in environmental external scope tests, five-year moving average

similar to the results for all of the studies. On a raw count basis for studies published in peer-reviewed literature, 37% have scope tests that pass, 18% have mixed scope tests, and 46% have scope tests that fail. After fractional allocation, the results are pass (48%) and fail (52%), similar to the results for all studies.

DO SCOPE TESTS DEMONSTRATE ADEQUATE SENSITIVITY TO SCOPE?

The NOAA Panel's concern over scope focused in part on whether CV studies demonstrate "adequate" sensitivity to scope. There is no analytical basis for determining how much scope sensitivity is "adequate" or "plausible." Defining sensitivity in terms of elasticity of scope, a scope elasticity of somewhat less than one would be viewed by most economists as plausible (in the presence of declining marginal utility, most environmental goods and services would have scope elasticities of less than one). It does not seem plausible that utility for environmental goods would be easily satiated, as might be the case for many use goods (such as ice cream cones at the beach to give an extreme example). If the value of preserving one species is $10, we think most observers would expect the value of preserving a second similar species would also be close to $10 (and similarly for acres of clean beaches and numbers of pristine lakes or forests). A judgment of plausibility of a scope test will understandably differ for different observers.

In the case of many of the CV surveys that pass a scope test, as in the case of the Araña and León (2008) study of walking path kilometers, WTP for the larger good is only slightly larger than WTP for the smaller good. For example, in Poe et al. (2005) the authors ask 369 survey respondents whether they would pay various costs to protect the Mexican spotted owl. A separate group of 363 respondents are asked about their WTP to protect the Mexican spotted owl and 62 additional threatened and endangered species. The study finds that mean WTP for protection of the Mexican spotted owl is $99.93 and mean WTP for protection of the Mexican spotted owl and 62 additional threatened and endangered species is $130.42. This study passes a directional scope test, but is this estimated scope "adequate"? The results imply that, on average, the typical respondent values each of the 62 additional species by an amount that is less than 1% of their valuation of the Mexican spotted owl.

There is a tendency for CV studies to demonstrate a kink in the demand for an environmental amenity at the base level of that amenity that is defined in the survey (see our earlier discussion of diminishing marginal utility and bounded substitution). For example, a study by Rollins and Lyke (1998) of national parks in Canada's Northwest Territories informs respondents that 29 of 39 natural regions are already national parks, and then asks respondents about WTP for additional parks. The reported WTPs are $105.45 for one additional park, $161.85 for two more parks, $191.07 for four more parks, and $188.44 for ten more parks. The increment from one to two additional parks is significant, but the increments from two to four and from four to ten additional parks are not. If these WTPs are correct representations of respondent utility, the demand curve for parks rapidly becomes flat in the range of 29–31 parks. It is conceivable (but not credible, in our view) that this is accurate for this particular study, but is it credible that in most such studies the kink in the demand curve is at or just above the base quantity in the study?

The majority of CV studies have scope tests that are either "categorical" in nature or do not provide information on the change in quantity in the survey, and therefore do not lend themselves to a quantitative analysis. Table 8 presents the non-failing (pass and mixed) scope tests in 24 "quantitative" scope studies that do lend themselves to an analysis of quantitative scope effects.[53] Table 9 reports scope results only for those tests that pass scope. For each scope test we identify the good, the baseline quantity, the scope quantity, the baseline WTP, the scope WTP, the scope elasticity, and the weight of the scope test used in our weighted average calculations. The reported WTPs are means, as this is the metric most commonly reported in CV studies and is available for virtually all the studies in our survey.

Figure 2 presents a histogram of the scope elasticity effects for the median result in each study using all reported scope results, including the fractional passes from papers that report mixed effects. For the 21 results we could include in this analysis,[54] nine have scope elasticities of less than 0.10 and 12 have scope elasticities of less than 0.2; only three have scope elasticities above 0.5. It is worth bearing in mind that only 46% of reported scope tests pass; if, say, scope elasticities above 0.5 are plausible, this means that only about 7% (3/21 × 46%) of reported scope studies pass with "adequate" scope. If an elasticity of 0.2 is the threshold for plausibility, only about 20% (9/21 × 46%) of reported scope tests pass with adequate scope.

The frequency of limited scope elasticities documented in this study suggests that warm glow is an important element of measured WTP for environmental amenities. Diminishing marginal utility and bounded substitution cannot credibly explain the low levels of scope responsiveness across all of the CV studies we measured. This justification would mean that these factors dominate WTP valuations at levels just larger than the smaller environmental good presented in each individual paper, chosen by each individual author, across a range of unique goods. Put differently, how is it possible that in our review of the entire scope literature we found so few examples of WTPs for incremental goods that are even commensurate with the initial valuation? Traditional scope tests (i.e., non-adding-up tests) cannot determine whether findings of limited or no scope sensitivity are explained by "warm glow," diminishing marginal utility, part-whole bias, disagreement with the survey's implied probability of provision of the larger good, cognitive shortcomings, or any other explanations that have been proffered.

---

[53] Two studies – Giraud et al. (1999) and Poe et al. (2005) – use the same survey data of Mexican spotted owls and each find elasticity of WTP of less than 0.2. These are treated as one study in Figure 2. We exclude two studies with absurdly high scope elasticities that are not credible: Ready et al. (1997, horse farms) with a median scope elasticity of 65.98 and Pattison et al. (2011, wetlands) with a scope elasticity of 3.8.

[54] Giraud et al. (1999) and Poe et al. (2005) are each weighted as 0.5.

Table 8 Quantitative tests of scope elasticities

Author	Year	Commodity	Base Quantity	Scope Quantity	Base WTP ($)	Scope WTP ($)	Elasticity
McDaniels et al.	2003	Rivers	1	10	36	95	0.18
Berrens et al.	2000	Miles of river	170	1,000	24	52	0.24
Berrens et al.	2000	Miles of river	170	1,000	26	58	0.24
Berrens et al.	2000	Miles of river	170	1,000	24	52	0.24
Berrens et al.	2000	Miles of river	170	1,000	662	79,328	24.33
Berrens et al.	2000	Miles of river	170	1,000	206	1,819	1.6
Berrens et al.	2000	Miles of river	170	1,000	26	72	0.35
Carson et al.	1994	Years of recovery period	50	15	63	34	0.66
Bowker and Didychuk	1994	Acres of farmland	71,250	95,000	78	86	0.29
Bowker and Didychuk	1994	Acres of farmland	47,500	71,250	68	78	0.32
Bowker and Didychuk	1994	Acres of farmland	23,750	47,500	49	68	0.38
Binger et al.	1995	Wilderness areas	1	57	29	79	0.03
Giraud et al.	1999	Specie	1	62	48	118	0.02
Araña and León	2008	Kilometers	30	300	20	28	0.05
Araña and León	2008	Kilometers	100	300	26	28	0.05
Araña and León	2008	Kilometers	30	100	20	26	0.13
Poe et al.	2005	Specie	1	62	100	130	0.01
Poe et al.	2005	Specie	1	62	116	156	0.01
Eom and Larson	2006	Reductions in biochemical oxygen demand level	4	7	10	18	1
Macmillan and Duff	1998	Forests to be saved	1	2	53	67	0.26
Macmillan and Duff	1998	Forests to be saved	1	2	35	67	0.91

Macmillan and Duff	1998	Forests to be saved	1	2	69	109	0.58
Macmillan and Duff	1998	Forests to be saved	1	2	51	109	1.14
Stanley	2005	Specie	1	32	30	56	0.03
Stanley	2005	Specie	1	32	31	64	0.04
Stanley	2005	Specie	1	32	31	64	0.03
Stanley	2005	Specie	1	32	21	38	0.03
Stanley	2005	Specie	1	32	28	59	0.04
Stanley	2005	Specie	1	32	25	52	0.04
Hsee and Rottenstreich	2004	Pandas	1	4	11	22	0.31
Nunes and Schokkaert	2003	Areas	1	2	3,500	6,000	0.71
Nunes and Schokkaert	2003	Areas	1	2	2,600	6,000	1.31
Hanemann	2005	Percentage of at-risk bird population saved	100,000	1,000,000	22	34	0.06
Jakobsson and Dragun	2001	Number of species	1	700	29	267	0.01
Hicks et al.	2004	Acres	1,000	10,000	11	24	0.13
Hicks et al.	2004	Acres	5,000	10,000	22	24	0.12
Hicks et al.	2004	Acres	2,500	5,000	20	22	0.09
Hicks et al.	2004	Acres	1,000	2,500	11	20	0.53
Ahearn et al.	2006	Bird species increase percentage	10	50	12	14	0.04
Ahearn et al.	2006	Bird species increase percentage	10	50	11	13	0.06
Ahearn et al.	2006	Bird species increase percentage	10	50	12	14	0.03
Ahearn et al.	2006	Bird species increase percentage	10	50	11	12	0.03

Table 8 (continued)

Author	Year	Commodity	Base Quantity	Scope Quantity	Base WTP ($)	Scope WTP ($)	Elasticity
Hite et al.	2002	Percentage decreases in river runoff	0	0	47	50	0.06
Alvarez-Farzio et al.	1999	Environmentally sensitive area	1	2	13	36	1.68
Alvarez-Farzio et al.	1999	Environmentally sensitive area	1	2	25	36	0.43
Brown and Duffield	1995	Rivers	1	5	7	12	0.21
Brown and Duffield	1995	Rivers	1	5	10	18	0.19
Whitehead et al.	1998	Bodies of water	1	2	113	137	0.21
Berrens et al.	1996	Miles of river	170	1,000	29	90	0.43
Schkade and Payne	1994	Bird deaths prevented	2,000	200,000	63	122	0.11
Schkade and Payne	1994	Bird deaths prevented	2,000	200,000	69	134	0.10
Diamond et al.	1993	Wilderness areas	1	57	29	79	0.03
Loomis et al.	1993	Hectares of land	6,000	70,000	57	103	0.08
Loomis et al.	1993	Hectares of land	70,000	122,000	103	100	−0.04

Table 9 Quantitative tests of scope elasticities (pure passes only)

Author	Year	Commodity	Base Quantity	Scope Quantity	Base WTP ($)	Scope WTP ($)	Elasticity
McDaniels et al.	2003	Rivers	1	10	36	95	0.18
Berrens et al.	2000	Miles of river	170	1,000	24	52	0.24
Berrens et al.	2000	Miles of river	170	1,000	2	58	0.24
Berrens et al.	2000	Miles of river	170	1,000	24	52	0.24
Berrens et al.	2000	Miles of river	170	1,000	662	79,328	24.33
Berrens et al.	2000	Miles of river	170	1,000	206	1,819	1.6
Berrens et al.	2000	Miles of river	170	1,000	26	72	0.35
Carson et al.	1994	Years of recovery period	50	15	63	34	0.66
Bowker and Didychuk	1994	Acres of farmland	71,250	95,000	78	86	0.29
Bowker and Didychuk	1994	Acres of farmland	47,500	71,250	68	78	0.32
Bowker and Didychuk	1994	Acres of farmland	23,750	47,500	49	68	0.38
Binger et al.	1995	Wilderness areas	1	57	29	79	0.03
Giraud et al.	1999	Specie	1	62	48	118	0.02
Eom and Larson	2006	Reductions in biochemical oxygen demand level	4	7	10	18	1
Macmillan and Duff	1998	Forests to be saved	1	2	53	67	0.26
Macmillan and Duff	1998	Forests to be saved	1	2	35	67	0.91
Macmillan and Duff	1998	Forests to be saved	1	2	69	109	0.58
Macmillan and Duff	1998	Forests to be saved	1	2	51	109	1.14
Stanley	2005	Specie	1	32	30	56	0.03
Stanley	2005	Specie	1	32	31	64	0.04

Table 9 (continued)

Author	Year	Commodity	Base Quantity	Scope Quantity	Base WTP ($)	Scope WTP ($)	Elasticity
Stanley	2005	Specie	1	32	31	64	0.03
Stanley	2005	Specie	1	32	21	38	0.03
Stanley	2005	Specie	1	32	28	59	0.04
Stanley	2005	Specie	1	32	25	52	0.04
Hanemann	2005	Percentage of at-risk bird population saved	100,000	1,000,000	22	34	0.06
Jakobsscn and Dragun	2001	Number of species	1	700	29	267	0.01
Hite et al.	2002	Percentage decreases in river runoff	0	0	47	50	0.06
Alvarez-Farzio et al.	1999	Environmentally sensitive area	1	2	13	36	1.68
Alvarez-Farzio et al.	1999	Environmentally sensitive area	1	2	25	36	0.43
Whitehead et al.	1998	Bodies of water	1	2	113	137	0.21
Berrens et al.	1996	Miles of river	170	1,000	29	90	0.43

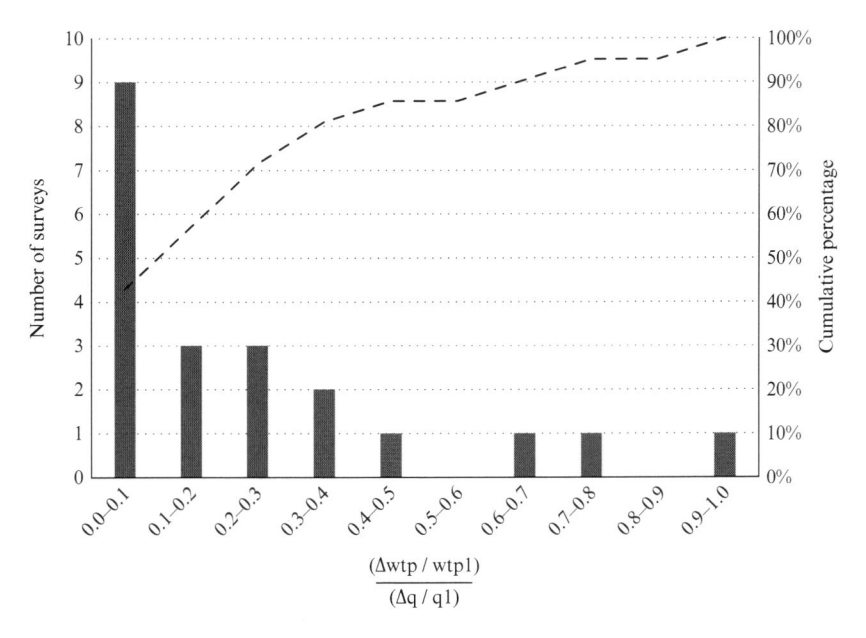

Figure 2 Elasticity of WTP median result per paper

ARE SCOPE PASS AND FAIL RESULTS AFFECTED BY MEASURABLE CHARACTERISTICS OF THE SURVEYS?

As we have shown, it is not uncommon for CV studies to fail a scope test. It would be useful to know how CV studies could be designed to pass scope (and presumably more reliably reflect underlying utility). In an effort to shed some light on this issue, we collected information on a variety of characteristics of the CV studies we reviewed. These include: sample size, year of publication (year of survey was not reported for many studies), elicitation methodology (dichotomous choice, multiple-bounded dichotomous choice, open ended, and payment card), survey method (in person, telephone, Internet, and mail), frequency of payment (single payment, annual, other), public/private, presence of cheap talk, presence of a budget reminder, certainty correction, removal of outliers, presence of dissonance minimization, and whether WTP was reported for a gain or a loss. The overall quality of the survey might be an important factor, but we have no direct measure of quality. Certain proxies are available, however. CV studies have presumably improved over time, so year of publication might be correlated with survey quality. Larger sample sizes and response rates may also be indicators of quality. We do have data on sample size, but most CV studies that report scope tests do not provide data on response rates for the scope split samples.

Table 10 presents the simple correlations between each individual variable and a dummy variable for pass. All of the simple correlation coefficients are small. The largest positive effects are for the presence of certainty corrections, WTP measured as a gain, and year of survey. In all of these cases, the direction of the effect is in the expected direction. Surprisingly, sample size has a negative simple correlation with pass. "Public" is negatively correlated (as expected if respondents have a less well-defined utility for public goods vs private goods). "Mandatory" payment and "open-ended" survey mode are negatively correlated with pass, neither of which is expected.

We also estimated probit multivariate regressions, reported in Table 10. With all explanatory variables included (column 1), the R^2 is only 0.07. The only significant variables are "public" (negative coefficient), and "online" survey methodology (negative); the interpretation of "public" is suspect because only four studies in our database estimated WTPs for private goods. Column 2 reports the results after dropping variables for which there were either few observations (certainty corrections, public, removal of outliers) or for which we were uncertain about the reporting accuracy of the variables (e.g., "budget reminder" and "cheap talk," as many articles were silent on these aspects of the survey). The only variable that is significant in this version is "online" survey mode. Column 3 reports the results in which the "public" variable is dropped (as all but four studies are public). In addition, the "mandatory" and "online" payment vehicle and "mail" and "phone" survey mode variables are dropped. In this version, only "online" survey mode is significant. Column 4 shows the results in which payment frequency "once" and "periodic" are dropped. In this version, only the "online" survey mode variable is significant. It is notable that in no version is the time trend or sample size significant, so the two variables that might be proxies for survey quality seem to have no explanatory power.

In sum, very little of the variance of pass/fail is explained by the measurable characteristics that we could identify for the CV studies we reviewed. The only variable that is consistently significant is "online" survey mode. This provides weak evidence that administrating a survey online may have some slight effect on the ability of the survey to pass scope.

Table 10 *Regressions examining factors that affect scope insensitivity*

Variable	Correlation	(1) Pass	(2) Pass	(3) Pass	(4) Pass
Intercept		−27.6331	−36.3914	−27.5609	−21.0349
		(45.8366)	(43.9923)	(42.0119)	(40.6707)
Samplesizetotal	−0.022825866	−0.00003	0.000024	0.000017	0.000017
		(0.000153)	(0.000146)	(0.00014)	(0.00014)
Gain	0.186205405	0.397	0.3144	0.3199	0.287
		(0.2914)	(0.2798)	(0.2707)	(0.267)
Pub_year	0.17989491	0.0141	0.0185	0.0134	0.0104
		(0.0229)	(0.022)	(0.021)	(0.0203)
Em_multiple	0.072486809	0.4179	0.6248	0.4187	0.4096
		(0.3967)	(0.3764)	(0.3633)	(0.3534)
Em_open	−0.265319614	−0.6479	−0.5093	−0.5017	−0.4565
		(0.3994)	(0.3807)	(0.3551)	(0.3471)
Em_paymentcard	0.138246794	0.0353	0.3429	0.1588	0.1962
		(0.4569)	(0.4022)	(0.3883)	(0.3836)
Em_single	0.112646765	Omitted	Omitted	Omitted	Omitted
Sm_person	0.101937002	−0.3016	−0.426	−0.0826	−0.1001
		(0.4268)	(0.4129)	(0.3037)	(0.3008)
Pv_voluntary	0.091034085	0.1519	0.1868	0.0571	−0.0168
		(0.3515)	(0.3399)	(0.3197)	(0.308)
Pv_NA	0.148859071	0.1656	0.3295	0.1664	0.1999
		(0.5519)	(0.5461)	(0.5291)	(0.5264)
Pf_once	0.013647689	0.9123	0.8841	0.393	
		(0.8718)	(0.8668)	(0.823)	
Pf_periodic	−0.012771008	0.9749	1.0128	0.5673	
		(0.8583)	(0.8516)	(0.8121)	
Pf_NA	−0.001102309	Omitted	Omitted	Omitted	
Public	−0.100940019	−1.5108*	−1.5162		
		(0.8155)	(0.8072)		
Pv_indirect	0.066137319	0.1577	0.303		
		(0.484)	(0.4479)		
Pv_mandatory	−0.206242136	Omitted	Omitted		
Sm_online	0.041647614	−1.733**	−1.4775**	−1.0901**	−1.0513*
		(0.6965)	(0.6312)	(−0.5543)	(0.5543)
Sm_mail	−0.045961431	−0.4985	−0.5421		
		(0.3952)	(0.3783)		
Sm_phone	−0.058656592	Omitted	Omitted		
Budget	0.018154951	−0.4105			
		(0.3379)			
Cheap	0.076138778	1.0716			
		(0.9813)			
Certain	0.189879845	0.5652			
		(1.0945)			

Table 10 (continued)

Variable	Correlation	(1) Pass	(2) Pass	(3) Pass	(4) Pass
Outlier	0.016710393	0.7365* (0.3864)			
R^2		0.0718	0.0526	0.0338	0.0317
Max-rescaled R^2		0.1907	0.1397	0.0897	0.0843
AIC		168.78	167.41	167.779	164.459
Observations		324	324	324	324
Sum of weights		111	111	111	111

Note: Standard errors in parentheses; *** $p < 0.01$, ** $p < 0.05$, * $p < 0.1$.

CONCLUSIONS

A fundamental tenet of consumer utility theory is that for most goods utility increases as consumption increases. The 1993 NOAA Panel report concluded that the findings of a CV study would be "unreliable" if the survey exhibited "inadequate responsiveness to the scope of the environmental insult." Four of the Panel members later stated that "had the panel thought that something as straightforward as statistical measurability were the proper way to define sensitivity, then we would (or should have) opted for language to that effect. A better word than 'adequate' would have been 'plausible'."

In spite of the importance of demonstrating that CV studies are adequately responsive to scope, and thus CV estimates of WTP are accepted as exhibiting rationality, there has been very little systematic review in the literature of the extent to which CV studies pass scope and the extent to which the scope findings in those studies that pass are "adequate" or "plausible." The literature also fails to tell us how CV studies can be designed to elicit rational WTPs that exhibit adequate scope responsiveness. An early study by Carson (1997) implies that 31 studies that he identifies all passed scope; his survey does not include at least 35 additional studies, most of which fail scope, and the studies he identifies include four that do not have a scope test, three that have mixed results, and two that fail scope. A later study by Desvousges et al. (2012) reports that more studies have mixed results or fail scope than pass scope.

A number of meta-studies review scope tests across studies; for amenities that are non-use or mixed non-use/mix, more report negative scope findings than positive scope findings. In addition, these studies are flawed because they include multiple data points from the same respondents and do not correct for the effects of the cost scale. In addition, most of the meta-studies include studies that use other techniques than CV, the only methodology that is appropriate for estimating WTP for non-use amenities.

We find that approximately 54% of a comprehensive set of 111 environmental CV studies fail to demonstrate scope. Studies dated in the last 15 years (2002–16) have a higher failure rate (59%) than studies dated in the prior 15-year period (1987–2001), suggesting that the significant advances in the sophistication of CV methodology from its early days have not improved the ability of this methodology to estimate rationally sound WTPs.

For the minority of papers that do pass, few of the studies that pass scope exhibit scope elasticities in a range that, in our judgment, is plausible. Just under half of the studies that provide scope results that can be quantified exhibit scope elasticities of less than 0.2, and less than one-fourth of the studies exhibit scope elasticities over 0.5.

The only characteristic of the studies we reviewed that seems to be weakly associated with passing scope is online administration of the survey. There is a need for additional analysis to determine how to improve the CV methodology so that it exhibits results that plausibly pass scope, a basic criterion of rationality.

REFERENCES

Ahearn, M., K. Boyle, and D. Hellerstein (2006), "Designing a contingent valuation study to estimate the benefits of the conservation reserve program," in A. Alberini and J. Kahn (eds), *Handbook of Contingent Valuation*, Cheltenham, UK and Northampton, MA, USA: Edward Elgar Publishing.

Ahlheim, M., O. Frör, G. Langenberger, and S. Pelz (2014), "Chinese urbanites and the preservation of rare species in remote parts of the country: The example of Eaglewood," *Environmental Economics*, **5**(4), 32–43.

Alvarez-Farizo, B., N. Hanley, R.E. Wright, and D. Macmillan (1999), "Estimating the benefits of agri-environmental policy: Econometric issues in open-ended contingent valuation studies," *Journal of Environmental Planning and Management*, **42**(1), 23–43.

Amiran, E. and D.A. Hagen (2010), "The scope trials: Variation in sensitivity to scope and WTP with directionality bounded utility functions," *Journal of Environmental Economics and Management*, **59**(3), 293–301.

Andreoni, J. (1990), "Impure altruism and donations to public goods: A theory of warm glow giving," *Economic Journal*, **100**(401), 464–77.

Araña, J.E. and C.J. León (2008), "Do emotions matter? Coherent preferences under anchoring and emotional effects," *Ecological Economics*, **66**(4), 700–711.

Arrow, K., E.E. Leamer, H. Schuman, and R. Solow (1994), *Comments on Proposed NOAA/DOI Regulations on Natural Resource Damage Assessment*, US Environmental Protection Agency.

Arrow, K., R. Solow, P. Portney, E. Leamer, R. Radner, and H. Schumanj (1993), *Report of the NOAA Panel on Contingent Valuation*, December 1, 2016 at http://www.economia.unimib.it/DATA/moduli/7_6067/materiale/noaa%20 report.pdf.

Banzhaf, H.S., D. Burtraw, D. Evans, and A. Krupnick (2006), "Valuation of natural resource improvements in the Adirondacks," *Land Economics*, **82**(3), 445–64.

Banzhaf, H.S., D. Burtraw, S. Chung, D.A. Evans, A. Krupnik, and J. Siikamaki (2011), "Valuation of ecosystem services in the Southern Appalachian Mountains," paper presented at the Annual Meeting of the Association of Environmental and Resource Economists.

Barrio, M. and M.L. Loureiro (2010), "A meta-analysis of contingent valuation forest studies," *Ecological Economics*, **69**(5), 1020–30.

Bateman, I. (2003), "Contrasting conventional with multi-level modeling approaches to meta-analysis: Expectation consistency in U.K. woodland recreation values," *Land Economics*, **79**(2), 235–58.

Bateman, I.J., A.A. Lovett, and J.S. Brainard (2003), *Applied Environmental Economics. A GIS Approach to Cost–Benefit Analysis*, Cambridge, UK: The Press Syndicate of the University of Cambridge.

Bateman, I.J., M. Cole, S. Georgiou, and D. Hadley (2006), "Comparing contingent valuation and contingent ranking: A case study considering the benefits of urban river water quality improvements," *Journal of Environmental Management*, **79**(3), 221–31.

Bateman, I.J., M. Cole, P. Cooper, S. Georgiou, D. Hadley, and G.L. Poe (2004), "On visible choice sets and scope sensitivity," *Journal of Environmental Economics and Management*, **47**(1), 71–93.

Bennett, J., M. Morrison, and R. Blamey (1998), "Testing the validity of responses to contingent valuation questioning," *The Australian Journal of Agricultural and Resource Economics*, **42**(2), 131–48.

Bergstrom, J.C. and J.R. Stoll (1987), "A test of contingent market bid elicitation procedures for piecewise valuation," *Western Journal for Agricultural Economics*, **12**(2), 104–8.

Berrens, R.P., P. Ganderton, and C.L. Silva (1996), "Valuing the protection of minimum instream flows in New Mexico," *Journal of Agricultural and Resource Economics*, **21**(2), 294–309.

Berrens, R.P., A.K. Bohara, C.L. Silva, D. Brookshire, and M. McKee (2000), "Contingent values for New Mexico instream flows: With tests of scope, group-size reminder and temporal reliability," *Journal of Environmental Management*, **58**(1), 73–90.

Binger, B.R., R.F. Copple, and E. Hoffman (1995), "The use of contingent valuation methodology in natural resource damage assessments: Legal fact and economic fiction," *Northwestern University Law Review*, **89**(3), 1029–53.

Bishop, Richard, Kevin, Boyle, Michael Welsh, Robert Baumgartner and Pamela Rathburn (1986), Glen Canyon Dam Releases and Downstream Recreation: An Analysis of User Preferences and Economic Values. Final Report to the Bureau of Reclamation. HBRS Madison, Wisconsin.

Bliem, M. and M. Getzner (2008), *Valuation of Ecological Restoration Benefits* in the Danube River Basin Using Stated Preference Methods – Report on the Austrian Case Study Results, Klagenfurt: Institute for Advanced Studies Carinthia, Department of Economics, Klagenfurt University.

Bliem, M. and M. Getzner (2012), "Willingness-to-pay for river restoration: Differences across time and scenarios," *Environmental Economics and Policy Studies*, **14**(3), 241–60.

Blomquist, G.C. and J.C. Whitehead (1998), "Resource quality information and validity of willingness to pay in contingent valuation," *Resource and Energy Economics*, **20**(2), 179–96.

Boman, M. and G. Bostedt (1999), "Valuing the wolf in Sweden: Are benefits contingent on the supply?," *Topics in Environmental Economics*, **17**, 157–74.

Bowker, J.M. and D.D. Didychuk (1994), "Estimation of the nonmarket benefits of agricultural land retention in Eastern Canada," *Agricultural and Resource Economics Review*, **23**(2), 218–25.

Boxall, P.C., W.L. Adamowicz, M. Olar, G.E. West, and G. Cantin (2012), "Analysis of the economic benefits associated with the recovery of threatened marine mammal species in the Canadian St. Lawrence Estuary," *Marine Policy*, **36**(1), 189–97.

Boyce, R.R., T.C. Brown, G.D. McClelland, G.L. Peterson, and W.D. Schulze (1989), "Experimental evidence of existence value in payment and compensation contexts," paper presented at the Joint Meeting of the Western Committee on the Benefits and Costs of Natural Resource Planning and the Western Regional Science Association, San Diego, CA.

Boyle, K.J., S.D. Reiling, and M.L. Phillips (1990), "Species substitution and question sequencing in contingent valuation surveys evaluating the hunting of several types of wildlife," *Leisure Sciences*, **12**(1), 103–18.

Boyle, K.J., M.P. Welsh, and R.C. Bishop (1993), "The role of question order and respondent experience in contingent valuation studies," *Journal of Environmental Economics and Management*, **25**(S), 8,064–99.

Boyle, K.J., W.H. Desvousges, F.R. Johnson, R.W. Dunford, and S.P. Hudson (1994), "An investigation of part-whole biases in contingent valuation studies," *Journal of Environmental Economics and Management*, **27**(1), 64–83.

Brander, L.M., P. van Beukering, and H.S.J. Cesar (2007), "The recreational value of coral reefs: A meta-analysis," *Ecological Economics*, **63**(1), 209–18.

Brookshire, D.S., L.S. Eubanks, and A. Randall (1983), "Estimating option prices and existence values for wildlife resources," *Land Economics*, **59**(1), 1–15.

Brouwer, R., I.H. Langford, I.J. Bateman, and R.K. Turner (1999), "A meta-analysis of wetland contingent valuation studies," *Regional Environmental Change*, **1**(1), 47–57.

Brown, T.C. and J.W. Duffield (1995), "Testing part-whole valuation effects in contingent valuation of instream flow protection," *Water Resources Research*, **31**(9), 2,341–51.

Brown, T.C., S.C. Barro, M.J. Manfredo, and G.L. Peterson (1995), "Does better information about the good avoid embedding effect?," *Journal of Environmental Management*, **44**(1), 1–10.

Cameron, T.A. and D.D. Huppert (1989), "OLS versus ML estimation of non-market resource values with payment card interval data," *Journal of Environmental Economics and Management*, **17**(3), 230–46.

Carlsson, F. and P. Martinsson (2008), "How much is too much? An investigation of the effect of the number of choice sets, context dependence and the choice of bid vectors in choice experiments," *Environmental Resource Economics*, **40**, 165–76.

Carson, R.T. (1994), *Prospective Interim Lost Use Value Due to PCB and DDT Contamination in the Southern California Bight, Volume 1*, report by Natural Resource Damage Assessment Inc. and Industrial Economics Inc. to the NOAA.

Carson, R.T. (1997), "Contingent valuation and tests of insensitivity to scope," in R.J. Kopp, W. Pommerhene, and N. Schwartz (eds), *Determining the Value of Non-Marketed Goods: Economic, Psychological, and Policy Relevant Aspects of Contingent Valuation Methods*, Boston, MA: Kluwer.

Carson, R.T. (2012), "Contingent valuation: A practical alternative when prices aren't available," *Journal of Economic Perspectives*, **26**(4), 27–42.

Carson, R.T. and W.M. Hanemann (2005), "Contingent valuation," in K.G. Maler and J.R. Vincent (eds), *Handbook of Environmental Economics, Volume 2: Valuing Environmental Changes*, Amsterdam: North-Holland.

Carson, R.T. and R.C. Mitchell (1989), *Using Surveys to Value Public Goods: The Contingent Valuation Method*, Washington, DC: Resources for the Future.

Carson, R.T. and R.C. Mitchell (1993), "The value of clean water: The public's willingness to pay for boatable, fishable, and swimmable quality water," *Water Resources Research*, **29**(7), 2,445–54.

Carson, R.T. and R.C. Mitchell (1995), "Sequencing and nesting in contingent valuation surveys," *Journal of Environmental Economics and Management*, **28**(2), 155–73.

Carson, R.T., R.C. Mitchell, and P.A. Ruud (1990), "Valuing air quality improvements: Simulating a hedonic equation in the context of a contingent valuation scenario," in C. Mathi (ed.), *Visibility and Fine Particles*, Pittsburgh, PA: Air and Waste Management Association.

Carson, R.T., L. Wilks, and D. Imber (1994a), "Valuing the preservation of Australia's Kakadu Conservation Zone," *Oxford Economic Papers*, **46**(Supplement), 727–49.

Carson, R.T., W.M. Hanemann, R.J. Kopp, J.A. Krosnick, R.C. Mitchell, S. Presser, P.A. Ruud, and V.K. Smith (1994b), *Prospective Interim Lost Use Value Due to PCB and DDT Contamination in the Southern California Bight*, report to National Oceanic and Atmospheric Administration by Natural Resource Damage Assessment Inc.

Caudill, S.B., P.A. Groothius, and J.C. Whitehead (2011), "The development and estimation of a latent choice multinomial logit model with application to contingent valuation," *American Journal of Agricultural Economics*, **93**(4).

Chapman, D.J., R.C. Bishop, W.M. Hanemann, B.J. Kanninen, J.A. Krosnick, E.R. Morey, and R. Tourangeau (2009), *Natural Resource Damages Associated with Aesthetic and Ecosystem Injuries to Oklahoma's Illinois River System and Tenkiller Lake. Expert Report for State of Oklahoma*, accessed December 1, 2016 at https://pprg.stanford.edu/wp-content/uploads/9-Natural-resource-damages-associated-with-aesthetic-and-ecosystem-injuries-to-Oklahomas-Illinois-river-system.pdf.

Choe, K., D. Whittington, and D.T. Lauria (1996), "The economic benefits of surface water quality improvements in developing countries: A case study of Davao, Philippines," *Land Economics*, **72**(4), 519–37.

Christie, M. (2001), "A comparison of alternative contingent valuation elicitation treatments for the evaluation of complex environmental policy," *Journal of Environmental Management*, **62**(3), 255–69.

Cooper, J. and J. Loomis (1992), "Sensitivity of willingness-to-pay estimates to bid design in dichotomous choice contingent valuation models," *Land Economics*, **68**(2), 211–24.

Cummings, R.G., D.S. Brookshire, and W.D. Schulze (1986), *Valuing Environmental Goods: An Assessment of the Contingent Valuation Method*, Totowa, NJ: Rowman & Allanheld.

Day, B. and S. Mourato (1998), "Willingness to pay for water quality maintenance in Chinese rivers," *CSERGE Working Paper*, Centre for Social and Economic Research on the Global Environment, University College London and University of East Anglia.

Desvousges, W., K. Mathews, and K. Train (2012), "Adequate responsiveness to scope in contingent valuation," *Ecological Economics*, **84**(1), 121–8.

Desvousges, W., K. Mathews, and K. Train (2016), "An adding-up test on contingent valuations of river and lake quality," *Land Economics*, forthcoming.

Desvousges, W.H., F.R. Johnson, R.W. Dunford, S.P. Hudson, K.N. Wilson, and K.J. Boyle (1992), *Measuring Non-use Damages Using Contingent Valuation: An Experimental Evaluation of Accuracy*, Research Triangle Institute Monograph No. 92-1, Research Triangle Park, NC.

Desvousges, W.H., F.R. Johnson, R.W. Dunford, S.P. Hudson, K.N. Wilson, and K.J. Boyle (1993), "Measuring natural resource damages with contingent valuation: Tests of validity and reliability," in J.A. Hausman (ed.), *Contingent Valuation: A Critical Assessment*, Amsterdam: Elsevier, pp. 91–164.

Diamond, P.A. (1996), "Testing the internal consistency of contingent valuation surveys," *Journal of Environmental Economics and Management*, **30**(3), 337–47.

Diamond, P.A., J.A. Hausman, G.K. Leonard, and M.A. Denning (1993), "Does contingent valuation measure preferences? Experimental evidence," in J.A. Hausman (ed.), *Contingent Valuation: A Critical Assessment*, Amsterdam: Elsevier, pp. 41–89.

Duffield, J. and C. Neher (1991), *A Contingent Valuation Assessment of Montana Waterfowl Hunting*, report prepared for the Montana Department of Fish Wildlife, and Parks, Montana Bioeconomics, Missoula, MT.

Duffield, J.W. and D.A. Patterson (1991), "Field testing existence values: An instream flow trust fund for Montana rivers," paper presented at the Association of Environmental and Resource Economics during the Valuing Environmental Goods with Contingent Valuation session.

DuPont, D.P. (2003), "CVM embedding effects when there are active, potentially active and passive users of environmental goods," *Environmental and Resource Economics*, **25**(3), 319–41.

DuPont, D.P. (2013), "Water use restrictions or wastewater recycling? A Canadian willingness to pay study for reclaimed wastewater," *Water Resources and Economics*, **1**(1), 61–74.

Eom, Y.-S. and D.M. Larson (2006), "Improving environmental valuation estimates through consistent use of revealed and stated preference information," *Journal of Economics and Environmental Management*, **52**(1), 501–16.

Fischhoff, B., M.J. Quadrel, M. Kamlet, G. Loewenstein, R. Dawes, P. Fischbeck, S. Klepper, J. Leland, and P. Stroh (1993), "Embedding effects: Stimulus representation and response mode," *Journal of Risk and Uncertainty*, **6**, 211–34.

Fredman, P. (1995), "The existence of existence value – study of the economic benefits of an endangered species," *Journal of Forest Economics*, **1**(3), 307–27.

Gerrans, P. (1994), "An economic valuation of the Jandakot wetlands," *Occasional Paper No. 1*, Perth: Edith Cowan University.

Ghermandi, A., J.C.J.M. van der Bergh, L.M. Brander, H.L.F. de Groot, and P.A.L.D. Nunes (2008), "The economic value of wetland conservation and creation: A meta-analysis," *Nota di Lavoro No. 79.2008*, Fondazione Eni Enrico Mattei.

Gilbert, A., R. Glass, and T. More (1991), "Valuation of eastern wilderness: Extramarket measures of public support," in C. Paine, J. Bowker, and P. Reed (eds), *The Economic Value of Wilderness*, Ashville, NC: US Department of Agriculture, Forest Service.

Giraud, K.L., J.B. Loomis, and R.L. Johnson (1999), "Internal and external scope in willingness-to-pay estimates for threatened and endangered wildlife," *Journal of Environmental Management*, **56**(3), 221–9.

Gong, M. and J. Baron (2011), "The generality of the emotion effect on magnitude sensitivity," *Journal of Economic Psychology*, **32**(1), 17–24.

Goodman, S.L., W. Seabrooke, and S.A. Jaffry (1998), "Considering conservation value in economic appraisals of coastal resources," *Journal of Environmental Planning and Management*, **41**(3), 313–36.

Haab, T.C., M.G. Interis, D.R. Petrolia, and J.C. Whitehead (2013), "From hopeless to curious? Thoughts on Hausman's 'dubious to hopeless' critique of contingent valuation," *Applied Economic Perspectives and Policy*, **35**(4), 593–612.

Halvorsen, B. (1996), "Ordering effects in contingent valuation surveys: Willingness to pay for reduced health damage from air pollution," *Environmental and Resource Economics*, **8**(4), 485–99.

Hammit, J.K., L. Jin-Tan, and L. Jin-Long (2001), "Contingent valuation of a Taiwanese wetland," *Environment and Development Economics*, **6**(2), 259–68.

Hanemann, M. (2005), "The bird study revisited," presentation, UC Berkeley.

Hanley, N., R.E. Wright, and B. Alvarez-Farizo (2005), "Estimating the economic value of improvements in river ecology using choice experiments: An application to the Water Framework Directive," *Journal of Environmental Management*, **78**(2), 183–93.

Hausman, J. and W. Newey (2016), "Individual heterogeneity and average welfare," *Econometrica*, **84**(3), 1225–48.

Heberlein, T.A., M.A. Wilson, R.C. Bishop, and N.C. Schaeffer (2005), "Rethinking the scope test as a criterion for validity in contingent valuation," *Journal of Environmental Economics and Management*, **50**(1), 1–22.

Hicks, R.L., T.C. Haab, and D. Lipton (2004), *The Economic Benefits of Oyster Reef Restoration in the Chesapeake Bay*, report for the Chesapeake Bay Foundation.

Hite, D., D. Hudson, and W. Intarapapong (2002), "Willingness to pay for water quality improvements: The case of precision application technology," *Journal of Agricultural and Resource Economics*, **27**(2), 433–49.

Hjerpe, E., A. Hussain, and S. Phillips (2015), "Valuing type and scope of eco-system conservation: A meta-analysis," *Journal of Forest Economics*, **21**(1), 32–50.

Hoehn, J.P. and J.B. Loomis (1993), "Substitution effects in the valuation of multiple environmental programs," *Journal of Environmental Economics and Management*, **25**(1), 56–75.

Hoevenagel, R. (1996), "The validity of the contingent valuation method: Perfect and regular embedding," *Environmental and Resource Economics*, **7**(1), 57–78.

Hsee, C.K. and Y. Rottenstreich (2004), "Music, pandas, and muggers: On the affective psychology of value," *Journal of Experimental Psychology*, **133**(1), 23–30.

Huang, J.-C., T.C. Haab, and J.C. Whitehead (1997), "Willingness to pay for quality improvements: Should revealed and stated preference data be combined?" *Journal of Environmental Economics and Management*, **34**(3), 240–55.

Irwin, J., G. McClelland, M. McKee, W.D. Schulze, and E. Norden (1998), "Payoff dominance vs. cognitive transparency in decision making," *Economic Inquiry*, **36**(2), 272–85.

Jakobsson, K.M. and A.K. Dragun (2001), "The worth of a possum: Valuing species with the contingent valuation method," *Environmental and Resource Economics*, **19**(3), 211–27.

Jakus, J.P. (1992), "Valuing the private and public dimensions of a mixed good: An application to pest control," PhD thesis, North Carolina State University.

Jin, J., A. Indab, O. Nabangchang, T.D. Thuy, D. Harder, and R.F. Subade (2010), "Valuing marine turtle conservation: A cross-country study in Asian cities," *Ecological Economics*, **69**(10), 2020–26.

Johnston, R.J. and J.M. Duke (2009), "Informing preservation of multifunctional agriculture when primary research is unavailable: An application of meta-analysis," *American Journal of Agricultural Economics*, **91**(5), 1353–9.

Johnston, R.J., E.Y. Besedin, R. Iovanna, C.J. Miller, R.F. Wardwell, and M.H. Ranson (2005), "Systematic variation in willingness to pay for aquatic resource improvements and implications for benefit transfer: A meta-analysis," *Canadian Journal of Agricultural Economics*, **53**(2–3), 221–48.

Kahneman, D. (1986), "Comments by Professor Daniel Kahneman," in R. Cummings, D. Brookshire, and W. Schulze (eds), *Valuing Environmental Goods: An Assessment of the Contingent Valuation Method*, Totowa, NJ: Rowman & Allanheld, pp. 185–94.

Kahneman, D. and J.L. Knetsch (1992), "Valuing public goods: The purchase of moral satisfaction," *Journal of Environmental Economics and Management*, **22**(1), 57–70.

Kahneman, K. and I. Ritov (1994), "Determinants of stated willingness to pay for public goods: A study in the headline method," *Journal of Risk and Uncertainty*, **9**(1), 5–38.

Kling, C.L., D.J. Phaneuf, and J. Zhao (2012), "From Exxon to BP: Has some number become better than no number?," *Journal of Economic Perspectives*, **26**(4), 3–26.

Kniivila, M., V. Ovaskainen, and O. Saastamoinen (2002), "Costs and benefits of forest conservation: Regional and local comparisons in Eastern Finland," *Journal of Forest Economics*, **8**(2), 131–50.

Kragt, M.E. (2013), "The effects of changing cost vectors on choices and scale heterogeneity," *Environmental and Resource Economics*, **54**(2), 201–21.

Krieger, D.J. (1994), "The economic value of environmental risk information: Theory and application to the Michigan sport fisher," dissertation, Michigan State University, Ann Arbor, MI: University Microfilms International.

Kwak, S., S. Yoo, and S. Han (2003), "Estimating public's value for urban forest in Seoul Metropolitan Area of Korea: A contingent valuation study," *Urban Studies*, **40**(11), 2,207–21.

Lindhjem, H. (2007), "20 years of stated preference valuation of non-timber benefits

from Fennoscandian forests: A meta-analysis," *Journal of Forest Economics*, **12**(4), 251–77.
Longo, A., D. Hoyos, and A. Markandya (2012), "Willingness to pay for ancillary benefits of climate change mitigation," *Environmental Resource Economics*, **51**(1), 119–40.
Loomis, J. and E. Ekstrand (1997), "Economic benefits of critical habitat for the Mexican spotted owl: A scope test using a multiple-bounded contingent valuation survey," *Journal of Agricultural and Resource Economics*, **22**(2), 356–66.
Loomis, J. and D.S. White (1996), "Economic benefits of rare and endangered species: Summary and meta-analysis," *Ecological Economics*, **18**(3), 197–206.
Loomis, J., A. González-Cabán and R. Gregory (1994), "Do reminders of substitutes and budget constraints influence contingent valuation estimates?," *Land Economics*, **70**(4), 499–506.
Loomis, J., L.T. Hung, and A. González-Cabán (2009), "Willingness to pay function for two fuel treatments to reduce wildfire acreage burned: A scope test and comparison of white and Hispanic households," *Forest Policy and Economics*, **11**(3), 155–60.
Loomis, J., M. Lockwood, and T. DeLacy (1993), "Some empirical evidence on embedding effects in contingent valuation of forest protection," *Journal of Environmental Economics and Management*, **24**, 44–55.
Macmillan, D.C. and E.I. Duff (1998), "Estimating the non-market costs and benefits of native woodland restoration using the contingent valuation method," *Forestry*, **71**(3), 247–59.
Macmillan, D., N. Hanley, and S. Buckland (1996), "A contingent valuation study of uncertain environmental gains," *Scottish Journal of Political Economy*, **43**(5), 519–33.
Magnussen, K. (1992), "Valuation of reduced water pollution using the contingent valuation method – testing for amenity misspecification," in S. Navrud (ed.), *Pricing the European Environment*, Oxford: Oxford University Press.
Markowski, M.A., K.J. Boyle, R.C. Bishop, D.M. Larson, and R.W. Paterson (2001), 'A cautionary note on interpreting meta analyses', unpublished paper, Industrial Economics Inc.
McDaniels, T.L., R. Gregory, J. Arvai, and R. Chuenpagdee (2003), "Decision structuring to alleviate embedding in environmental valuation," *Ecological Economics*, **46**(1), 33–46.
McFadden, D. (1994), "Contingent valuation and social choice," *American Journal of Agricultural Economics*, **76**(4), 689–708.
McFadden, D. and G. Leonard (1993), "Issues in the contingent valuation of environmental goods: Methodologies for data collection and analysis," in J.A. Hausman (ed.), *Contingent Valuation: A Critical Assessment*, Amsterdam: Elsevier, pp. 177–207.
Metcalfe, P.J. (2012), "Non-market valuation using stated preferences: Applications in the water sector," thesis submitted to the Department of Geography and Environment, the London School of Economics and Political Science.
Mill, G.A, T.M. van Rensburg, S. Hynes, and C. Dooley (2007), "Preferences for multiple use forest management in Ireland: Citizen and consumer perspectives," *Ecological Economics*, **60**(3), 642–53.
Mørkbak, M.R., T. Christensen, and D. Gyrd-Hansen (2010), "Choke price bias in choice experiments," *Environmental Resource Economics*, **45**(4), 537–51.

Mullarkey, D.J. (1997), "Contingent valuation of wetlands: Testing sensitivity to scope," dissertation submitted to the Graduate School of the University of Wisconsin-Madison.

Mullarkey, D.J. and R.C. Bishop (1999), "Sensitivity to scope: Evidence from a CVM study of wetlands," presented at the American Agricultural Economics Association Annual Meeting.

Navrud, S. (1989), "Estimating social benefits of environmental improvements from reduced acid rain deposition: A contingent valuation survey," in H. Folmer and E.C. van Ierland (eds), *Valuation Methods and Policy Making in Environmental Economics*, Amsterdam: Elsevier.

Nunes, P.A.L.D. and E. Schokkaert (2003), "Identifying the warm glow effect in contingent valuation," *Journal of Environmental Economics and Management*, **45**(2), 231–45.

Ojea, E. and M.L. Loureiro (2011), "Identifying the scope effect on a meta-analysis of biodiversity studies," *Resource and Energy Economics*, **33**(3), 706–24.

Ojea, E., P.A.L.D. Nunes, and M.L. Loureiro (2010), "Mapping biodiversity indicators and assessing biodiversity values in global forests," *Environmental and Resource Economics*, **47**(3), 329–47.

Pattison, J., P.C. Boxall, and W.L. Adamowicz (2011), "The economic benefit of wetland retention and restoration in Manitoba," *Canadian Journal of Agricultural Economics*, **59**(2), 223–44.

Petrolia, D.R. and T. Kim (2009), "What are barrier islands worth? Estimates of willingness to pay for restoration," *Marine Resource Economics*, **24**(2), 131–46.

Poe, G.L., K.J. Boyle, and J.C. Bergstrom (2001), "A preliminary meta analysis of contingent values for ground water quality revisited," in J.C. Bergstrom, K.J. Boyle, and G.L. Poe (eds), *The Economic Value of Water Quality*, Cheltenham, UK and Northampton, MA, USA: Edward Elgar Publishing.

Poe, G., K.L. Giraud, and J.B. Loomis (2005), "Computational methods for measuring the difference of empirical distributions," *American Journal of Agricultural Economics*, **87**(2), 353–65.

Pouta, E. (2003), "Attitude-behavior framework in contingent valuation of forest conservation," dissertation submitted to the University of Helsinki.

Pouta, E. (2005), "Sensitivity to scope of environmental regulation in contingent valuation of forest cutting practices in Finland," *Forest Policy and Economics*, **7**(4), 539–50.

Powe, N.A. and I.J. Bateman (2004), "Investigating insensitivity to scope: A split-sample test of perceived scheme realism," *Land Economic*, **80**(2), 258–71.

Prelec, D., J. Burrows, and P. Dixon (forthcoming), "Context sensitivity in stated preference experiments."

Rahmatian, M. (1986), "Extensions of the disaggregate bid experiment: Variations in framing," *Journal of Environmental Management*, **22**(3), 191–202.

Randall, A., J.P. Hoehn, and G.S. Tolley (1981), "The structure of contingent markets: Some results of a recent experiment," paper presented at the annual meeting of the American Economic Association, Washington, DC.

Rathnayake, R.M.S. (2016), "Willingness to pay for a novel visitor experience: Ecotourism planning at Kawdulla National Park in Sri Lanka," *Tourism Planning and Development Journal*, **13**(1), 37–51.

Ready, R.C., M.C. Berger, and G.C. Blomquist (1997), "Measuring amenity benefits from farmland: Hedonic pricing vs. contingent valuation," *Growth and Change*, **28**(4), 438–58.

Ressurreição, A., J. Gibbons, T.P. Dentinho, M. Kaiser, R.S. Santos, and G. Edwards-Jones (2011), "Economic valuation of species loss in the open sea," *Ecological Economics*, **70**(4), 729–39.

Richardson, L. and J. Loomis (2009), "The total economic value of threatened, endangered and rare species: An updated meta-analysis," *Ecological Economics*, **68**(5), 1535–48.

Rollins, K. and A. Lyke (1998), "The case for diminishing marginal existence values," *Journal of Environmental Economics and Management*, **36**(3), 324–44.

Rosenberger, R.S. and J.B. Loomis (2000a), *Benefit Transfer of Outdoor Recreation Use Values: A Technical Document Supporting the Forest Service Strategic Plan (2000 Revision)*, final report for the USDA Forest Service.

Rosenberger, R.S. and J.B. Loomis (2000b), "Using meta-analysis for benefit transfer: In-sample convergent validity tests of an outdoor recreation database," *Water Resources Research*, **36**(4), 1097–107.

Rowe, R.D., W.D. Shaw, and W. Schulze (1992), "Nestucca oil spill," in K.M. Ward and J.W. Duffield (eds), *Natural Resource Damages: Law and Economics*, New York: John Wiley, pp. 527–54.

Ryan, M. and S. Wordsworth (2000), "Sensitivity of willingness to pay estimates to the level of attributes in discrete choice experiments," *Scottish Journal of Political Economy*, **47**(5), 504–24.

Samples, K.C. and J.R. Hollyer (1990), "Contingent valuation of wildlife resources in the presence of substitutes and complements," in R.L. Johnson and G.V. Johnson (eds), *Economic Valuation of Natural Resources: Issues, Theory, and Applications*, Boulder, CO: Westview Press, pp. 177–92.

Schkade, D.A. and J.W. Payne (1993), "Where do the numbers come from? How people respond to contingent valuation questions," in J.A. Hausman (ed.), *Contingent Valuation: A Critical Assessment*, Amsterdam: Elsevier, pp. 271–93.

Schkade, D.A. and J.W. Payne (1994), "How people respond to contingent valuation questions: A verbal protocol analysis of willingness to pay for an environmental regulation," *Journal of Environmental Economics and Management*, **26**(1), 88–109.

Schulze, W.D., R.D. Rowe, and G.H. McClelland (1995), *Contingent Valuation of Natural Resource Damages Due to Injuries to the Upper Clark Fork River Basin*, report prepared for the State of Montana Natural Resource Damage Litigation Program.

Shrestha, R.K. and J.B. Loomis (2003), "Meta-analytic benefit transfer of outdoor recreation economic values: Testing out of sample convergent validity," *Environmental and Resource Economics*, **25**(1), 79–100.

Smith, A.E., M.A. Kemp, T.H. Savage, and C.L. Taylor (2005), "Methods and results from a new survey of values for eastern regional haze improvements," *Journal of Air and Waste Management Association*, **55**(11), 1767–79.

Smith, K.V. and L.L. Osborne (1996), "Do contingent valuation estimates pass a 'scope' test? A meta-analysis," *Journal of Environmental Economics and Management*, **31**(3), 287–301.

Smith, V.K. and Y. Kaoru (1990), "Signals or noise? Explaining the variation in recreation benefit estimates," *American Journal of Agricultural Economics*, **72**(2), 419–33.

Smith, V.K., X. Zhang, and R.B. Palmquist (1997), "Marine debris, beach

quality, and non-market values," *Environmental and Resource Economics*, **10**(3), 223–47.
Stanley, D.L. (2005), "Local perception of public goods: Recent assessments of willingness-to-pay for endangered species," *Contemporary Economic Policy*, **23**(2), 165–79.
Stevens, T.H., S. Benin, and J.S. Larson (1995), "Public attitudes and values for wetland conservation in New England," *Wetlands*, **15**(3), 226–31.
Stevens, T.H., N.E. DeCoteau, and C.E. Willis (1997), "Sensitivity of contingent valuation to alternative payment schedules," *Land Economics*, **73**(1), 140–48.
Streever, W.J., M. Callaghan-Perry, A. Searles, T. Stevens, and P. Svoboda (1998), "Public attitudes and values for wetland conservation in New South Wales, Australia," *Journal of Environmental Management*, **54**(1), 1–14.
Sturtevant, L.A., F.R. Johnson, and W.H. Desvousges (1998), "A meta-analysis of recreational fishing," unpublished manuscript, Durham, NC: Triangle Economics Research.
Svedsäter, H. (2000), "Contingent valuation of global environmental resources: Test of perfect and regular embedding," *Journal of Economic Psychology*, **21**(6), 605–23.
Tanguay, M., W. Adamowicz, P. Boxall, W. Phillips, and W. White (1993), *A Socio-Economic Evaluation of Woodland Caribou in Northwestern Saskatchewan*, Project Report No. 93-04.
Total Value Team (2015a), "Draft Technical Memo TM-10: Econometric analysis of choice questions," in the US Department of the Interior's Deepwater Horizon Response & Restoration Administrative Record.
Total Value Team (2015b), "Draft Technical Memo TM-5: Development and testing of the survey questionnaire," in the US Department of the Interior's Deepwater Horizon Response & Restoration Administrative Record.
Van Houtven, G., J. Powers, and S.K. Pattanayak (2007), "Valuing water quality improvements in the United States using meta-analysis: Is the glass half-full or half-empty for national policy analysis?," *Resource and Energy Economics*, **29**(3), 206–14.
Veisten, K., H.F. Hoen, S. Navrud, and J. Strand (2004a), "Scope insensitivity in contingent valuation of complex environmental amenities," *Journal of Environmental Management*, **73**(4), 317–31.
Veisten, K., H.F. Hoen, S. Navrud, and J. Strand (2004b), "Sequencing and the adding up property in contingent valuation of endangered species: Are contingent non-use value economic values?," *Environmental and Resource Economics*, **29**, 419–33.
Vo, D.T. and K.V. Huynh (2014), "Estimating residents' willingness to pay for groundwater protection in the Vietnamese Mekong Delta," *Applied Water Science*, November, DOI: 10.1007/s13201-014-0257-8.
Walsh, R.G., D.M. Johnson, and J.R. McKean (1992), "Benefit transfer of outdoor recreation demand studies, 1968–1988," *Water Resources Research*, **28**(3), 707–13.
Walsh, R., J. Loomis, and R. Gillman (1984), "Valuing option, existence, and bequest demands for wilderness," *Land Economics*, **60**(1), 14–29.
Welsh, M.P., R.C. Bishop, R.M. Baumgartner, and M.L. Phillips (1994), *Pilot Test Non-use Value Study (draft final report), Glen Canyon Environmental Studies Technical Report*, Madison, WI: HBRS Inc.
Welsh, M.P., R.C. Bishop, M.L. Phillips, and R.M. Baumgartner (1995), *Glen*

Canyon Environmental Studies Non-Use Value Study, final report prepared for Glen Canyon Environmental Studies Non-Use Value Committee, Madison, WI: RCG/Hagler-Bailly Inc.

White, P.C.L., K.W. Gregory, P.J. Lindley, and G. Richards (1997), "Economic values of threatened mammals in Britain: A case study of the otter *Lutra lutra* and the water vole *Arvicola terrestris*," *Biological Conservation*, **82**(3), 345–54.

Whitehead, J.C. (1992), "Ex ante willingness to pay with supply and demand uncertainty: Implications for valuing a sea turtle protection programme," *Applied Economics*, **24**(9), 981–8.

Whitehead, J.C. (2016), "Plausible responsiveness to scope in contingent valuation," *Ecological Economics*, **128**, 17–22.

Whitehead, J.C. and T.L. Cherry (2007), "Willingness to pay for a green energy program: A comparison of ex-ante and ex-post hypothetical bias mitigation approaches," *Resource and Energy Economics*, **29**(4), 247–61.

Whitehead, J.C. and S. Finney (2003), "Willingness to pay for submerged maritime cultural resources," *Journal of Cultural Economics*, **27**(3), 231–40.

Whitehead, J.C., P.A. Groothius, and R. Southwick (2007), "Linking recreation demand and willingness to pay with the inclusive value: Valuation of Saginaw Bay coastal marsh," presented at the US Environmental Protection Agency Workshop (Valuation for Environmental Policy: Ecological Benefits Workshop).

Whitehead, J.C., T.C. Haab, and J.-C. Huang (1998), "Part-whole bias in contingent valuation: Will scope effects be detected with inexpensive survey methods?," *Southern Economic Journal*, **65**(1), 160–68.

Whitehead, J.C., P.A. Groothius, R. Southwick, and P. Foster-Turley (2009), "Measuring the economic benefits of Saginaw Bay coastal marsh with revealed and stated preference methods," *Journal of Great Lakes Research*, **35**(3), 430–37.

Wilson, M.A. (2000), 'Rethinking scope sensitivity and contingent valuation surveys: Strong environmental attitudes and contingent economic values', dissertation submitted to the Graduate School of the University of Wisconsin-Madison, UMI Number: 9981890.

Woodward, R.T. and Y. Wui (2001), "The economic value of wetland services: A meta-analysis," *Ecological Economics*, **37**(2), 257–70.

Wu, P. (1993), "Substitution and complementarity in commodity space: Benefit evaluation of multidimensional environmental policy," *Academia Economic Papers*, **21**(1), 151–82.

Zandersen, M. and R.S.J. Tol (2009), "A meta-analysis of forest recreation values in Europe," *Journal of Forest Economics*, **15**(1–2), 109–30.

6. Stated preference methods and their applicability to environmental use and non-use valuations

Daniel McFadden[1]

> [...]it appears that the CVM is likely to work best for those kinds of problems where we need it least; that is, where respondents' experience with changes in the level of the environmental good have left a record of trade-offs, substitutions, and so forth, which can be the basis of econometric estimates of value. But for the problems for which we need something like the CVM most, that is, where individuals have little or no experience with different levels of the environmental good, CVM appears to be least reliable.
> (Freeman, 1986, p.160)

INTRODUCTION

Stated preference (SP) methods collect data on consumer tastes by direct elicitation, in contrast to *revealed preference* (RP) methods that infer tastes from observed market demand behavior. Leading SP methods are *choice-based conjoint* (CBC) experiments and surveys, widely used in market research to forecast demand for new or modified products, and *contingent valuation method* (CVM) elicitations, employed by environmental economists to estimate use, non-use, or total values of non-marketed natural resources. CBC and CVM are defined and illustrated in the second section of this chapter. The main subject of this book is CVM, and since the critique of CVM in Hausman (1993), the progress, or lack of progress, in refining this method to the point where it can produce reliable, reproducible, and plausible valuations. This chapter is different, concentrating instead on SP studies of demand for ordinary consumer goods and services where actual market experience provides a proving ground for accuracy of SP methods, and drawing lessons from these market applications for use and non-use valuation of environmental goods.

---

[1] E. Morris Cox Professor of Economics, University of California, Berkeley.

There are several reasons experience with SP methods in market research matters for CVM. First, one can ask whether the users of CVM could improve their valuations by adopting more of the CBC technology. Second, proponents of CVM for environmental valuations have defended the method by claiming on one hand that CVM is sufficiently close to CBC applied to ordinary market goods so that the demonstrated successes of the latter are support for CVM, and on the other hand that hypersensitivity to context and behavioral inconsistencies found in CVM responses are also seen in CBC studies of ordinary market goods. There is some truth to both premises – CBC studies of demand for ordinary market goods often do exhibit context and behavioral effects, and despite these problems have been relatively successful in demand forecasting for ordinary market goods. However, a closer examination of SP methods for market goods finds a sharp reliability gradient. Forecasts that are comparable in accuracy to RP forecasts can be obtained from well-designed SP studies for familiar, relatively simple goods that are similar to market goods purchased by consumers, particularly when calibration to market benchmarks can be used to correct experimental distortions. However, studies of unfamiliar, complex goods give erratic, unreliable forecasts. For relatively simple environmental goods such as hunting licenses and beach access that are similar to regular market goods, it seems possible to obtain reliable, reproducible use values from well-designed SP studies. However, valuations of relatively complex and unfamiliar environmental goods, particularly for non-use values that have no real market equivalents, are at the bad end of the reliability gradient, and neither CVM nor more robust CBC methods seem capable of producing consistent results. A deeper understanding of the relationship between consumer well-being and stated choices or votes, and major innovations in SP methodology, are needed before SP methods can hope to reliably value complex goods that do not have close market analogues.

Looking back over the 30 years since the Freeman quote that starts this chapter, it is disappointing that CVM has not evolved to overcome its performance issues, so that the concerns of that time are still on the table.[2] Perhaps this is because the task that CVM takes on to elicit consistent non-use values from consumers is in truth impossible to complete – consumers may simply not be up to the job of forming consistent preferences for unfamiliar environmental goods in an experimental setting. Some

---

[2] The outstanding issues addressed in this book were already concerns expressed by Cummings et al. (1986, pp. 106–9), Freeman (1986), Bishop and Heberlein (1986), Smith et al. (1986), a panel composed of Kenneth Arrow, Danny Kahneman, Sherwin Rosen, and Vernon Smith (in Cummings et al., 1986, pp. 181–236), and Diamond and Hausman (1993).

of the lack of CVM innovation may also be due to over-optimistic assessments by environmental economists of the potential of CVM, followed by a "circling-of-the-wagons" defense against legitimate as well as off-the-mark criticisms.[3] A history of skepticism about stated preference methods within the economics community, described next, may have contributed to the defensiveness of CVM proponents, and to their reluctance to incorporate developments and insights from cognitive psychology, behavioral economics, survey research, and market research that might improve the reliability of at least some environmental valuation tasks.

HISTORY OF SP METHODS

Stated preference methods date back to the 1930s, when the iconic psychologist Leon Thurstone (1931) made a presentation to the second meeting of the Econometric Society proposing direct elicitation of indifference curves:

> Perhaps the simplest experimental method that comes to mind is to ask a subject to fill in the blank space [to achieve indifference] in a series of choices of the following type: "eight hats and eight pairs of shoes" versus "six hats and ___ pairs of shoes". . . One of the combinations such as eight hats and eight pairs of shoes is chosen as a standard and each of the other combinations is compared directly with it.

Thurstone introduced psychophysical axioms for preferences that led, via Fechner's law,[4] to indifference curves that could be interpreted as coming from a log-linear utility function. He collected experimental data on hats vs shoes, hats vs overcoats, and shoes vs overcoats, fit the parameters of the log-linear utility function to data from each comparison, treating responses as bounds on the underlying indifference curves, and used these estimates to test the consistency of his fits across the three comparisons.

At the time of Thurstone's presentation, empirical demand analysis was in its early days. Frisch (1926) and Schultz (1925, 1928) had published pioneering studies of market demand for a single commodity (sugar), but there were no empirical studies of demand for more than one product. Least-squares estimation was new to economics, and required tedious hand

---

[3] See, for example, Randall (1986), Mitchell and Carson (1989, pp. 295–7), Carson et al. (2001), and Carson (2012).

[4] Fechner's law (propounded in *Elemente der Psychophysik*, 1860), also called Weber's law, states that subjective sensation, quantified in terms of just noticeable differences, is proportional to the logarithm of stimulus intensity. The law was advanced for perceptions of weights and auditory and visual stimuli, and has been verified for a variety of human perceptions, with some exceptions at extremes.

calculation. Consolidation of the theory of demand for multiple commodities was still in the future; for example, Hicks (1939) and Samuelson (1947). Given this setting, Thurstone's approach was path-breaking. Nevertheless, his estimates were rudimentary, and he failed to connect his fitted indifference curves to market demand forecasts and changes in well-being. In retrospect, these flaws were correctable: denote by H, S, C, respectively, the numbers of hats, pairs of shoes, and coats consumed, let M denote the money remaining for all other goods and services after paying for the haberdashery, and let Y denote total income. If Thurstone had asked subjects for the amounts of M that made comparison bundles (H,S,C,M) indifferent to a standard bundle (H_0, S_0, C_0, M_0), he could have estimated the parameters of the log-linear utility function $u = \log M + \theta_H \log H + \theta_S \log S + \theta_C \log C$ by a least squares regression of $\log(M/M_0)$ on $\log(H_0/H)$, $\log(S_0/S)$, and $\log(C_0/C)$, and from this forecast the demand for hats at price p_H and income Y using the formula $H = \frac{\theta_H}{1 + \theta_H + \theta_S + \theta_C} \cdot \frac{Y}{p_H}$ derived by utility maximization subject to the budget constraint, with similar formulas for the other goods. He could have plugged these demand functions into the utility function to obtain the log-linear indirect utility function, and from this determined the *net* reduction in income *after* a change in the price of hats from p_H' to p_H'' that leaves the consumer indifferent to the change, $HCV = Y\left[1 - (p_H''/p_H')^{\theta_H/(1+\theta_H+\theta_S+\theta_C)}\right]$ the *Hicksian compensating variation*. Technical questions could have been raised about the applicability of Fechner's law and the restrictiveness and realism of the log-linear utility that it implies, lack of accounting for heterogeneity in tastes across consumers, and lack of explicit treatment of consumer response errors. Decades later, these issues did arise when the Stone-Geary generalization of this demand system was applied to revealed preference (RP) data.

According to Moscati (2007), Harold Hotelling and Ragnar Frisch panned Thurstone's presentation from the floor. They objected that Thurstone's indifference curves as constructed were insufficient to forecast market demand response to price changes, failing to recognize that extending Thurstone's elicitations to include residual expenditure would have solved the problem. They also pointed out that the knife-edge of indifference that Thurstone tried to elicit is not well determined in comparisons of bundles of discrete commodities. Beyond these objections, Frisch and Hotelling were generally skeptical that experimental, non-market data could be used to predict market behavior. The orthodoxy of that era, formed partly as a reaction to the casual introspections of Bentham and the utilitarians, was that empirical economics should rely solely on revealed market data. Wallis and Friedman (1942) summarized this attitude in an attack that forcefully dismissed Thurstone's method or any other attempt to use experimental data for market demand analysis, pointing out difficulties in designing experiments that mimic the environment of real market choices: "[Thurstone's] fundamental shortcomings probably cannot be overcome in any experiment involving economic stimuli and human beings."

Following the Thurstone presentation, there was no mention of his method in the demand analysis literature until MacCrimmon and Toda (1969). Looking back, this seems narrow-minded, but there was some reason for it. The language of economic analysis, then and now, is prediction of market demand, and assessment of market failures in terms of dollars of equivalent lost income deduced from demand as consumer surplus. Any measurement method that uses experimental data on preferences has to produce convincing results in this language by showing that stated preferences collected outside the market have the same predictive power for market behavior as implied preferences reconstructed from market data. With the advent of behavioral economics, we have learned that people are often not relentless utility maximizers, either in markets or in experiments, undermining the tight links neoclassical consumer theory postulates between consumer utility and demand behavior.[5] This has led to calls for less focus on market demand behavior, and assessment of consumer welfare in terms other than dollars of lost income; see Kahneman et al. (1999) and Kahneman and Krueger (2013). This approach may eventually gain acceptance, but at present market prediction and valuation remain the yardsticks against which any method for eliciting consumer preferences and inferring consumer welfare has to be judged.

The first sustained use of SP methods came out of the theory of conjoint measurement derived from psychophysical axioms by Luce and Tukey (1964) and Luce and Suppes (1965). This method was adapted and named "conjoint analysis" by market researchers like Green and Rao (1971), Johnson (1974, 1999), Shocker and Srinivasan (1974), Green and Srinivasan (1978), Green et al. (1981), Louviere (1988), and Srinivasan (1988) and applied to the study of consumer preferences among familiar market products (e.g., carbonated beverages, automobiles); see Louviere et al. (2000), Rossi et al. (2005), and Ben-Akiva et al. (2016). A central feature of conjoint analysis is use of experimental designs that allow at least a limited mapping of the preferences of each subject, and multiple measurements that allow estimates of preferences to be tested for consistency.

Early conjoint analysis experiments described hypothetical products in terms of levels of attributes in various dimensions, and asked subjects to rank attributes in importance, and rate attribute levels. Market

---

[5] See, for example, Fischhoff and Manski (1999), Kahneman and Tversky (2000), Camerer et al. (2004), and McFadden (2014a).

Table 1   A typical CBC menu: paper towels

Attribute	Alternative 1	Alternative 2	Alternative 3
Price/roll	$2.29	$1.54	$1.25
Sheets/roll	110	58	117
Absorptive capacity (oz. of water per sheet)	2X	3X	1X
Strength when wet (compared to standard towels)	2.5X	1X	1.5X
Brand	Bounty	Viva	Brawny
Check here _____ if you would not pick any of these. Otherwise, check your choice on the right	___	___	___

researchers used these measurements to classify and segment buyers, and target advertising, but they proved to be unreliable tools for predicting market demand. However, Louviere and Woodworth (1983) and Hensher and Louviere (1983) introduced CBC elicitations that directly mimicked market choice tasks, offering respondents repeated menus of products with various attribute levels and prices, and asking them for the choice they would make if the menu offering was fulfilled. McFadden et al. (1986) and McFadden (1986) showed how these elicitations could be analyzed using the tools of discrete choice analysis and the theory of random utility maximization. Subjects would be presented with a series of menus of products. Each product offered in each menu would be described in terms of price and levels of attributes, and perhaps be offered as a sample to handle or taste. Subjects would be asked to choose their most preferred product in each menu. For example, as illustrated in Table 1, subjects might be offered menus of paper towels, with each product described in terms of price, number of towel sheets per roll, a measure of the absorption capacity, a measure of strength when wet, and brand name. Choice data from these menus, within and across subjects, could then be handled in the same way as real market choice data to estimate money-metric indirect utility functions and use them to calculate Hicksian compensating variations for changes in product availability, attributes, and prices. Choice-based conjoint surveys analyzed using discrete choice methods have become widely used and accepted in market research to predict the demand for consumer products, with a sufficient track record so that it is possible to identify many of the necessary conditions for successful prediction; see Green et al. (2001), Cameron et al. (2013), and McFadden (2014b).

Environmental economists developed independently an SP technique

> **BOX 1   A TYPICAL CVM REFERENDUM ELICITATION**[a]
>
> There is a population of several million seabirds living off the Pacific coast, from San Diego to Seattle. The birds spend most of their time many miles away from shore and few people see them. It is estimated that small oil spills kill more than 50,000 seabirds per year, far from shore. Scientists have discussed methods to prevent seabird deaths from oil, but the solutions are expensive and extra funds will be required to implement them. It is usually not possible to identify the tankers that cause small spills and to force the companies to pay. Until this situation changes, public money would have to be spent each year to save the birds. We are interested in the value your household would place on saving about 50,000 seabirds each year from the effects of offshore oil spills.
>
> If you could be sure that 50,000 seabirds would be saved each year, would you agree to pay $5 in extra federal or state taxes per year to support an operation to save the seabirds? (The operation will stop when ways are found to prevent oil spills, or to identify the tankers that cause them and make their owners pay for the operation.)
> Yes _____ No _____
>
> *Note:* a. The specified payment in each elicitation was a randomly assigned value in $5, $25, $60, $150, $400.

termed the *contingent valuation method* (CVM), and applied it to valuing natural resources. For a complete definition of CVM see Randall et al. (1974) or Cummings et al. (1986). In a typical example, taken from Green et al. (1998), CVM asks each respondent one question, in what is termed "referendum format," as illustrated in Box 1.

CVM questions are typically embedded in a survey that instructs the respondent on the nature of the good, payment arrangements and the circumstances under which the hypothetical offer might be fulfilled, and also collects data on the respondent's background. This method traces its beginnings to a proposal by Ciriacy-Wantrup (1947) and an article and PhD thesis by Robert Davis (1963a, 1963b) on the use-value of Maine woods. The development of CVM in essentially its current form was due to Randall et al. (1974). Its first published applications for valuation of environmental public goods seem to have been Hammack and Brown (1974), Brookshire et al. (1976, 1980), and Bishop and Heberlein (1979). While CVM has been widely used in environmental economics and beyond, its methodological development has occurred almost entirely within a tight circle of environmental economists who emphasize the unique features of environmental applications and have been selective in incorporating findings from research in marketing, cognitive psychology, and behavioral economics; see Carson et al. (2001).

CVM can be viewed as a truncated form of CBC analysis with three important differences. First, CVM most commonly elicits a single or a small number of stated votes on hypothetical referendums, and consequently does not have the experimental design features of CBC that allow extensive tests for the structure and consistency of stated preferences. Second, CVM as it has developed has been utilized primarily for valuation of environmental public goods, and as a consequence often does not have predictive accuracy in markets as a direct yardstick for reliability. Third, the environmental goods in a CVM experiment are usually complex and unfamiliar, and are described in words, numbers, and/or pictures that are very difficult to present in a way that is complete and balanced, and at the same time sufficiently succinct and graphic to keep the subjects' attention.

Other elicitation methods for stated preferences, termed "vignette analysis" and measurement of "subjective well-being," have become popular among some applied economists and political scientists; see Rossi (1979), King et al. (2004), Caro et al. (2012), Kahneman and Krueger (2013). Vignette analysis uses detailed story descriptions of alternatives, often visual, and may improve consumer information and understanding. Vignette presentations of alternatives can be used within conjoint analysis experiments, and may improve subject attention and understanding of alternatives.

Subjective well-being methods elicit overall self-assessments of welfare, often on Likert or rating scales similar to those used in the early days of conjoint analysis; see Kahneman and Krueger (2013). The conditions under which these methods are reliable enough for policy conclusions are still largely undetermined. In the instances where vignette and subjective well-being methods have been tested, they have proven to be strongly influenced by context and anchoring effects that would tend to reduce forecast accuracy in market demand forecasting applications; see Deaton (2012).

To this day, SP methods, and particularly CVM, remain controversial in the economics community, and SP results are often dismissed, frequently with cause but sometimes without. In the remainder of this chapter, I discuss the track record of CBC for forecasting demand for ordinary market products, and experimental design features and circumstances that seem to be required for reliable demand forecasts. I conclude by drawing lessons from this record for applications of CBC and CVM methods for use and non-use valuations of environmental public goods.

CHOICE-BASED CONJOINT STUDY DESIGN

A CBC analysis offers subjects a series of menus of alternative products with profiles giving levels of their attributes, including price, and asks them to identify which product they most prefer in each menu. The menus of products and their descriptions are designed to realistically mimic a market experience, where a consumer is presented with various competing alternatives and chooses one of the options. By changing the attribute levels available for the included products and presenting each consumer with several menus, the researcher obtains information on the relative importance that the consumer places on each of the attributes. The classic CBC setup in marketing might be a laboratory experiment where subjects are asked to sample actual products with the different profiles, and then asked for their choices from different menus. For example, subjects might be given tastes of cola drinks from menus, with various degrees of sweetness, carbonation, flavor, and price for the different products, and asked to pick one from each menu. However, CBC can also be used for familiar products whose features are simply described in words and pictures, with subjects asked to choose from a menu of products based on these descriptions. The paper towel example in Table 1 mimics the menus a consumer sees when going to Amazon.com to look for these products. A major application of CBC in market research has been to experiment on automobile brand and model choice. These studies describe alternatives in terms of price and attributes such as horsepower, fuel consumption, number of seats, and cargo space, and in some cases give subjects experience in a driving simulator and the opportunity to consult reviews and man-on-the-street opinions. These studies can determine with considerable predictive accuracy the distributions of preference weights that consumers give to various vehicle features, and the automobiles they will buy; see Urban et al. (1990, 1997); Brownstone and Train (1999), Brownstone et al. (2000), and Train and Winston (2007).

The levels of attributes of the products offered on different menus can be set by experimental design so that it is possible to separate statistically the weights that consumers give to the different attributes. In the early days, menu designs were often of a "complete profile" form that mimicked classical experimental design and allowed simple computation of "part-worths" from rating responses, but currently the emphasis is simply on ensuring that menus are realistic and incorporate sufficient independent variation in the attributes so that the impact of each attribute on choice can be isolated statistically.

Conjoint analysis methods can be expected to work relatively well for preferences among consumer market goods when the task is choice among a small number of realistic, relatively familiar, and fully described alternatives, with clear and well-understood incentives for truthful response. The idea behind incentives is that when subjects have a realistic chance of really getting what they say they prefer, and they understand this, they have a positive disincentive to misrepresent their preferences and risk getting an inferior outcome. Studies of conjoint methods show that they are in general less reliable and less directly useful for predicting behavior when the task is to rate products on some scale, or to adjust some attribute (e.g., price) to make alternatives indifferent; these seem to induce cognitive "task-solving" responses different from the task of maximizing preferences; see Wright and Kriewall (1980), Chapman and Staelin (1982), and Elrod et al. (1992). Asking follow-up questions within a single menu also seems to induce a different mind-set than simple choice. For example, a study might follow up a stated choice with a question about the second-best choice among the remaining alternatives, a question as to whether the consumer would stay with first stated choice if the price of one of the alternatives were reduced, or questions about the perceived attributes of various alternatives. Empirical experience is that such follow-up questions elicit responses that are not always consistent with the initial stated choices, even though they do not differ much in their framing from market experiences; see Beggs et al. (1981). The explanation may be that the initial menu "anchors" perceptions and shadows subsequent responses, or that follow-up questions induce a "bargaining" mind-set that invites strategic responses; see Hanemann et al. (1991) and Green et al. (1998). Responses to follow-up questions on preferences can also be colored by self-justification.

Conjoint methods can be expected to be less reliable when the products are unfamiliar or incompletely described, or involve public good aspects that induce respondents to incorporate social welfare judgments; for example, when preferences for automobile models are stated in an elicitation that emphasizes the energy footprint of the models, and environmental consequences. Valuation of non-use aspects of natural resources are particularly challenging for conjoint methods because these applications seek to measure preferences that are outside normal market experiences of consumers.

There are six important issues that need to be considered when designing a CBC study. These also apply to CVM considered as a variety of CBC analysis, although the focus on market forecasting reliability applies only to CVM valuation of lost use, since non-use valuations are neither constrained nor disciplined by market benchmarks:

- Familiarity is important. If subjects are experienced with the products or services, and the attributes that are being assessed, then they seem to make more consistent and predictive choices. If possible, subjects should have the opportunity to test for themselves their subjective sensations from different attribute levels. For example, in a study of consumer choice among streaming music services with various attributes, it should improve prediction to give subjects a hands-on experience with different features. These opportunities to acquire and validate information and impressions of products should resemble their opportunities to investigate and experience these features in a real market. This might be done with mock-up working models of the products, or with computer simulation of their operation. However, there is a trade-off: attempting to train consumers, and providing mock-ups, can inadvertently create anchoring effects. Consumers who are unfamiliar with a product may take the wording in the training exercises about the attributes, and the characteristics of the mock-ups, as clues to what they should feel about each attribute. Even the mention of an attribute can give it more prominence in a subject's mind than it would have otherwise. The researcher needs to seriously weigh the often-conflicting goals of making the subject knowledgeable about the products and avoiding influencing their relative values of attributes.

- The researcher needs to decide whether to offer an "outside alternative" in the choice sets, and, if so, how to characterize it to the subjects. The inclusion of a realistic "no purchase" option allows estimation of market shares and price elasticities, while experiments without this option can only be used to estimate demand conditioned on a purchase. If the outside option is included, it is important that the meaning of the option be clearly delineated to subjects. For example, in a car choice exercise, does "no purchase" mean that the subject would use a vehicle that the household currently owns and reconsider options next year, or what? In a CVM referendum response, will there be opportunities later to support interventions the subject considers more appropriately scaled or more cost-effective? A danger is that the "no purchase option" can be interpreted differently by different subjects, and can easily become a way for subjects to avoid the effort of resolving difficult trade-offs. Whether and how to include an outside option is an important experimental design decision. If it is not included, it will be necessary to use external market share data to constrain or calibrate the choice model fitted to the CBC data so that it can make complete market demand predictions.
- If possible, the conjoint study should be "incentive compatible"; that is, subjects should have a positive incentive to be truthful in their responses. For example, suppose subjects are promised a Visa cash card, and then offered menus and asked to state whether or not they would purchase a product with a profile of attributes and price, with the instruction that at the end of the experiment, their choice from

one of their menus will be delivered, and the price of the product in that menu deducted from their cash card balance. If they never choose a product, then they get the full Visa balance. If subjects learn, perhaps with training or experience, that it is in their interest to say they would choose a product if and only if its value to them is higher than its price, then they have a positive incentive to be truthful, and the experiment is said to be "incentive aligned" or "incentive compatible."

- In many situations it will not be practical to provide an incentive-compatible format while maintaining the objectives of the analysis. The researcher might want to consider combinations of attributes that are not currently available, such as testing consumers' reactions to new features during the design phase of a manufacturers' product development. For existing but expensive products, a lottery that offers a chance of receiving a chosen alternative may be incentive compatible in principle, but the probabilities required to make it practical may be so low that subjects do not take the offer seriously. For example, suppose a CBC experiment on preferences for automobiles asks a subject to choose between a car with a selling price of $40,000 and $40,000 in cash, and told that she has a 1 in 10,000 lottery chance of receiving her choice. If she declines the car when her true value $V > $40,000, then her *expected* loss is $V/10,000 − $4, a small number. This incentive is still enough in principle to induce a rational consumer to state truthfully whether she prefers the car. However, misperceptions of low-probability events, mistrust of lotteries, and attitudes toward risk may in practice lead the consumer to ignore this incentive or view it as insufficient to overcome other motivations for misleading statements.
- The researcher needs to decide how "far down" to explore stated preference orderings. Subjects' first choice (i.e., most preferred option) is most natural to consumers, since it mimics their regular purchasing task. Second choice, third choice, and so on, can be colored by framing dynamics and may be less reliable for predicting market behavior; see Beggs et al. (1981), McFadden (1981), Louviere's (1988) "best-worst" choice setup, Green et al. (1998), Hurd and McFadden (1998), and List and Gallet (2001).
- Where possible, CBC results should be tested against and calibrated to consumer behavior in real markets. In some cases, CBC menus will coincide with product offerings in existing markets. In this case, it is useful to compare models estimated from the CBC study and the market data to assess whether people are weighing attributes similarly. Improved forecasts may be obtained by imposing real market

constraints such as product shares on the estimation of choice models from CBC data, by calibrating CBC model parameters to satisfy market constraints, or by combining CBC and market choice data and estimating a combined model with scaling and shift parameters for CBC data as needed; see Hensher et al. (1999).
- CBC studies should when possible embed tests for response distortions that are commonly observed in cognitive experiments, such as anchoring to cues in the elicitation format, reference point or status quo bias, extension neglect, hypersensitivity to context, and shadowing from earlier questions and elicitations. While some of these cognitive effects also appear to influence market choices, many are specific to the CBC experience and have the potential to reduce forecasting accuracy. Ideally, a well-designed CBC study will not show much sensitivity of its bottom-line willingness-to-pay (WTP) values to these sources of possible response distortion.

The following subsections expand on some of these conditions and other important requirements for reliable demand prediction using CBC data.

Sampling and Recruitment

Target populations may differ depending on the objectives of the study – for example, current users, current and potential users, and the general population. An important consideration is whether the target population is individuals, families considered as unitary decision-makers, or family or social group with related but not identical preferences, and in the latter cases how to identify a knowledgeable spokesperson for the group. It is important that the sampling frame draw randomly from the target population, without excessive weighting to correct for stratification and non-response, or use of convenience samples that can contain unobserved sampling biases. However, not all members of the target population may have the background needed to make informed product choices. Then it may be more informative to study the preferences of experienced users, and separately study the differences in users and non-users. An example might be study of consumer demand for relatively esoteric technical attributes of products, say the levels of encryption built into telecommunications devices, where only technically savvy device users will appreciate the meaning of different encryption levels. In this case, a good study design may be to conduct an intensive conjoint analysis on technically knowledgeable users, and separately survey the target population to estimate the extent and depth of technical knowledge, and the impact of technical information on the purchase propensities of general users and non-users.

Relatively universal Internet access has led to less expensive and more effective surveying via the Internet than by telephone, mail, or personal interview. However, it is risky to use Internet convenience samples recruited from volunteers, as even with weighting to make them representative in terms of demographics, they can behave quite differently than a target population of possible product buyers. Better practice is to use a reliable method such as random sampling of addresses, then recruit subjects for the Internet panel from the sampled addresses. It is important to compensate subjects for participation at sufficient levels to minimize selection due to attrition; see McFadden (2012). Experience with "professional" subjects who are paid to participate in Internet panels is positive: subjects who view responding as a continuing "job" with rewards for effort are more attentive and consistent in their responses.

Experimental Design

The design of a conjoint experiment establishes the number of menus offered to each subject, the number of products on each menu, the number of attributes and attribute levels introduced for each product, and the design of the profiles of the products placed on each menu. Some other aspects of a conjoint study, the setup and introduction to the experiment given to each subject, subject training, and incentives, might be considered components of the design, but will here be treated separately. There are four distinct considerations that enter conjoint experimental designs.

The first consideration is that for good statistical identification of the valuations of separate attributes, the design needs to allow considerable linearly independent variation in the levels of different attributes, and a considerable span of attribute levels. The classical statistical literature on experimental design focused on analysis of variance and emphasized orthogonality properties that permitted simple computation of effects, and treatments that provided minimum variance estimates. Designs that reduce some measure of the sampling variance under specified model parameters (such as the determinant of the covariance matrix for "D-efficiency") have been implemented in market research by Kuhfield et al. (1994), Bliemer and Rose (2009), Rose and Bliemer (2009), and others. It is important that conjoint studies be designed to yield good statistical estimates, but there is relatively little to be gained from adherence to designs with classical completeness and orthogonality properties. First, with contemporary computers, the computational simplifications from orthogonal designs are usually unimportant. Second, for the non-linear models used with CBC, orthogonality of attributes does not in general minimize sampling variance. Unlike classical analysis of variance problems, it is not usually possible in non-linear choice models to specify efficient designs in advance of knowing the parameters that are the target of the analysis.

The second consideration is the formatting, clarity, and prominence of attributes and prices of products presented in CBC studies. These presentations are critical aspects of real market environments, and are correspondingly important in realistic hypothetical markets. Advertising and point-of-sale product presentations in real markets often feature "hooks" that attract the consumers' attention and make products appealing, and understate or shroud attributes that may discourage buyers. Thus, prices may not be prominently displayed, or may be presented in a format that shrouds the final cost; for example, promotions of "sales" or "percent-off" discounts without stating prices, statements of prices without add-ons such as sales taxes and baggage fees, and subscriptions at initial "teaser" rates. Products like mobile phones, automobiles, and hospital treatments are often sold with total cost obscured or shrouded, often through ambiguous contract terms, through a two-part tariff that combines an access price and a usage fee, or through framing (e.g., "pennies a day"). A CBC study that is reliable for forecasting evidently needs to mimic the market in its presentation of product costs, incorporating the same attention-getting, persuasion, ambiguities and shrouding that consumers see in the real market.

The third consideration is that relatively mechanistic statistical approaches to setting attribute levels may lead to profiles that are unrealistic, or are dominated by the profiles of other products on a menu. Considerable care is needed to balance statistical objectives with realism of the experiment; see Huber and Zwerina (1996). Menus and their framing that are unlike familiar market settings invite cognitive responses that differ from those that appear to determine preferences and drive choices in market settings. There is a tendency for subjects to approach surveys as if they were school exams – they cast about for "correct" answers by making inferences on what the experimenter is looking for. While some may use their responses to air opinions, most give honest answers, but not necessarily to the question posed by the experimenter. They may "solve" problems other than recovering and stating their true preferences, indicating instead the alternative that seems the most familiar, the most feasible, the least cost, the best bargain, or the most socially responsible; see Schkade and Payne (1993).

The fourth consideration is that prominence and ease of comparison are known to be factors that influence the attention subjects give to different aspects of decision problems; for example, there is a claim that subjects in their stated choices systematically place more weight on price relative to other product attributes than they do in real markets, perhaps because this dimension is clearly visible and comparisons are easy in a conjoint analysis menu, whereas prices in real markets often come with qualifications and may not be displayed side by side. Widespread folklore in marketing is that subjects have trouble processing more than six attributes and more than four or five products, and begin to exhibit fatigue when making choices from more than 20 menus; see Johnson and Orme (1996). Beyond these limits, they appear to use *filtering* heuristics, taking "short cuts" by eliminating consideration of some products and attributes using simple heuristics, and considering trade-offs only on the remainder. Often conjoint analysts will address this behavior by limiting the dimensionality of the attribute profile, explicitly or implicitly asking subjects to assume that in all other dimensions, the products are comparable to brands currently in the market. This leaves subjects free to make possibly heterogeneous and unrealistic assumptions about these omitted attributes, or requires them to digest and remember lengthy specifications for omitted attributes and their assumed levels. These design restrictions may make responses more consistent and easy to analyze, but they may not improve prediction. Filtering heuristics also seem to be used in real markets with many complex products, such as the market for houses. If the primary focus of the conjoint study is prediction, then the best design may be to make the experiment as realistic as possible, with approximately the same numbers and complexity of products as in a real market with similar products, and possibly sequential search, so that consumers face similar cognitive challenges and respond similarly even if decision-making is less single-minded than neoclassical preference maximization. However, if the primary focus is measurement of consumer welfare, there are deeper problems in linking well-being to demand behavior influenced by filtering. While it may be possible to design simple choice experiments that eliminate filtering and give internally consistent statements of consumer welfare, there is currently no good theoretical or empirical framework for using filtering-influenced consumer choice in either real or hypothetical markets to calculate neoclassical economic measures of well-being.

Subject Training

Extensive experiments from cognitive psychology show that context, framing, and subject preparation can have large, even outsize, effects on subject response. It is particularly important that subjects have familiarity with the products and features they are being asked to evaluate that is comparable to their real market experiences, as attention, context, and framing effects are particularly strong when subjects are asked to respond in unusual or unfamiliar circumstances. Familiarity may be automatic if the target population is experienced users of a particular line of products. For inexperienced users, tutorials on the products and hands-on experience can reduce careless or distorted responses, but may also influence stated preferences in ways that reduce forecasting accuracy.

It is useful to recognize that training of subjects can occur at several levels, and that training can manipulate as well as educate, leading to unreliable demand predictions. First, subjects have to get used to answering questions that may be difficult or intrusive, and learn that it is easier or more rewarding to be truthful than to prevaricate. Some of this is mechanical: practice with using a computer for an Internet-based conjoint survey, and moving through screens, buttons, and branches in a survey instrument. Second, subjects need to be educated as to what the task of stating preferences is. Subjects can be taught in "Decision-Making 101" how to optimize outcomes with assigned preferences, and how to avoid mistakes such as confusing the intrinsic desirability of a product with process issues such as availability or dominance by alternatives. Such training can be highly manipulative, leading to behavior that is very different from and not predictive for real market choices. But real markets are also manipulative, providing the "street" version of "Decision-Making 101" that teaches by experience the consequences of poor choices. The goal of a conjoint study designed for prediction should be to anticipate and mimic the training that real markets provide. Third, the study designer needs to determine what information will be conveyed to the subject, in what format, and assess what information the subject retains and understands. Typically a conjoint survey begins by describing the types of products the subject will be asked to evaluate, their major attributes, and the structure of the elicitation, asking for most preferred alternatives from a series of menus. Details may be given on the nature and relevance of particular attributes. Instructions may be given on the time the subject has to respond, and what rules they should follow in answering. For example, the survey may either encourage or discourage the subject from consulting with other family members, finding and operating past products in the same line, or consulting outside sources of information such as Internet searches. Finally, subjects need to be instructed on the incentives they face, and the consequences of their stated choices. At various stages in subject training, they may be monitored or tested to determine if they have acquired information and understand it. For example, a protocol in market research called "information acceleration" gives subjects the opportunity to interactively access product descriptions, consumer reviews, and media reports, and through click-stream recording and inquiries during the choice process collects data on time spent viewing information sources and its impact on interim propensities. This protocol seems to improve subject attention and understanding of product features, and also identify the sources and content of information that has high impact on stated choices; see Urban et al. (1990, 1997).

In summary, while training may educate subjects so they are familiar with the products being compared, it is difficult to design training that is neutral and non-manipulative. Real markets are in fact often manipulative, via advertising and peer advice, and one goal for CBC is to achieve accurate prediction by mimicking the advertising and other elements of persuasion the consumer will encounter in the real market. One caution is that particularly in cases where preferences are not well formed in advance, subjects will be particularly vulnerable to manipulation, and training that embodies manipulation that is not realistic risks inducing stated responses that are not predictive for real market behavior.

Training and context seem to have particularly strong effects on subjects asked to value complex and unfamiliar environmental goods, particularly non-use valuations. The suggested benchmark for market goods, that training and information presentations in hypothetical elicitations be designed to mimic these processes in real markets, is obviously not available for non-use valuations. A fundamental question in this case is whose preferences are being solicited, the perhaps poorly formed and unformed preferences of untrained consumers in the general population, or the presumably informed, but possibly not representative, educated preferences of trained jurists. In the first case, CVM mimics direct democracy by referendum, as practiced in Switzerland or California, and in the second case, elicitations from trained respondents mimic the choices of presumably informed grand jurors, judges, or legislators. In practice, direct referendums and decisions by untrained juries are seldom cited as models for thoughtful, consistent public decision-making, although our judicial system mandates their use to avoid systematic biases that can enter the decisions of professional experts. If one is in a well-functioning, effective, and informed representative democracy, admittedly a big if, then one would expect that professional legislators aided by their experts would understand the issues and the preferences of their constituents, and would provide the most reliable mechanism for expressing values for environmental goods. Then, well-trained respondents in carefully designed SP experiments might be envisioned as providing the "expert valuations" that legislators need as input to rational public policy decisions on environmental issues.

Incentive Alignment

Economic theorists have developed mechanisms for incentive-compatible elicitation of preferences for both private and public goods. The simplest offer the subject a positive probability that every stated choice will be *pivotal* and result in a real transaction. If subjects understand the offer, the probabilities are sufficiently high so that the subject does not dismiss them as negligible, and subjects view the transactions as being paid for from their own budgets rather than in terms of "house money" that they feel is not really theirs, then it is a dominant strategy for the subject to honestly state whether or not a product with a given profile of attributes is worth more to them than its price; this is shown by Randall et al. (1974) and Green et al. (1998) for a leading variant of this mechanism due to Becker et al. (1964). For more general settings, including menus with multiple alternatives, McFadden (2012) shows that the Groves-Clarke mechanism (Groves and Loeb, 1975) is incentive-compatible when consumers empaneled in an informed jury embrace the incentives. However, the experimental evidence is that people have difficulty understanding, accepting, and acting on the incentives in these mechanisms. Thus, it can be quite difficult in practice to ensure incentive alignment in a CBC, or to determine in the absence of strong incentives whether subjects are responding truthfully. Fortunately, there is also considerable evidence that while it is important to get subjects to pay attention and answer carefully, they are mostly honest in their responses irrespective of the incentives offered or how well they are understood; see Bohm (1972), Bohm et al. (1997), Camerer and Hogarth (1999), Yadav (2007), and Dong et al. (2010). This provides some encouragement for applications where it is impractical to provide effective incentives. However, the argument for a simple link between stated choices or referendum votes and consumer welfare is particularly weak in the absence of incentives to be truthful.

Incentive compatibility has been a particular issue for CVM. While it is not difficult in principle to design incentive-compatible elicitation mechanisms, the biggest problem is to get subjects to understand and accept the offered incentives. This is particularly problematic for elicitations of values for large-scale environmental goods, such as protection of endangered species, where subjects are likely to be justifiably skeptical that the environmental change as stated would actually be delivered at the stated cost, or that their response has a non-negligible chance of being pivotal.

Reconciliation and Validation

An advantage of CBC experimental designs is that through the presentation of a slate of menus, there is an opportunity to test the consistency of individual stated choices with neoclassical preference theory, to confront respondents and ask them to explain and reconcile stated choices, and to incorporate menus that allow direct cross-validation between stated and revealed market choices. For example, menus can be offered that allow for the possibility of testing whether stated choices are consistent with the axioms of revealed preference, and specifically whether they violate the transitivity property of preferences. Even under the more relaxed standard that consumers have stochastic preferences with new preference draws for each choice, their responses can be tested for the regularity property that adding alternatives cannot increase the probability that a previous alternative is chosen. If menus contain current market alternatives, and past purchase behavior of the subjects is known, then one can test whether revealed and stated preferences for the same alternatives are consistent in their weighting of attributes. For example, Morikawa et al. (2002) find that there are systematic differences in weights given to attributes between stated and revealed choices, and that predictions from stated choices can be sharpened by calibrating them to revealed preferences; see also Ben-Akiva and Morikawa (1990), Hensher and Bradley (1993), and Brownstone et al. (2000). This step of testing and validating CBC is important particularly in studies where verisimilitude of the conjoint menus and congruity of the cognitive tools respondents use in experimental and real situations are in question, for example when the products being studied are complex and unfamiliar, such as choices of college, house to purchase, cancer treatment to pursue, or remedies for environmental damages. A large literature compares and tests stated preference elicitation methods, and is relevant to questions of CBC reliability: see Huber (1975, 1987), Rao (1977, 2014), Carmone et al. (1978), Hauser and Koppelman (1979), Hauser and Urban (1979), Jain et al. (1979), Acito and Jain (1980), Neslin (1981), Segal (1982), Akaah and Korgaonkar (1983), Bateson et al. (1987), Train et al. (1987), Louviere (1988), Reibstein et al. (1988), Srinivasan (1988), Huber et al. (1993), McFadden (1994), Huber and Zwerina (1996), Orme (1999), Huber and Train (2001), Hauser and Rao (2002), Raghavarao et al. (2010), and Miller et al. (2011).

In marketing applications, it is possible to validate CBC forecasts against actual market performance of new or modified products, judged by market shares in the population or in population segments. I have found only selective surveys of the performance of forecasts from CBC studies. Natter and Feurstein (2002) compare consumer-level CBC forecasts with scanner data on actual purchases, and conclude that accounting for individual heterogeneity leads to market-level forecasts no better than aggregate models. However, they do not use a statistical method that accounts for the unreliable estimation of individual preference weights. Moore (2004) compares CBC with other elicitation and forecasting methods, and concludes that CBC data analyzed using the methods described in this chapter outperformed the alternatives. Wittick and Bergestuen (2001) cite studies in which CBC forecasts of market shares of data terminals, commuter modes, state lottery products, personal computers, and fork-lift trucks are close to actual results, and conclude that "[t]hese results provide strong support for the validity of self-explicated conjoint models in predicting marketplace choice behavior." At a disaggregate level, Wittink and Montgomery (1979) use CBC data to estimate individual weights on eight attributes of jobs open to MBA graduates, and four months later observe actual job choices and the actual attributes of jobs offered. They report 63% accuracy (percentage of hits) in predicting the jobs students chose out of those offered, compared to a 26% expected hit rate if the students had chosen randomly. They attribute the failure to achieve higher accuracy to noise in estimates of weights for individuals, and to the influence of job attributes not included in the CBC study. They conclude: "On balance, the published results of forecast accuracy are very supportive of the value of conjoint results." They do caution that "[o]ne should keep in mind that positive results (conjoint analysis providing accurate forecasts) are favored over negative results for publication. Nevertheless, the evidence suggests that marketplace forecasts have validity."

Based on my own experience with CBC and review of the marketing literature, I conclude that CBC-based market demand forecasts for the population or for large consumer segments are reasonably predictive for familiar products, or products whose attributes are easily extrapolated from past experience. Further, I conclude that uneven performance in some studies is likely due to failure to follow the design principles given in this section, and failures at the stages of modeling, estimation, and forecasting, rather than any intrinsic inability of subjects to state preferences accurately. On the other hand, the evidence is that when respondents have not had market experience with products similar to the ones being studied, or the products in the study have attributes or attribute levels that are unfamiliar, CBC responses are often hypersensitive to framing and context effects, making it very difficult to design elicitations that will give reliable market demand forecasts.

Making CBC Menus Realistic

The CBC design discussion has emphasized product familiarity and menu realism as key ingredients in successful demand forecasting studies. To explore these problems at a concrete level, consider the problem of estimating consumer preferences for red table wines in order to guide blending and pricing decisions. Suppose that in preliminary focus groups, it is found that in addition to *price* per 750ml bottle the attributes that consumers mention as important are *appearance* (brilliant, clear, hazy, cloudy), *bouquet* (outstandingly complex and balanced, distinguished, pleasant, flat, offensive), *aroma/scent* (Figure 1), *taste and texture* (smooth and full-bodied, good balance with some imperfections, undistinguished, noticeable off-flavors, objectionable flavors), *aftertaste* (outstanding, pleasant, undistinguished, unpleasant), *dryness* (crisp, sensation of residual sugar, sweet), *acidity* (sour, bright, soft), *alcohol content* (percent by volume), *Wine Spectator* magazine rating (60–100), and whether the grapes used to make the wine come from an *organic* vineyard. In a typical CBC study, subjects intercepted in a supermarket would be asked to make choices from eight menus, with each menu containing a no-purchase alternative and

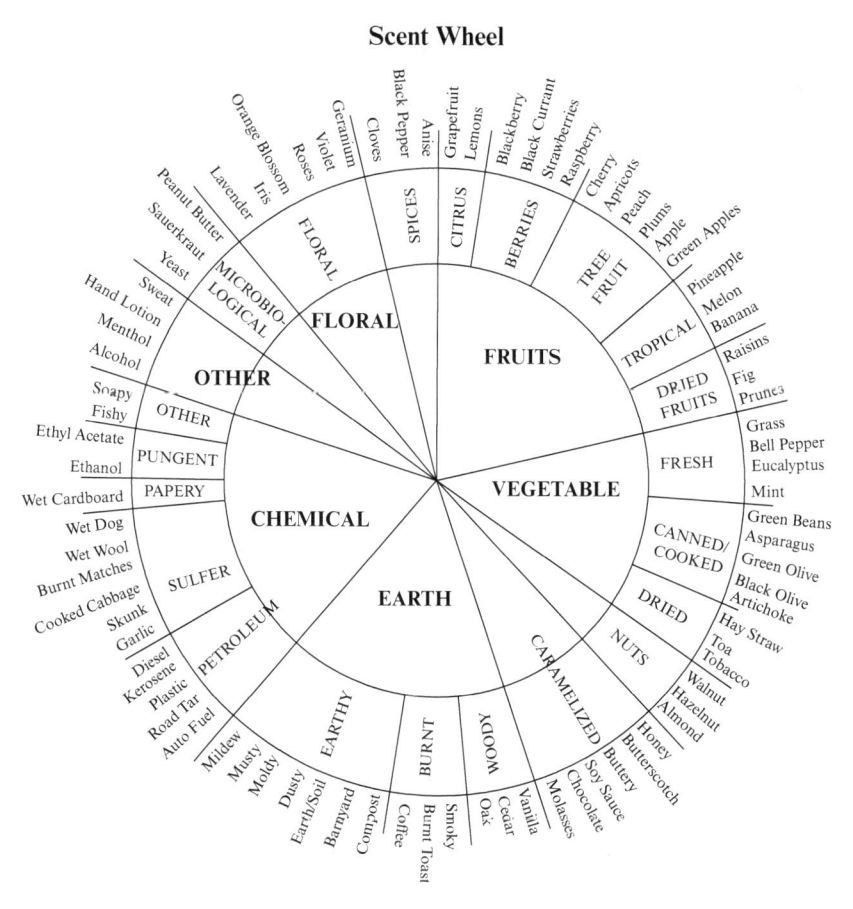

Scent Wheel

Source: Accessed December 5, 2016 at http://www.nathankramer.com/wine/wine_lists/smelling.htm.

Figure 1   Aroma/scent attributes of wine

three alternative bottles of wine, described in pictures and in words giving price and attributes, and/or offered in tastes. To motivate participation and for incentive alignment, subjects might be instructed that at the end of the experiment, they will receive one of their eight menu choices plus a Visa cash card for the balance after paying for the product they choose (or the full balance if they chose the no-purchase option on this menu).

A first question in the design of the CBC experiment is how to describe attributes, and set price and attribute levels. Three (sometimes conflicting) criteria are realism, inclusion of existing products (to aid physical tasting, fulfillment of the incentive scheme, and calibration to market data), and sufficient independent variation to allow estimation of the distribution of consumer trade-offs across attributes. Realism requires that prices be in the general range of the subject's experience, and that menus exclude obviously dominated products; for example, the same wine at two different prices. A second question is how to map attributes consumers can understand and relate to, or sensations that consumers experience and consider in making choices, into technical attributes of wines that can be controlled in the production process, such as pH (unbuffered acidity), total acidity (g/L), volatile acidity (g/L), alcohol content (volume percentage), residual sugar (Brix), levels (mg/L) of compounds that influence aroma and taste (e.g., total monomers, total tannins, malic and lactic acid balance, pigmented polymers, catechin, sulfates, free sulfur), and levels of undesirable compounds (ethyl acetate, 2,4,6-trichloroanisole). Most consumers will not be familiar with these technical attributes, and would be unable to incorporate them consistently into stated tastes for different products. One solution is to train subjects to evaluate the products on the basis of these dimensions. For example, with a great deal of wine consumption, subjects may learn to map wine tastes into the scent wheel in Figure 1, and conversely to anticipate accurately the taste of a wine characterized by adjectives in this figure. A panel of experts may be able to map attribute levels that consumers have learned to consistently evaluate and report into technical attributes controlled in the process of making the product; thus, the mapping between chemical scents reported by consumers and flaws in the production process. However, these complex steps may still fail to forecast correctly consumer choices in real market settings in response to the selective information these markets provide, and it may be beyond the capacities of CBC survey design to describe attributes such as the scents in Figure 1 in menus that subjects can understand.

The incentive alignment described above, offering a chosen alternative from one of the menus each subject faces, will be feasible only if one of the stated choices is an existing product. Otherwise, it may not be possible to fulfill a promised transaction. Incentives can be aligned through more general promises to deliver an available product (or cash) consistent with the subject's stated preferences, but it is likely to be more difficult for the subject to recognize that this makes it in their interest to be truthful.

Whether subjects view the offered prices as reasonable, or a purchase as tempting, will depend on their unknown shopping histories and wine inventories, their expectations regarding availability and prices of wine elsewhere, particularly awareness of and response to real market promotions and sales, and their anticipations of how they will feel if they receive wine from the experiment. In particular, it is important how a "no purchase" option is framed and interpreted. Without prompts, subjects will probably think of the offered menus in the context of their past consumption and current stock of wine at home, and of their options for purchasing wine when they next go to the market. These factors also enter real market purchase decisions, so this context may be realistic, but without measurement or control it is risky to assume that the real environment of the CBC experiment will also prevail in future real markets. Alternately, subjects could be prompted to "think only in terms of what combination of money and wine you leave the experiment with today," but clearly this prompt may elicit different behavior than a prompt such as "Suppose you are on your way to get-together with friends, wine is one of the possible things you could bring, and the menus you see in this experiment are your only opportunity to buy wine" or a prompt such as "You can always take your cash card and buy wine from the regular supermarket shelves if that is more appealing to you than the wines available through this experiment." Some benchmarking to real market penetration rates for wine purchases is likely to be needed to correct for distortion in wine-buying propensity induced by the experience of participating in the experiment and the prompts it contains. Overall, the usefulness of having the "no purchase" option will depend on its being given a sufficiently specific description and context so that it corresponds realistically to the options and attention the consumer will have in the forecast market.

Data Analysis

The CBC elicitation format produces data on choices from hypothetical market experiments that must then be analyzed to model preferences. Simulations from these preferences can then be used to predict market demands for products in the future with different attribute profiles or prices, and if stated consumer behavior is judged to be consistent with (random) utility maximization, used to measure the impact on consumer welfare of changes in product prices and attributes. In marketing, the most widely used model for this analysis is a mixed (or random coefficients) multinomial logit form, with hierarchical Bayes estimation; see McFadden (1986), Allenby and Rossi (1999, 2006), McFadden and Train (2000), Train and Winston (2007), and Ben-Akiva et al. (2016). The population preference heterogeneity in this model seems to be necessary to reliably predict demands. Further, a number of details seem to be important. It is important to allow correlation in random parameters attached to different product attributes; see Haaijer et al. (1998). It is often important to allow the possibility of market segmentation in which some attributes or products are of no value for some segments of the population. For stable and reliable estimates of WTP for various product attributes, it is useful to model consumer utility in what is termed "money metric" or "WTP" form; see Train and Weeks (2005) and Ben-Akiva et al. (2016). Finally, it is important to be careful in translating changes in attributes of products into changes in consumer well-being when tastes are heterogeneous so that selection becomes an issue, and to define welfare changes consistent with policy alternatives considered and transfers made prior to choice. Hierarchical Bayes estimation methods combined with realistically flexible distributions of model parameters across people then allow simulation-based prediction of market demand. It is then relatively straightforward to infer the impact on utility, or consumer surplus, from adding or altering a product in the market; McFadden (2016) discusses the details of the welfare calculus. The most serious defect in this program comes when consumer choice behavior is so inconsistent and context dependent that the logical connection between consumer choice and well-being breaks down. This is a problem for all of welfare economics predicated on the neoclassical assumptions of maximization of predetermined preferences, but it is particularly acute in SP studies where market discipline of deviations from self-interest breaks down.

CBC Failures

There are a number of things that can go wrong with a CBC experiment and render it unreliable, even when the "necessary" experimental conditions described in this section are met. Mostly, these come from inconsistencies in consumer choice behavior, and in failures of consumers to attend to or understand the task, the alternatives, or the offered incentives. For example, McFadden et al. (1988) find a strong "status quo bias" in a CBC study of electricity reliability choices – there are consistent trade-offs between reliability and cost for alternatives other than the subject's status quo, but a strong distaste for moving away from the status quo, no matter what its initial level. McFadden (1994) finds "extension bias" in CBC responses, a phenomenon related to preferences over alternatives of different scope – subjects discount the size dimension of product comparisons. Green et al. (1998) find strong "anchoring biases" that are similar in both estimation and valuation tasks, suggesting that subjects think about and estimate uncertain facts and uncertain preferences in similar ways. Morikawa et al. (2002) merge stated and revealed preference data, and find evidence that subjects make *similar but not identical trade-offs* in the two circumstances. Ariely (2009) and McFadden (1998, 1999, 2014a, 2014b) give a broader list of cognitive effects on consumer behavior. Researchers collecting stated preference data need to be keenly aware of how cognitive effects can influence subject's responses, develop elicitation methods that minimize the distortions in apparent preferences these effects can produce, and find testing and calibration methods that detect and correct for the presence of these effects.

There is a qualitative difference between the impact of inconsistencies in stated or revealed consumer choice behavior on the reliability of demand forecasts and on the reliability of measures of consumer well-being. Market demand forecasting has the relatively robust feature that so long as the distribution of decision-making rules in the population is stationary and a CBC experiment is realistic, mimicking well the information, manipulations, incentives, and social context of choices in real markets, then models fitted to the CBC data will usually forecast successfully even if consumers systematically deviate from neoclassical utility maximization so that the forecasting model predicated on utility maximization is only an approximation. However, the tight neoclassical link between choice behavior and consumer welfare that holds under utility maximization, allowing changes in well-being to be inferred from consumer surplus calculations, breaks down when choices are inconsistent with utility maximization. In this case, there is no foundation for a supposition that neoclassical consumer surplus measures are reliable indicators of well-being.

The question remains whether stated WTP or well-being might provide satisfactory measures of consumer welfare even if choice behavior is inconsistent with neoclassical utility maximization. The answer in short is that there are currently no accepted scientific principles that support such an inference. In particular, the economic theory of markets, and the methods of neoclassical economics, provide no support for direct elicitation of well-being. While it is possible that psychological scales of well-being, such as those promoted by Kahneman and Krueger (2013), may develop to the point where they can pass reasonable tests for reliability and plausibility, their current implementations are far too sensitive to context and framing to be useful now; see Deaton (2012). It is also possible that in the future the tools of neuroeconomics can provide a physiological basis for measures of well-being that can be tied to stated choices and WTP. Khaw et al. (2015) find that elicitations of values for ordinary market goods and for use values of environmental goods provoke similar brain activity in MRI scans, but elicitations for non-use values are processed differently. However, this is an early paper, and a full investigation will require substantial progress in brain science. Pending such developments, there is no scientific basis for a claim that in situations where choice behavior cannot pass tests for consistency with utility maximization, stated WTP for changes in attributes of alternatives is reliable.

LESSONS FOR VALUATION OF ENVIRONMENTAL PUBLIC GOODS

Applications of SP methods to environmental use values raise similar questions to applications of CBC to conventional products and services. Carson (2012), Hausman (2012), and Kling et al. (2012) discuss the particular challenges of using CVM for natural resource valuation. To the extent that consumers are unfamiliar with market transactions for environmental goods, the challenges are similar to those of forecasting demand for unfamiliar consumer products. Extensive training is likely to be necessary to get subjects to think of their CBC offerings in the same way they do personal market purchases, and the framing and context provided by this training itself can manipulate stated preferences. Issues are (1) that preferences may not be well formed, and consequently may be particularly susceptible to manipulation coming from the framing of attributes and ranges of attribute levels, and order and emphasis that influence prominence of different attributes, (2) that personal preferences are sensitive to social judgments that are difficult to frame and control in an experiment, and (3) subjects may not be persuaded that the incentive alignment they are offered is real. For these reasons, CBC or CVM elicitation of WTP for use of environmental goods face major hurdles to the achievement of consistency and reproducibility.

For valuation of lost use, such as lost opportunities for anglers when streams are closed due to hazardous waste, the services involved may be sufficiently familiar, and the elicitations may be sufficiently similar to ordinary market opportunities, so that the CBC methods may prove reliable. However, all the cautions that apply to conventional marketing applications of CBC also apply here, and these environmental good applications will often be low on the reliability gradient, involving public good and social aspects that can interfere with individual utility assessments, and requiring unfamiliar stated purchase choices. At best, CBC elicitations of use values are likely to require extensive validation through merger of stated and revealed preference data. For example, Myer et al. (2010) summarize findings from CVM studies of the recreational use value of birdwatching, and show a great range of valuations. Some of this variation is due to differences in bird populations and birdwatching opportunities, but the greatest part of the variation seems to come from apparently modest differences in CVM study design and analysis methods. A question for future research is whether moving from CVM and econometric methods appropriate for such data (e.g., Cameron and James, 1987; Cameron, 1988; Cameron and Quiggin, 1994) to CBC designs and hierarchical Bayes methods would reduce the variations in stated use values for environmental services like birdwatching.

The greatest need for stated preference data is in application to environmental non-use values, but here all the circumstances that make market research–oriented CBC unreliable are reinforced. My judgment is that to this point no one has been able to develop and demonstrate stated preference methods that are reliable for valuation of non-use claims. For example, consider the demonstrated ability of market researchers to nail down predictions of demand for products such as smartphones with specific attributes and prices. I am not aware of parallel success stories for environmental non-use values. Seemingly innocuous and inconsequential changes in stated preference study designs that should have little influence on neoclassical consumers with well-formed preferences induce major changes in valuations, and there are no good yardsticks for either "correct" study design or results. The combination of consumers who are hypersensitive to context and susceptible to manipulation, and SP analysts who lack market benchmarks to constrain their experimental designs, is toxic for reliability. As noted in the last section for marketing applications, and with more emphasis here for non-use values, I believe that a great deal of scientific work, and some major breakthroughs, will be needed before stated WTP or well-being measures have a sufficient foundation in neuroscience so that they can be measured reliably without close links to revealed market behavior. In my judgment, environmental economists should be more scientifically cautious in weighing the evidence for and against the reliability of stated preference methods, and more prudent in the claims they make for these methods in environmental non-use valuations.

REFERENCES

Acito, F. and A. Jain (1980), "Evaluation of conjoint analysis results: A comparison of methods," *Journal of Marketing Research*, **17**(1), 106–12.

Akaah, I. and P. Korgaonkar (1983), "An empirical comparison of the predictive validity of self-explicated, Huber-hybrid, traditional conjoint, and hybrid conjoint models," *Journal of Marketing Research*, **20**(2), 187–97.

Allenby, G. and P. Rossi (1999), "Marketing models of consumer heterogeneity," *Journal of Econometrics*, **89**(1–2), 57–78.

Allenby, G. and P. Rossi (2006), "Hierarchical Bayes models: A practitioner's guide," in R. Grover and M. Vriens (eds), *The Handbook of Marketing Research*, Thousand Oaks, CA: Sage Publications.

Ariely, D. (2009), *Predictably Irrational*, New York: Harper-Collins.

Bateson, J., D. Reibstein, and W. Boulding (1987), "Conjoint analysis reliability and validity: A framework for future research," in M. Houston (ed.), *Review of Marketing*, Chicago, IL: American Marketing Association, pp. 451–81.

Becker, G., M. DeGroot, and J. Marschak (1964), "Measuring utility by a single-response sequential method," *Behavioral Science*, **9**(3), 226–32.

Beggs, S., S. Cardell, and J. Hausman (1981), "Assessing the potential demand for electric cars," *Journal of Econometrics*, **17**(1), 1–19.

Ben-Akiva, M., D. McFadden, and K. Train (2016), "Foundations of stated preference elicitation," *UC Berkeley Working Paper*, accessed December 4, 2016 at http://eml.berkeley.edu/~train/foundations.pdf.

Ben-Akiva, M. and T. Morikawa (1990), "Estimation of switching models from revealed preferences and stated intentions," *Transportation Research A*, **24**(6), 485–95.

Bishop, R. and T. Heberlein (1979), "Measuring values of extramarket goods: Are indirect measures biased?," *American Journal of Agricultural Economics*, **61**(5), 926–30.

Bishop, R. and T. Heberlein (1986), "Does contingent valuation work?," in R.G. Cummings, D.S. Brookshire, R.C. Bishop, and K.J. Arrow (eds), *Valuing Environmental Goods: An Assessment of the Contingent Valuation Method*, Totowa, NJ: Rowman & Allanheld, pp. 123–47.

Bliemer, M. and J. Rose (2009), "Designing stated choice experiments: The state of the art," in R. Kitamura, T. Yoshi, and T. Yamamoto (eds), *The Expanding Sphere of Travel Behaviour Research*, Kyoto: International Association for Travel Behaviour Research, pp. 499–538.

Bohm, P. (1972), "Estimating the demand for public goods: An experiment," *European Economic Review*, **3**(2), 111–30.

Bohm, P., J. Linden, and J. Sonnegard (1997), "Eliciting reservation prices: Becker-DeGroot-Marschak mechanisms vs. markets," *The Economic Journal*, **107**(443), 1079–89.

Brookshire, D., B. Ives, and W. Schultze (1976), "The valuation of aesthetic preferences," *Journal of Environmental Economics and Management*, **3**(4), 325–46.

Brookshire, D., A. Randall, and J. Stoll (1980), "Valuing increments and decrements in natural resource service flows," *American Journal of Agricultural Economics*, **62**(3), 478–88.

Brownstone, D. and K. Train (1999), "Forecasting new product penetration with flexible substitution patterns," *Journal of Econometrics*, **89**(1–2), 109–29.

Brownstone, D., D. Bunch, and K. Train (2000), "Joint mixed logit models of stated and revealed preferences for alternative-fuel vehicles," *Transportation Research B*, **34**, 315–38.

Camerer, C. and R. Hogarth (1999), "The effects of financial incentives in experiments: A review and capital-labor-production framework," *Journal of Risk and Uncertainty*, **19**(1–3), 7–42.

Camerer, C., G. Lowenstein, and M. Rabin (2004), *Advances in Behavioral Economics*, Princeton, NJ: Princeton University Press.

Cameron, L., M. Cragg, and D. McFadden (2013), "Determining reasonable royalty damages: the role of conjoint surveys," *Law360*, October 16, accessed December 4, 2016 at http://www.law360.com/articles/475390/the-role-of-conjoint-surveys-in-reasonable-royalty-cases.

Cameron, T. (1988), "A new paradigm for valuing non-market goods using referendum data: Maximum likelihood estimation by censored logistic regression," *Journal of Environmental Economics and Management*, **15**(3), 355–79.

Cameron, T. and M. James (1987), "Efficient estimation methods for closed-ended contingent valuation survey data," *Review of Economics and Statistics*, **69**(2), 269–76.

Cameron, T. and J. Quiggin (1994), "Estimation using contingent valuation data from a 'dichotomous choice with follow-up' questionnaire," *Journal of Environmental Economics and Management*, **27**(3), 218–34.

Carmone, F.J., P.E. Green, and A.K. Jain (1978), "Robustness of conjoint analysis: Some Monte Carlo results," *Journal of Marketing Research*, **15**(2), 300–303.

Caro, F., T. Ho, D. McFadden, A. Gottleib, C. Yee, and T. Chan et al. (2012), "Using the Internet to administer more realistic vignette experiments," *Social Science Computer Review*, **30**(2), 184–201.

Carson, R. (2012), "Contingent valuation: A practical alternative when prices aren't available," *Journal of Economic Perspectives*, **26**(4), 27–42.

Carson, R., N. Flores, and N. Meade (2001), "Contingent valuation: Controversies and evidence," *Environmental and Resource Economics*, **19**(2), 173–210.

Chapman, R. and R. Staelin (1982), "Exploiting rank ordered choice set data within the stochastic utility model," *Journal of Marketing Research*, **19**(3), 288–301.

Ciriacy Wanthrup, S.V. (1947), "Capital returns from soil-conservation practices," *Journal of Farm Economics*, **29**(4), 1181–96.

Cummings, R., D. Brookshire, and W. Schulze (1986), *Valuing Environmental Goods*, Totowa, NJ: Rowman & Allanheld.

Davis, R. (1963a), "Recreation planning as an economic problem," *Natural Resources*, **3**, 239–49.

Davis, R. (1963b), "The value of outdoor recreation: An economic study of the Maine woods," PhD dissertation, Harvard University.

Deaton, A. (2012), "The financial crisis and the well-being of America," in D. Wise (ed.), *Investigations in the Economics of Aging*, Chicago, IL: University of Chicago Press, pp. 343–76.

Diamond, P.A. and J.A. Hausman (1993), "On contingent valuation measurement of non-use values," in J. Hausman (ed.), *Contingent Valuation: A Critical Assessment*, Amsterdam: North Holland, pp. 3–38.

Dong, S., M. Ding, and J. Huber (2010), "A simple mechanism to incentive-align conjoint experiments," *International Journal of Research in Marketing*, **27**(1), 25–32.

Elrod, T., J. Louviere, and K. Davey (1992), "An empirical comparison of ratings-based and choice-based conjoint models," *Journal of Marketing Research*, **29**(3), 368–77.

Fischhoff, B. and C. Manski (1999), *Elicitation of Preferences*, Boston, MA: Kluwer Academic Publishers.

Freeman, R. (1986), "On assessing the state of the arts of the contingent valuation method of valuing environmental change," in R. Cummings, D. Brookshire,

and W. Schulze (eds), *Valuing Environmental Goods*, Totowa, NJ: Rowman & Allanheld, pp. 148–61.
Frisch, R. (1926), "Sur un problème d'économie pur," *Norsk Matematisk Forenings Skrifter*, **16**, 1–40; translation in J. Chipman, L. Hurwicz, M. Richter, and H. Sonnenschein (eds), *Preferences, Utility, and Demand*, New York: Harcourt.
Green, D., K. Jacowitz, D. Kahneman, and D. McFadden (1998), "Referendum contingent valuation, anchoring, and willingness to pay for public goods," *Resource and Energy Economics*, **20**(2), 85–116.
Green, P. and V. Rao (1971), "Conjoint measurement for quantifying judgmental data," *Journal of Marketing Research*, **8**(3), 355–63.
Green, P. and V. Srinivasan (1978), "Conjoint analysis in consumer research: Issues and outlook," *Journal of Consumer Research*, **5**(2), 103–23.
Green, P., D. Carroll, and S. Goldberg (1981), "A general approach to product design optimization via conjoint analysis," *Journal of Marketing*, **45**(3), 17–37.
Green, P., A. Krieger, and Y. Wind (2001), "Thirty years of conjoint analysis: Reflections and prospects," *Interfaces*, **31**(Supplement), S56–S73.
Groves, T. and M. Loeb (1975), "Incentives and public inputs," *Journal of Public Economics*, **4**(3), 211–26.
Haaijer, R., M. Wedel, M. Vriens, and T. Wansbeek (1998), "Utility covariances and context effects in conjoint MNP models," *Marketing Science*, **17**(3), 236–52.
Hammack, J. and G. Brown (1974), *Waterfowl and Wetlands: Toward Bioeconomic Analysis*, Baltimore, MD: Johns Hopkins Press.
Hanemann, M., J. Loomis, and B. Kanninen (1991), "Statistical efficiency of double-bounded dichotomous choice contingent valuation," *American Journal of Agricultural Economics*, **73**(4), 1255–63.
Hauser, J. and F. Koppelman (1979), "Alternative perceptual mapping techniques: Relative accuracy and usefulness," *Journal of Marketing Research*, **16**(4), 495–506.
Hauser, J. and G. Urban (1979), "Assessment of attribute importances and consumer utility functions: Von Neumann-Morgenstern theory applied to consumer behavior," *Journal of Consumer Research*, **5**(4), 251–62.
Hauser, J. and V. Rao (2002), "Conjoint analysis, related modelling, and applications," in Y. Wind and P.E. Green (eds), *Market Research and Modeling: Progress and Prospects*, New York: Springer, pp. 141–68.
Hausman, J. (ed.) (1993), *Contingent Valuation: A Critical Assessment*, Amsterdam: North-Holland.
Hausman, J. (2012), "Contingent valuation: From dubious to hopeless," *Journal of Economic Perspectives*, **26**(4), 43–56.
Hensher, D. and M. Bradley (1993), "Using stated response data to enrich revealed preference discrete choice models," *Marketing Letters*, **4**(2), 139–52.
Hensher, D. and J. Louviere (1983), "Identifying individual preferences for international air travel: An application of functional measurement theory," *Journal of Transport Economics and Policy*, **17**(3), 225–45.
Hensher, D., J. Louviere, and J. Swait (1999), "Combining sources of preference data," *Journal of Econometrics*, **89**(1–2), 197–221.
Hicks, J. (1939), *Value and Capital*, Oxford: Clarendon Press.
Huber, J. (1975), "Predicting preferences on experimental bundles of attributes: A comparison of models," *Journal of Marketing Research*, **12**, 290–97.
Huber, J. (1987), "Conjoint analysis: How we got here and where we are," in

Proceedings of the Sawtooth Software Conference on Perceptual Mapping, Conjoint Analysis, and Computer Interviewing, pp. 237–52.

Huber, J. and K. Train (2001), "On the similarity of classical and Bayesian estimates of individual mean partworths," *Marketing Letters*, **12**(3), 259–69.

Huber, J. and K. Zwerina (1996), "The importance of utility balance in efficient choice designs," *Journal of Marketing Research*, **33**(3), 307–17.

Huber, J., D. Wittink, J. Fiedler, and R. Miller (1993), "The effectiveness of alternative preference elicitation procedures in predicting choice," *Journal of Marketing Research*, **30**(1), 105–14.

Hurd, M. and D. McFadden (1998), "Consumption and savings balances of the elderly: Experimental evidence on survey response bias," in D. Wise (ed.), *Frontiers in the Economics of Aging*, Chicago, IL: University of Chicago Press, pp. 353–87.

Jain, A., F. Acito, N. Malhotra, and V. Mahajan (1979), "A comparison of the internal validity of alternative parameter estimation methods in decompositional multiattribute preference models," *Journal of Marketing Research*, **16**(3), 313–22.

Johnson, R. (1974), "Trade-off analysis of consumer values," *Journal of Marketing Research*, **11**(2), 121–7.

Johnson, R. (1999), "The joys and sorrows of implementing HB methods for conjoint analysis," *Working Paper*, Sequim, WA, Sawtooth Software.

Johnson, R. and B. Orme (1996), "How many questions should you ask in choice-based conjoint studies?," *Research Paper Series*, Sequim, WA: Sawtooth Software, Inc.

Kahneman, D. and A. Krueger (2013), *Developments in the Measurement of Subjective Well-Being*, Cheltenham, UK and Northampton, MA, USA: Edward Elgar Publishing.

Kahneman, D. and A. Tversky (eds) (2000), *Choices, Values, and Frames*, New York: Sage.

Kahneman, D., E. Diener, and N. Schwarz (eds) (1999), *Well-Being: The Foundations of Hedonic Psychology*, New York: Sage.

Khaw, M., D. Grab, M. Livermore, C. Vossler, and P. Glimcher (2015), "The measurement of subjective value and its relation to contingent valuation and environmental public goods," *PLOS ONE*, **10**(7).

King, G., C. Murray, J. Salomon, and A. Tandon (2004), "Enhancing the validity and cross-cultural comparability of measurement in survey research," *American Political Science Review*, **98**(1), 191–207.

Kling, C., D. Phaneuf, and J. Zhao (2012), "From Exxon to BP: Has some number become better than no number?," *Journal of Economic Perspectives*, **26**(4), 3–26.

Kuhfield, W., R. Tobias, and M. Garratt (1994), "Efficient experimental design with marketing research applications," *Journal of Marketing Research*, **31**(4), 545–57.

List, J. and C. Gallet (2001), "What experimental protocol influences disparities between actual and hypothetical stated values?," *Environmental and Resource Economics*, **20**(3), 241–54.

Louviere, J. (1988), *Analyzing Decision Making: Metric Conjoint Analysis*, Newbury Park, CA: Sage.

Louviere, J.J. and G.G. Woodworth (1983), "Design and analysis of simulated consumer choice or allocation experiments: An approach based on aggregate data," *Journal of Marketing Research*, **20**(4), 350–67.

Louviere, J., D. Hensher and J. Swait (2000), *Stated Choice Methods: Analytics and Applications*, New York: Cambridge University Press.
Luce, D. and P. Suppes (1965), 'Preferences, utility and subjective probability', in R. Luce, R. Bush, and E. Galanter (eds), *Handbook of Mathematical Psychology*, New York: John Wiley & Sons, pp. 249–410.
Luce, D. and J. Tukey (1964), "Simultaneous conjoint measurement: A new type of fundamental measurement," *Journal of Mathematical Psychology*, **1**(1), 1–27.
MacCrimmon, K. and M. Toda (1969), "The empirical determination of indifference curves," *Review of Economic Studies*, **36**(4), 433–51.
McFadden, D. (1981), "Econometric models of probabilistic choice," in C. Manski and D. McFadden (eds), *Structural Analysis of Discrete Data*, Cambridge, MA: MIT Press, pp. 198–272.
McFadden, D. (1986), "The choice theory approach to market research," *Marketing Science*, **5**(4), 275–97.
McFadden, D. (1994), "Contingent valuation and social choice," *American Journal of Agricultural Economics*, **76**(4), 689–708.
McFadden, D. (1998), "Measuring willingness-to-pay for transportation improvements," in T. Garling, T. Laitila, and K. Westin (eds), *Theoretical Foundations of Travel Choice Modeling*, New York: Elsevier.
McFadden, D. (1999), "Rationality for economists?" in B. Fischoff and C. Manski (eds), *Elicitation of Preferences*, Boston, MA: Kluwer, pp. 73–106.
McFadden, D. (2012), "Economic juries and public project provision," *Journal of Econometrics*, **166**(1), 116–26.
McFadden, D. (2014a), "The new science of pleasure: Consumer behavior and the measurement of well-being," in S. Hess and A. Daly (eds), *Handbook of Choice Modelling*, Cheltenham, UK and Northampton, MA, USA: Edward Elgar Publishing, pp. 7–48.
McFadden, D. (2014b), "An economist's perspective on environmental damages," paper at The Eighth Annual Advanced Conference on Litigating Natural Resource Damages, Law Seminars International.
McFadden, D. (2016), "Welfare economics with partially-observed consumers," *UC Berkeley Working Paper*.
McFadden, D. and K. Train (2000), "Mixed MNL models for discrete response," *Journal of Applied Econometrics*, **15**(5), 447–70.
McFadden, D., A. Goett, and C.-K. Woo (1988), "Estimating household value of electric service reliability with market research data," *Energy Journal: Special Electricity Reliability Issue*, **9**, 105–20.
McFadden, D., M. Ben-Akiva, A. Goett, and D. Bolduc (1986), *The Choice Theory Approach to Analyze the Preferences and Choices of Electric Utility Consumers*, EPRI Final Report RP2671-1.
Miller, K., R. Hofstetter, H. Krohmer, and Z.J. Zhang (2011), "How should consumers' willingness to pay be measured? An empirical comparison of state-of-the-art approaches," *Journal of Marketing Research*, **48**(1), 172–84.
Mitchell, R. and R. Carson (1989), *Using Surveys to Value Public Goods: The Contingent Valuation Method*, Washington, DC: Resources for the Future.
Moore, W. (2004), "A cross-validity comparison of rating-based and choice-based conjoint analysis models," *International Journal of Research in Marketing*, **21**(3), 299–312.
Morikawa, T., M. Ben-Akiva, and D. McFadden (2002), "Discrete choice models incorporating revealed preferences and psychometric data," in P. Franses and

A. Montgomery (eds), *Econometric Models in Marketing*, Amsterdam, London and New York: Elsevier Science, pp. 29–55.

Moscati, I. (2007), "Early experiments in consumer demand theory: 1930–1970," *History of Political Economy*, 39(3), 359–401.

Myer, K., G. Parsons, and P. Edwards (2010), "Measuring the recreational use value of migratory shorebirds on the Delaware Bay," *Marine Resources Economics*, 25(3), 247–64.

Natter, M. and M. Feurstein (2002), "Real world performance of choice-based conjoint models," *European Journal of Operational Research*, 117, 448–58.

Neslin, S. (1981), "Linking product features to perceptions: Self-stated versus statistically revealed importance weights," *Journal of Marketing Research*, 18(1), 80–86.

Orme, B. (1999), "ACA, CBC, or both? Effective strategies for conjoint research," *Working Paper*, Sequim, WA: Sawtooth Software.

Raghavarao, D., J. Wiley, and P. Chitturi (2010), *Choice-Based Conjoint Analysis: Models and Designs*, Boca Raton, FL: CRC Press.

Randall, A. (1986), "The possibility of satisfactory benefit estimates with contingent markets," in R. Cummings, D. Brookshire, and W. Schulze (eds), *Valuing Environmental Goods*, Totowa, NJ: Rowman & Allanheld, pp. 114–22.

Randall, A., B.C. Ives, and E. Eastman (1974), "Bidding games for valuation of aesthetic environmental improvements," *Journal of Environmental Economics and Management*, 1(2), 132–49.

Rao, V. (1977), "Conjoint measurement in marketing analysis," in J. Sheth (ed.), *Multivariate Methods for Market and Survey Research*, Chicago, IL: American Marketing Association, pp. 257–86.

Rao, V. (2014), *Applied Conjoint Analysis*, Berlin: Springer.

Reibstein, D., J. Bateson, and W. Boulding (1988), "Conjoint analysis reliability: Empirical findings," *Marketing Science*, 7(3), 271–86.

Rose, J. and M. Bleimer (2009), "Constructing efficient stated choice experimental designs," *Transport Reviews*, 29(5), 587–617.

Rossi, P. (1979), "Vignette analysis: Uncovering the normative structure of complex judgments," in R.K. Merton, J.S. Coleman, and P.H. Rossi (eds), *Qualitative and Quantitative Social Research: Papers in Honor of Paul Lazarsfeld*, New York: Macmillan, pp. 175–88.

Rossi, R., G. Allenby, and R. McCulloch (2005), *Bayesian Statistics and Marketing*, New York: John Wiley & Sons Ltd.

Samuelson, P. (1947 [1983]), *Foundations of Economic Analysis*, Cambridge, MA: Harvard University Press.

Schkade, D. and J. Payne (1993), "Where do the numbers come from? How people respond to contingent valuation questions," in J. Hausman (ed.), *Contingent Valuation: A Critical Assessment*, Amsterdam: North-Holland, pp. 271–93.

Schultz, H. (1925), "The statistical law of demand as illustrated by the demand for sugar," *Journal of Political Economy*, 33(5), 481–504 and 577–637.

Schultz, H. (1928), *Statistical Laws of Demand and Supply with Special Application to Sugar*, Chicago, IL: University of Chicago Press.

Segal, M. (1982), "Reliability of conjoint analysis: Contrasting data collection procedures," *Journal of Marketing Research*, 19, 139–43.

Shocker, A. and V. Srinivasan (1974), "A consumer-based methodology for the identification of new product ideas," *Management Science*, 20(6), 921–37.

Smith, K., W. Desvousges, and A. Fisher (1986), "A comparison of direct and indirect methods for estimating environmental benefits," *American Journal of Agricultural Economics*, **68**(2), 280–90.

Srinivasan, V. (1988), "A conjunctive-compensatory approach to the self-explication of multiattributed preferences," *Decision Sciences*, **19**(2), 295–305.

Thurstone, L.L. (1931), "The indifference function," *Journal of Social Psychology*, **2**(2), 139–67.

Train, K. and C. Winston (2007), "Vehicle choice behavior and the declining market share of U.S. automakers," *International Economic Review*, **48**(4), 1469–98.

Train, K., D. McFadden, and A. Goett (1987), "Consumer attitudes and voluntary rate schedules for public utilities," *Review of Economics and Statistics*, **LXIX**, 383–91.

Train, K. and M. Weeks (2005), "Discrete choice models in preference space and willingness-to-pay space," in R. Scarpa and A. Alberini (eds), *Applications of Simulation Methods in Environmental and Resource Economics*, Dordrecht: Springer, pp. 1–16.

Urban, G., J. Hauser, and J. Roberts (1990), "Prelaunch forecasting of new automobiles: Models and implementation," *Management Science*, **36**(4), 401–21.

Urban, G., J. Hauser, W. Qualls, B. Weinberg, J. Bohlmann, and R. Chicos (1997), "Validation and lessons from the field: Applications of information acceleration," *Journal of Marketing Research*, **34**(1), 143–53.

Wallis, A. and M. Friedman (1942), "The empirical derivation of indifference functions," in O. Lange, F. McIntyre, and T.O. Yntema (eds), *Studies in Mathematical Economics and Econometrics*, Chicago, IL: University of Chicago Press, pp. 175–89.

Wittink, D. and T. Bergestuen (2001), "Forecasting with conjoint analysis," in J. Armstrong (ed.), *Principles of Forecasting: A Handbook for Researchers and Practitioners*, New York: Springer, pp. 147–67.

Wittink, D. and D. Montgomery (1979), "Predicting validity of trade-off analysis for alternative segmentation schemes," paper at the American Marketing Association Educator's Conference, pp. 69–73.

Wright, P. and M. Kriewall (1980), "State-of-mind effects on accuracy with which utility functions predict marketplace utility," *Journal of Marketing Research*, **17**(3), 277–93.

Yadav, L. (2007), "Hypothetical bias in contingent valuation," dissertation, University of Massachusetts Amherst.

7. Some findings from further exploration of the "composite good" approach to contingent valuation[1]

Michael Kemp, Edward Leamer, James Burrows, and Powell Dixon[2]

THE CONTEXT AND RATIONALE FOR THIS INVESTIGATION

In this chapter, we report on some components of a larger study addressing "budget awareness" considerations in contingent valuation ("CVM") studies. The study explored general population willingness to pay ("WTP") for essentially the same environmental resource under several different budget awareness approaches, using a split-sample design. In the fall of 2014 (after substantial development work), we undertook a survey with a total achieved sample size of almost 4,000 households. This chapter reports two of those approaches, based on subsamples totaling approximately 2,400 households: the use of within-questionnaire "wording additions" and the disaggregation of a value obtained for a larger composite good.[3]

As well as the budget awareness focus, our study had a second major emphasis: on respondent cognition and on other survey design considerations in the use of CVM techniques to estimate non-use (or "existence")

---

[1] The authors are grateful for contributions provided in the course of this study by Hasat Cakkalkurt, Hiu Man Chan, Harry Foster, Jerome Genser, Stamatia Kostakis, Paul Labys, Daniel Ladd, Josh Lustig, Renée Miller-Mizia, Rebecca Newman, Jeff Plewes, Anne Smith, and Connor Tobin.

[2] Respectively, Senior Consultant, Charles River Associates; Chauncey J. Medberry Professor in Management and Professor in Economics and Statistics at UCLA; Vice Chairman, Charles River Associates; Associate Principal, Charles River Associates.

[3] The survey additionally included a subsample presented with three comparable goods, and our analysis has also employed parametric methods (alongside the non-parametric analysis techniques presented in this chapter). It is anticipated that these aspects of the overall study will be reported in other papers.

values[4] among representative samples of the general public. Empirically, it has long been recognized that reminding respondents about their household budget constraints can sometimes significantly affect responses to valuation questions.[5] Specifically, there has been an effort to design surveys in ways that induce respondents to view their responses as *consequential* in terms both of contributing significantly to the framing of public policy, and of the financial impacts on their own households. The NOAA Blue Ribbon Panel explicitly endorsed such concerns too.[6]

To this end, a variety of approaches has been used within valuation questionnaires to intensify the perceived consequentiality of responses to the posited hypothetical. We refer to these within-questionnaire tactics as "wording additions." These approaches have often appeared to lower *some* of the hypothetical bias,[7] typically by reducing valuation estimates by levels in the 5% to 40% range, but rarely to an extent approaching the levels of "over-statement" observed in the meta-analyses of marketplace valuations.[8]

The Single-focus and "Composite Good" Approaches

The budget constraint that should underlie the answer to a single-focus willingness-to-pay question holds total spending constant so that the purchase of the item being studied comes at the cost of one or more goods currently consumed. WTP survey methods – whether involving direct (CVM) or indirect (choice experiment, or "CE") questioning techniques – usually embody this budget constraint by having respondents promise to give up cash to acquire the good or service being studied. That cash is probably interpreted by respondents in terms of the private goods it represents, since trading cash for public goods is an unfamiliar experience.

However, the cheapest way to pay for a public good might be by giving up an equivalent or a close substitute public good. Furthermore, the amount of the private goods one would surrender to fund a public good

---

[4] While it is sometimes helpful to think of a non-use value (or "existence value") as just another public good, there are very fundamental differences. A non-use value cannot be observed from *any* marketplace behaviors, and (unlike other public initiatives) it has no substantive manifestation except in the *minds* of the affected population. The non-use valuation task is essentially one of finding credible, robust, reliable methods of eliciting those thoughts, when survey respondents have no prior experience (or marketplace frames of reference) for articulating any values for them.

[5] See, for example, Kotchen and Reiling (1999) and Whitehead and Cherry (2007).

[6] See Arrow et al. (1993).

[7] See Morrison and Brown (2009) and Loomis (2014).

[8] See Foster and Burrows (Chapter 10, this volume).

depends on the existence of already available close substitutes for the new public good, which may not be present (or prominent) in the respondent's thinking. For both of these reasons, it seems wise to encourage respondents to think about a *variety* of public goods as an alternative to the traditional single-focus survey.

Our study pursued this idea with a survey exploring the WTP *in aggregate* for a large basket of alternative public goods, including one specific program for which (with a separate sample) we conducted a single-focus valuation survey. We put the respondents through a top-down budget-allocation exercise in which they first prioritized the components of an extensive composite of environmental goods, before eliciting their WTP for the complete basket.[9] They were then given, as *one example* of the kinds of things the portmanteau program would do, the same details of the specific program of interest as were provided to the single-focus split sample. Following this extra information, respondents were given opportunities to adjust their binary-choice WTP responses and/ or their priority allocations among the components of the composite good.

A single-focus valuation method might be intended to estimate the amount that would be needed to compensate for some accidental damage (using WTP as a conservative approximation of willingness to *accept*). This single-focus question involves a different budget constraint that does not include public goods currently unavailable, but it does include public goods currently provided, and one might reasonably expect that WTP should depend on the existence of these close substitutes.[10]

As Hoehn and Randall (1989) and others have pointed out, the entities being valued by a single-focus survey and a composite good survey are not identical, and it should not be expected that the WTP value for the bundle equal the sum of the single-focus WTPs for each of the goods in

---

[9] This exercise is close in spirit to traditional public budgeting, in which elected officials typically allocate a given tax revenue over a broad set of expenditure items, and consider tax increases only when the revenue seems inadequate to fund all the appealing programs. This contrasts with the (relatively unfamiliar) single-focus referendum that proposes a new tax specifically for funding one new public good. If the single-focus question were intended for public policy it would be essential that respondents recognize that this use of the tax revenue precludes other uses, something that is an explicit feature of the multi-good budget exercise.

[10] Our study explored the possibility that the budgeting exercise makes respondents more aware of substitute public goods, and that a single-focus question asked after the budgeting exercise might produce a different (lower) valuation than the single-focus question without the budgeting exercise. In a sense, this is an alternative to the various "wording addition" treatments. Another potential benefit of a multi-good survey is that it may reduce the "importance" bias by including a very broad set of alternatives instead of one special one.

the bundle. Valuing a single good implicitly assumes that all other goods are being held constant, while valuing a bundle does not share the same constraint.

Both CVM and CE valuation methods are based on the assumption of rational and well-behaved neoclassical utility maximization by respondents, which is a questionable assumption in the case of unfamiliar, non-traded goods such as existence values for environmental amenities. There are several empirical reasons to be skeptical about the validity of the basic assumptions underlying this model. For instance, qualitative research associated with similar respondent tasks[11] frequently shows that, no matter how carefully a hypothetical scenario is crafted to present a credible *mandatory* payment mechanism, many respondents have a pervasive difficulty interpreting the valuation questions in ways other than being asked to consider a *voluntary* contribution.[12] And detailed post-valuation debriefing questions often show that relatively few respondents pass *all* of the criteria thought necessary for a valid interview, and specifically, few may pass a consequentiality filter.[13]

A different cognitive approach for exploring public valuations posits that, faced with a task to respond financially to a completely novel, hitherto unconsidered category of commodities, some respondents might prefer to tackle the task from a different perspective. Consistent with the "mental accounting" approach to the analysis of consumer choices,[14] several environmental valuation researchers[15] have explored constructs in which respondents determine their WTP by budgeting their wants in categories of similar goods or services. Not surprisingly, the quantitative values resulting from this approach can be considerably smaller than those from the single-focus methods.

---

[11] See particularly the "cognitive interviews" (or "verbal protocols") reported by Schkade and Payne (1993). Similar evidence is frequently seen in focus groups or one-on-one intensive interviews.
[12] Respondents often use terms like "give" or "donate" in this context, probably in part because being asked about how much one is prepared to pay for some governmental action is such an uncommon, perhaps unrealistic, phenomenon.
[13] See, for example, Schläpfer and Brauer (2007) and Myers et al. (Chapter 9, this volume).
[14] See, for example, Thaler (1985).
[15] See Kahneman and Knetsch (1992), Magnussen (1992), Kemp and Maxwell (1993), Brown et al. (1995), Li et al. (2005), and Smith et al. (2005).

The Design of Our Study

We used Carson et al. (2004) as a "test bed" for our work, exploring how that project's findings might change were different approaches to budget awareness adopted in the study's survey. This "California oil spill" study ("COS") addressed the prevention and remediation of oil spills off the central California coast.[16] Based on a spring 1995 home-interview survey of a probability sample of about 1,000 English-speaking California households, the survey followed a dichotomous choice quasi-referendum structure.

The questionnaire described a scenario in which, as a direct result of oil spills anticipated off the central coast over the next ten years without further action by the State of California, 12,000 sea birds would be killed, 1,000 more birds would be injured but survive, and many small animals and saltwater plants would die over a total of about ten miles of shoreline. None of the involved species were considered "threatened," and these numbers represent minuscule proportions of the species populations. All projected harms would recover, naturally and fully, within ten years at the most, and the state initiative would no longer be necessary after ten years because of the full implementation by then of federal double-hulling mandates for oil tankers.[17]

Survey respondents were asked how they would vote on a state referendum about a hypothetical program that would provide for escort ships for *every* oil tanker sailing there.[18] The operating costs of this initiative would be borne by "the oil companies." However, "(b)ecause individual oil companies cannot legally be required to pay the cost of setting up the program, all California households would pay a special *one* time tax for this purpose." The referendum essentially offered complete and certain avoidance of the specified ten-year harms in return for approving a one-year state tax surcharge on the respondent's household.

The values that the 1995 survey sought to measure comprise *both* use

---

[16] The methodologically detailed report allowed us to follow the design closely. Moreover, as an example of CV methodology, the COS study claimed to be "arguably the first and only valuation study to meet in full the reference study standards set by NOAA's Blue Ribbon Panel on Contingent Valuation...effectively a 'how-to' guide for undertaking state-of-the-art contingent valuation studies."

[17] This scenario distorted the actual legal situation. The Oil Pollution Act of 1990 ("OPA") required single-hull oil tankers operating in US waters to be phased out, *starting* in 2005, with achievement deadlines set for 2010 and 2015. Thus, in 1995 the OPA requirement set a 20-year time horizon, not ten years.

[18] Additionally, the program would establish three oil spill prevention and response centers along the central coast. Sea fences and skimmers would be used quickly by the escort ships to contain and remove any spilled oil, augmented by other response ships.

and non-use values for residents of California. However, since onshore effects are limited to the oiling of "about ten miles of shoreline," the level of harm that can be associated with "use" would be relatively small for the overriding proportion of the state's residents.

Reflecting interim changes in survey research methods, our own 2014 survey was carried out *online*. *Version 1* ("V1") of the study translated the 1995 COS questionnaire into an online, computer-assisted form, staying as close to the original as possible. It was completed by an achieved total sample of about 1,200 respondents. *Within* V1 we used split samples to investigate three different budget awareness-related enhancements to the original survey: a "cheap talk" entreaty consistent with modern practice, an "environmental contributions" script reminding respondents of their disposable income and allocation to environmental concerns, and a "dissonance minimization" variant of the referendum question (that gives a respondent the opportunity to indicate agreement with the identified cause while giving justification for voting *no*). We also tested a variant using a much shortened scenario description, necessary for use in other versions of the questionnaire.

The *Version 2*[19] ("V2") questionnaire also had an achieved sample size of almost 1,200 respondents. It presented a composite environmental good – a prospective "California Environmental Improvement Program" – and asked the respondent to prioritize spending under that program among several tiers of competing elements (including, in the last tier, "Reduce the risk of oil spills at sea off the California Coast").[20]

After the prioritization exercise, a referendum valuation question was asked in a manner closely analogous to that of the test bed study.[21] The 1995 oil spill prevention and remediation scenario was next introduced (in its shortened form), as an example of just one of the many programs that the proposed California Environmental Improvement Program might include, and (after that added detail) respondents were offered the opportunity to amend either or both of their earlier referendum response or their earlier priority allocations. Finally, the questionnaire asked respondents how they would vote in a referendum about the oil spill program alone,

---

[19] In the questionnaire specification and all other survey documents, available on request to the lead author (MKemp@crai.com), this version is labeled Version 3. We use Version 2 in this chapter solely to avoid confusion here.

[20] The questionnaire design was based largely on Kemp and Maxwell (1993), which reports a 1991 *pilot* study, carried out (after qualitative development work) using only a convenience sample. The matter settled before an anticipated subsequent production survey was undertaken.

[21] Version 2 did not employ any of the budget awareness wording variants tested in Version 1.

if it were to appear on the ballot *in place of* the much larger portmanteau program.

THE SINGLE-GOOD VERSION

Similarities with and Differences from the 1995 Test-bed Study

To take advantage of the substantial development work carried out for the 1995 COS survey, we designed our own V1 baseline survey to align as closely as possible to the original, particularly with respect to question wordings and the choice of bid levels ("design points"). However, with a 19-year gap since the original fieldwork, some changes and differences in survey methods were inevitable.

First, we changed the mode of administration from an in-home face-to-face interview to an online, self-administered survey, using a high-quality online survey platform designed to provide a probability sample representative of the general population of California households, regardless of their telephone, computer, or online access status.[22]

Second, presenting the detailed COS scenario had occupied a large proportion of the 1995 interview time, with several scripted points at which the interviewer would engage the respondent by asking a general interest question or checking on comprehension. Such personal interactions could not be emulated fully online. And the 1995 survey used procedures designed to minimize non-committal "don't know" ("DK") responses to the referendum valuation question. After the lengthy COS scenario exposition, respondents were asked just "[. . .]would you vote *for* the program or would you vote *against* it?" It seems impolite (at a minimum) – or unengaged, unintelligent, or lazy – to respond after that effort that one had no opinion about voting for or against the proposed program.[23]

---

[22] We used the pre-recruited KnowledgePanel[SM], maintained by GfK Custom Research (formerly Knowledge Networks), which recruits participants using an address-based random sampling technique and provides Internet access free of charge to any recruit who doesn't already have such access. In recent years, the same panel has been used for several large-sample environmental valuation studies on behalf of NOAA and other governmental agencies (see, for example, Bishop et al., 2011 and Wallmo and Lew, 2011). Our sample used *all* available California respondents in the KnowledgePanel[SM], and screened to ensure that the respondent was "one of the people who make most of the decisions about major purchases and other financial matters for your {household}."

[23] Moreover, to such responses as "I don't vote," "I'm not registered," "I'm not a citizen," the interviewer was instructed to probe with "If you did vote. . .would you vote for the program or against it?"

The NOAA Blue Ribbon Panel had recommended a referendum format valuation question, with the inclusion of an *explicit* "no-answer" option.[24] There has been considerable debate in the survey research literature about the pros and cons of including explicit "no-opinion filters,"[25] and the balance of much current commercial market research practice appears to favor excluding them. We judge this practice troubling on several grounds. Most importantly, we worry about the (conscious or subconscious) alienation of those respondents who do not find an acceptable, truthful choice among the range of options proffered them, and how such alienation might affect their overall perception of the researchers' interest in accuracy and truthfulness throughout other parts of the questionnaire.[26]

Accordingly, we opted to include an explicit "I'm not sure" response option for our valuation questions, which led to a significantly higher level of non-committal responses. In the 1995 survey, about 4% of respondents gave a DK response; for our V1 respondents, the proportion choosing "I'm not sure" for the same question was over 19%.[27]

Other wording changes reflected developments in the interim between the two surveys. The COS study scenario had envisaged a ten-year program that would then become redundant by the federally mandated migration to double-hulled tankers. While information about the extent of double-hulling along the Central California coast by 2014 was sparse, we changed the proposed program slightly (lest some respondents should doubt the scenario's credibility) to include some additional dredging work and changes in navigational rules.[28]

The 1995 survey had employed five "design points" (or "bid levels") at which different subsamples were offered the subject environmental good.[29] We generally inflated the 1995 survey by about 55% to reflect

---

[24] See Arrow et al. (1993).

[25] See Krosnick and Presser (2010), at §9.6, for a review of this literature. In connection with CVM studies specifically, see Krosnick et al. (2002).

[26] Also, the inclusion of an explicit DK option more realistically represents the real-world situation of a statewide referendum, where a voter may opt not to vote at all in a particular election, or if voting, not to provide a response to any specific initiative question on the ballot. We note also that the circumstances of an *online survey* much more closely resemble those of an actual referendum than does a lengthy, in-home, face-to-face *oral interview*.

[27] As with the 1995 survey, the proportion of DK responses increased with the bid level.

[28] Additional changes from the 1995 survey design expanded the sample scope to include Spanish-speaking (as well as English-speaking) households, and removed any reference to the participation of state and federal agencies in the sponsorship of the study.

[29] While mentioning that the five points were selected on the basis of the questionnaire development work, the COS report does not identify the specific criteria used in making those decisions, nor justify the critical choice of $220 as the uppermost design point, an amount

interim inflation,[30] resulting in Version 1 design points of $7.50, $40, $95, $185, and $340.

Some Comparisons with the 1995 Study Findings

In analyzing their referendum responses, Carson et al. (2004) use a non-parametric, maximum likelihood estimator of the lower bound on the mean WTP, following Turnbull (1976).[31] This statistic is derived from the response curve of the subsamples voting "*not-for*" the hypothetical referendum at each of the proffered design points. In both the 1995 and 2014 surveys, the *not-for* respondents are those who did not vote an explicit *yes* to the referendum, and they comprise both explicit *no* votes and those who did not express an opinion.

Theoretically, one would expect the proportion of *not-for*s to increase monotonically as the design point increases. But natural sampling variations and number cognition–related effects may mean that this is not always the case, and we refer to such a situation as the "non-monotonicity issue."[32] In the analysis of the 2014 survey data, we frequently encountered subsamples of interest for which the *not-for* responses were non-monotonic. Following a now common practice in the non-market valuation literature to cope with this situation, we used the ABERS approach.[33]

---

that does not appear to have been tested in any of the development work. See Carson et al. (2004), at pp. 20–21 and 225–8.

[30] As measured by the consumer price index for all urban consumers (CPI-U) as the 2014 questionnaire was being finalized. Inflated values were mostly rounded to the closest $5, except that the lowest value was kept at $7.50 and the value that would otherwise have been $100 was set at $95 as a result of non-monotonicity issues detected in our pilot survey.

[31] See Carson et al. (2004), at Appendix F.

[32] The original COS study did not have this problem, because *all* of the *not-for* distributions reported were monotonic. Given the magnitude of the confidence intervals for the individual design point *not-for* percentages, this outcome is somewhat surprising.

[33] Ayer et al. (1955) – often referenced in the literature as "ABERS" – and Turnbull (1974, 1976) describe non-parametric estimators for the lower bound on the mean WTP that have frequently appeared in the environmental literature. ABERS provide a method for smoothing non-monotonic empirical distributions. Turnbull extends ABERS and Kaplan and Meier (1958) to accommodate doubly bounded data, but for single-bounded dichotomous choice data, the ABERS and Turnbull techniques yield identical results. The ABERS algorithm compares proportions for adjacent design points, and when the *not-for* proportion does not increase monotonically as the design point increases, the affected subsamples are pooled. That pooled proportion is then compared to the proportion for the next higher design point. This "pooled-adjacent-violators" algorithm continues until the estimated empirical cumulative distribution is monotonic. Not surprisingly, the resulting estimates are sensitive to the actual categories pooled by the algorithm, and it is not clear how best to compare estimates derived from different patterns of pooling of adjacent design point subsamples.

Three different "choice measures" were discussed in the report of the 1995 survey. The first (labeled **B1**) was based on the answers originally given by respondents to the referendum question, while measure **B1CH** (the one most relied upon by the authors) reflected two possible subsequent changes to the initial vote. The third measure (**B1CHNT**) also used the amended votes but additionally edited any *for* votes from households who were not currently paying California income taxes to *not-for* votes.

For the **B1** measure, we estimate[34] that the lower bound on the sample mean WTP per household was $90.32, which translates to $141.1 in 2014 prices.[35] This estimate fell to $85.39 ($133.4 in 2014 prices) for the **B1CH** measure, and fell further to $76.45 ($119.4 in 2014) when non-taxpayer *for* votes were also changed to *not-for*.

One-eighth of our 2014 V1 sample (153 respondents) had a questionnaire most closely matching the 1995 survey. These were the respondents for whom the COS scenario was described using the "long" form, and who did not experience any "wording additions" intended to enhance budget awareness.[36] For this group, using initial referendum responses in accordance with the 1995 study's **B1** measure, we estimated a lower bound on the sample mean WTP per household of $100.5,[37] about 70% of the 1995 study value at 2014 prices.

Our closest feasible replication[38] of **B1CH** from those 2014 respondents answering the most analogous questionnaire was $92.6. And the closest replication of **B1CHNT** for those same respondents was $68.1.[39] These estimates (both of which use *unweighted* data, to align with the 1995 survey treatment, and derive from monotonic distributions) are approximately 69% and 57% of the 1995 survey values expressed in 2014 prices.

---

[34] The COS report does not explicitly present this figure, but we have estimated it from the underlying frequency of *not-for* votes by design point.

[35] The 2014 estimates for values derived from the 1994 survey reflect an approximately 56.2% increase in the consumer price index (CPI-U) between the two surveys.

[36] However, this subsample did include some interviews completed in the Spanish language, excluded by design from the 1995 survey.

[37] This estimate derived from a non-monotonic distribution, and involved pooling. To match the 1995 treatment, it is derived from *unweighted* data.

[38] Because our questionnaire did not include the original survey's opportunity to revise the referendum vote at the very end of the interview, we were unable to match the 1995 **B1CH** and **B1CHNT** choice measures exactly.

[39] 15.9% of the sample were non-taxpayers, and the fraction of these making *for* votes (after any vote revisions) was 13.3%.

It appears, therefore, that the net effect of all of the factors that differentiate the 2014 survey methodology from the 1995 original has been to *lower* these key WTP statistics by roughly 30% to 45%.[40]

Moving from just the one-eighth of the V1 sample that most closely matched the 1995 treatment to the full Version 1 sample of a little over 1,200 respondents, the estimated lower bound on the sample mean WTP for the full sample was $105.5.[41] This full sample comprised subsamples given both long and short forms of the COS scenario, and (orthogonally) four different "wording addition" treatments (including one with *no* wording additions).

We investigated the effect of using the long and short COS scenario descriptions.[42] The weighted WTP statistic (based on original, unadjusted responses) was $93.0 for the long scenario and $118.8 for the short scenario, both derived from monotonic, unpooled response data. And the proportions of *for* votes were higher for the short scenario at all five design points. If the only response effect at play here were an importance bias, then one might expect that the longer, more detailed exposition would increase the expressed value. But other factors also appear to be at work. Perhaps some specific language omitted from the longer version reduced the respondents' perception of possible reasons to reject the project (concerning, for example, the abundance of the damaged species, the rate of natural restoration, or the substitution possibilities), or perhaps some aspect of the greater detail impaired credibility, or increased respondent frustration with the exercise, for example.[43]

---

[40] These factors include, most importantly (we would judge), the translation from a face-to-face to a (more "anonymous") online administration mode, the use of computer-assist to greater personalize the questionnaire, the adoption of an explicit "I'm not sure" voting option, and the 19-year gap between the two survey periods.

[41] The *issued* sample was designed to provide an accurate representation of the California non-institutionalized population, but differential non-response can lead an *achieved* sample to differ from reference proportions derived from Census data. Individually for each of the V1 and V2 samples, we weighted the achieved sample composition to more closely align with geographic, demographic, and socioeconomic reference proportions for the state. Here and subsequently throughout this chapter, unless otherwise indicated, the presented statistics are those for the *weighted* sample. Weighting effects were small in most instances, and typically did not materially influence our conclusions.

[42] In these comparisons, the wording addition variations were distributed very close to equally for both the long and short scenario descriptions.

[43] While the shorter version included all salient facts regarding expected harms (in the absence of the COS program) and the specific initiatives proposed to prevent or remediate any spills, it lacked (1) a number of diagrams and maps from the longer version, (2) some repetition and added emphasis around the types of shoreline and species affected, and (3) intermediate questions designed to maintain respondent interest and attention.

THE COMPOSITE GOOD VERSION

Valuing the Version 2 Composite Good

Since single-focus, direct questioning CVM methods are known to be very sensitive to context and survey design considerations,[44] it is sensible to anticipate that the composite good approach would be similarly sensitive to design artifacts. It seems highly likely that the results from a disaggregation survey are significantly sensitive to the somewhat arbitrary assumptions used in defining both the parent good and the disaggregation structure.

The V2 questionnaire incorporated several changes from the Kemp and Maxwell pilot study for a variety of reasons, not least that the switch to a *computer-assisted* questionnaire provides the possibility of framing the questions in a much more personalized way than was feasible with in-person, pencil-and-paper methods. More recent empirical explorations of applying CV methods to composite and component goods[45] have focused on much more tightly defined situations, with relatively constrained sets of choices among which to allocate the funds.

The 1991 experiment had asked its valuation question early in the questionnaire, *before* setting out the list of specific issues or programs that the aggregate good might include. It is possible that the specific details provided later in the disaggregation tree might incline respondents to indicate a greater WTP if the valuation question (changed to a referendum, dichotomous choice format) were delayed until *after* the disaggregation information, and this is the approach we took in the 2014 survey.

Version 2 of the questionnaire posited a very expansive new environmental program on the part of the State of California.[46,47] Then, after

---

[44] Not least, because a non-trivial proportion of respondents appear ready to assent to the proffered good no matter how high the price is set, the selection of the highest design point is a crucial determinant of the measured WTP. See, for example, Parsons and Myers (2016, and Chapter 2, this volume).

[45] See, for example, Magnussen (1992), Bateman et al. (2003), and Boxall et al. (2012).

[46] "Consideration is being given to introducing a new program – the *"California Environmental Improvement Program"* – that will help *protect California's environment and natural areas* over the next ten years. We will ask some questions to find out which environmental issues are most important to {your household}, to find out what types of environmental improvements should be included in the program if it is to appeal to the majority of California's residents.

To pay for starting up the program, and for costs that cannot legally be charged to private companies, there would be a special *one-time* tax for this purpose."

[47] The computer-assisted questionnaire tailored second person references to the most appropriate form for the circumstances of the particular respondent: "you," "your household," or "your family unit." In footnote 46, and subsequently when quoting from the

respondent prioritization of the wide spectrum of environmental initiatives that such a program might comprise (listed in Table 1), the V2 respondents were asked a valuation referendum question similar in form to the V1 valuation.[48]

The payment scenario was directly analogous to that posited in the original COS study: the responsible government entity would impose a *one-year* income tax surcharge to fund a *ten-year* government program. The V2 design points were set at four times those used for V1: $30, $160, $380, $740, and $1,360. We added a sixth design point, set at $2,500, to accommodate the greater scope of the proposed portmanteau good.

For the 1,172 completed V2 interviews, the *not-for* vote percentage ranged from 52% at the lowest ($30) amount to 90% at the highest ($2,500) level. However, there was non-monotonicity for the $740 and $1,360 bid levels, which necessitated pooling of those two subsamples to estimate the proportion of *not-for*s. The ABERS estimate for the lower bound on the sample mean WTP is $413.2^p.[49] Hence this statistic for the large portmanteau program is about 3.8 times that for the COS program alone from the V1 sample[50] (a multiplier not much different from the factor of four used to inflate the design points).

---

questionnaire, for ease of reading we use the "your household" form, and indicate the existence of the tailoring {thus}.

[48] "Now that you and other survey participants have told us what environmental improvements would be most important to {your household}, we want to find out how California residents would be likely to vote on the *California Environmental Improvement Program* if it were put on the ballot in a California election.

Even though (to shorten the interview) we have only asked you about just *some* of the environmental improvements that you think are important, we want you to assume that the ballot proposition on which you would be asked to vote will make significant improvements, over the next ten years, on the environmental issues that are important to you and to other California residents. Please assume also that it would do so efficiently, without wasting money.

Remember that to pay for setting up and administering the program, and for costs that cannot legally be charged to private companies, there would be a special *one time* tax *added to* your California income tax for one year. You would pay this tax increase in the same way as you usually pay any California income tax now, so for many people the extra amount would increase the amount that is withheld from their pay checks...but the extra tax withholding would end after one year.

If the *California Environmental Improvement Program* were put into place, it would cost {your household} $X in a special *one time* tax *added to* your next year's California income tax.

If a California-wide ballot proposition about this proposal were on an election being held today, and the total cost in extra tax to {your household} for the program would be $X, would you vote *for* the program or would you vote *against* it? [*Select one only.*]"

[49] Here and subsequently, we use the superscript ^{p} to identify any WTP estimate based on pooling of design point subsamples.

[50] To make best use of the available 1,213-member V1 sample, here (and in the discussion that immediately follows), we used the *whole* of the sample, including both long and short COS scenarios and all of the tested wording additions, rather than just those 153 V1 respondents whose questionnaires most closely followed the 1995 survey.

Priority Allocations for Components of the Composite Good

Similar to the disaggregation structure developed (on the basis of qualitative survey research) for the 1991 experiment, respondents were asked to allocate the total funding for the proposed California Environmental Improvement Program in three stages. At each stage, the allocation question involved assigning 100 cents across a range of specified choices.[51] Figure 1 summarizes the logical structure that was followed to disaggregate from the complete California Environmental Improvement Program down to the share for marine oil spills off the California coast.

If at any stage a respondent chose *not* to allocate any money to the category that was of particular interest – that is, in the direct path to the next stage of the disaggregation – the questionnaire conservatively tried to ensure that this decision was not due to a lack of understanding about that category.[52] Other language was used to suggest that the particular disaggregation path chosen for questioning was randomly determined,[53] or to justify following a path for which the respondent had previously allocated a zero amount.[54] All of these features had been developed for the 1991 pilot.

With the translation to a *computer-assisted* online survey we were able to *offer* respondents the opportunity to learn further details about the alternative choices that they were being asked to prioritize at each stage of the disaggregation. A respondent could find out more about the allocation options (definitions, examples, and representative "prices") in two ways. Hovering the cursor over applicable text on the screen brought up a small

---

[51] "Out of *every additional dollar* – that is, 100 cents – that {your household} would have to pay in a one-time state tax to fund the program, how many of the extra cents should go to each of the issues on the list below?"

[52] "Some people think that California should do more to...[expanded explanation of the category of interest]. We see that you have allocated none of {your household's} additional tax to that category. Is that what you intended, or would like to make some changes to how you allocated your payments?"

[53] "To keep this survey from being too long, we will focus on just one of the environmental issues for each of the people taking the survey.

In your case, we are going to ask for your opinions about: [short delay before adding remaining text]{Protecting non-endangered animals, birds, fish, and plants, on the land and in the ocean off the California coastline}."

[54] "Even though you've told us that you do not want any of your money to go to this particular issue, we're going to suppose that some of your one-year tax surcharge would in fact be spent on that category." In this way, unless the respondent replies with a "not sure" answer at any of the disaggregation stages, the questionnaire still obtains each respondent's allocation priorities throughout the full structure.

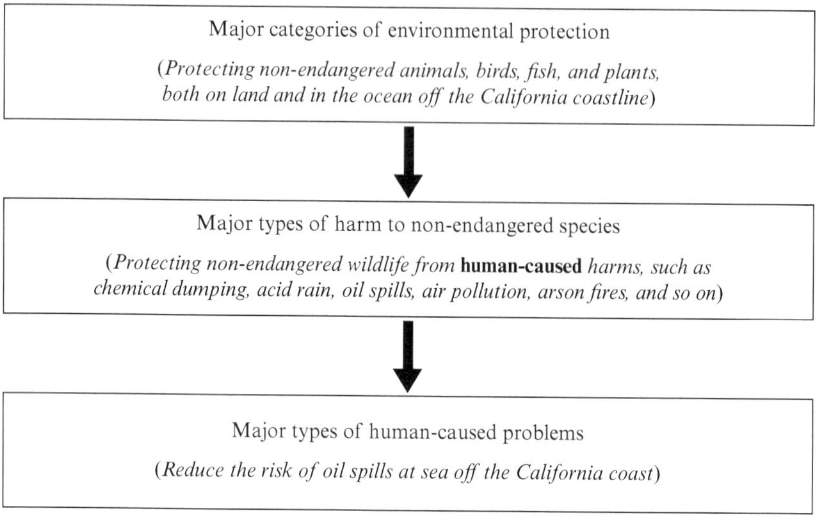

Major categories of environmental protection

(*Protecting non-endangered animals, birds, fish, and plants, both on land and in the ocean off the California coastline*)

↓

Major types of harm to non-endangered species

(*Protecting non-endangered wildlife from* **human-caused** *harms, such as chemical dumping, acid rain, oil spills, air pollution, arson fires, and so on*)

↓

Major types of human-caused problems

(*Reduce the risk of oil spills at sea off the California coast*)

Note: The particular category identified in italics is the one of primary interest at each stage of the disaggregation.

Figure 1   Logical structure used for the disaggregation

box with a brief amplification, or still more detail could be obtained (on a separate screen) by clicking on the text as a hot link.[55]

Table 1 shows the alternative environmental improvement categories offered at each stage of the disaggregation, and summarizes the mean allocations of resources for each of the three tiers of the disaggregation process. The data in the table imply that the proportion of the total California Environmental Improvement Program that respondents would, on average, dedicate to the category of interest – "[r]educe the risks of oil spills at sea off the California coast"[56] – was (~0.071 × ~0.329 × ~0.258 =) 0.60% (with a standard error of 0.03%). For just those people who (later)

---

[55] A similar approach to providing details that respondents might or might not wish to learn was used in a recent, large, online choice experiment study sponsored by NOAA. See Wallmo and Lew (2011).

[56] Note that, for tractability reasons, this category of interest is a little different from the focus of the original COS study (and our own V1 replication) in two principal ways. First, "at sea off the California coast" is a more expansive geographical region than that defined for the COS program. Second, "Reduce the risk of oil spills at sea" makes no reference to the *remediation* activities described as part of the program, just as other details (e.g., the cause and magnitude of the harms, projected recovery times, and the program scale) also exceed the detail feasible in this approach.

Table 1   Initial mean allocations across environmental categories

Subsample	Allocation (%)	St. Err. (%)
First tier allocation:		
Protecting the quality of California's drinking water	19.1	0.7
Developing renewable sources of energy, like solar and wind power	14.2	0.5
Encouraging greater energy conservation	10.3	0.3
Improving disposal of household/industrial wastes, encouraging recycling	9.3	0.3
Protecting types of animals, birds, fish, and plants that are endangered	8.8	0.3
Enhancing the safety of nuclear power plants in California	9.3	0.4
Reducing air pollution (other than greenhouse gases)	8.6	0.3
Reducing the production of "greenhouse gases"	7.8	0.3
Protecting non-endangered animals, birds, fish, and plants, both on land and in the ocean off the California coastline	7.1	0.2
Other (write-in) topics	5.5	
Total	100.0	
Allocation of "protecting non-endangered species":		
Protecting non-endangered wildlife from human-caused harms (such as chemical dumping, acid rain, oil spills, air pollution, arson fires, and so on)	32.9	0.7
Preserving habitats in a wild state rather than land development	28.5	0.6
Protecting undeveloped areas or wildlife from harm from natural causes	21.3	0.5
Wildlife reduced through hunting or fishing for food or sport	17.2	0.5
Total	100.0	
Allocation of "protecting non-endangered wildlife from human-caused harms":		
Wildlife harmed from chemical or oil spills on the land or in rivers	31.4	0.6
Reduce the risks of oil spills at sea off the California coast	25.8	0.5
Human-caused fires in California wilderness areas	25.3	0.6
Other human-caused harms to California wilderness areas and wildlife	17.5	
Total	100.0	

Note: Descriptors of categories have sometimes been shortened, except for those (italicized) descriptors on the disaggregation path.

voted *for* the referendum, the overall allocation to the COS good was similarly 0.60%.

So the lower bound on the sample mean WTP for the portmanteau good was $413.2^p (based on pooled design points), and the mean allocation of composite program dollars to marine oil spills was 0.60%. Under this particular disaggregation structure, therefore, the lower bound mean WTP to reduce the risks of oil spills off the California coast is approximated by (~$413.2^p × ~0.006 =) $2.47^p.[57]

Reactions to the Standalone COS Scenario

At a later stage of the V2 interview, respondents were given an opportunity to revise their referendum votes and/or their allocations of portmanteau program revenues. In both cases, these revisions followed the presentation of the short version of the COS scenario, described as "an example of just *one* of the many ideas that have been proposed for funding under the program."

In total, just over a quarter of unweighted V2 respondents revised their referendum votes following the COS scenario.[58] The net effect of presenting the COS scenario was to increase the *for* proportion at the expense of both the *against* and *not sure* votes. In general, the propensity to shift votes was slightly higher at the higher bid levels, resulting in a relatively large impact on the WTP statistic. Using the revised referendum responses, the ABERS estimate for the lower bound on the sample mean WTP for the portmanteau program adjusted to $639.5^p.

After any revision made to the referendum vote, respondents were shown the "bottom line" monetary implications (that is, the percentage allocation multiplied by the design point) of their previous allocation decisions, focusing in particular on the last tier of the allocation but with amounts also representing the totals from higher tiers of the disaggregation. We displayed these amounts, and provided the opportunity for the respondent to adjust the allocation.

About 40% of the unweighted respondents (45% of those voting *for* the program, after reconsideration) decided to make some adjustments to their implicit monetary allocations. Of those choosing to adjust their

---

[57] Statistical dangers lurk in the combination of two independently determined distribution means. Depending on how the two variables are distributed interactively across the sample, the product of the means for each variable may not equal the mean of the products calculated individually for every sample member. Other factors equal, such a discrepancy is likely to be greater as the correlation between the two variables increases. This was not a significant problem in the current case.

[58] The 24% of respondents who had originally voted *not sure* were responsible for the highest number of changes, with about 72% of their changed votes moving to *for*. The second largest number of vote shifts was among the respondents initially voting *against* the composite good referendum – almost 21% of those votes were changed, and almost three-quarters of the changed votes went to *not sure*. The initial *for* votes were least affected. Only 11% of those votes were switched, with 71% of the changes ending up as *not sure*.

allocations, 67% *increased* the amount apportioned to "oil spills at sea," while 9% *decreased* the amount and 24% left that particular item unchanged. The proportion of respondents not allocating anything to marine oil spills fell from 22% to 15%.

The general pattern of allocation shifts was to move money (in net) to *all* of the bottom tier options. "Oil spills at sea" benefited the most, but the amounts assigned to chemical/oil spills on land, human-caused fires, and other human-caused problems increased as well. At the next tier up, even the average amount allocated to protecting wilderness areas and wildlife from *natural harms* increased. All of these increases came at the expense of the catch-all category "All other environmental problems" – the respondents "went to the bank" to benefit the issue that had just been described to them, along with others sharing some similar characteristics.

How far the incidence and magnitude of the adjustments are ascribable to specific features of the COS scenario, or would be replicated for *any* single-focus environmental initiative that might have been presented at that point, is impossible to say, since we did not vary the scenario that we chose to present as "an example of just *one* of the many ideas that have been proposed for funding under the program."

Accepting *all* of the reallocations of budget share to marine oil spills, the mean share of the portmanteau program revenues increases to 3.9%, roughly 6½ times the original allocation. But this figure is highly influenced by a relatively small number of people making very large shifts to increase the marine oil spills share (as we later amplify). For example, if one edits to exclude the 6.4% of revised responses that allocated 20% or more of their total bid level amounts to marine oil spills, this adjusts the mean revised allocation to 2.4%, and if revised allocations of 10% or over are excluded (15% of the sample), the mean allocation for the rest of the sample is 1.0%.

Values for the Standalone COS Program

At the end of the Version 2 questionnaire, immediately before the debriefing and classification questions, respondents were asked how they would vote if, instead of the portmanteau California Environmental Improvement Program, the referendum were limited to just the COS scenario alone.[59]

---

[59] Among other things, we were interested to explore whether and how the "training aspects" of the top-down disaggregation logic – the fact that respondents had been exposed to a much broader litany of environmental concerns (many with potential harms of a much greater magnitude than those described in the COS scenario) – might affect their valuations of COS as a "standalone" good. For the standalone COS question, we used the five COS design points from V1.

Table 2 V2 ABERS estimates of the lower bound on the sample mean WTP for "standalone COS"

Subsample	Unweighted n	WTP ($)	St. Err. ($)
Version 1 respondents with short scenario:			
All (including wording additions)	603	118.8	10.0
No wording additions	153	146.9^p	na
Version 2 "standalone COS" responses:			
All respondents	1,172	107.9	7.0
All voting *for* the portmanteau program	853	86.2	8.0
All voting *not for* the portmanteau program	319	159.8	14.7
All except those with $\Phi \geq 0.75$	900	126.7	10.0
All except those with $\Phi \geq 0.25$	786	132.6^p	na
All except those with $\Phi \geq 0.10$	429	91.7^p	na
All except for "yea-sayers"	654	79.4	8.1
All with marine oil spill share < median value	586	93.0^p	na
All with marine oil spill share ≥ median value	586	121.7^p	na

Note: The variable Φ is defined as the ratio between the (randomly assigned) design point for the standalone COS exercise and the previously seen, randomly assigned design point for the portmanteau program. Estimates with the superscript ^{p} are derived from pooled models, and no standard errors were computed in those cases.

Table 2 summarizes the ABERS estimates derived from responses to the standalone COS referendum. Across the full V2 sample the *not-for* proportions rose monotonically with the bid level, and consequently no pooling across adjacent design points was necessary. The WTP estimate (again, the lower bound for the sample mean) for the most comparable unweighted subsamples from Version 1 were around the $120 to $150 level. By comparison, for the full, unweighted V2 sample the equivalent WTP measure falls to about $108.

KEY FINDINGS OF THIS STUDY

1. **The study evidenced a very marked lack of sensitivity to a huge scope difference.**

We reported earlier that the ABERS estimate for the lower bound on the sample mean WTP for the V2 California Environmental Improvement Program was $413.2^p, about 3.8 times that for the COS program alone from the V1 sample.[60] Recall that the bid levels for the composite good were set at four times those for V1 COS, with the addition of an extra bid level at the top of the scale. The similarity between the ratio of design points and the ratio of estimated WTP is remarkable. Such a result echoes the finding of Burrows et al. (Chapter 1, this volume) that a fourfold increase in the cost scale for endangered and threatened species resulted in an approximate tripling in estimated WTP. Results like these strongly suggest that there is a scope failure, with respondents providing WTPs for the lower-scope good as if they were valuing the larger-scope good.

Closer examination revealed that this fourfold difference between the WTP statistics for the composite good and the much smaller COS good is driven by the three highest bid levels for the portmanteau good, and *not* by any apparent difference in the WTP responses at similar price levels. Figure 2, which shows the proportion of *not-for* votes by design point for both cases, reveals an effect that is masked when just the WTP summary statistics alone are compared.[61] Where the two bid level ranges overlap in the lower part of the response curve, the two graphs are barely distinguishable after considering sampling errors.

The similarity of these two response curves reveals a colossal scope failure. If the survey responses are to be believed, at least for the overlapping portions of the cost scales the expressed WTP for a good that effectively encompasses the entire environment is virtually identical to the expressed WTP for a trifling fraction of the larger good: avoiding harms to minuscule proportions of the populations of a small number of non-threatened species, that will all recover naturally by no later than ten years.[62] In other words, within the $30–380 bid level range (which accounts for 100% of the V1 sample and 50% of the V2 sample) respondents apparently see very little difference to them in the value of this single-good COS program and the substantially more ambitious California Environmental Improvement Program.

Clearly, it cannot be the case that the "true" utility of the COS good alone is the same as the larger good incorporating the whole gamut of

---

[60] To make best use of the available 1,213-member V1 sample, here (and in the discussion that immediately follows), we used the *whole* of the sample, including both long and short COS scenarios and all of the tested wording additions, rather than just those 153 V1 respondents whose questionnaires most closely followed the 1995 survey.

[61] Figure 2 displays the one standard error confidence bands of *not-for* votes at each design point for both the V1 and the V2 composite good referenda. This figure uses a logarithmic transformation of the design point axis to improve clarity in the region of greatest interest.

[62] As Table 1 shows, V2 respondents initially allocated only 0.6% of their composite program budget to marine oil spills off the California coast.

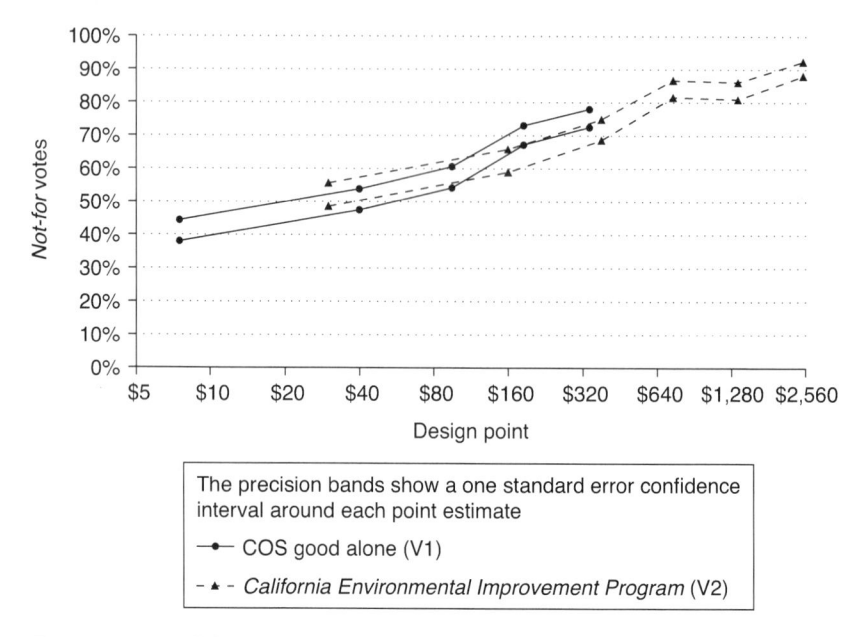

Figure 2 Confidence bands for referendum responses to COS and the composite good, by design point (log scale)

state environmental policies. The only interpretation that makes sense is that in the V1 COS referendum a sizeable proportion of the sample is providing a WTP response for environmental goods in general, or perhaps for "good deeds" in general, and not the WTP for COS specifically. It is not credible that the anomalous findings are the result of a monumental embedding problem in which respondents *mistake* the COS good for the portmanteau good. As the respondents valuing the COS good are provided information only about that single good, it is not likely that their responses are really providing a value for the whole environment. An alternative and much more credible explanation is that respondents are providing a symbolic measure of the warm glow benefit of making a contribution (*any* contribution) to "the environment."

2. **The composite good estimate of WTP allocated to marine oil spills is markedly smaller than the single-focus estimate.**

The composite good approach used in Version 2 resulted in estimates of the WTP statistics that were considerably smaller than those obtained from the single-focus CVM questionnaire of Version 1 (from around

$120[63] for the single-focus estimate to, from disaggregation, $2 to $3 before reallocation and $15 to $20 after reallocation).

This conclusion per se is neither particularly novel nor surprising. Consistent with the analysis of Hoehn and Randall (1989), the two different approaches are measuring two different *entities*. For one of them, respondents are shown just a single public good in isolation, and are expected to articulate whether its non-use value to them is greater or less than a given amount. For the second, the subject public good is but one possibility among a plethora of similar goods (including possible substitutes), part of a larger category for which the respondents might have an aggregate non-use value.

A potentially valuable side benefit of the disaggregation approach is that it allows us to identify other environmental goods that have utility levels *less* than COS (consider giving these up to fund COS) and other environmental goods that have utility levels *greater* than COS (consider these as ways to compensate for COS-like environmental damage). Our results showed that when respondents had the opportunity to allocate dollars over a wide range of different potential state environmental initiatives, they did not find "Reduce the risks of oil spills at sea off the California coast" to be very appealing in comparison to the other public goods being considered, allocating only 0.6% of the total budget to that category. This means that there is not much scope for giving up other environmental goods to fund a COS-like initiative, but there are lots of ways of compensating for COS-like damage with more attractive alternative environmental goods.

3. Sizeable proportions of respondents reported cognition difficulties in their responses, and the resulting WTP estimates are sensitive to those difficulties.

As had the original COS Study,[64] we explored the sensitivity of the WTP estimates to excluding from the analysis various categories of respondents who might, for various reasons, be judged of particular interest. For the 2014 survey, we added a markedly more extensive battery of post-valuation debriefing questions to those used in 1995.[65]

---

[63] This estimate is specifically for those V1 respondents who saw the "short scenario" also used for V2.

[64] See Carson et al. (2004), at Table 6.4.

[65] Most of the additional questions used this rubric:

"We have a few more questions about what things were important to you as you answered our earlier questions about voting for or against the proposed {insert program name}.

Different people go about answering questions like these in different ways. On the screens that follow, we will show a number of statements that other people have made about *how* and *why* they answered the questions in the way that they did."

For each of the V1 and V2 samples, Table 3 summarizes the effect on the lower bound of the sample mean WTP value (using the original, unadjusted referendum responses) as various types of respondents are removed from consideration. Several features of this table merit discussion. First, one is struck by the high variability of the WTP lower-bound estimates as the various groups are excluded. For V1, for example, the resulting estimates range from 40%[66] to 134% of the "all respondents" value. Second, the pattern of variations for the V2 values apportioned to marine oil spills appears to be broadly similar to that observed with the V1 values.[67]

In reviewing other aspects of the table, we will focus attention on those categories that either (1) remove the highest proportions of responses, or (2) result in the largest adjustments to the WTP statistic, mostly using the V1 sample data for illustration. Of particular note in both regards are the effects of eliminating those respondents who might be judged to have misconstrued the COS good in some way (row a).[68] In total, about 85% of the full Version 1 sample indicated "misconstruction" in at least one way or another. Some of the people eliminated might (for example) be just expressing a general skepticism about what they are told about government programs, or be exhibiting acquiescence response bias when presented with rationales that in reality may not have occurred to them. But the large percentage per se will come as little or no surprise to those who have viewed

---

When each statement appears, please select a number between 1 and 5 to indicate how well that statement describes the way in which *you personally* thought about your own answers to those questions. A '5' answer means that the statement 'describes me perfectly,' and a '1' answer means the statement 'doesn't describe me at all'."

The battery of statements relating to Versions 1 and 2 comprised 29 in total, not all of which applied to any one respondent. Presented in randomized order, each statement would appear alone across the top of the screen, with a five-point numerical scale arrayed horizontally beneath it. Consistent with our strong belief in allowing respondents to indicate uncertainty or discomfort about a question, an "I'm not sure" response option was also provided.

When using this form of debriefing question in the sensitivity analyses, we based the classification on the two points at the appropriate end of the scale; that is, scale positions 4 and 5 (or 1 and 2).

[66] Excluding the atypical row h entry.

[67] The sizes of the variations shown in Table 3 generally increase when unweighted data are used instead of the weighted statistics shown in the table. We also note that the 1995 survey's exclusion of Spanish-only households does not appear, on this evidence, to be material: the V1 Spanish language interviews showed only a slightly lower WTP statistic than the English language interviews.

[68] These people reported either (1) that they thought the harm from oil spills would be "a lot *more*" than presented in the questionnaire; or (2) that they thought that they would have to pay the special tax "for more than one year;" or (3) that they "were *consciously* thinking" that the hypothetical program was in some way more beneficial than had been described (either "other types of animals or plants. . .would also benefit," or that the program infrastructure "might also be useful if a spill occurred along *other parts* of the California coast," or "if a spill occurred at an oil drilling well or because of a broken underwater pipeline").

Table 3 *Sensitivity of the lower-bound mean WTP estimates to respondent exclusion criteria*

Subsample	V1 Single-focus COS Un-weighted n	V1 WTP ($)	V2 Marine Oil Spills Un-weighted n	V2 WTP ($)
Original referendum responses for all respondents:	1,213	105.5	1,172	2.47[p]
*Comparable estimates, **excluding**:*				
a. Respondent misconstrues the COS good	179	49.9	410	1.16[p]
b. COS scenario judged not fully credible	441	138.5	348	3.74[p]
c. Survey judged inconsequential	993	113.3	954	2.93[p]
d. Surveys, ballots shouldn't be used in this case	612	99.6	414	2.37[p]
e. "Protest no" votes	948	141.6	778	4.21[p]
f. Costs shouldn't (or didn't) matter	643	42.1	654	1.09[p]
g. "Not sure" referendum responses:	986	130.5	888	3.49[p]
Respondent is not a taxpayer	924	112.0	879	2.86[p]
Changed from *for* to *not-for* on re-ask	1,165	98.7	1,121	2.59[p]
WTP more than 5% of income	1,204	100.2	1,151	2.51[p]
Respondent compares bid level to donations	692	99.7	641	2.02[p]
Survey too long or too complicated	835	106.5	752	2.37[p]
Survey gave too much or too little information for the allocation task			637	2.52[p]
Survey pushed one way or another	1,023	106.8	921	3.07[p]
Survey pushed to vote for	1,085	106.3	993	2.93[p]
Respondent not currently registered to vote	992	109.2	973	2.76[p]
Respondent unlikely to vote	900	89.4	826	2.85[p]
Spanish language interviews	1,033	105.7	1,023	2.69[p]
h. Any one or more of the above criteria	4	12.5[p]	12	3.21[p]

Note: WTP amounts are estimates of the lower bound on the sample mean. Estimates with the superscript [p] are derived from pooled models.

video recordings of "cognitive interviews" or "verbal protocols" used as respondents complete CVM tasks,[69] and it is also notable that for the people *not* admitting to any of the misconstruction indicators, the WTP statistic falls markedly, by over a half of the reference value.

[69] Such as those filmed in connection with Schkade and Payne (1993).

Eliminating the respondents who in some way do not find the scenario fully credible (row b)[70] also reduces the available sample markedly, by about 64%. Having credibility concerns apparently lowers WTP, because removing such respondents from consideration *increased* the WTP statistic by a little over 31%. Relatedly, removing the roughly 17% of respondents appearing to view the survey as inconsequential (those *dis*agreeing that "my answers to this survey will help state government decision-makers to make better decisions about new environmental programs like the one described in the survey", row c) increased the WTP statistic by almost 7½%.

However, there were other respondents agreeing with statements that, for issues like these, the state should rely more on scientists and other trained experts than on either "surveys (like this one) of the general public" or "how California voters vote on ballot propositions." Row d shows that just under half of the sample, in total, agreed with one or other of those statements, and when those people were excluded the WTP statistic fell by roughly 5½%.

CVM practitioners have long sought to identify "protest *no*" votes, and remove them from consideration. In our case, we classified about 22% of the respondents as giving protest *no* votes (row e),[71] and eliminating those respondents increased the WTP statistic by roughly a third. At the opposite end of the spectrum are respondents – sometimes characterized as "*yea*-sayers" – who will agree to proposed environmental improvements no matter how high the price attached to the proposal (row f).[72] We classified 47% of the V1 sample in this category, and when those respondents were removed, the WTP statistic fell by 60%.

Removing the people giving "not sure" referendum responses (row g, almost 19% of the sample) increases the WTP statistic by about 24%, to $130.5.[73]

---

[70] These were people who agreed with statements indicating that some aspect of the COS scenario was either "not factually correct" or "just didn't make sense to me," or who were not sure the proposed program would be able to prevent oil spills.

[71] These respondents voted *no* in the referendum and expressed agreement with statements either that "I would not vote in favor of any tax increase, no matter how worthy the program" or that the oil companies should pay.

[72] These were respondents agreeing with either (1) "In decisions about preserving and protecting our environment, the costs shouldn't really matter;" or (2) "I voted for the *Central California Coast oil spill prevention program* mostly because we need to do more to care for our environment. I was less interested in the actual details of the program, or its cost to {my household}, than the fact that it would help the environment."

[73] The similarity of this estimate to the comparable one from the 1995 survey, expressed in 2014 prices ($141.1), is most likely a chance outcome, but it does suggest that the different treatment of DK responses (strongly discouraged in 1995, despite the Blue Ribbon Panel's advocacy, while offered as an acceptable response in 2014) may be a significant element in the differences between the two surveys' numerical results.

In the V1 survey, the proportion of respondents who opined that the survey had "pushed me to vote for" the proposal was about 10.5%. For the California Environmental Improvement Program in V2, the proportion expressing the same sentiment rose to over 15% (p value for the difference = 0.001), not surprising given the additional time spent in describing the COS program and voting on it as a standalone proposition.

Other researchers[74] have observed that the cumulative effect of eliminating all those CVM respondents whose answers, in one respect or another, do not conform with the theoretical notions of what constitutes a "good respondent" can result in very few remaining observations. In our case, of the 1,213 California residents interviewed in Version 1, only four of them were not removed in *any* of our sensitivity tests (row h).

For practically every one of the rows in Table 3, there could be justification for using *that* particular entry as *the* non-use value estimate best representative of the general California population. . .for framing public policy, or for damages estimation, or for whatever purpose. Yet the variation in the implicit aggregate monetary values, when multiplied by the applicable number of households (currently approaching 13 million in California), can be very large.

In coming up with an appropriate estimate, the researcher needs not only to fix on design details for the survey itself – which, as we see in this study, have great potential to influence the results[75] – but also on which responses should be edited out.[76] Since the resultant value estimate can vary greatly with such decisions, those choices merit greater attention and justification than appears common in many CVM study reports.

4. **Respondents who were presented the single-focus COS referendum after having done the budget exercise were slightly less favorable to COS than those who did not have the budget exercise.**

After completing the composite good allocation and valuation tasks, V2 respondents were asked to vote on an alternative referendum for the COS good alone. This resulted in an estimate for the lower bound on the sample mean WTP of $107.9. One hypothesis shaping our study design was that the budgeting exercise might serve effectively as "training," helping respondents to better understand the part-whole relationship

---

[74] See, for example, Myers et al. (Chapter 9, this volume).

[75] Consider, for instance, the effects of using a long or short version of the scenario, including or excluding an explicit "not sure" option, or opting for one specific type of wording addition.

[76] Because, say, the respondent is a non-taxpayer, a non-voter, a tax-protester, a yea-sayer, or does not view the survey as consequential.

between COS and the portmanteau program, and the relative scale of the two initiatives. We plotted the precision bands for the V1 sample response curve and for the V2 sample's standalone COS question, showing that the *not-for* vote proportion had increased in V2 at all design points. While the confidence intervals were not greatly separated, and the implied reduction in the WTP was not large, the budget exercise does appear to have had a modest effect.

The limited impact of the budget exercise on the WTP for COS may come from the fact that there are two different substitutions that underlie the two types of questions. The response to the standalone version should depend on the existence of close substitutes for COS that are already available, but the budget exercise deals with substitution among public goods that are not presently available. Recent experience with the latter seems not to have had much effect on the awareness of the former.

5. A sizeable proportion of respondents experiences cognition difficulties with part-whole relationships.

As well as the evidence provided by the immediately preceding conclusion, this finding reflects two additional empirical observations revealed by our study when (after the composite good allocation and valuation tasks) Version 2 respondents were given the COS scenario as an example of just one component of the portmanteau good. First, when allowed to reallocate budget shares, some respondents exhibited behaviors suggesting little conception of the part-whole relationship between the example component and the portmanteau good. Second, the valuation estimate for the COS standalone good also points to a similar problem.

Some V2 respondents changed their allocations markedly after being presented the COS scenario. For the original allocation to marine oil spills, 98.6% of the implied amounts were $50 or less, and 99.9% were $100 or less. After reallocation, these proportions changed to 88.7% and 95.4% respectively, but 2.9% of the sample now had implied amounts of over $200. At the extreme, three respondents increased their marine oil spills allocation from an original zero to *100%* of their bid levels, and a fourth adjusted from zero to *95%*.

Arraying respondents by the percentage and dollar values of their adjustments shows, in the upper tail of the distribution, a spectrum of respondents who clearly are responding to the stimulus of the most recently presented COS scenario without placing it in any perspective of the much larger scope of the portmanteau program on which they had previously voted. For these outliers, the experiment has effectively ceased to be a disaggregation survey.[77] Retaining the relative advantage of the disaggregation survey in reducing importance bias obviously requires some editing of allocation adjustments allowed after introducing a single-focus scenario, but where to draw the line for that editing is an arbitrary decision.

Viewed in the context of the various "wording additions" explored in subsamples of Version 1 (to be discussed subsequently), the systematic delineation of possible other environmental issues that might compete for a share of the respondent's total WTP appears to be comparably effective in reducing valuations to the "cheap talk," "environmental contributions," or "dissonance minimization" approaches.

But from a different viewpoint, one might ask why the value obtained from the standalone COS exercise is as *large* as this.[78] Part of the standalone COS valuation might reasonably be ascribed to "anchoring effects." There is considerable evidence in the non-market valuation literature that responses to later valuation exercises can often be strongly influenced by the prices that respondents see in their *first* (or *any* prior) exercise.[79] For that reason, many studies examine the findings from an initial valuation exercise separately from those derived from any subsequent exercises, and prefer to use split samples rather than multiple valuations from the same respondents. In our case, 80% of standalone COS respondents had been shown a higher bid level for their earlier valuation of the composite good, and for those people the ratio between the composite good price and the standalone COS price, while highly variable, averaged about 38. For a respondent paying more attention to the price than to the specifics of the environmental good under offer, standalone COS would frequently appear to be a comparative bargain.[80]

When respondents express a WTP value for the *first* environmental good with which they are presented, they may be using a large portion of their

---

[77] In one sense, this portion of the sample can be regarded as operating in a zone between a single-focus survey – to which they are being drawn perhaps because of the recency, specificity, substance, or some other feature of the COS good – and a composite good survey.

[78] After all, the "COS alone" referendum question came *immediately* after respondents were shown (in dollar terms) the size of their allocation to marine oil spills under the California Environmental Improvement Program. Across the full range of design points for the portmanteau program, the monetary allocation to marine oil spills (before any respondent adjustments of the allocations) ranged from zero (for over 23% of the respondents) to about $56 at the 99th percentile, with a mean of $5.3 and a median of $1.3.

[79] Burrows et al. (Chapter 5, this volume) provide a list of studies drawing this conclusion.

[80] Relatedly, the independent randomization of design points allocated for the two very different program scopes in Version 2 potentially creates a credibility issue for the minority of respondents offered a bid level for standalone COS that is relatively high compared with the bid level offered earlier for the portmanteau program. For each respondent we computed a variable ϕ as the ratio between the standalone COS design point and that for the composite good. But as Table 2 shows, the effects of removing those respondents with the highest values for ϕ do not indicate that those respondents were much affected by that design artifact.

"budget for good deeds," so that this value is essentially a warm glow value. This explanation is also consistent with our finding that large proportions of the respondents do not find the survey consequential or fully credible,[81] so they are spending essentially "free" virtual dollars to achieve their warm glow.

6. Within-questionnaire "wording additions" intended to enhance budget awareness had a relatively small effect on WTP estimates.

Employing various within-questionnaire "wording additions" touching on budget awareness, intended to reduce some of the budget-related hypothetical bias, produced results that are broadly in line with the literature reports for such techniques. Version 1 of our survey tested three different types of wording additions within the interview. Each treatment (including the "no wording additions" baseline) was allocated randomly to a quarter of the total V1 sample.

References to household budget matters in the 1995 questionnaire were quite sparse, limited to some text on one visual aid that was also read out to the respondent,[82] and all three of the 2014 subsamples receiving wording additions also retained this 1995 language. For two of the three subsamples, the additional text came immediately after the 1995 summarization of reasons for voting for and against the proposal. The first variant of additional text was a "cheap talk" entreaty in the spirit of Cummings and Taylor (1999), but shortened somewhat in a manner used for a recent, large, online choice experiment study sponsored by NOAA.[83] This variant also emphasized that respondents might have non-use values for *other* environmental goods as well as for the subject program.[84]

---

[81] Across the full V1/V2 sample, about 29% agreed with "In decisions about preserving and protecting our environment, the costs shouldn't really matter," and 39% agreed with "When I thought about whether to vote for or against the proposed program. . .I was *consciously* thinking about the amounts I typically give when asked to *donate* to a good cause that I believe in." Roughly 57% of the respondents voting in favor of the program agreed with "I voted for the {program} mostly because we need to do more to care for our environment. I was less interested in the actual details of the program, or its cost to {my household}, than the fact that it would help the environment."

[82] The visual aid card summarized two reasons why the respondent might want to vote for the proposal and three reasons to vote against it. The second and third reasons for "voting against" were expressed in the (slightly longer) oral script as "Your household might prefer to spend the money to solve *other* social or environmental problems *instead*" and "The program might *cost more* than your household wants to spend for this."

[83] See Wallmo and Lew (2011).

[84] "As you consider how you would vote on the Central Coast oil spill prevention program, please take into account the following considerations. The extra one-time tax funds that {your own household} and all other California households would have to pay would help to prevent oil spills off the Central Coast over the next ten years, and to prevent the harm if spills do occur."

The second tested wording addition focused on the respondent's perceived disposable income and on the current budget allocation to environmental concerns.[85] The fourth subsample of Version 1 changed the response options for the valuation question itself. In the other three variants, the response options were just "FOR," "AGAINST," and "I'm not sure." For the "dissonance minimization" variant, following Morrison and Brown (2009), three additional "AGAINST + excuse" response options were added.[86]

Table 4 summarizes the estimated WTP statistics for each of the wording

---

For survey questions like these, studies have shown that many people *say* they are willing to pay more for new environmental protection programs than they actually *would pay* out of their pockets. We believe this happens because, when answering these types of questions, people do not really consider how big an impact an extra cost actually has to their {household's} budget. It is easy to be generous when you do not really need to open your wallet.

To avoid this, as you consider each question please suppose that {your household} will actually have to pay the cost indicated in the question, out of your {household's} budget.

There are *other* environmental improvements that you might like to see made, both here in California and elsewhere in the United States. There are *other* areas of public policy that you might also like to influence, both here in California and nationally. Those other programs might also imply increases in the amount of State or federal income tax that {your household} would have to pay, either as a one-time tax or annually. You may or may not prefer that the State or the federal government spend your money on other things, if those other things have a higher priority for you than the proposed Central Coast oil spill prevention program.

The proposed one-time tax increase might also require {your household} to spend less on other items that you need or want, or to put less money into your savings."

[85] Following Li et al. (2005), this "environmental contributions" variant read: "But before we ask you how you would vote on this ballot proposition, please think about your {household's} average monthly income and expenses. After you have paid all the necessary bills for such things as housing, transportation, groceries, insurance, debt, and taxes, what percent of your income is left over for optional uses on things like recreation, savings, and giving for charity and other causes?

Now please think about the portion of your {household's} total monthly income available for "optional uses" (like recreation, savings, and giving for charity and other causes). On average, what percent *of that amount* do you use for contributions to environmental causes, such as donations for specific programs or contributions and memberships to environmental advocacy groups?"

[86] "If a California-wide ballot proposition about this proposal were on an election being held today, and the total cost to {your household} for the program would be $X, which one of these statements best describes your own reaction to the ballot proposition? [*Select one only.*]

I would vote FOR the proposition.

I support the goal of the Central Coast oil spill prevention program, but I'm not prepared to pay that much and so I would vote AGAINST.

I support the goal of the Central Coast oil spill prevention program, but I cannot afford to pay that much and so I would vote AGAINST.

I support the goal of the Central Coast oil spill prevention program, but I prefer that my money be spent on other priorities and so I would vote AGAINST.

I support the goal of the Central Coast oil spill prevention program, but I would vote AGAINST for the following reason [*Please enter:* _____].

I would vote AGAINST the proposition.

I'm not sure."

Table 4 Version 1 ABERS estimates of the lower bound on the sample mean WTP

Subsample	Unweighted n	WTP ($)	St. Err. ($)
All Version 1 respondents:	1,213	105.5	7.2
All Version 1, by wording addition variant:			
No wording addition	306	109.8^p	na
"Cheap talk" wording added	307	118.8	14.0
"Environmental contributions" wording added	300	103.4^p	na
"Dissonance minimization" wording added	300	85.1^p	na
All Version 1, by scenario length:			
Long scenario version (as 1995)	610	93.0	9.2
Short scenario version (as used for V2)	603	118.8	10.0

Note: The estimates in this table are based on initial responses, equivalent to the measure **B1** in the 1995 study. Estimates with the superscript ^{p} are derived from pooled models, and no standard errors were computed in those cases.

addition treatments.[87] The situation was confounded somewhat by uncertainty around our baseline ("no treatment") measure, caused by non-monotonicity that required the pooling of the highest two design points for that subsample.

For respondents who saw the "cheap talk" variant before the referendum question, the WTP statistic is surprisingly *higher.* While an occasional few other studies have observed a similar effect,[88] the preponderant result in the literature is that "cheap talk" scripts *do* tend to lower the WTP estimate.[89]

In addressing non-monotonicity when comparing WTP estimates, we found it valuable to plot the one-standard error confidence bands for *not-for* vote percentages by design point, because with the added assumption that the true curve should increase monotonically, neighboring points add statistical support (over and above the precision provided by just each point's sample observations considered independently). This approach would appear to be more insightful than the "level step" diagrams typically generated for singly bounded dichotomous choice responses.

For example, Figure 3 plots the precision bands for our cheap talk and baseline cases. It also shows for each design point the estimate when the

---

[87] Each of the table rows comprises approximately equal numbers of respondents given the long and short COS scenario descriptions.
[88] See, for example, Aadland and Caplan (2006).
[89] See Loomis (2014) at Table 1, and Morrison and Brown (2009).

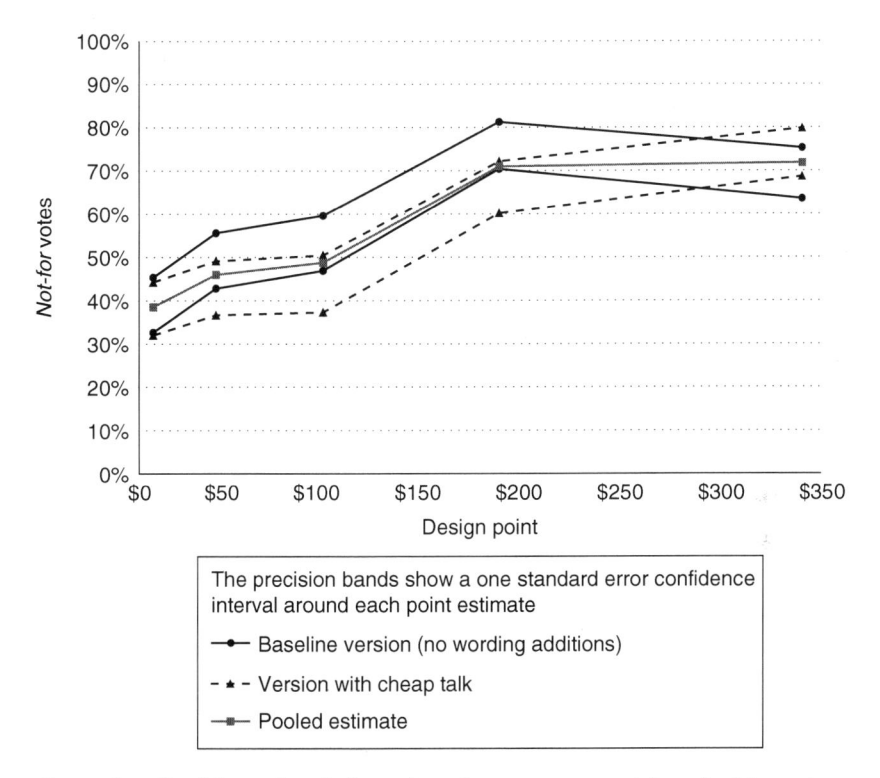

Figure 3 Confidence bands for referendum responses with and without cheap talk, by design point

baseline and cheap talk subsamples are pooled, and these always lie within the one standard error precision bands for both of the two subsamples. On this evidence, the baseline and cheap talk responses appear statistically indistinguishable.

The response curves for both the "environmental contributions" and "dissonance minimization" methods were (barely) non-monotonic for the weighted sample, but not for the unweighted sample (which yielded WTP statistic estimates of $102.8 and $92.4 respectively). Perhaps because of the issue with the non-monotonic baseline, the impact of our tested wording additions appeared somewhat lower than those reported by the original developers of the two techniques.[90] Our general ranking of the tested

---

[90] For "environmental contributions," Li et al. (2005) observed a drop in their estimate of *median* WTP of between 50% and 60% from their base, untreated case. For "dissonance minimization" Morrison and Brown (2009) measured a 32% reduction in their Turnbull

techniques did appear to support the literature experience – "dissonance minimization" produced the most marked reduction in the WTP statistic, followed by "environmental contributions" and "cheap talk" – but examination of the confidence bands for our response curves makes it hard to conclude that these differences are statistically significant.

A PLAUSIBLE RATIONALIZATION FOR SEVERAL OF THESE FINDINGS

The evidence from our study that many respondents are more focused on the type of message that their answers convey than on balancing a household budget call into question whether cognitive disjunctions threaten the validity of trying to improve the financial consequentiality of CVM responses.

As a thought experiment, consider the following simple hypothetical. The survey sample comprises two segments, one of which has respondents who do their very best to consider carefully all of the information they are given, and try their hardest to answer the questions as accurately and realistically as possible, just as the CVM theoreticians would want them to do. The second group – the polar opposite – has people with a much simpler set of decision rules. Is the proffered public good (without getting into all of that superfluous detail) one of which I broadly *approve* or *disapprove*? Is the price at which I'm being offered that good acceptable to me, as a once-only payment with no longer-term commitment (just like a one-off charitable donation)? If I approve, and the price is OK, then I'll vote *for*. Task completed; move on to the next question when I will apply the same approach again a priori, regardless of any part-whole or other association between this public good and any previous one.

Such a hypothetical would explain not only our V2 "standalone COS" result but also the disconnect that a proportion of V2 respondents showed when allowed to adjust their portmanteau program allocations after being shown the COS program scenario. It would help explain the serious scope failure when the V1 responses are compared with those for the much more expansive V2 cornucopia of environmental initiatives. Indeed, the hypothetical also would rationalize many of the other hypothetical bias phenomena observed with CVM surveys, such as "warm glow altruism" and the pervasive and persistent similarities between WTP findings and average charitable donations.

WTP estimate from including the same number of *no* categories. The resulting measure was slightly below a revealed preference estimate of WTP, but not by a significant amount. See also Loomis (2014), at pp. 38–9.

If something like that hypothetical (albeit in reality, doubtless a more subtle and complicated version of it) is, in fact, at work here, one key problem for the survey designer and the analyst is how to identify the different sub-samples, and how best to interpret their various responses once having identified them.[91] Some clues can come from a comprehensive debriefing battery (as was used with this survey), and thorough sensitivity testing.

REFERENCES

Aadland, D. and A.J. Caplan (2006), "Cheap talk reconsidered: New evidence from CVM," *Journal of Economic Behavior and Organization*, **60**(4), 562–78.
Arrow, K., R. Solow, P.R. Portney, E.E. Leamer, R. Radner, and H. Schuman (1993), "Report of the NOAA Panel on contingent valuation," *Federal Register*, **58**, 4,601–14.
Ayer, M., H.D. Brunk, G.M. Ewing, W.T. Reid, and E. Silverman (1955), "An empirical distribution function for sampling with incomplete information," *Annals of Mathematical Statistics*, **26**(4), 641–7.
Bateman, I.J., M. Cole, P. Cooper, S. Georgiou, D. Hadley, and G.L. Poe (2003), "On visible choice sets and scope sensitivity," *Journal of Environmental Economics and Management*, **47**(1), 71–93.
Bishop, R.C., D.J. Chapman, B.J. Kanninen, J.A. Krosnick, B. Leeworthy, and N.F. Meade (2011), *Total Economic Value for Protecting and Restoring Hawaiian Coral Reef Ecosystems: Final Report*, Silver Spring, MD: NOAA Office of National Marine Sanctuaries.
Boxall, P.C., W.L. Adamowicz, M. Olar, G.E. West, and G. Cantin (2012), "Analysis of the economic benefits associated with the recovery of threatened marine mammal species in the Canadian St. Lawrence Estuary," *Marine Policy*, **36**(1), 189–97.
Brown, T.C., S.C. Barro, M.J. Manfredo, and G.L. Peterson (1995), "Does better information about the good avoid the embedding effect?," *Journal of Environmental Management*, **44**(1), 1–10.
Carson, R.T., M.B. Conaway, W.M. Hanemann, J.A. Krosnick, R.C. Mitchell, and S. Presser (2004), *Valuing Oil Spill Prevention: A Case Study of California's Central Coast*, Dordrecht: Kluwer Academic Publishers.
Cummings, R.G. and L.O. Taylor (1999), "Unbiased value estimates for environmental goods: A cheap talk design for the contingent valuation method," *American Economic Review*, **89**(3), 649–65.
Hoehn, J.P. and A. Randall (1989), "Too many proposals pass the benefit cost test," *American Economic Review*, **79**(3), 544–51.
Kahneman, D. and J.L. Knetsch (1992), "Valuing public goods – the purchase of moral satisfaction," *Journal of Environmental Economics and Management*, **22**(1), 57–70.

---

[91] Leamer and Lustig (Chapter 8, this volume), who use latent class models to explore the heuristic decision rules that respondents may adopt in addressing non-market valuation questions, address a similar hypothesis.

Kaplan, E.L. and P. Meier (1958), "Nonparametric observation from incomplete observations," *Journal of the American Statistical Association*, **53**(282), 457–81.

Kemp, M.A. and C. Maxwell (1993), "Exploring a budget context for contingent valuation estimates," in J.A. Hausman (ed.), *Contingent Valuation: A Critical Assessment*, Amsterdam: North-Holland, pp. 217–65.

Kotchen, M. and S. Reiling (1999), "Do reminders of substitutes and budget constraints influence contingent valuation estimates? Another comment," *Land Economics*, **75**(3), 478–82.

Krosnick, J.A. and S. Presser (2010), "Question and questionnaire design," in P.V. Marsden and J.D. Wright (eds) (2010), *Handbook of Survey Research*, 2nd edition, Bingley, UK: Emerald Group Publishing, pp. 263–313.

Krosnick, J.A., A.L. Holbrook, M.K. Berent, R.T. Carson, W.M. Hanemann, and R.J. Kopp et al. (2002), "The impact of 'no opinion' response options on data quality: Non-attitude reduction or an invitation to satisfice?," *Public Opinion Quarterly*, **66**(3), 371–403.

Li, H., R.P. Berrens, A.K. Bohara, H.C. Jenkins-Smith, C.L. Silva, and D.L Weimer (2005), "Testing for budget constraint effects in a national advisory referendum survey on the Kyoto Protocol," *Journal of Agricultural and Resource Economics*, **30**(2), 350–66.

Loomis, J.B. (2014), "Strategies for overcoming hypothetical bias in stated preference surveys," *Journal of Agricultural and Resource Economics*, **39**(1), 34–46.

Magnussen, K. (1992), "Valuation of reduced water pollution using the contingent valuation method – testing for mental accounts and amenity misspecification," in S. Navrud (ed.), *Pricing the European Environment*, Oxford: Oxford University Press, pp. 195–220.

Morrison, M. and T.C. Brown (2009), "Testing the effectiveness of certainty scales, cheap-talk, and dissonance minimization in reducing hypothetical bias in contingent valuation studies," *Environmental and Resource Economics*, **44**(3), 307–26.

Parsons, G. and K. Myers (2016), "Fat tails and truncated bids in contingent valuation: An application to an endangered shorebird species," *Ecological Economics*, **129**(C), 210–19.

Schkade, D.A. and J.W. Payne (1993), "Where do the numbers come from? How people respond to contingent valuation questions," in J.A. Hausman (ed.) (1993), *Contingent Valuation: A Critical Assessment*, Amsterdam: North-Holland, pp. 271–93.

Schläpfer, F. and I. Brauer (2007), "Theoretical incentive properties of contingent valuation questions: Do they matter in the field?," *Ecological Economics*, **62**, 451–60.

Smith, A.E., M.A. Kemp, T.H. Savage, and C.L. Taylor (2005), "Methods and results from a new survey of values for eastern regional haze improvements," *Journal of the Air and Waste Management Association*, **55**(11), 1767–79.

Thaler, R.H. (1985), "Mental accounting and consumer choice," *Marketing Science*, **4**(3), 199–214.

Turnbull, B.W. (1974), "Nonparametric estimation of a survivorship function with doubly censored data," *Journal of the American Statistical Association*, **69**(345), 169–73.

Turnbull, B.W. (1976), "The empirical distribution function with arbitrarily grouped, censored and truncated data," *Journal of the Royal Statistical Society B*, **38**, 290–95.

Wallmo, K. and D.K. Lew (2011), "Valuing improvements to threatened and endangered marine species: An application of stated preference choice experiments," *Journal of Environmental Management*, **92**(7), 1793–801.

Whitehead, J.C. and T.L Cherry (2007), "Willingness to pay for a green energy program: A comparison of ex-ante and ex-post hypothetical bias mitigation approaches," *Resource and Energy Economics*, **29**(4), 247–61.

8. Inferences from stated preference surveys when some respondents do not compare costs and benefits[1]

Edward Leamer and Josh Lustig[2]

INTRODUCTION

Stated preference surveys are often used to estimate willingness to pay (WTP) for environmental improvements. These surveys typically ask respondents to choose between the status quo and one or more environmental improvements at hypothetical costs. The feature of these survey data that determines the estimate of the WTP is the declining fraction of respondents who choose an environmental improvement as the hypothetical cost increases. But data alone are not enough. A formal choice model is also needed to turn these data into WTP estimates. The traditional model presumes that all respondents know the gain in utility that they would experience if the environmental improvement were enacted, and they also know how much utility would be lost if they were compelled to pay the hypothetical cost. They then are assumed to choose the option with the greatest hypothetical net benefit, or choose the status quo if all the hypothetical net benefits are negative.

The WTP estimates derived from this traditional analysis are valid only if respondents are actually behaving in a way consistent with the utility maximization assumption, and in particular are making the kind of thoughtful trade-offs between costs and benefits that would have them choosing the environmental improvement if the cost is low and rejecting it if the cost is high. Rather than presupposing this ideal behavior, this

---

[1] The authors gratefully acknowledge the essential contributions made to this chapter by Drazen Prelec, Powell Dixon, James Burrows, Renée Miller-Mizia, Stamatia Kostakis, Hiu Man Chan, Jerome Genser, and Hasat Cakkalkurt.
[2] Respectively, Chauncey J. Medberry Professor in Management and Professor in Economics & Statistics at UCLA; Principal, Charles River Associates, Boston.

chapter offers models that allow for the possibility that some respondents may ignore costs while others may ignore benefits.

The fraction of respondents who behave according to the traditional utility maximization model is an estimated parameter in our model, as are the fractions of respondents whose decisions are better described by one of the heuristic decision rules. This statistical model can be thought to be a way of purging from the data suspicious responses, thus providing a formal basis for the common practice of excluding "protestors" who would oppose any environmental improvement regardless of cost (e.g., Meyerhoff et al., 2012). Protestors who ignore the benefits inappropriately drag down the estimated WTP if they are included in the data set, but there may also be respondents who want to improve the environment but do not weigh the costs and benefits of doing so. For example, some respondents may ignore the costs of environmental improvements and others may make choices only on the basis of costs. Therefore, it takes a model with at least three heuristics to identify protestors and respondents whose preferences for environmental improvements do not reflect trade-offs between costs and benefits, and to do statistically valid and conceptually unbiased two-sided trimming of responses. Inevitably, as we allow more heuristic rules into the model, the data trimming becomes more substantial and the estimated fraction of respondents whose choices reflect cost–benefit trade-offs declines but the estimated WTP of these respondents can go either up or down.

We apply our methodology to data collected by a National Oceanic and Atmospheric Administration ("NOAA") survey designed to value eight threatened and endangered marine species. We discover that many of the NOAA survey respondents' choices are more consistent with one or more heuristic rules than with a model of utility maximization. Using a model that includes a mixture of five heuristic decision rules competing with utility maximization, we estimate that only 23.4% of survey respondents answer the survey in a manner consistent with utility maximization. This estimated model offers a substantially improved fit of the data over the traditional mixed logit model that assumes all respondents maximize utility. We also discover that as the list of included heuristics is varied, there is considerable variability in the estimate of the fraction of utility maximizers and the estimate of their WTP. This variability of conclusions is troubling because we have not attempted to identify a full set of heuristics and if more heuristics are included in the model the range of alternative estimates would inevitably increase. The operative concluding words are thus: credibility and fragility. A credible analysis of data from stated preference surveys needs to allow formally for aberrant decision-makers, but attempts to increase credibility are likely to uncover an uncomfortable amount of fragility.

The rest of this chapter proceeds as follows. The next section briefly reviews related literature. The third section describes the stated preference survey we exploit. In sections four and five, we present our model and describe our estimation strategy. The sixth section presents our results and the seventh concludes.

RELATED LITERATURE

Latent class models allow survey respondents to use different rules or strategies when responding to surveys. For example, one class we assume below will absorb survey respondents who weigh the costs and benefits of marine species improvements when responding to the survey. What class a particular respondent belongs to is hidden to the researcher. But the latent class model infers probabilistically which class each respondent likely belongs to. Below, we use latent class models to infer which NOAA stated preference survey respondents likely make trade-offs between species improvement costs and benefits and which respondents likely use alternative choice rules. Other researchers have also used latent class models to make this distinction. In this section, we briefly review this literature.

First is a recent literature that uses latent class models to study attribute non-attendance.[3] Attribute non-attendance is present when some respondents ignore one or more attributes of the good or service when making choices. To accommodate multiple classes of respondents, these papers modify the multinomial and mixed logit models and allow for separate utility specifications for each class of respondents.[4] The literature on attribute non-attendance allows some respondents to have zero coefficients for the neglected attributes, but those respondents are otherwise identical to utility maximizers. We depart from this literature by allowing respondents who use heuristic decision rules to be entirely different, with no parameters in common with the utility maximizers who trade off costs and benefits.[5]

The attribute non-attendance literature comes to the same conclusion

---

[3] See, for example, Hensher et al. (2005, 2012), Scarpa et al. (2009), Hensher (2010), Hensher and Greene (2010), McNair et al. (2010), Campbell et al. (2011), and Greene and Hensher (2013).

[4] All but one of the papers cited above estimate multinomial logit models with latent classes. Hensher et al. (2005) estimate a multinomial *mixed* logit model with latent classes.

[5] Another difference between our chapter and the non-attendance literature is that all but one of the heuristic rules in our model are deterministic in the sense that the choices made by respondents following the heuristic rules can be perfectly predicted based on the observed characteristics of the options.

we do. Many individuals do not weigh the costs and benefits of improvement options when responding to stated preference surveys. For example, in a survey intended to elicit WTP for rural landscape improvements in Ireland, Campbell et al. (2011) find that 65.2% of survey respondents ignore costs. Using a model that does not allow non-attendance, they estimate WTP for landscape improvements between from $163 to $221. After accounting for attribute non-attendance, estimated WTP ranged from $49 to $109. In other words, WTP falls by more than 50% after adjusting the model to allow for the possibility that not all respondents are attentive to the costs of landscape improvements. Below, we will find a similar downward adjustment to WTP when the model allows a set of heuristics as alternatives to utility maximization.

A second related literature uses latent class models to identify "protestors" based on serial non-participation.[6] See, for example, Von Haefen et al. (2005), Burton and Rigby (2009) or Cunha-e-Sa et al. (2012). In these analyses, a class of respondents is assumed to reject environmental improvements (or other improvements) regardless of their benefits and costs. Inferring "protest" responses using latent class models complements the standard approach that identifies "protestors" based on their responses to follow-up questions. For example, Lew and Wallmo (2011) and Wallmo and Lew (2011, 2012)[7] also rely on the NOAA survey and define protestors as (1) respondents who choose the status quo in all three questions and (2) indicate they are not confident in their responses or their answers to other follow-up questions indicate the respondent is not making cost–benefit trade-offs. For example, respondents who distrust the government or are unwilling to pay higher taxes for any reason are classified as protestors if they choose the status quo in all three questions.

Other applications of latent class models do not neatly fall into the two categories described above. For example, McNair et al. (2012) use a latent class model to identify survey respondents who learn their preferences while completing the survey and respondents who behave strategically (i.e., misrepresent their preferences to manipulate the survey outcome). Similarly, Hess et al. (2012) use a latent class model to distinguish between respondents who use reference points when completing stated preference surveys and respondents whose choices reflect lexicographic preferences.

---

[6] This literature also uses the term "hurdle" model to refer to latent class models.
[7] Throughout the text, we refer to the definition of protestors used by Lew and Wallmo. In each of these instances we are referring to the definition of protester adapted by Lew and Wallmo (2011), Wallmo and Lew (2011), and Wallmo and Lew (2012).

NOAA SURVEY DATA

Our analysis relies on survey data from Phase I of the Protected Species Valuation Survey undertaken by the National Marine Fisheries Service of the National Oceanic and Atmospheric Administration ('NOAA survey'). The purpose of the NOAA survey was to value potential improvements in the Endangered Species Act (ESA) status of eight threatened and endangered ('T&E') marine species – the North Pacific right whale, the North Atlantic right whale, the loggerhead sea turtle, the leatherback sea turtle, the Hawaiian monk seal, the wild Upper Willamette River Chinook salmon, the wild Puget Sound Chinook salmon, and the smalltooth sawfish. Each version of the survey offered respondents the opportunity to improve three of these eight species.

Before answering choice questions about species improvements, respondents were first shown information about the ESA and the three species in their version, as well as what actions are currently being done to protect them and what additional actions could be undertaken. They were then asked to select their most preferred option in three choice questions. Each question offered respondents three alternatives to choose from: a status quo option and two alternative options offering additional protection actions for at least one of the three T&E species. Respondents were asked to select the option they would most prefer. Figure 1 shows an example choice screen. Each option is described by the ESA status of each species (endangered, threatened, or recovered) before and after the option is implemented and the amount of added household cost per year over a period of ten years. The three options are labeled A, B, and C from left to right, with Option A always being the status quo option, with no added household cost.

The NOAA survey was conducted by Knowledge Networks using a random sample of their Internet panel of US households.[8] A pretest including only three of the eight T&E species was fielded in December 2008 and January 2009. The main survey was fielded in June and July of 2009, yielding 13,684 completed surveys with a completion rate of 70.8%. There are 44 versions of the main survey, differing by species combination, species order, which cost scale was used, and whether a "cheap talk" script was given to the respondent. Each version is further divided into 16 sub-versions with different levels of ESA status and costs.[9]

---

[8] We obtained the NOAA survey data through a Freedom of Information request.
[9] We chose not to weight the Knowledge Networks (2009) survey data for several reasons. First, Wallmo and Lew did not use weighted data, and we wanted to do our analysis using the

As in the previous question, please compare Options A, B, and C in this table and select the option you most prefer.

Remember that any money you spend on these options is money that could spent on other things.

Expected result in 50 years for each option

	Option A *No additional protection actions*	Option B *Additional protection actions*	Option C *Additional protection actions*
Loggerhead sea turtle ESA status	Threatened	Recovered	Recovered
North Pacific right whale ESA status	Endangered	Threatened	Endangered
Leatherback sea turtle ESA status	Endangered	Threatened	Recovered
Cost per year Added cost to your household each year for 10 years	$0	$100	$60
Which option do you prefer?	○	○	○

Figure 1   Example of choice experiment

We restrict our analysis to survey respondents who provide answers to each of the three choice tasks assigned to them. Imposing this restriction reduces the number of respondents from 13,684 to 11,459 and the number of observed choices from 41,052 to 34,377.

same data they used to allow direct comparison of our results. Second, the data sample used in the survey was enormous, so any distortions caused by not weighting should be minimal. Third, our focus in our analysis was to show that estimated WTPs vary depending on the inclusion of different heuristics classes in the estimation methodology; weighting the data was not required for this purpose.

MODEL

In this section we describe the model we use to explain respondents' answers to the NOAA stated preference survey. Our model allows a number of alternative choice rules that respondents could have used to solve this task. These include choice rules in which survey respondents make rational trade-offs between the costs and benefits of environmental improvements and choice rules where choices do not reflect such trade-offs. This distinction is important because survey responses are informative about willingness to pay only if they reflect rational cost–benefit trade-offs.

We note where the choice rules we include in the model are similar to choice rules used in previous analyses of stated preference surveys. Although our set of alternative rules spans a wide range of behaviors, we have not attempted to include all likely choice rules, and in particular we do not study context effects here.[10,11]

Trade-off Respondents

We assume a fraction π_{TO} of respondents make rational trade-offs between the costs and benefits of species improvements. A "trade-off" respondent i is assumed to choose option j that maximizes utility v_{ij}:

$$v_{ij} = \sum_s \beta_{is} * d_{js} - \alpha Cost_j + \varepsilon_{ij}$$

Utility v_{ij} includes the benefits from species improvements, the costs of species improvements, and an idiosyncratic zero mean error term ε_{ij}. The error term represents either unobserved utility or personal indecision (wavering). If ε_{ij} is unobserved utility with mean zero it does not affect mean WTP and if ε_{ij} is wavering it does not affect individual WTP. The average WTP calculations we perform below that exclude the error terms are correct in either case.

The binary indicator d_{js} turns on when a species improvement is offered and the parameter β_{is} is the "utility" that respondent i would experience given a particular species improvement. The coefficient on cost α measures the utility of income, which is implicitly assumed to be constant over the chosen cost scale and the same for all individuals. Since option A (the

---

[10] We study the context effects in the NOAA survey in a companion paper.
[11] We also chose not to use the NOAA stated preference survey to study learning (e.g., Plott, 1996). Researchers typically identify learning by looking for changes in respondents' behavior as they proceed through the survey. However, the NOAA survey only asks respondents three questions. Learning studies typically use surveys with more than three questions.

status quo option) offers no species improvements and imposes no costs, we use the normalization $v_{iA} = 0$.

WTP is the level of the cost that perfectly offsets the benefits and makes the respondent indifferent between paying for a species improvement and the status quo. This cost is the solution to $0 = \beta_{is} - \alpha Cost$, namely $WTP_{is} = \beta_{is}/\alpha$.

We model utility maximizers' behavior with a mixed logit specification similar to that used by Wallmo and Lew (2012) to analyze the same survey data.[12] The mixed logit model has been widely adopted to analyze stated preference survey data in the recent literature.[13] Similar to other studies, we assume that each level of marginal utility for species improvements, β_{is}, is drawn from a normal distribution with mean $\overline{\beta}_s$ and standard deviation σ_s. We assume the marginal utility of income, α, is fixed across respondents, leading to WTP that is also normally distributed.[14] Finally, the mixed logit model carries the assumption that ε_{ij} is drawn from an *iid* extreme value distribution.

Alternatives to Benefit–Cost Trade-offs: Heuristic Decision Rules

We consider several heuristic decision rules that capture three broad categories of respondents who do not compare and make trade-offs between costs and benefits – respondents who consider costs but not benefits, respondents who consider benefits but not costs, and respondents who consider neither costs nor benefits. We make no claims that the set of heuristics we consider is comprehensive, and the heuristic rules that we describe below represent only a subset of all the heuristics that respondents may be using.[15] However, even a small set of heuristics is sufficient to demonstrate that there are a large number of responses that are more consistent with heuristic decision rules than with utility maximization:

---

[12] Wallmo and Lew also used a similar model in the analysis of the NOAA survey's pre-test data (Lew and Wallmo, 2011; Wallmo and Lew, 2011).

[13] Examples in the environmental literature include studies on global climate change (Layton and Brown, 2000), biodiversity (Cerdaa et al., 2013), river ecology (Hanley et al., 2006), coral reef ecosystems (Parsons and Thur, 2008), landscape (Olsen, 2009), and endangered species (Lew et al., 2010), and wetlands (Kaffashi et al., 2012).

[14] When estimating mixed logit models, researchers do not typically assume random coefficients for all product characteristics. All contingent evaluation studies cited above as examples in the environmental literature assume a fixed cost or price coefficient, while allowing the coefficients of all other attributes to be random.

[15] The rules we use are intended as examples of heuristic rules in which respondents are not attentive to costs or benefits. There are alternative heuristic rules we could have tested in which respondents are also not attentive to costs and/or benefits. However, identifying the heuristic rules that best explain respondents' choices is beyond the scope of this chapter.

1 Status quo only

A fraction π_{SQ} of respondents are assumed to be protestors who always choose the status quo option no matter what other alternatives are offered in the survey question. These respondents are not attentive to costs or benefits when responding to the survey. Thus, the probability an individual i chooses an option k in question q conditional on following the protestor heuristic is given by:

$$Prob(y_{iq} = k | Status\, Quo) = \begin{matrix} 1 \; if\, k = A \\ 0 \; if\, k \neq A \end{matrix}$$

In a secondary specification, we remove survey respondents identified by Wallmo and Lew (2012) as protestors before estimating the model. These include the choices made by 2,800 respondents who chose the status quo in all three questions and whose responses to follow-up questions suggest protest behavior. While this secondary specification yields results that are similar to our main specification, we prefer a latent class approach to identifying protest behavior because it does not require a priori exclusion of respondents based on ad hoc protestor definitions. This view is supported in the literature. See, for example, Meyerhoff and Liebe (2006, 2008) and Meyerhoff et al. (2012).

2 Attentive to environmental improvements only ("steps only" respondents)

We assume that a fraction of the population π_{Steps} is composed of respondents who follow the "improvement steps only" heuristic. These respondents support environmental improvements but do not make benefit–cost trade-offs. Instead, they first identify how many steps of improvement are offered by each option in their choice set. For example, an option that improves the North Pacific right whale from endangered to recovered and leatherback turtle from endangered to threatened offers three steps of improvement. These respondents then choose the option that offers the greatest total number of steps of species improvements, irrespective of costs. If options B and C offer the same number of steps of improvements, "max steps" respondents are assumed to randomly choose between the two options with probability 0.5 on both.

"Steps only" respondents' choice probabilities are as follows. Since the status quo option offers no species improvements, for all questions:

$$Prob(y_{iq} = A | Steps\, Only) = 0$$

Instead, respondent i chooses the option that offers the most steps of improvement. If options B and C offer the same number of steps of improvement, respondents' choices are determined by a coin flip. Therefore, the probability that individual i chooses B is given by:

$$Prob(y_{iq} = B|\text{Steps Only}) = \begin{array}{l} 0 \text{ if } Steps_{qB} < Steps_{qC} \\ .5 \text{ if } Steps_{qB} = Steps_{qC} \\ 1 \text{ if } Steps_{qB} > Steps_{qC} \end{array}$$

The probability that i chooses C in any question is defined analogously.

3 Attentive to environmental costs only ("costs only" respondents)

We include a heuristic that captures respondents who want to improve the status of marine species but at the lowest cost possible. We assume these respondents choose the environmental improvement option with the lower cost, and randomly choose between the two improvement options if they share the same cost. Since the status quo option offers no species improvements, for all questions:

$$Prob(y_{iq} = A|\text{Costs Only}) = 0$$

Instead, i chooses the option that offers some form of improvement at the lowest cost. Like the steps only heuristic, if options B and C are equally costly, respondents' choices are determined by a coin flip. Therefore, the probability that individual i chooses B is given by:

$$Prob(y_{iq} = B|\text{Costs Only}) = \begin{array}{l} 0 \text{ if } Cost_{qB} > Cost_{qC} \\ .5 \text{ if } Cost_{qB} = Cost_{qC} \\ 1 \text{ if } Cost_{qB} < Cost_{qC} \end{array}$$

The probability that i chooses C in any question is defined analogously. This heuristic represents a fraction π_{Costs} of the population.[16] For example, some respondents might have "attribute non-attendance" with a zero coefficient on cost in their utility function but might have

---

[16] We have also experimented with a "high cost only heuristic." High cost only respondents always choose the species improvement with the highest cost. If options B and C have the same cost, high cost only respondents are assumed to randomly choose between the two options with probability 0.5 on both. We do not include this heuristic in our main specification because the set of respondents compatible with the high cost only heuristic overlaps the set compatible with the improvement steps only heuristic. More than twice as many respondents make choices that are consistent with the steps only heuristic than the high cost only heuristic and there are very few respondents who make choices that are consistent with the high cost only heuristic but inconsistent with the steps only heuristic. In a sensitivity analysis below, we include the high cost only heuristic in order to demonstrate how our results are affected by the inclusion of an unnecessary heuristic.

all the species improvement coefficients in common with the trade-off respondents.

4 Choose environmental improvements ignoring costs and benefits

Some survey respondents may want to indicate support for the environment and get the survey over as rapidly as possible. These respondents may always choose the first improvement, option B, and others may always choose the second (and last) improvement, option C. These heuristics represent π_B and π_C of the population. The probability an individual i chooses an option k in question q conditional on following one of these two heuristics is given by:

$$Prob(y_{iq} = k|B\ Only) = \begin{cases} 1 & if\ k = B \\ 0 & if\ k \neq B \end{cases}$$

$$Prob(y_{iq} = k|C\ Only) = \begin{cases} 1 & if\ k = C \\ 0 & if\ k \neq C \end{cases}$$

5 Randomizers ignoring costs and benefits

Last is a set of respondents who ignore the costs and the proposed improvements and act as if they were randomly choosing a response. This heuristic represents a fraction π_{Random} of the population. The other heuristics predict behavior with probability either one or zero depending on whether the decisions conform or not with the rule. Both the utility maximization rule and the random rule predict observed behavior with a probability between zero and one. An individual is judged by the estimation routine likely to be a randomizer if his or her decisions are incompatible with the other deterministic rules and also if the random model predicts better than utility maximization. Under this heuristic individuals choose options A, B, and C with probabilities π_{RandA}, π_{RandB}, and π_{RandC}, respectively.[17] Thus, the probability an individual i makes a sequence of choices Y_i is given by:

$$Prob(Y_i|Randomizer) = \pi_{RandA}^{\Sigma_{=1}(y_{iq}=A)} \pi_{RandB}^{\Sigma_{=1}(y_{iq}=B)} \pi_{RandC}^{\Sigma_{=1}(y_{iq}=C)}$$

---

[17] An alternative would be to model randomizers as having an equal probability of choosing A, B, or C. We chose to use the less restrictive rule of allowing the data to determine the probabilities of choosing each option.

ESTIMATION

A critical modeling assumption that we make is that individuals use the same decision rule for all three choice sets.[18] Therefore, the unconditional probability of observing individual i make a sequence of choices Y_i is a probabilistic mixture of the shares (π) and conditional probabilities (*Prob* (Y_i|*Choice Rule*)) described in the fourth section:

$Prob(Y_i) = \pi_{TO}Prob(Y_i|Trade\text{-}offs) + \pi_{SQ}Prob(Y_i|Status\ Quo) + \pi_{Steps}Prob(Y_i|Steps\ Only) + \pi_{Costs}Prob(Y_i|Costs\ Only) + \pi_B Prob(Y_i|B\ Only) + \pi_C Prob(Y_i|C\ Only) + \pi_{Random}Prob(Y_i|Randomizer).$

We multiply these probabilities across respondents and take the log to form the likelihood function:

$$Ln(Prob(Y_1, Y_2, ..., Y_n|\pi, \theta)) = \sum_i \log\left[\sum_{s=1}^{S} \pi_s Prob_s(Y_i|\theta_s)\right].$$

We estimate the model by via maximum likelihood in Matlab.[19,20] Maximum likelihood estimation of this model has the same estimating equations for respondents' preferences and WTP (α and β) as the standard mixed logit model, except that respondents' choices are weighted on the basis of whether they are likely to be utility maximizers. Below we demonstrate this result and provide additional intuition underlying identification of the model's parameters.

Let $\Theta \equiv (\alpha, \beta, \sigma)$ represent the parameters entering the mixed logit component of our model. Recall that these are the parameters determining WTP. Below, we compare the first-order conditions that characterize

---

[18] Mariel et al. (2011) allow choice rules to vary across questions for the same respondent. The authors allow respondents to attend to attributes in some questions but not others. In our analysis we make the assumption that individuals use the same decision rule in each choice set because of the data limitations of having only three choice sets per individual. In addition, the focus of our study was on showing the importance of including in the estimation methodology latent classes of individuals using heuristic decision rules not based on cost–benefit rules and not on identifying the optimal set of heuristics. We demonstrate that under the assumption that each individual's decision rules are fixed that our estimates are statistically superior to standard mixed logit results. A fertile area for future research would be to investigate whether respondents' decision rules change across choice sets.

[19] To determine the reliability of our estimation routine, we applied it to simulated data. Our estimation routine was able to recover the parameters used to simulate the data (subject to sampling error).

[20] We based our Matlab estimation routine on code provided by Professor Kenneth Train (accessed December 7, 2016 at http://eml.berkeley.edu/Software/abstracts/train1006mxlmsl.html). To incorporate heterogeneity into the mixed logit component of the model, we used shuffled Halton draws.

Θ when heuristics are included in the model to the first-order conditions when heuristics are excluded. Below $L_{MixLogit + Heuristics}$ represents the log-likelihood function when heuristics are added to the mixed logit model and $L_{MixLogit}$ represents the log-likelihood function when heuristics are not included.

In our model and the mixed logit model, Θ is chosen to maximize the probability of respondents' observed choices generated by the model. Both first-order conditions are satisfied by a Θ such that a weighted sum of $\frac{\partial Prob(Y_i|Trade\text{-}offs)}{\partial \Theta}$ across respondents equals zero. The first-order conditions associated with our model and the mixed logit model differ only in how respondents' choices are weighted:

$$\frac{\partial L_{MixLogit + Heuristics}}{\partial \Theta} = \sum_{i=1}^{N} w_{MixLogit + Heuristics, i} \frac{\partial Prob(Y_i|Trade\text{-}offs)}{\partial \Theta} = 0$$

$$\frac{\partial L_{MixLogit}}{\partial \Theta} = \sum_{i=1}^{N} w_{MixLogit, i} \frac{\partial Prob(Y_i|Trade\text{-}offs)}{\partial \Theta} = 0$$

Thus, the nature of variation in the data used to identify Θ (and, WTP) in the mixed logit model and a model merging the mixed logit with heuristics is the same. The parameters are chosen so the observed propensity of respondents to choose species improvements at stated costs over the status quo is best explained by the model.

However, the measures of WTP emerging from the mixed logit and our model will differ because of differences in how the models weigh respondents. A careful examination of the weights in the first-order conditions illustrates differences in identification across the two models. For individual i:

$$w_{MixLogit, i + Heuristics, i} = \frac{\pi_{TO}}{Prob(Y_i)}$$

$$= \frac{\pi_{TO}}{\pi_{TO} Prob(Y_i|Trade\text{-}offs) + \cdots + \pi_{Random} Prob(Y_i|Randomizer)}$$

and

$$w_{MixLogit, i} = \frac{1}{Prob(Y_i|Trade\text{-}off\,Rule)}$$

Dividing $w_{MixLogit + Heuristics, i}$ by $w_{MixLogit, i}$ and applying Bayes' rule yields:

$$\frac{w_{MixLogit + Heuristics, i}}{w_{MixLogit, i}} = Prob(i\ is\ a\ Trade\text{-}off\ Respondent|Y_i)$$

Given i's choices, *Prob(i is a Trade-off Respondent $|Y_i$)* expresses the probability that i is maximizing a neoclassical utility function. When a respondent's choices are easily rationalized by the mixed logit model, this probability is high. When i's choices cannot be easily rationalized by the mixed logit model, and it appears that i is following a heuristic rule, this probability is low. In contrast to the mixed logit model, our estimation routine places greater weight on respondents who appear to be more likely to be maximizing utility. Our routine appropriately places less weight on respondents whose choices appear less likely to reflect trade-offs between species improvements and costs.[21]

Next, we discuss identification of the heuristic shares. Let π_h denote the share of respondents following an arbitrary heuristic. The first-order condition associated with $\pi_{heuristic\ h}$ is:[22]

$$\sum_{i=1}^{N} \frac{Prob(Y_i|heuristic\ h)}{Prob(Y_i)} = \sum_{i=1}^{N} \frac{Prob(Y_i|Trade\text{-}offs)}{Prob(Y_i)}$$

For any individual i, $Prob(Y_i)$ is equal to the portion of i's choice explained by the estimated model and $\frac{Prob(Y_i|heuristic\ h)}{Prob(Y_i)}$ equals the fraction of the model's fit attributable to heuristic h. The heuristic shares are chosen so the marginal contribution of each heuristic in explaining respondents' behavior (averaged across respondents) is equal across choice rules.

Intuitively, the estimation routine evaluates each heuristic's marginal contributions using variations in choice sets across respondents. Recall that each respondent is given one of 44 versions and 16 sub-versions of the NOAA survey so that there is extensive variation in the species status improvements and costs offered to the respondents. Each choice rule makes unique predictions about how patterns in respondents' choices should vary across choice sets. We identify heuristic shares on the basis of whether these unique predictions are confirmed in the data. For example, we identify the share of respondents following the status quo heuristic (π_{SQ}) by examining changes in respondents' choice patterns when choice sets' species status improvements are fixed but their costs vary. Respondents following the status quo heuristic will indiscriminately choose option A regardless of whether species improvements are offered at low or high costs. Trade-off respondents, however,

---

[21] When choosing the parameters that determine WTP, the estimation routine does place weight on all respondents. This is because all respondents' choices are potentially explained by the trade-off rule. No respondents are assigned to a decision rule with certainty.

[22] This formulation of the first-order conditions relies on the identity $\pi_{TO} = 1 - \pi_{Steps} - \pi_{Costs} - \cdots - \pi_{Random}$

will choose the status quo more often when they are presented choice sets with relatively high costs. Our estimation routine chooses π_{SQ} so that the estimated model best explains changes in respondents' observed behavior related to this choice set variation. If the share of respondents choosing option A in all three questions varies little with options B and C's costs, the model will infer that a large fraction of respondents consistently choose option A because they follow the status quo heuristic. Similar intuition explains identification of the other heuristic shares.

RESULTS

In this section we first describe the estimates implied by a model that includes all the heuristics, and then we show how much these estimates change if the set of alternative heuristics is varied. We argue that the estimates lack credibility if the set of alternative heuristic decision rules is too narrow (e.g., none), and we show that the estimates are fragile (very dependent on the particular mix of heuristics that is allowed) when the set of heuristics is wide enough to be credible.

Estimated Population Shares of Choice Rules

Our main specification is a probabilistic mixture of all the heuristics described above plus a mixed logit group of trade-off respondents. The first column of Table 1 reports estimates of the population shares of the seven choice rules of this specification and also the choice probabilities of the maximizers.[23]

The six simple heuristic rules absorb a large majority of respondents and only 22.4% are better explained by the trade-off rule.[24] A larger fraction is estimated to follow the status quo and randomizer heuristics (24.6% and 27.8% respectively) and large fractions of respondents (12.4% and 8.7%) are estimated to behave according to the steps only and costs only heuristics. According to the estimated model, few

---

[23] The results in Table 1 and all subsequent tables are based on a sample of 11,459 respondents who answer all three survey questions. The choices of 1,822 respondents who did not answer all three survey questions were excluded from the analysis. Of these respondents 1,478 failed to answer one question. The remaining 344 respondents failed to answer two of the three questions.

[24] We expect that incorporating a more comprehensive set of heuristic rules will reduce this share further; in addition, using heuristic rules that assume errors in respondents' choices would likely increase the estimated heuristics shares and reduce the estimated trade-off share.

Table 1   Estimated choice rule shares

	Heuristic Shares (%)	St. Err. (%)
Trade-off	22.40	0.80
Status quo only (Always A)	24.60	0.90
Steps only	12.40	0.40
Costs only	8.70	0.40
B or C only	4.20	0.30
Randomizers	27.80	0.80
Probability of A	4.70	0.30
Probability of B	44.50	0.60
Probability of C	50.80	0.60

respondents systematically choose options B and C and belong to the B and C only heuristics (4.2%). Finally, the estimates imply that respondents following the randomizer heuristic tend to ignore option A. They randomly choose between the two improvement options, with a higher tendency to choosing the middle option B (50.8% of respondents following the randomizer heuristic) rather than option C (44.5% of respondents following the randomizer heuristic). In other words, this turns out to be describing random environmentalists. If we sum the shares of the steps only heuristic (12.4%), the costs only heuristic (8.7%), and the randomizer heuristic (27.8%), we find that 48.9% of survey respondents reject the status quo regardless of how expensive the two environmental options may be.

These population shares are estimated with high precision, per the standard errors reported in column two. These standard errors imply, for example, that there is a 90% chance that the share of respondents following a trade-off decision rule is between 21% and 24.5%.

A deterministic heuristic rule predicts behavior with probability one or zero. For example, the status quo rule perfectly predicts the choices if the status quo was chosen for all three choice sets, but otherwise is incompatible with these choices. This allows us to separate the observations into those that are perfectly compatible with the rule and those that are incompatible. Table 2 compares the estimated heuristic shares with the % of respondents whose responses were perfectly compatible with the rule.

Responses that are compatible with more than one decision rule are counted more than once in the percentage of respondents column and these have to be allocated probabilistically across the alternatives including the utility maximization rule to compute the estimated population shares. Consequently, in all cases the estimated population share is

Table 2 Percentage of respondents whose behavior is consistent with heuristic rules

	% Respondents	(%) Estimated Heuristic Share
Status quo only (Always A)	27.0	24.6
Steps only	24.4	12.4
Cost only	18.2	8.7
B or C only	16.7	4.2

smaller than the fraction of compatible respondents. This has the smallest effect on the protestors (who always choose the status quo) because most of the cases in which the status quo was chosen all three times are not well explained by any of the other rules, which is a partial justification for the common procedure of dropping these "protestors."

While the data cannot reveal exactly which of the decision rules each respondent followed, the estimated model and data do allow us to compute an estimated probability that a respondent was following one of the decision rules.[25] Estimates of the parameters of the trade-off rule with maximum likelihood place more weight on respondents who were probably using the trade-off rule. Since respondents who chose the status quo in all three questions are unlikely to have done so while following the trade-off decision rule, the estimation routine discounts these respondents' choices when determining the trade-off rule parameters and WTP.

Next, we turn to our measures of WTP for various species status improvements that are calculated from estimates of species valuations ($\bar{\beta}_{sk}$ and σ_{sk}) and cost sensitivity (α) parameters of the mixed logit model. It is important to emphasize these are the WTPs of trade-off respondents, who constitute fewer than one-quarter (22.4%) of respondents.[26]

Estimated Willingness to Pay for Species Status Improvements

Table 3 presents estimates of WTP for species status improvements. These measures reflect the choices of respondents whose patterns of

---

[25] Intuitively, the more favorable the improvement options are in the respondent's choice set (large improvements at low costs), the less likely it is that the respondent picked the status quo because the respondent was rationally weighing costs and benefits.

[26] Moreover, these WTP estimates would change if more heuristic rules were added and if we took into account the types of context effects we analyze in a companion paper, Prelec et al. (forthcoming).

Table 3 *Estimated mean willingness to pay for species improvements*

	Trade-off Respondents		Population	
	Mean WTP ($)	Standard error ($)	Mean WTP ($)	Standard error ($)
One step from endangered to threatened				
Smalltooth sawfish	10.30	2.30	2.41	0.54
Leatherback turtle	11.08	3.12	2.59	0.73
Hawaiian monk seal	15.60	2.02	3.65	0.47
North Pacific right whale	14.13	2.04	3.31	0.48
North Atlantic right whale	12.15	2.47	2.84	0.58
One step from threatened to recovered				
Upper Willamette River Chinook salmon	15.78	2.53	3.69	0.59
Puget Sound Chinook salmon	17.92	2.37	4.19	0.55
Loggerhead	18.55	1.61	4.34	0.38
Two steps from endangered to recovered				
Smalltooth sawfish	16.98	2.03	3.97	0.71
Hawaiian monk seal	23.93	2.63	5.60	0.62
Leatherback turtle	27.00	3.00	6.32	0.70
North Pacific right whale	23.52	4.32	5.50	1.01
North Atlantic right whale	23.92	4.12	5.60	0.96
Average one-step	14.44		3.38	
Average two-step	23.07		5.40	

Note: The population WTP is equal to the trade-off respondents' WTP multiplied by the share of respondents following the trade-off rule. The population WTP estimates assume that the non-trade-off respondents have zero WTP because there is no evidence in the data to support non-zero WTPs for these respondents.

responses indicate that they are likely to use a trade-off decision rule.[27] While the mixed logit model generates a distribution of WTP across individuals (reflecting the distributions of β), we only present the estimated means of these distributions below and the standard errors of the means.[28]

[27] Since all respondents' choice rules are unobserved, technically all respondents' choices enter the WTP calculation. However, the estimation routine places much more weight on respondents likely to be maximizing utility. For example, a respondent following the trade-off choice rule with 75 percent probability will receive 15 times as much weight as a respondent following the trade-off rule with 5 percent probability.

[28] For each species improvement, we report $\frac{\hat{\bar{\beta}}_s}{\hat{\alpha}}$ where $\bar{\beta}_s$ and $\hat{\alpha}$ are point estimates of $\bar{\beta}_s$ and α. To calculate the standard error of mean willingness to pay, we perform a bootstrap

The first set of columns reports mean WTP estimates of the trade-off respondents. The mean WTP estimates range from $10.30 (WTP for the smalltooth sawfish improvement from endangered to threatened) to $27.00 (WTP for the leatherback turtle improvement from endangered to recovered). The second set of columns presents average WTP across all respondents. This overall WTP estimate is obtained by multiplying the estimated WTP of trade-off respondents by the estimated share of respondents who are utilizing the trade-off rule, thus assigning zero WTP to all non-trade-off respondents. While some of these non-trade-off respondents may have positive WTP, the model and the database we are using do not allow us to infer their WTP from their responses.

Additional Specifications: Sensitivity Analysis

It seems clear that analyses of stated preference surveys have to allow for protestors and other types of non-conforming respondents. But what other types should be considered? That is not at all clear. While the utility maximization hypothesis does not dictate all the features of the logit or mixed logit models, the extent of model ambiguity in a utility maximization model seems very small compared with the model ambiguity that afflicts studies that allow for non-conforming respondents. Inferential fragility thus becomes a very serious issue. Do minor changes in the model lead to major changes in the inferences? To explore the fragility of estimates of WTP, we present in this section results from models with different sets of included heuristics, beginning with the traditional model that includes no heuristics.

Tables 4 and 5 contain results of ten models that have different lists of included heuristics. Table 4 reports the estimated heuristic shares and measures of mean WTP (averaged across species improvements and respondents) implied by each model. Table 5 reports measures of fit (likelihood value and Bayesian information criterion [BIC]) for each model. The mixed logit trade-off rule is included in all ten models and the estimated fraction of the population using this rule is reported in the first column of Table 4 labeled "Trade-off." The intent of Table 4 is to help discover how much the estimates of WTP depend on the choice of heuristics and which heuristics matter most. Table 5 supplements Table 4 with information on measures of fit.

The first two rows of Table 4 contain the results of traditional mixed logit models with and without the Lew and Wallmo "protestors" included.

using the estimated distributions of $\hat{\bar{\beta}}_s$ and $\hat{\alpha}$. These standard errors are measures of how precisely mean willingness to pay is estimated and not the amount of heterogeneity across respondents.

The third row refers to a model that includes only the mixed logit model and the status quo heuristic. Row (4) includes all of the heuristics plus a high cost only heuristic.[29] Rows (5) through (10) refer to models that include all the heuristics but one.

The first seven columns of numbers are the estimated fractions of each of the heuristic types, and columns (8) to (10) report the estimated choice probabilities for the randomizers. The last two columns report average WTP, first for the trade-off respondents and then for the population overall, assigning zero WTP to non-trade-off respondents.

The purpose of rows (1) through (3) is to evaluate the implications of different treatments of protestors. In row (1), we report estimates using the choices of all 11,459 respondents.[30] In row (2), we exclude from the data set the 24.4%[31] of respondents labeled "protestors" by Lew and Wallmo. These Lew and Wallmo "protestors" are respondents who both chose the status quo in all three choice sets and also revealed in follow-up questions confusion regarding the task they had performed. In row (3), we include all 11,459 respondents in the data set but use a model that adds the status quo heuristic to the mixed logit model. Notice how similar are rows (2) and (3), the former using the Lew and Wallmo definition of protestors and the latter using the protestor heuristic to drive the trimming. The estimated fractions of trade-off respondents are 75.6% and 73.5%, and the estimates of mean willingness to pay of the trade-off respondents are $45.80 and $51.20 compared with $21.34 for the row (1) case with all the data included. Also note that the population WTP estimates in row (2) and row (3) are both substantially larger than the row (1) estimate based on all the data, because the increase in the estimated WTP for the trade-off respondents in rows (2) and (3) more than offsets the reduced fraction of respondents to which the estimated WTP applies.

Although rows (2) and (3) yield very similar conclusions, it is important to understand that the model-driven results in row (3) do not exclude respondents who always chose the status quo since respondents who in all three choice sets saw high prices for the environmental improvements may be well explained by the utility maximization model. The model-driven estimates of WTP put lower weights but not zero weights on the respondents who are reasonably well explained by the utility maximization model. To put it another way, row (3) uses the choice model to infer the likelihood a respondent's status quo choices result from cost–benefit trade-offs and

---

[29] See footnote 18 for a description of the high cost heuristic.
[30] The NOAA data actually contain 13,684 respondents. However, we exclude respondents who do not answer each of the three questions posed to them.
[31] 2,800.

Table 4 Sensitivity analyses

Model Specifications	Estimated Heuristic Shares (%)							Randomizers' choice probabilities			WTP ($)	
	Trade-off	Status quo only (always A)	Steps only	B or C only	Costs only	High cost option only	Randomizer	Status quo	Option B	Option C	Trade-off respondents	Population
(1) Traditional mixed logit with all data	100										21.34	21.34
(2) Traditional mixed logit excluding protestors	76										45.80	34.61
(3) Include status quo heuristic only	73.5	26.5									51.20	37.62
(4) All heuristics including high cost only heuristic	22.4	24.6	12.4	4.2	8.7	0.0	27.8	4.7	44.5	50.8	17.28	3.87
(5)	41.7		10.8	10.0	3.1	1.8	30.5	96.1	2.1	1.8	39.38	16.41
(6)	33.9	26.2		3.5	9.8	3.5	23.0	32.9	32.8	34.3	59.03	20.00
(7) Include all	25.0	24.8	12.8		8.7	0.2	28.6	3.2	48.9	47.9	18.70	4.67
(8) heuristics but one	29.1	24.9	10.9	4.5		0.0	30.7	3.1	45.6	51.4	20.48	5.95
(9)	22.4	24.6	12.4	4.2	8.7		27.8	4.7	44.5	50.8	17.28	3.86
(10)	44.6	25.9	12.1	5.1	10.2	2.0					33.44	14.90

Notes:
Mean WTP is averaged across both species improvements and respondents.
Non-conforming respondents assigned zero WTP.
The row labeled Always B or C combines the Always B and Always C heuristics.
The population WTP estimates assume that the non-trade-off respondents have 0 WTP because there is no evidence in the data to support non-zero WTPs for these respondents.

Table 5 Sensitivity analyses measures of fit

Model Specifications	Measures of Fit	
	Mean likelihood value	BIC criterion
(1) Traditional mixed logit with all data	−2.934	5.886
(2) Traditional mixed logit excluding protestors	−2.828	5.678
(3) Include status quo heuristic	−2.566	5.151
(4) All heuristics including high cost only heuristic	−2.377	4.777
(5)	−2.415	4.840
(6)	−2.433	4.889
(7) Include all heuristics but one	−2.395	4.811
(8)	−2.405	4.833
(9)	−2.377	4.777
(10)	−2.446	4.914

Notes:
Mean WTP is averaged across both species improvements and respondents.
Non-conforming respondents assigned zero WTP.
The row labeled Always B or C combines the Always B and Always C heuristics.

"trims" the data by placing lower weight on respondents whose status quo choices cannot be rationalized by utility maximization, while row (2) uses responses to ad hoc follow-up questions to exclude status quo choices that may be the result of utility maximization.

It is noteworthy that we obtain similar results in (2) and (3) using alternative strategies to deal with protestors. However, comparing rows (1) with either (2) or (3) reveals the large impact of protestor treatment, either by excluding them (row 2) or by absorbing them into a protestor heuristic (row 3), in both cases substantially increasing the estimated WTP of the trade-off respondents.

The model represented in row (4) contains the same heuristics as our main specification and an additional heuristic for respondents who systematically choose the species improvement alternative with the highest cost instead of making cost–benefit trade-offs. Survey respondents might adopt this choice strategy if they believe the highest cost option always does the most to improve the environment. Including the high cost only heuristic doesn't really matter much if it is accompanied by other heuristics. This reminds us that adding additional heuristics won't matter if the new behavior can be mimicked by one of the heuristics already in the model.[32] Because of this, the high cost only heuristic has a near-zero share in the all-heuristics model reported in row (4).

In rows (5) through (10) of Tables 4 and 5, we remove heuristics from the model one at a time. There are two purposes behind this exercise. First, we evaluate the contribution from each heuristic to goodness of fit. Second, we evaluate whether measures of willingness to pay are reliable when an incomplete set of heuristics is used.

Table 5 indicates that models with heuristics better explain respondents' choices than models without heuristics.[33] We have used maximum likelihood estimation, and the likelihood value at the maximum is a standard measure of the fit of the model. The model that includes all heuristics (row 4) has a maximum likelihood value equal to -2.377, better than traditional mixed logit models or models using sets of heuristics known to be incomplete. This, however, is a simple consequence of the fact that all the other models are special cases of this general model. The issue is not whether this model allows a greater likelihood value; the issue is whether the increment is great enough when adjusted for the number of parameters included. To account for the size of the models we report the Bayesian information criterion (BIC) (or, Schwarz criterion). The BIC is one of several measures of fit that adjust for the number of parameters with more parameters.[34] Models with small BIC measures better fit the data than models with large BIC measures. Here, the smallest BIC equal to 4.77 applies to the general model in row (4) and the model without the high cost only heuristic in row (9). On this basis, we conclude it is appropriate to include each of the heuristics used in our main specification.

The measures of willingness to pay we report in Table 3 are reliable only if one of two conditions hold. First, our measured willingness to pay is reliable if our underlying model is properly specified and we have included in our model all relevant heuristics survey respondents rely upon when not making cost–benefit trade-offs. As this set of potential heuristics is very large, we believe it is very unlikely our model includes every possible heuristic.[35] Unfortunately, it is not practical to test our first condition

---

[32] Of the 11,459 respondents, 2,795 respondents' choices are consistent with the steps only environmentalist heuristic and 1,353 respondents' choices are consistent with the high cost heuristic. Of these 1,353 respondents, only 172 respondents make choices that are inconsistent with the steps only environmentalist heuristic.

[33] The WTPs reported in Table 5 are averages across both species improvements and respondents.

[34] Greene (2002), at p. 160.

[35] Indeed, we do not include heuristics that absorb respondents who behave strategically or who have poorly formed preferences as in McNair et al. (2012). Nor do we include heuristics to absorb respondents whose trade-offs are affected by context as in Prelec et al. (forthcoming). Many other heuristics are described in Gilovich et al. (2002).

because it is not possible to list all possible heuristics, much less incorporate them into an econometric model of choice. If our first condition is not satisfied or untestable, however, it might be the case that biases in willingness to pay that emerge from models with incomplete sets of heuristics are small in practice. If this second condition is satisfied, the measures of willingness to pay reported in Table 3 are reliable.

In Table 4, we investigate the second condition listed in the preceding paragraph by estimating models with sets of heuristics known to be incomplete. Using this top-down approach, except for the case of the high cost only heuristic, which has a near zero estimated share in row (4), omitting any one of the heuristics increases both the WTP of the trade-off respondents and the WTP of the population. A reduction in the list of included heuristics inevitably increases the estimated fraction of trade-off respondents because there are fewer competitors for the trade-off rule but the effect on the estimated WTP is not clear-cut. The estimated trade-off fraction in the complete model in row (4) is 22.4%, in contrast to the range of estimates from 22.4%, to 44.6% in rows (5) to (10).

When heuristics are removed from the model one at a time, estimated WTP increases from $17.28 to values between $18.70 and $59.03 depending on which heuristic is removed from the model.[36] The biggest effect on WTP occurs in row (6) when the steps only heuristic is omitted and mean willingness to pay increases from $17.28 to $59.03. This increase occurs because the model needs to explain the observed B and C choices without the benefit of the 12.4% of the respondents who are steps only respondents in the all-heuristics model and it does this by both increasing the percentage of respondents who are trade-off respondents and by reducing the cost sensitivity of those respondents (resulting in more B and C choices by that class). The exclusion of the status quo only heuristic in row (5) also substantially increases WTP, from $17.28 to $39.38. To understand the source of this increase, consider the randomizers' choice probabilities before and after the status quo only heuristic is excluded. Before the exclusion, randomizers accept species improvements (options B and C) in 95.3% of questions. After the exclusion, randomizers choose the status quo in 96.1% of questions. In other words, the randomizer heuristic mimics the status quo only heuristic in row (5) and respondents who were classified as randomizers in row (4) are classified as trade-off respondents in row (5). The model now needs to explain the observed B and C choices, which it

---

[36] We do not include the model when we exclude the high cost only heuristic (row 9) in this range since the estimated share on the high cost only heuristic in row (4) is zero. So it is no surprise that WTP in rows (4) and (9) are identical.

does by increasing the share of trade-off respondents and reducing their cost-sensitivity by lowering the absolute value of the cost coefficient.

Table 4 indicates that reliance on incomplete sets of heuristic potentially introduces substantial biases into measures of willingness to pay. These results demonstrate the challenge of using stated preference surveys to measure WTP. The set of heuristics included in row (4) of Table 4 is incomplete and to some extent arbitrary and accidental. Although this initial foray into alterations of the model to allow non-conforming respondents offers explains choices better than traditional mixed logit models, it has an "accidental" feel to it, meaning that a different set of analysts would likely propose a different list of heuristics. Unfortunately, no one can say with confidence what estimates would result if different or more complete sets of heuristics are employed. Perhaps the bias in row (4) from omitted heuristics is small and relying on a more complete set of heuristics would decrease WTP by 7.5% or less, which occurred when add the B only or C only heuristics to the model (i.e., we go from row 7 to row 4). But the bias from relying on an incomplete set of heuristics could be much larger, as was the case in rows (5) and (6) when the status quo only and steps only heuristics were excluded from the model. On the other hand, there is a downside to including too many heuristic rules. With only three choices per respondent some utility maximizing individuals will match the choice profile of one of the heuristics by chance. Including more heuristic rules increases this probability, reducing the fraction of the population estimated to be utility maximizers. Exploring the issues how to determine the "best" heuristic rules and the optimal number of heuristic rules are beyond the scope of this chapter. For these and other reasons, we regard the results reported in Table 4 to be suggestive but they are not definitive estimates of WTP.

CONCLUSIONS

Wallmo and Lew (2011) have offered a traditional mixed logit analysis of the stated preference data collected by a NOAA endangered species survey. After excluding what they regard to be protestors, they find an estimated WTP averaged across respondents and species improvements equal to $45.80. We have analyzed the same data using models that allow various types of non-conforming respondents – those who do not behave according the traditional utility maximization model. Our most general model has a mixture of six heuristic rules and also the traditional mixed logit utility maximization rule. This model estimates that only 23.4% of respondents were conforming with the utility maximization model. The randomizers have the largest estimated population share equal to 24.8%.

These respondents choose the status quo in 3.7% of questions, the species improvement in column B in 53.4% of questions, and column C in 43.0% of questions – basically flipping a coin to decide which of the species options to select.

This model offers a substantially improved fit of the data relative to the mixed logit model and is the best fitting model according to the BIC criterion of any considered here. It supports an estimate of WTP equal to $17.28 for the 22.4% of respondents who are maximizing utility and $3.87 for the population as a whole after assigning $0 WTP to the other respondents.

We emphasize that our model is not intended as a realistic and comprehensive description of the survey respondents' decisions. The heuristic decision rules we have included are stylized and limited in number. Together with our companion paper, Leamer (2016), which extends the heuristic decision rules to allow individual wavering, what we have accomplished is a demonstration of the inadequacy of the traditional utility maximization model for estimation of environmental valuation. But this isn't news to analysts who omit subsets of aberrant respondents, including Lew and Wallmo who omit the non-conforming respondents they call protestors. To those who omit protestors, we offer the rhetorical question: "Why not more?" and we demonstrate the very large impact when more heuristics are included in the model and when the effective trimming of the sample is two-sided, not just protestors.

REFERENCES

Burton, M. and D. Rigby (2009), "Hurdle and latent class approaches to serial non-participation in choice models," *Environmental and Resource Economics*, **42**(2), 211–26.

Campbell, D., D.A. Hensher, and R. Scarpa (2011), "Non-attendance to attributes in environmental choice analysis: A latent class specification," *Journal of Environmental Planning and Management*, **54**(8), 1061–76.

Cerdaa, C., A. Ponceb, and M. Zappic (2013), "Using choice experiments to understand public demand for the conservation of nature: A case study in a protected area of Chile," *Journal of Nature Conservation*, **21**(3), 143–53.

Cunha-e-Sa, M., L. Madureira, L. Nunes, and V. Otrachshenko (2012), "Protesting and justifying: A latent class model for contingent valuation with attitudinal data," *Environmental and Resource Economics*, **52**(4), 531–48.

Gilovich, T., D. Griffin, and D. Kahneman (2002), *Heuristics and Biases: The Psychology of Intuitive Judgement*, Cambridge, UK: Cambridge University Press.

Greene, W. (2002), *Econometric Analysis*, 5th edition, New York: New York University Press.

Greene, W.H. and D.A. Hensher (2013), "Revealing additional dimensions of preference heterogeneity in a latent class mixed multinomial logit model," *Applied Economics*, **45**(14), 1897–902.

Hanley, N., R.E. Wright, and B. Alvarez-Farizo (2006), "Estimating the economic value of improvements in river ecology using choice experiments: An application to the water framework directive," *Journal of Environmental Management*, **78**(2), 183–93.

Hensher, D.A. (2010), "Attribute processing, heuristics and preference construction in choice analysis," in S. Hess and A. Daly (eds), *Choice Modelling: The State-of-the-Art and the State-of-Practice – Proceedings from the Inaugural International Choice Modelling Conference*, Bingley, UK: Emerald Group Publishing, pp. 35–70.

Hensher, D.A. and W.H. Greene (2010), "Non-attendance and dual processing of common-metric attributes in choice analysis: A latent class specification," *Empirical Economics*, **39**(2), 413–26.

Hensher, D.A., J.M. Rose, and W.H. Greene (2005), "The implications on willingness to pay of respondents ignoring specific attributes," *Transportation*, **32**(3), 203–22.

Hensher, D.A., J.M. Rose, and W.H. Greene (2012), "Inferring attribute non-attendance from stated choice data: Implications for willingness to pay estimates and a warning for stated choice experiment design," *Transportation*, **39**(2), 235–46.

Hess, S., D.A. Hensher, and A. Daly (2012), "Not bored yet – revisiting respondent fatigue in stated choice experiments," *Transportation Research*, **46**(A), 626–44.

Hess, S., A. Stathopoulos, D. Campbell, V. O'Neill, and S. Caussade (2012), "It's not that I don't care, I just don't care very much: Confounding between attribute non-attendance and taste heterogeneity," *Transportation*, **40**(3), 583–607.

Kaffashi, S., M.N. Shamsudin, A. Radam, M.R. Yacob, K.A. Rahim, and M. Yazid (2012), "Economic valuation and conservation: Do people vote for better preservation of Shadegan International Wetland?," *Biological Conservation*, **150**(1), 150–58.

Knowledge Networks (2009), *Field Report, Protected Species Valuation Survey Conducted Under Contract to Pacific States Marine Fisheries Commission and OAK Management, Inc., Submitted to Dr. Kristy Wallmo, Ph.D., July 31, 2009*.

Layton, D.F. and G. Brown (2000), "Heterogeneous preferences regarding global climate change," *The Review of Economics and Statistics*, **82**(4), 616–24.

Leamer, E.E. (2016), "Tradeoffs between costs and benefits in choice experiments, or not," working paper.

Lew, D.K. and K. Wallmo (2011), "External tests of scope and embedding in stated preference choice experiments: An application to endangered species valuation," *Environmental and Resource Economics*, **48**(1), 1–23.

Lew, D.K., D.F. Layton, and R.D. Rowe (2010), "Valuing enhancements to endangered species protection under alternative baseline futures: The case of the Steller sea lion," *Marine Resource Economics*, **25**(2), 133–54.

Mariel, P., J. Meyerhoff, and D. Hoyos (2011), "Stated or inferred attribute non-attendance? A simulation approach," working paper presented at International Choice Modelling Conference, Leeds, UK.

McNair, B.J., D.A. Hensher, and J. Bennett (2010), "Modelling heterogeneity in response behaviour towards a sequence of discrete choice questions: A latent class approach," *Environmental Management & Development Occasional Paper, No. 16*, Crawford School of Economics and Government, The Australian National University.

McNair, B., D.A. Hensher, and J. Bennett (2012), "Modelling heterogeneity in response behaviour towards a sequence of discrete choice questions: A probabilistic decision process model," *Environmental and Resource Economics*, **51**(4), 599–616.

Meyerhoff, J. and U. Liebe (2006), "Protest beliefs in contingent valuation: explaining their motivation," *Ecological Economics*, **57**(4), 583–94.

Meyerhoff, J. and U. Liebe (2008), "Do protest responses to a contingent valuation question and a choice experiment differ?," *Environmental and Resource Economics*, **39**(4), 433–46.

Meyerhoff, J., A. Bartczak, and U. Liebe (2012), "Protester or non-protester: A binary state? On the use (and non-use) of latent class models to analyse protesting in economic valuation," *The Australian Journal of Agricultural and Resource Economics*, **56**(3), 438–54.

Olsen, S.B. (2009), "Choosing between Internet and mail survey modes for choice experiment surveys considering non-market goods," *Environmental and Resource Economics*, **44**(4), 591–610.

Parsons, G.R. and S.M. Thur (2008), "Valuing changes in the quality of coral reef ecosystems: A stated preference study of SCUBA diving in the Bonaire National Marine Park," *Environmental and Resource Economics*, **40**(4), 593–608.

Plott, C.R. (1996), "Rational individual behavior in markets and social choice processes: The discovered preference hypothesis," in K. Arrow, E. Columbatto, M. Perlman, and C. Schmidt (eds), *The Rational Foundations of Economic Behavior*, London: Macmillan.

Prelec, D., J. Burrows, and P. Dixon (forthcoming), "Context sensitivity in stated preference experiments," available from the paper's authors on request.

Scarpa, R., T.J. Gilbride, D. Campbell, and D.A. Hensher (2009), "Modelling attribute non-attendance in choice experiments for rural landscape valuation," *European Review of Agricultural Economics*, **36**(2), 151–74.

Wallmo, K. and D.K. Lew (2011), "Valuing improvements to threatened and endangered marine species: An application of stated preference choice experiments," *Journal of Environmental Management*, **92**(7), 1793–801.

Wallmo, K. and D.K. Lew (2012), "Public willingness to pay for recovering and downlisting threatened and endangered marine Species," *Conservation Biology*, **26**(5), 830–39.

9. Assessing the validity of stated preference data using follow-up questions

Kelley Myers, Doug MacNair, Ted Tomasi, and Jude Schneider[1]

INTRODUCTION

Stated preference (SP) studies such as contingent valuation (CV) and discrete choice experiments (DCEs) are often used to attempt measurement of willingness to pay (WTP) for environmental goods. However, concern exists that these methods do not provide data that can support valid, reliable, and meaningful WTP estimates, especially in the context of estimating non-use values for environmental goods. The foundation of all survey-based exercises is that the questions as asked by the researcher and answered by the respondent share a common understanding. This common understanding is difficult to achieve. In WTP studies, additional criteria must be met if the results are to provide data for estimating Hicksian welfare measures.[2] The criteria that must be satisfied if SP data are to be theoretically interpreted via the standard microeconomic rational choice model (RCM) have been widely discussed in the literature (e.g., Mitchell and Carson, 1989; Carson and Groves, 2007; US EPA SAB, 2009; Carson and Louviere, 2011; Bateman, 2011). General consensus exists on these criteria: that the respondents believe the information in the survey and base their responses solely on outcomes described in the survey,

---

[1] Respectively, Senior Economist, Cardno, Newark, DE (corresponding author, Kelley Myers@cardno.com); Technical Director, Economics and Decision Sciences, ERM, Raleigh, NC; Vice President, Cardno, Newark, DE; Senior Consultant, Cardno, Santa Barbara, CA.

[2] Economists, psychologists and others have developed more behaviorally based theories that depart from the standard microeconomic model of rational choice. While welfare measures may be developed for such theories, we focus here on the standard interpretation of rational choice and Hicksian WTP measures associated with such choice.

they treat the exercise posed in the survey as they would a real decision that affects their budget, and they answer valuation questions as rational economic agents with well-defined preferences who are trading money for economic goods.

One approach for assessing whether respondents satisfy these criteria is to use follow-up, debriefing questions. The earliest and most ubiquitous follow-up questions were "Yes/No" follow-ups based on recommendations from the National Oceanic and Atmospheric Administration (NOAA) Blue Ribbon Panel on contingent valuation. As part of a review of the use of contingent valuation to estimate lost non-use values in the context of natural resource damage assessments (NRDAs), the NOAA panel recommended the use of "Yes/No" follow-ups to determine the type of response (i.e., protest vote, yea-saying, etc.). However, the scope of follow-up questions has expanded over time (Krupnick and Adamowicz, 2006 provide a discussion). These questions may be used to "shore up the credibility of the survey" (ibid.), "to modify the estimate derived from one or more SP questions in some way" (Carson and Louviere, 2011), or to identify "problematic responses" in order to delete some responses or respondents or treat them as zeros for analysis purposes.

Despite their ubiquity, there is little consistency to either the questions posed or their use to modify analyses. First, no consensus exists on what or how many questions to ask in order to identify problematic responses. Second, most studies report results by question rather than by respondent; thus, the literature does not evaluate how many respondents had a general understanding of the tasks asked of them. Third, other than those respondents who protest the SP exercise as a whole and typically are dropped from the analysis sample, no consensus exists on what to do about problematic answers. This lack of consistency in the use of follow-up questions is troubling, as substantial proportions of respondents may give problematic answers to some of the follow-up questions and welfare estimates may be sensitive to decisions made regarding such answers.

This chapter does not solve this problem; we do not propose a theory of "problematic responses" and a practice for what to do about them. We do, however, provide some new insights into the potential prevalence of problematic responses and assess whether *respondents* are providing valid information. We focus on the pattern of responses by individual respondents to follow-up questions across a suite of debriefing questions. These questions identify whether respondents are failing to meet the criteria for satisfactory SP responses discussed above. This approach allows us to assess whether respondents "fail" on a large number of questions or only one, fail on one or many validity criteria, give responses that are correlated with observable demographic variables, and whether validity failures are related to answers to valuation questions.[3]

The subject of our survey is valuing wetland restoration projects to reduce the effects of hypoxia in the Chesapeake Bay. The survey was Internet based and uses a sample of respondents from a web-based panel. The results show that most respondents do not meet the fundamental SP assumption that responses to valuation questions reflect carefully considered, rational economic values for the goods being evaluated in the survey. In fact, if one uses the answers to our suite of follow-up questions as a whole to identify a "core"[4] group of respondents who give unambiguously valid responses, the core would include two respondents out of a total of 1,224, both of whom were not willing to pay for environmental improvements in any of their votes. We also find that people are likely to fail more than one question within a single validity criterion. In other words, when using different types of questions to address the same topic (i.e., various types of questions and response formats that address scenario attendance), people still fail, thus reducing the likelihood that the failing response was due to response error (e.g., misinterpreting questions, marking the wrong response).[5] Further, we find little relationship between the tendency to fail the criteria and demographic variables. Hence, applying some sort of weight to the sample to match the population based on census data does not appropriately weight for the proportion of those in the population that would fail to meet the SP validity criteria. This undermines the ability to apply "econometric fixes" to problematic answers.

The rest of the chapter is organized as follows. The next section provides examples of SP studies that use debriefing questions. The third section describes our study design and data. The fourth summarizes the results, while the fifth describes the implications and paths for further research.

---

[3] Of course, asking a follow-up question about what a respondent was thinking when answering the primary valuation question has its methodological deficiencies. An alternative is a "think aloud" protocol in real time (e.g., Schkade and Payne, 1994) as the respondent is answering the question. However, follow-up questions are frequently used to identify "problem responses" and can trigger alternative estimators of welfare. It is this practice we address here.

[4] Bishop et al. (2011) refer to those satisfying criteria as being part of a "rational core" of respondents; here, we call those passing all questions as part of the "core."

[5] For example, we ask respondents seven different questions to assess whether they attend to the voting scenarios and outcomes described in the survey and not others. The average number of failed questions is three, and 75% of respondents fail between two and five questions.

LITERATURE REVIEW

This section discusses the use of follow-up questions in the SP literature and describes how they map to the basic principles of validity (i.e., respondents take the exercise seriously and treat it as they would a real decision, believe the information in the survey and answer valuation questions as rational economic agents with well-defined preferences). The goal is not to provide a comprehensive assessment of whether or not validity has been found to be a significant problem. Instead, we provide a description of some of the ways that it has been assessed as background information to illustrate how we developed our approach. Table 1 provides examples of the results of follow-up questions reported in the SP literature.

The most common approach to assessing whether respondents take the SP exercise seriously (i.e., view their responses as consequential) is to use questions that ask about response certainty. Using this approach, respondents are asked how certain they are that they would actually pay the amount, or vote as they indicated they would in the survey. Scenario acceptance, or belief in the information provided, requires that respondents value the good described in the survey (and not some other good of their own construction) based on the stated price (and not some other price they believe they would pay). A number of studies ask follow-up questions to test whether respondents believe the survey scenario (Carson et al., 1994, 2003; Krupnick et al., 2002; Banzhaf et al., 2006, 2011; Bishop et al., 2011). These studies ask whether the individual believed the outcomes described would occur, if they believed they would have to pay the amount shown, or if they valued something larger than the good in question.

Finally, the third criterion requires that respondents exhibit utility maximizing behavior and make trade-offs according to standard compensatory methods. Examples of behaviors that violate this criterion include problematic attitudes such as yea-saying or purchasing moral satisfaction, protest responses, using simplifying decision heuristics rather than careful evaluations, and ignoring certain attributes of the SP question. Follow up questions are often used to identify these types of behaviors and adjust the WTP values accordingly.

Our literature review yields three insights that guided our study design. First, because of the widespread use of follow-up questions in CV surveys, we expected that almost all recent DCE studies would use follow-up questions to test validity comprehensively. However, the proportion of DCE studies using follow-up questions to test validity is smaller than we expected,[6] and most studies that do use follow-up questions only focus

---

[6] In their review of supporting questions in DCEs, Krupnick and Adamowicz (2006)

Table 1 Summary of SP studies that use debriefing questions

Author(s) and Year	Good	Question Topic(s)	Percentage of Problematic Responses[a]
Contingent valuation studies			
Li and Mattson (1995)	Forests	Response certainty	64
Champ et al. (1997)	Open space	Response certainty	Not reported
Champ and Bishop (2001)	Wind-generated electricity	Response certainty	48
Poe et al. (2002)	Green electricity	Response certainty	21
Banzhaf et al. (2006)	Ecosystem services	"Yea-saying" and protest no's	59
Carson et al. (2003)	Damages from oil spill	Scenario acceptance	Not reported
Carson et al. (1994)	Damages from DDT and PCBs	Scenario acceptance	48
Krupnick et al. (2002)	Mortality risk	Scenario acceptance	40
Discrete choice experiments			
Olsson (2005)	Cod	Response certainty	71
Ready et al. (2010)	Wild animals	Response certainty	Mean certainty 6.5 reported
Bishop et al. (2011)	Hawaiian coral reefs	Scenario acceptance	54
Scarpa et al. (2009)	Alpine grazing areas	Ignoring attributes	40–80
Carlsson et al. (2010)	Environmental quality	Ignoring attributes	54
Banzhaf et al. (2011)	Ecosystem services	"Yea-saying" or hypothetical bias	9[b]
Cameron et al. (2010)	Major illness/injury	Scenario replacement/adjustment	Not reported
Kataria et al. (2012)	Water quality	Scenario acceptance	64

Notes:
a. Represents the highest number reported from all questions.
b. Only report frequency of responses to one out of 34 questions.

on one test of validity. Establishing the validity of a stated choice survey is fundamental, but assessing validity does not appear to be a standard practice in DCE studies. Second, numerous studies report results that show significant portions of the population giving a problematic response to the follow-up question, casting doubt on the DCE's validity. Third, these studies tend to report sample proportions answering a question in an invalid fashion for each question separately. The pattern of responses across questions and across question topics by an individual respondent is not investigated.

STUDY DESIGN AND DATA

Our study developed follow-up questions as part of a stated choice survey about reducing hypoxia in Chesapeake Bay. Survey development occurred between August 2010 and September 2011 with the aid of two focus groups and four one-on-one interview sessions. The survey has four sections, which is consistent with current practices in DCEs (see Bateman et al., 2002 for more information).

The first section introduces respondents to Chesapeake Bay and describes the causes and impacts of hypoxia and how restoring coastal wetlands can reduce these effects. The first section also asks some general warm-up questions about environmental attitudes. The second section describes a potential program for reducing hypoxia in Chesapeake Bay by restoring coastal wetlands. This section includes a description of the policy change, the institution for providing this change, and the payment mechanism. In our survey, the policy change is a second phase of restoration to build on restoration that has already occurred in Phase 1 (thus mitigating the desire to vote yes to "do something" for the environment, since something already has been done). If approved, Phase 2 would require a one-time payment through increased income taxes for all US households. We select a national income tax as the payment mechanism since the benefits of the restoration are not limited by geographic location.[7] The pages that follow describe the attributes affected by the program, which include acres of restored wetlands, bird diversity, days without excess algae, fish and shellfish abundance, public access to wetlands, and a Chesapeake Bay

---

state that "[a] surprisingly large number of stated choice surveys do not use debriefing questions...that ask respondents what they felt or thought as they read text or answered questions." Our review also supports this finding.

[7] Using a general tax as a payment mechanism is one of two types of coercive payment mechanisms commonly used in DCEs (see Carson and Louviere, 2011 for a discussion).

ecosystem health score.[8] The attributes were developed over the course of a year through a combination of consultation with ecologists, subject matter experts, and focus group respondents.

We also designed several of the ecological attributes, including the Chesapeake Bay ecosystem health score, by following guidelines for ecological indicators in SP valuation developed by Johnston and collaborators (Johnston et al., 2011, 2012).

The third section describes the voting format and includes a reminder about some of the pros and cons of voting for a restoration program. The pros include belief that reducing hypoxia in the Chesapeake Bay is worth the cost and is a good use of tax dollars, and that the cost of the tax increase is within a respondent's budget. The reasons to vote against the program include belief that it is not worth the cost, not a good use of tax dollars, and not within the respondent's budget. After a sample vote, each respondent votes on five different combinations of restoration outcomes. In each vote, respondents have the option to choose the status quo (keep the amount of restoration completed in Phase 1 and pay nothing) or to choose one of two alternative restoration programs at an additional cost to their household. To generate the choice sets, we used SAS market research macros to generate a D-Optimal fractional factorial design out of the full factorial ($4^6 * 2^1 = 8{,}192$ alternatives). This generation produced 24 choice pairs that we blocked into six groups of four.[9] A sample choice set is shown in Figure 1.

The fourth and final section of the survey contains the debriefing questions, followed by standard socioeconomic and demographic questions.

Our data come from 1,224 respondents enrolled in a web-enabled panel maintained by Research Now.[10] Of the sampled respondents, 27% said they had visited Chesapeake Bay. The average income of our sample was generally in line with 2010 census data, but the income range from $25,000 to $74,900 was slightly over-represented and the higher ranges were

---

[8] For a list of the attributes, their descriptions, and their respective levels, please contact the corresponding author.

[9] Each respondent saw four choice pairs that came from the experimental design plus a fifth pair that was common across all respondents. The decision to use five choice sets was based on a review of environmental studies that use DCEs to value similar goods. For example, Carlsson et al. (2003) present respondents with four choice sets each, while Hoehn et al. (2005) use five. Although it is not uncommon to use more choice sets (i.e., Birol et al., 2006 use eight), some empirical evidence suggests that cognitive burden increases with the number of choice sets (Bech et al., 2011).

[10] Research Now uses a "by-invitation only" methodology to member selection by partnering with a variety of businesses. Invitees already have a pre-existing relationship with the company that invited them, guaranteeing a high-quality panel while minimizing duplication, fraudulent responses, and professional survey takers.

Outcomes	Current Situation Without Phase 2	Design A	Design B
Wetland acres	52% of goal 13,000 acres out of 25,000 acres (0 more acres)	60% of goal 15,000 acres out of 25,000 acres (2,000 more acres)	90% of goal 22,750 acres out of 25,000 acres (9,250 more acres)
Bird diversity	30 species	30 species	36 species
Days without excess algae	20% of summer days 20 out of 100 days	20% of summer days 20 out of 100 days	80% of summer days 80 out of 100 days
Public access to wetlands	Some areas have access	Additional access	No additional access
Fish and shellfish abundance score	59 out of 100	59 out of 100	76 out of 100
Chesapeake Bay ecosystem function score	46 out of 100	46 out of 100	55 out of 100
Total one-time cost per US household	$0	$50	$295
Please make your selection (Choose one):	○	○	○

Figure 1 Example valuation question

slightly under-represented; 51% were males compared to 49.2% from the census data.[11]

METHODS AND RESULTS

Our analysis has three basic components. First, we review the frequency distributions of responses to each of the debriefing questions and impose three degrees of rigor for specifying whether a respondent satisfies the validity criteria.[12] Second, we examine each respondent's answers to see if

---

[11] Our sample was drawn from a nationwide population, stratified by 30% from the Mid-Atlantic region, 30% from the West, and 40% from the rest of the country.
[12] The frequency distributions are available upon request from the corresponding author.

a pattern exists by respondent (across the follow-up questions). Third, we use multivariate regression analysis to investigate whether the tendency to meet the validity criteria is associated with a particular type of response to the voting question (i.e., all yes votes, etc.), and to see if respondent characteristics can predict whether a respondent is more or less likely to pass the validity criteria.

Descriptive Statistics

Our analyses are based on a portion of the full sample (960 out of 1,224) as we exclude protest no's (i.e., people who stated they did not trust the government, did not believe in tax increases of any kind, or did not feel they should have to pay for the good). Based on our focus groups and one-on-ones, we use various types of questions and response formats, which include multiple choice, open-ended, and contrasting statements (a question that asks respondents to indicate whether they agree with contrasting statements on either end of a five-point scale) and use several different question types to address the same topic (i.e., attending to the scenario, believing responses will affect the outcome, etc.).

Clearly our response options give some leeway in determining what constitutes a "problem" in a response. For some of the questions, we construct three classes of "rigor" for specifying when a respondent satisfies the validity criteria: *stringent*, *average*, and *lenient*.[13] The stringent approach leads to the smallest number of respondents meeting the validity criteria: respondents meet the criteria only if their answers are unambiguously valid. These respondents are most clearly part of the "core" of respondents. For example, respondents were asked several questions with a contrasting statement response format where an unambiguously valid response was to the far left (response option A) and an invalid response was on the far right (response option E), with five total response categories from A to E. In the stringent approach, respondents who chose A or B are regarded as satisfying the validity criterion for this type of question. The lenient approach accepts more response categories as meeting the criteria and so expands the size of the core. The average approach is in the middle of these two.

In general, for questions that have only two response options (one that is unambiguously valid and one that is not), we do not specify a degree of rigor. A respondent either gives a valid response, or does not. Also, we do not specify a degree of rigor if a question is only shown to a subset of the

---

[13] A detailed description about what constitutes a stringent, average, and lenient classification for each question is available upon request from the corresponding author.

entire sample (i.e., a follow-up question based on a response to a previous question). In both cases, this is illustrated in Table 2 where the frequency of response is the same across all categories (lenient, average, and stringent).

Table 2 provides a complete list of valid responses to each of the questions and the percentage meeting the validity criterion for each question. Looking at some of the responses that did not vary by the degree of rigor, Table 2 shows that 20% of the sample gives a valid response to a question regarding how they considered costs of the restoration program when making a choice. A valid response to this question includes "I thought only about how I and/or my family would be affected by the cost," whereas an invalid response includes "I thought about an amount that would be fair for most people to pay" and "I thought about an amount that would get a lot of people to vote yes." Additionally, less than 40% valued the program as described (i.e., did not consider health effects when deciding their votes, which the survey explicitly excluded as a benefit of the program), thought they would have to pay the amount shown, did not include other outcomes like reducing toxic chemicals not part of the scenario, and did not consider that voting for the program would increase the chances of the government starting a similar program near them.

Using the stringent approach to identifying valid responses, 28% of respondents saw the results as consequential (i.e., thought that the survey responses would be used to decide whether taxes would be collected). Twenty-one percent of the sample thought program outcomes should be chosen based on people's answers to questions in surveys like this one and 25% thought that survey sponsors want to find out how much the public values the program.

Cumulative Assessment of the Validity of Responses

Next, we examine responses to the follow-up questions at the respondent level. Figure 2 provides the cumulative percentage of the respondents who give invalid responses by degree of rigor. Using the most lenient assessment, 50% of the respondents failed at least six questions. Using the most stringent assessment, 50% of the respondents fail at least nine questions.

We next identify respondents who provide valid responses to all questions and, therefore, make up the "core" of respondents. Table 3 shows that only two people are in the core using the lenient approach to inclusion, one person is in the core using the average approach, and the stringent core is empty. Moreover, the two people who do remain in the lenient core (and therefore clearly can be judged to engage in the survey as real, understand the choices being asked of them, and respond in accord with economic

Table 2 Percentage of sample that gives a valid response by question (n = 960)

Valid Response	Percentage of Sample		
	Stringent	Average	Lenient
Thought only about how I and/or my family would be affected by the cost	20	20	20
I think the survey responses will be used to decide if taxes will be collected for the program	28	56	81
My votes will affect the size and scope of the program	35	69	87
When I voted for a design that costs money it was to show support for the program and I am willing to pay the tax	55	79	93
Thought about things that I would not be able to buy for my family or about the other causes that I would not be able to support in order to pay for the program	62	62	62
I would vote the same way if the program were actually on the ballot (Certainty > 50%, > 30%, > 0%)	71	91	97
I did NOT consider that the program would protect the health of the people who eat fish from the Bay when deciding my votes	34	34	34
If this design is implemented, I think I would end up actually paying the amount shown	35	35	35
When I voted, I thought the wetland restoration program would only have a significant effect on reducing the excess phosphorus and nitrogen that causes hypoxia	36	36	36
I did NOT consider that if enough people voted for the program, it would increase the chances that the government would start a program to restore wetlands near me when deciding my votes	40	40	40
I hope and believe that the tax money spent will only be spent on the program	41	41	41
I hope and believe that the program will provide the restoration outcomes as described in the survey	62	62	62
I hope and believe that the program will reduce hypoxia in Chesapeake Bay as described in the survey	71	71	71
If the designs for the programs described here all cost the same amount and were funded by existing sources they should be chosen based on people's answers to questions in surveys like this one	21	51	75

Table 2 (continued)

Valid Response	Percentage of Sample		
	Stringent	Average	Lenient
Sponsors of the survey don't know whether to fund the program and want to find out how much the public values this program	25	55	79
When I made my choices in each of the votes I found the choices straightforward and carefully compared all of the outcomes as described in the survey	43	58	58

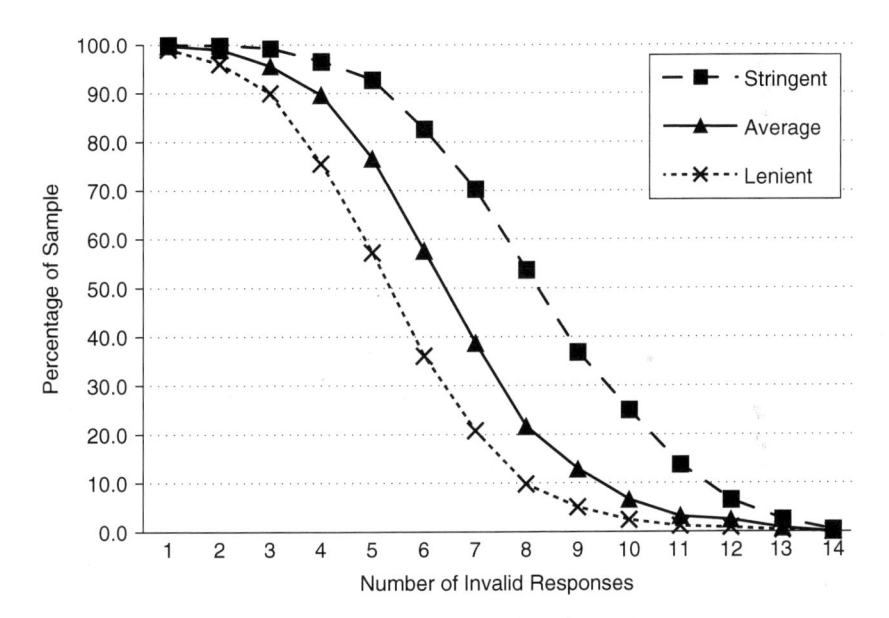

Figure 2 Cumulative percentage of sample that fails at least one question

rationality) voted against contributing taxes for environmental improvements in all five votes.

These results demonstrate that substantial proportions of the respondents do not provide responses to the follow-up questions that comport with the validity criteria. Of course, asking a large set of questions increases the chances that a respondent gives at least one invalid response. Hence, we do not necessarily propose that those not in the core be dropped from the

Table 3   Number of respondents in core

Vote Type	Lenient	Average	Stringent
Voted yes at least once	0	0	0
Voted all no	2	1	0
Total	2	1	0

analysis sample.[14] However, we find the portion of responses indicating a failure to meet validity criteria very troublesome.

Regression Analysis

This section examines the relationship between the follow-up questions and how people respond to the voting scenarios. It also explores whether respondent characteristics are reasonable predictors as to whether people will give valid or invalid responses to the follow-up questions. Table 4 shows the results of a zero-inflated Poisson model that regresses the responses to the follow-up questions for each individual on the number of status quo votes. We use the average approach to identifying responses as valid, and code each variable so that a 1 equals a valid response, 0 otherwise. The top half of the table indicates whether the response to the follow-up question has an influence on the total number of status quo votes, whereas the bottom half of the table is a logit regression that indicates whether a respondent is more likely to be a certain zero (i.e., "all yes" voter) based on their response to the question. The results show that seven questions influence the probability of being a certain zero (i.e., someone who votes yes to all five votes). The results also show that a subset of these questions influences the number of no votes.

For example, giving the following valid responses lowers the probability of voting yes to the restoration program in all five votes: considering *only* how their family would be affected by the taxes when voting (*Family_only*), and not how other people would be affected, that the votes will affect the size and scope of the restoration program (*Vote_affectscope*), and that the survey responses will be used to decide if taxes will be collected for the program (*Vote_affecttaxes*). In other words, respondents who give valid responses to these questions are less likely to be "yes" voters. Table 4 also indicates that valid responses to *Family_only* and *Vote_affecttaxes*

[14] With potential for response errors, as the number of questions increases, the probability of answering all correctly goes to zero even if the respondent is in the core. This outcome begs the question of what to do with respondents that fail some significant fraction of follow-up questions assessing validity, which is beyond the scope of this chapter.

Table 4 Zero-inflated Poisson regression by valid responses on number of "no" votes

Variable[a]	Coefficient	t-Statistic
NP_only	−0.01	−0.09
Family_only	0.16	2.53**
Didnotconsider_chances	0.05	0.68
Didnotconsider_health	0.02	0.26
40%_certain	−0.15	−1.94*
Hope_programworks	−0.13	−1.64
Hope_moneyspent	0.01	0.78
Hope_outcome	0.06	0.19
People_choose	0.02	0.38
Sponsors_dontknow	0.03	0.51
Vote_affecttaxes	0.05	0.76
Vote_affectscope	0.11	1.76
Willingtopay_tax	−0.41	−4.79**
No_decisionstrategy	0.07	1.2
Believe_payamtshown	−0.25	−2.33*
Constant	1.10	9.58
Inflate (Logit regression)		
NP_only	−0.11	−0.62
Family_only	−0.82	−3.76**
Didnotconsider_chances	−0.40	−2.17*
Didnotconsider_health	−0.33	−1.73
40%_certain	1.47	3.56**
Hope_programworks	0.51	2.17*
Hope_moneyspent	−0.06	−0.3
Hope_outcome	0.17	0.89
People_choose	−0.23	−1.35
Sponsors_dontknow	−0.05	−0.28
Vote_affecttaxes	−0.37	−2.17*
Vote_affectscope	−0.51	−2.85**
Willingtopay_tax	1.21	6.49**
No_decisionstrategy	−0.01	−0.08
Believe_payamtshown	0.02	0.10
Constant	−1.31	−2.83

Notes:
* Indicates significance at the 95% level of confidence; ** indicates significance at the 99% level of confidence.
a. A description of each variable is available upon request from the corresponding author.

increases the number of "no" votes. The overall conclusion from this analysis is that it takes more than just a single follow-up question or a single type of question (i.e., response certainty, etc.) to evaluate how people respond to the voting question. Our results indicate that many of our questions either affect how people responded to the vote (i.e., were all yes voters) or affect the number of times a person chooses the status quo.

In a review of alternative methods of valuing environmental goods and services, US EPA SAB (2009) stated that a key criterion for choosing an approach was whether or not the method provides a reliable way to extrapolate from the respondents to the target population. The regression analysis below provides evidence that a reliable extrapolation approach may not exist. First, one needs to be reasonably certain that the respondents are a true random sample of the population. However, if people who fail to satisfy validity criteria are more likely to vote for a tax for an environmental program, it is reasonable to believe they may also be more likely to respond to the survey. Therefore, randomness cannot be assumed. However, if the propensity to pass validity tests is closely linked to demographics, then sampling weights could be used to adjust the results. Unfortunately, no strong link exists between demographics and propensity to satisfy the criteria and, thus, no such simple weighting scheme to match the sample to the population is available.

To explore this, we use a binary logit model to regress demographics (age, income, and gender) on the response to each of the follow-up questions listed in Table 4. All of the adjusted R^2s are low and in most cases, an F-test indicates that the coefficients on at least two of the variables (age, income or gender) are not significantly different from zero in each of the regressions. However, this is not consistent across questions, making it difficult to identify a consistent pattern of respondent characteristics that explains responses to any of the follow-up questions. DCE studies have used a wide variety of techniques to make "adjustments" for respondents who don't appear to be providing valid responses. Reviewing and evaluating those approaches is beyond the scope of this chapter. Our point here is that the propensity to satisfy validity criteria may be so idiosyncratic that no reliable method may exist for determining the appropriate percentage of results to adjust to extrapolate to the population.

DISCUSSION AND CONCLUSIONS

General consensus exists in the literature that respondents to SP studies should attend to the scenarios and outcomes described in the survey and not others, take the exercise seriously and treat it as they would a real decision that affects their budget, and answer valuation questions as rational economic agents with well-defined preferences who are trading money for specific economic goods. In our survey, a large portion of our sample fails to meet these criteria. In fact, when examining all of each respondent's responses to the entire suite of follow-up questions, our sample yielded no more than two respondents out of 1,224 who answered the follow-up questions in a manner consistent with meeting the validity criteria; the average respondent failed to give a valid response, on average, to six or nine questions depending on degree of rigor in coding responses.

The majority of respondents (more than 50%) in our survey valued something other than reducing the effects of hypoxia, considered other elements of cost than how their family would be affected by the cost of the program, did not believe they would have to pay the amount shown in the vote, and/or thought that voting for the program would increase the chances of starting a similar program near them. We also find that people who vote yes for a program at least once are less likely to give a valid response and both of the respondents in the core that do give valid responses voted not to pay for the environmental program in all five votes.

Should policy decisions and legal damages be assessed using information obtained from people who appear to give invalid responses to follow-up questions such as these? What should be done with the results of answers to follow-up questions such as those we obtained? We do not propose answers to these questions, but our analysis suggests the questions are important.

It has been argued that when "state of the art" survey design and administration is employed, the results from SP studies can represent the population's true monetary values in an unbiased fashion (Ryan and Spash, 2011). However, existing literature and the results of this study may show that the inconsistent and invalid responses may be more endemic to SP methods and potentially resistant to changes in survey designs.

REFERENCES

Banzhaf, H.S., D. Burtraw, D.A. Evans, and A. Krupnick (2006), "Valuation of natural resource improvements in the Adirondacks," *Land Economics*, **82**(3), 445–64.

Banzhaf, H.S., D. Burtraw, S. Chung, D.A. Evans, A. Krupnick, and J. Siikamaki (2011), "Valuation of ecosystem services in the southern Appalachian Mountains," paper presented at the Annual Meeting of the Association of Environmental and Resource Economics, Seattle, WA.

Bateman, I.J. (2011), "Valid value estimates and value estimate validation: Better methods and better testing for stated preference research," in J. Bennett (ed.), *The*

International Handbook on Non-Market Environmental Valuation, Cheltenham, UK and Northampton, MA, USA: Edward Elgar Publishing, pp. 322–52.

Bateman, I.J., R.T. Carson, B. Day, M. Hanemann, N. Hanley, and T. Hett et al. (2002), *Economic Valuation with Stated Preference Surveys: A Manual*, Cheltenham, UK and Northampton, MA, USA: Edward Elgar Publishing.

Bech, M., T. Kjaer, and J. Lauridsen (2011), "Does the number of choice sets matter? Results from a web survey applying a discrete choice experiment," *Health Economics*, **20**(3), 273–83.

Birol, E., K. Karousakis, and P. Koundouri (2006), "Using a choice experiment to account for preference heterogeneity in wetland attributes: The case of Cheimaditida wetland in Greece," *Ecological Economics*, **60**(1), 145–56.

Bishop, R.C., D.J. Chapman, B. Kanninen, J.A. Krosnick, B. Leeworthy, and N.F. Meade (2011), *Total Economic Value for Protecting and Restoring Hawaiian Coral Reef Ecosystems: Final Report*, Silver Spring, MD: NOAA Office of National Marine Sanctuaries, Office of Response and Restoration, and Coral Reef Conservation Program.

Cameron, T.A., J.R. DeShazo, and E.H. Johnson (2010), "Scenario adjustment in stated preference research," *Journal of Choice Modelling*, **4**(1), 9–43.

Carlsson, F., P. Frykblom, and C. Liljenstolpe (2003), "Valuing wetland attributes: An application of choice experiments," *Ecological Economics*, **47**(1), 95–103.

Carlsson, F., M. Kataria, and E. Lampi (2010), "Dealing with ignored attributes in choice experiments," *Environmental and Resource Economics*, **47**(1), 65–89.

Carson, R. and T. Groves (2007), "Incentive and informational properties of preference questions," *Environmental and Resource Economics*, **37**(1), 181–210.

Carson, R. and J. Louviere (2011), "A common nomenclature for stated preference elicitation approaches," *Environmental and Resource Economics*, **49**(4), 539–59.

Carson, R., M. Hanemann, R.J. Kopp, J.A. Krosnick, R. Mitchell, and R. Presser et al. (1994), *Prospective Interim Lost Use Value Due to DDT and PCB Contamination in the Southern California Bight: Volume II*, La Jolla, CA: US Department of Commerce (NOAA).

Carson, R., R. Mitchell, M. Hanemann, R.J. Kopp, S. Presser, and P.A. Ruud (2003), "Contingent valuation and lost passive use. Damages from the Exxon Valdez oil spill," *Environmental and Resource Economics*, **25**(3), 257–86.

Champ, P. and R. Bishop (2001), "Donation payment mechanisms and contingent valuation: An empirical study of hypothetical bias," *Environmental and Resource Economics*, **19**(4), 383–402.

Champ, P., R. Bishop, T. Brown, and D. McCollum (1997), "Using donation mechanisms to value nonuse benefit from public goods," *Journal of Environmental Economics and Management*, **33**(2), 151–62.

Hoehn, J., F. Lupi, and M. Kaplowitz (2010), "Stated choice experiments with complex ecosystem changes: The effect of information formats on estimated variances and choice parameters," *Journal of Agricultural and Resource Economics*, **35**(3), 568–90.

Johnston, R.J., E.T. Schultz, K. Segerson, and E.Y. Besedin (2011), "Bioindicator-based stated preference valuation for aquatic habitat and ecosystem service restoration," in J. Bennett (ed.), *The International Handbook on Non-Market Environmental Valuation*, Cheltenham, UK and Northampton, MA, USA: Edward Elgar Publishing.

Johnston, R.J., E.T. Schultz, K. Segerson, and E.Y. Besedin (2012), "Enhancing the content validity of stated preference valuation: The structure and function of ecological indicators," *Land Economics*, **88**(1), 102–20.

Kataria, M., I.J. Bateman, T. Christensen, A. Dubgaard, B. Hasler, and S. Hime et al. (2012), "Scenario realism and welfare estimates in choice experiments – a non-market valuation study on the European water framework directive," *Journal of Environmental Economics and Management*, **94**(1), 25–33.

Krupnick, A. and V. Adamowicz (2006), "Supporting questions in stated choice studies," in B. Kanninen (ed.), *Valuing Environmental Amenities Using Stated Choice Studies*, Dordrecht: Springer.

Krupnick, A., A. Alberini, M. Cropper, N. Simon, B. O'Brien, and R. Goeree et al. (2002), "Age, health and willingness to pay for mortality risk reductions: A contingent valuation survey of Ontario residents," *Journal of Risk and Uncertainty*, **24**(2), 161–86.

Li, C.Z. and L. Mattsson (1995), "Discrete choice under preference uncertainty: An improved structural model for contingent valuation," *Journal of Environmental Economics and Management*, **28**(2), 256–69.

Mitchell, R. and R. Carson (1989), *Using Surveys to Value Public Goods: The Contingent Valuation Method*, Washington, DC: Resources for the Future.

Olsson, B. (2005), "Accounting for response uncertainty in stated preference methods," paper presented at the EAERE Congress, Bremen, Germany.

Poe, G.L., J.E. Clark, D. Rondeau, and W.D. Schulze (2002), "Provision point mechanisms and field validity tests of contingent valuation," *Environmental and Resource Economics*, **23**(1), 105–31.

Ready, R.C., P. Champ, and J. Lawton (2010), "Using respondent uncertainty to mitigate hypothetical bias in a stated choice experiment," *Land Economics*, **86**(2), 363–81.

Ryan, A. and C. Spash (2011), "Is WTP an attitudinal measure? Empirical analysis of the psychological explanation for contingent values," *Journal of Economic Psychology*, **32**(5), 674–87.

Scarpa, R., T. Gilbride, D. Campbell, and D.A. Hensher (2009), "Modelling attribute non-attendance in choice experiments for rural landscape valuation," *European Review of Agricultural Economics*, **36**(2), 151–74.

Schkade, D. and J. Payne (1994), "How people respond to contingent valuation questions: A verbal protocol analysis of willingness to pay for an environmental regulation," *Journal of Environmental Economics and Management*, **26**(1), 88–109.

United States Environmental Protection Agency (EPA) Scientific Advisory Board (SAB) (2009), *Valuing the Protection of Ecological Systems and Services*, Washington, DC: EPA.

10. Hypothetical bias: a new meta-analysis

Harry Foster and James Burrows[1]

INTRODUCTION

Participants in hypothetical surveys or referenda typically express higher values for goods than do participants faced with similar choices in which the stakes involve real money. Previous meta-analyses have confirmed the widespread presence of hypothetical bias in stated preference studies and have identified certain factors associated with higher or lesser degrees of bias. These studies, and indeed the broader stated preference valuation literature, have not offered any definitive insights that can reliably be used to eliminate these biases. The earlier meta-analyses are now dated and were based on a limited number of studies.

In this chapter we assess the evidence from the literature up to the present time on hypothetical bias. We include many more papers touching on hypothetical bias than were available to or used by the authors of the prior meta-analyses. We also add two variables (not analyzed in the existing literature) to our meta-analysis: one that is designed to capture whether the good in question is likely to be perceived as familiar or unfamiliar to the study's survey participants and a second that indicates whether or not the valuation of the good in question is largely or exclusively generated by non-use considerations.

In the remainder of this chapter, we first discuss how our meta-data were created. We then identify and briefly discuss some of the issues in survey design that have been hypothesized to contribute to the presence or extent of the hypothetical bias exhibited in various studies. We then present results from a regression analysis of the meta-data, and follow with some concluding remarks.

---

[1] Respectively, Principal, and Vice Chairman, Charles River Associates, Boston.

DATA

Our initial sample for our meta-analysis includes all of the relevant comparisons of mean willingness to pays (WTPs) between hypothetical and real survey treatments that we were able to draw from the papers cited in one or more of three previous meta-analyses: those of List and Gallet (2001), Little and Berrens (2004), and Murphy et al. (2005).[2] Similar to the practice adopted in the first two of these studies and in one of the analyses done in Murphy et al. (2005), we analyze only those comparisons from studies that included explicit calculations of mean WTPs across both hypothetical and real treatments. We thus eliminated from further analysis those studies that merely provide percentage yes/no results drawn from dichotomous choice referendum questions and that did not go on to calculate population mean WTPs. To this sample of results drawn from previously cited papers, we added data comparing WTPs drawn from additional papers not cited in prior meta-analyses.[3] The unit of observation is a comparison between a hypothetical WTP and a corresponding real WTP for the same good drawn from the same paper. Any particular paper could contribute one or multiple observations to the dataset, with the number depending on the number of survey variants conducted as a part of the paper's survey design. All told, our sample includes 432 comparisons between hypothetical and real results drawn from 77 studies. These studies are listed in the Bibliography with an asterisk.

For each of the comparisons of inferred WTP from CV surveys to inferred WTP from real transactions involving money, we calculate a "bias ratio" (BR) defined as the ratio of the mean WTP drawn from the hypothetical treatment to the mean WTP drawn from the real treatment. A histogram of the BRs found in Figure 1 provides summary data on the bias ratios we derived from the observations contained in our meta-data. The median value in the distribution is 1.39, while the mean value is 2.33.

---

[2] In addition to these three papers, we consulted two more recently published meta-analyses as potential sources of papers to our database. Schläpfer and Fischhoff (2010) relies upon the same sample of papers as was used in Murphy et al. (2005), while Little et al. (2012) does not provide a list of the studies it relied upon in creating its dataset.

[3] To assemble our database of studies related to measuring hypothetical bias ratios, we supplemented the articles cited in the prior meta-analyses and in another published overview of the hypothetical bias literature (Harrison and Rutström, 2008) by searching the EVRI (Environmental Valuation Reference Inventory) and NOEP (National Ocean Economics Program – Middlebury College) databases, government websites and publication sources (including NOAA, EPA, and the US Fisheries and Wildlife Agency, among others), academic websites (including Richard Carson's invaluable website for collected studies, accessed December 9, 2016 at https://ideas.repec.org/i/p.html), the mammoth bibliography in Carson, 2012, EBSCO, Econlit, and Google Scholar. In addition to these sources, we also cross-referenced citations in all the articles we identified.

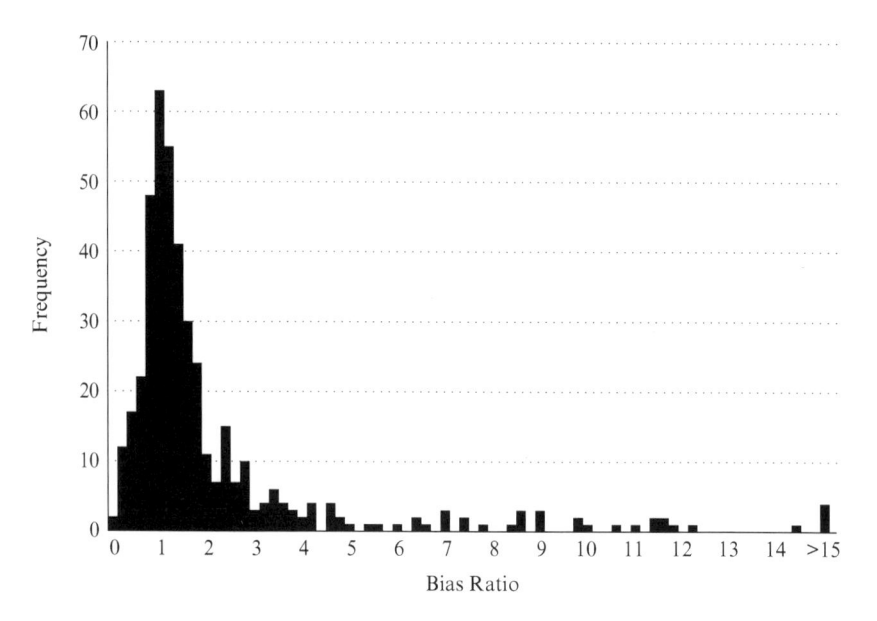

Figure 1 Bias ratio frequency distribution

The range of BRs exhibited in the distribution is relatively large, with a 5th percentile BR of 0.50 and a 95th percentile value of 8.66. Notably, the shape of the distribution of BRs provided in Figure 1 suggests that the values found in the dataset follow something like a log-normal distribution. Figure 2, which displays a histogram of the BRs arrayed on a logarithmic scale, confirms that the BRs are indeed consistent with a log-normal distribution.

We calculate a bias ratio (BR) for each observation retained in our data and assign a series of indicator variables to each comparison reflecting factors present or absent in the study's design that have been hypothesized in the literature to influence the extent of hypothetical bias. These factors are:

- whether or not the BR was calculated through use of an ex-post certainty correction;
- the presence or absence of a cheap talk script in the survey instrument;
- whether the hypothetical and real observations are drawn from a survey in which a single group of participants are asked to respond to both hypothetical and real treatments (same) or are drawn from two separate survey panels (different);
- whether or not the study uses a conjoint/choice experiment framework rather than any other type of contingent valuation;

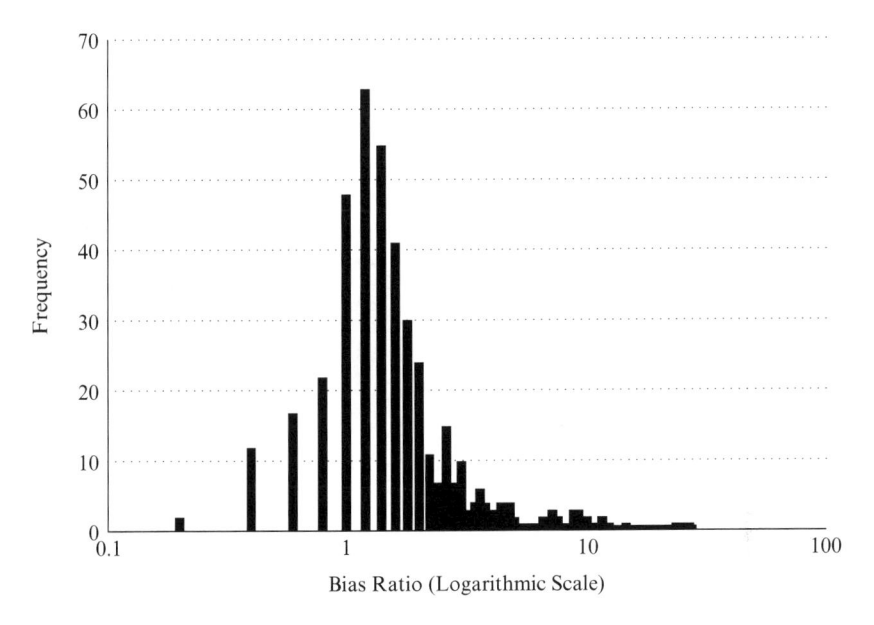

Figure 2 Bias ratio frequency distribution

- whether or not the survey group consists entirely of students;
- whether or not the survey was administered in a laboratory setting;
- whether the good is a public good or a private good;
- whether the good is likely to be perceived as a familiar or an unfamiliar one by the survey's participants;
- whether the perceived benefits to the survey participants of providing the good are generated primarily by non-use considerations.

Each of these nine factors can be used by itself to divide the full dataset into a pair of non-overlapping and fully inclusive subsamples. Table 1 provides summary statistics on the median, mean, and standard deviations for all of the 18 subsamples that can be created in this way. In addition to the median, Table 1 also provides the 5th percentile and 95th percentile BRs for each subsample and *p*-values associated with an equality of the means test across each relevant pairing.

Certainty correction

Certainty correction takes a value of one if the observation is derived from a hypothetical treatment employing an ex post certainty correction and is set to zero otherwise. This variable is meant to control for the

Table 1 Summary statistics for bias ratio by observation type

	Full Dataset
Mean	2.329
Median	1.388
Standard deviation	3.138
5–95%	0.495–8.659
Number of observations	432
P-value for two independent samples t-test	N/A

	Cheap Talk	No Cheap Talk	Same	Not Same	Lab	Non-lab
Mean	1.620	2.422	2.088	2.428	1.779	2.722
Median	1.410	1.381	1.214	1.471	1.275	1.424
Standard deviation	1.306	3.294	2.374	3.399	1.609	3.833
5–95%	0.205–4.156	0.531–8.778	0.698–8.500	0.422–8.659	0.507–4.203	0.422–10.188
Number of observations	50	382	125	307	180	252
P-value	0.0016		0.2385		0.0005	

	Private	Public	Conjoint	Non-conjoint	Student	Non-student
Mean	2.458	2.240	1.798	2.456	2.410	2.286
Median	1.630	1.260	1.419	1.378	1.233	1.456
Standard deviation	3.176	3.115	1.493	3.404	3.714	2.787
5–95%	0.700–7.912	0.402–8.778	0.333–4.156	0.545–9.083	0.495–9.167	0.554–7.067
Number of observations	177	255	83	349	151	281
P-value	0.4790		0.0077		0.7212	

Table 1 (continued)

	Familiar	Unfamiliar	Non-use	Use	Certainty correction	Non-certainty correction
Mean	2.213	2.423	2.631	2.076	0.875	2.578
Median	1.362	1.411	1.412	1.359	0.769	1.499
Standard deviation	3.030	3.226	3.501	2.781	0.513	3.327
5–95%	0.698–7.067	0.409–9.471	0.417–10.667	0.513–5.417	0.299–1.573	0.789–9.053
Number of observations	192	240	197	235	63	369
P-value	0.4872		0.0726		0.0000	

use in several studies of certainty correction techniques in an attempt to reconcile the differences between mean WTPs exhibited in paired hypothetical and real survey treatments by using data drawn from follow-up questions asking survey recipients to rate how sure they are in the answer they gave to the valuation question. Most commonly, this certainty question asks recipients to rate their degree of certainty in their answers to a hypothetical valuation question on a numerical scale, typically running from one to ten, with one representing "very uncertain" and ten representing "very certain." Alternatively, some studies dispense with creating a numerical scale, instead asking survey participants to indicate the degree of certainty in their responses by choosing the phrase that best describes their level of certainty from a set of qualitative options (for example, "very uncertain," "somewhat uncertain," "somewhat certain" or "highly certain") presented to them in the survey instrument. Such studies typically find that reasonable agreement between hypothetical and real treatments can be obtained if the set of hypothetical responses used to calculate WTPs is limited to only the survey responses given by those who indicate a degree of certainty that meets or exceeds some cut-off value or, alternatively, opt for qualitative descriptions of their levels of certainty that indicate a relatively high level of certainty. The researcher chooses the appropriate cut-off point for degree of certainty through an ex post determination of which particular value brings the certainty-corrected hypothetical WTP into closest agreement with the WTP derived from a real treatment. The particular cut-off value that is determined in this manner is survey specific and cannot be predicted a priori. For example, of six studies cited in Morrison and Brown (2009) that employed a ten-point certainty scale, two found closest agreement between real and hypothetical values if the analysis of WTP was limited to only responses associated with a degree of certainty of seven or greater, while two other studies found an optimal cut-off at eight, and two found that including only responses equal to ten brought the best fit between hypothetical and real WTP values. Because researchers actively choose, on an ex post basis, the certainty cut-off to be applied to the hypothetical treatment data to mimic the results obtained from an analogous real treatment, calibration factors between certainty-corrected hypothetical WTP results and real treatment WTP values will by design cluster near a value of one. For this reason, our regression models control for observations drawn from "certainty-corrected" or "certainty-calibrated" results. We are unaware of any paper that has analyzed how to set a certainty correction ex ante – that is, there is no procedure available to know what the "right" certainty correction is in advance.

Cheap talk
Cheap talk is set at 1 if the hypothetical treatment used in comparing hypothetical and real responses utilized a "cheap talk" script and set to zero otherwise. In this approach, survey respondents in the hypothetical treatment group are asked to answer any valuation questions only after they have first been presented with a script informing them of the tendency of participants in prior hypothetical surveys to overstate WTPs and asking them to keep this fact in mind when answering the survey's questions. Most, though not all, studies on the efficacy of cheap talk scripts have found that mean WTPs derived from treatments utilizing cheap talk scripts tend to be lower than those derived from similar hypothetical treatments lacking a cheap talk script, although the differences in the results obtained between the treatments may or may not be statistically significant. Consistent with the expectation that cheap talk scripts should generally dampen the extent of hypothetical bias, we find that the mean BR for study treatments included in our meta-analysis that include a cheap talk script (1.62) is lower than the mean bias ratio for study treatments lacking a cheap talk script (2.42). This difference is significant at any conventional level of statistical significance.

Same respondents vs different respondents
The indicator variable *Same* is set to one if the survey design has the same person answering the hypothetical and real survey treatments – that is, each participant is first asked to answer hypothetical valuation questions and then is asked to make a real purchase or contribution for the same good. In the alternative "different" sample treatment, participants are divided into two groups, with one group answering only a hypothetical survey and the other group subjected to only the real treatment. Treatments that rely on the same individuals to provide responses for both the hypothetical and then the real valuation exercises are believed to generate smaller bias ratios than treatments that rely on separate and different hypothetical and real treatment groups. When the same participants are asked to respond to a hypothetical treatment and then to a real treatment, their real purchase behavior may be influenced in an upward direction by anchoring or by conscious or unconscious desires to have their real decisions bear a relationship to their answers to the questions asked them in the prior hypothetical treatment. In our sample, the mean bias ratio for within-sample comparisons is just slightly lower than that for between comparisons (2.09 vs 2.43), and the difference between these two values is not statistically significant.

Conjoint/choice experiment

The indicator variable *Conjoint* is set to one if the observation comes from a study using conjoint or choice experiment techniques in which WTPs are derived indirectly from the pattern of choices individual participants express when asked to choose among hypothetical goods that differ in their product attributes. *Conjoint* is otherwise set to zero otherwise, as is the case for studies using some variant of a contingent valuation survey. Some proponents of the choice experiment framework have claimed that it is less susceptible to hypothetical bias than are contingent valuation techniques. In our sample, the mean bias ratio for conjoint/choice experiment elicitation formats is 1.80, versus a mean value of 2.46 for studies using any one of several other elicitation techniques. The difference between these two means is statistically different at any conventional level of statistical significance.

Student

The indicator variable *Student* is set to 1 if a study's participants consist entirely of students and to zero otherwise. It has been hypothesized that survey responses from panels comprised of students are likely to reflect a greater degree of hypothetical bias than are those from panels drawn from predominantly non-student populations. In our sample, the mean bias ratio derived from experiments using only student participants is 2.41, while the mean bias ratio derived from studies that used non-student or mixed survey populations is slightly smaller at 2.29. The difference between these two means is not statistically significant.

Lab experiment

The indicator variable *Lab* is set to one if the hypothetical and real survey instruments were administered in a laboratory study and to zero otherwise. In our sample, the mean bias ratio derived from experiments conducted in laboratory settings is 1.78, while that derived from studies conducted in other settings is larger, at 2.72. The difference between these two subsamples means is statistically significant at all conventional levels of statistical significance.

Private good/public good

The indicator variable *Private* is set to one if the good that is the subject of the study is a private good and to zero otherwise. Valuations for public goods might be expected to exhibit greater hypothetical bias than those for private goods, given the far greater familiarity survey participants have in engaging in transactions for the purchase of private goods. Contrary to these expectations, in our subsamples the mean value of BR derived from experiments valuing private goods (2.46) is slightly greater than that derived from the public goods subsample (2.24). The difference between these two means is not statistically significant.

Familiar good

Based upon our own best judgment, we have classified observations into those we believe are for goods that are familiar to the population being surveyed and those that are unfamiliar to them. As might be expected, the mean bias ratio derived from experiments valuing familiar goods is lower than that from experiments valuing unfamiliar goods (2.21 vs 2.42, respectively), although the difference in means is not statistically significant. As far as we are aware, this study is the first of its kind to rely upon this distinction to create an explanatory variable for use in a meta-analysis.

Non-use

This variable, the assignment of which is based upon our best judgment, is set to one for goods that we believe generate all or most of their perceived value from non-use considerations. The mean correction factor in our survey is 2.63 for non-use-value goods and 2.08 for use-value goods. The difference between these two means is statistically significant at the 10% level. As is the case for the creation of the familiar/unfamiliar distinction described above, we believe that this study is the first to use this distinction to create an explanatory variable to be used in a meta-analysis.

REGRESSION ANALYSIS

Base Model

Having assigned the appropriate indicator variable values to each observation retained in our data we then estimated an equation of the form:

$$\ln(BR) = \alpha + \beta_1 * Certaintycorrection + \beta_2 * Cheap\ talk + \beta_3 * Same + \beta_4 * Conjoint + \beta_5 * Student + \beta_6 * Lab + \beta_7 * Private + \beta_8 * Familiar + \beta_9 * Non\text{-}use$$

where ln (BR), the natural logarithm of the bias ratio for each observation, is the dependent variable and the explanatory variables are a constant and the various indicator variables are as defined in the previous section.

Results of this initial OLS regression analysis are displayed in columns 1 and 2 of Table 2. Because some studies contribute multiple observations to the data, we follow the practice of Little and Berrens (2004) and estimate and report clustered standard errors, with each paper represented in the

Table 2 Regression coefficients for reference and linear specifications

Variable	(1) ln(BR) Unweighted Non-use	(2) ln(BR) Weighted Non-use	(3) BR Unweighted Non-use	(4) BR Weighted Non-use
Certaintycorrection	−0.8907***	−0.8845***	−1.8919***	−2.0200***
	(0.10)	(0.15)	(0.37)	(0.46)
Cheaptalk	−0.3627**	−0.4547**	−0.8145	−1.1727*
	(0.17)	(0.22)	(0.56)	(0.63)
Same	−0.1069	0.0175	−0.3865	0.1047
	(0.20)	(0.15)	(0.71)	(0.60)
Conjoint	−0.0331	−0.0748	−0.0507	−0.1277
	(0.11)	(0.19)	(0.42)	(0.64)
Student	0.1070	0.1879	1.4867	1.4773
	(0.23)	(0.21)	(1.08)	(0.94)
Lab	−0.1564	−0.3133*	−1.5703	−1.9390**
	(0.21)	(0.19)	(0.95)	(0.82)
Private	0.5205***	0.6246***	1.1969**	1.7810**
	(0.14)	(0.16)	(0.51)	(0.75)
Familiargood	−0.0871	−0.2716*	−0.2516	−0.6334
	(0.14)	(0.15)	(0.45)	(0.53)
Non-use	0.3716*	0.4503**	0.8287	1.6961**
	(0.19)	(0.18)	(0.63)	(0.77)
Constant	0.3447*	0.4379**	2.1994***	2.0305**
	(0.20)	(0.19)	(0.70)	(0.78)
Observations	432	432	432	432
R-squared	0.2349	0.2329	0.1112	0.1556
RMSE	0.706	0.726	2.990	3.104
Degrees of freedom	422	422	422	422

Note: Robust standard errors in parentheses; *** $p < 0.01$, ** $p < 0.05$, * $p < 0.1$.

data forming a separate cluster. In addition, we estimate the equation using both an unweighted and a weighted sample; in the former version, each observation carries equal weight in the estimation, no matter how many other observations may be drawn from the same paper, while in the latter each observation derived from a single study is weighted by the inverse of the number of comparisons in the dataset derived from the same study; that is, for each comparison from a paper contributing n observations to the dataset is weighted by a factor of $1/n$.

In general, most of the coefficients have the signs previously hypothesized for them in the literature. The coefficient on the *Certainty correction* variables in the unweighted models is relatively large, negative, and statistically significant at the 1% level. The *Cheap talk*, *Same*, and *Conjoint* variables are associated with lower bias ratios, as is the variable meant to indicate whether or not the good being valued is a familiar one. The use of student subjects is associated with higher bias ratios. Potentially offsetting the effects of the *Student* variable, the coefficient on the lab variable is negative, indicating that conducting experiments in a lab setting is associated with lowered bias ratios.[4] The coefficient on the *Private* variable is positive in sign, as is the coefficient on *Non-use*. The coefficients on the *Certainty correction*, *Cheap talk*, *Private* and *Non-use* variables are the only ones to achieve statistical significance at conventional levels ($p < 0.05$) in both the weighted sample and unweighted sample regressions. The coefficient on the *Lab* variable is of marginal statistical significance ($p < 0.10$) in only the weighted sample regression. All of the other indicator variable coefficients fail to achieve statistical significance at conventional levels.

Functional Form

We explore whether the results displayed in columns 1 and 2 of Table 2 are robust with respect to choice of functional form by estimating regressions in which BR replaces ln (BR) as the dependent variable. The original specification is appropriate under an assumption that the effects of the explanatory variables on observed bias ratios are multiplicative in nature, while the choice of BR as dependent variable implicitly assumes that the effects of the same variables in determining observed bias ratios are additive in nature. Results from regression form in which BR serves as the dependent variable can be found in columns 3 and 4 of Table 2. All of the coefficients in the regressions in which BR is the dependent variable exhibit the same signs as those of their counterparts in the ln (BR) specification. With the sole exception of the *Cheap talk* variable in the unweighted BR specification, all of the indicator variables that achieve statistical significance in the ln (BR) specifications also achieve some level of statistical significance in the corresponding BR specifications, with only two exceptions (the *Cheap talk* variable in the unweighted models and the *Familiar* variable in the weighted models). The same relationship holds in the reverse comparison, as all of the variables that achieve statistical significance in the BR specifications also are of statistical significance in the ln (BR) regressions. The

---

[4] This negative coefficient could reflect differences between the relative frequencies with which lab-administered surveys and field experiments are designed to elicit valuation responses having a basis in "induced values" supplied by the experimenter rather than in survey participants' "homegrown" preferences.

consistency in the patterns of coefficient signs and significance across the two sets of specifications provides reassurance that the results produced with ln (BR) as the dependent variable are not driven by this particular choice of functional form.

Time Trend

We also explore whether the results produced by the reference specification are robust to the inclusion of a *Time trend* variable. Including a time variable in the regression specification controls for the possibility that, after controlling for the effects of the other explanatory variables, at least some of the variation in bias ratios might reflect ongoing refinements in methodology and the gradual adoption of "best practices" in conducting valuation studies. The *Time trend* variable is based on year of publication[5] and is set at 1 for the year 1972, increasing by one unit with each subsequent year.

Table 3 displays a comparison of the results derived from estimating the reference model against those obtained when the *Time trend* variable is included as an additional explanatory variable. The coefficients on the *Time trend* variable are relatively small and are not statistically significant in either the unweighted sample or weighted sample regression and are both positive. The coefficients on the other explanatory variables are little changed by the inclusion of a *Time trend* variable and the pattern of which variables are statistically significant does not change at all, with the exception of the lab variable in the weighted models. Any changes in either the R-squared or root mean-squared error (RMSE) statistics produced by the addition of the *Time trend* variable to the regression equation are sufficiently small as to leave the rounded values reported in Table 3 unchanged. In short, the addition of a *Time trend* variable adds nothing to improve either the explanatory or predictive powers of the reference regression specification.

The results of this latest meta-analysis are broadly consistent with the findings of previous meta-analyses with respect to the pattern of coefficient signs. The regression equations we estimate explain, in the best of circumstances, only about 23% of the overall variance we observe in BRs. ($R^2 = 0.2329$ for the weighted regression and $R^2 = 0.2349$ for the unweighted regression.) Notable, too, is the low predictive power of these regressions, as evidenced by the relatively large RMSEs in both the

---

[5] We choose to use year of publication to assign time trend values to each study rather than the year in which the underlying research took place. The choice is driven by the availability of year of publication data for each of the studies included in our sample. Commonly, these studies also describe when the underlying survey or experiment was conducted, but this information is not provided in all cases.

Table 3 Time trend regression coefficients

Variables	(1) ln (BR) Unweighted Non-use	(2) ln (BR) Weighted Non-use	(3) ln (BR) Unweighted Non-use Time	(4) ln (BR) Weighted Non-use Time
Certaintycorrection	−0.8907***	−0.8845***	−0.8989***	−0.9045***
	(0.10)	(0.15)	(0.10)	(0.15)
Cheaptalk	−0.3627**	−0.4547**	−0.3795**	−0.4919**
	(0.17)	(0.22)	(0.17)	(0.22)
Same	−0.1069	0.0175	−0.1049	0.0226
	(0.20)	(0.15)	(0.20)	(0.14)
Conjoint	−0.0331	−0.0748	−0.0605	−0.1359
	(0.11)	(0.19)	(0.14)	(0.20)
Student	0.1070	0.1879	0.1028	0.1745
	(0.23)	(0.21)	(0.24)	(0.21)
Lab	−0.1564	−0.3133*	−0.1440	−0.2925
	(0.21)	(0.19)	(0.22)	(0.19)
Private	0.5205***	0.6246***	0.5261***	0.6418***
	(0.14)	(0.16)	(0.13)	(0.16)
Familiargood	−0.0871	−0.2716*	−0.0835	−0.2563
	(0.14)	(0.15)	(0.14)	(0.16)
Non-use	0.3716*	0.4503**	0.3835**	0.4708**
	(0.19)	(0.18)	(0.19)	(0.18)
Time_trend			0.0033	0.0066
			(0.01)	(0.01)
Constant	0.3447*	0.4379**	0.2407	0.2349
	(0.20)	(0.19)	(0.36)	(0.38)
Observations	432	432	432	432
R-squared	0.2349	0.2329	0.2355	0.2353
RMSE	0.706	0.726	0.706	0.726
Degrees of freedom	422	422	421	421

Note: Robust standard errors in parentheses; *** $p < 0.01$, ** $p < 0.05$, * $p < 0.1$.

weighted and unweighted sample regressions, 0.726 and 0.706, respectively. This represents the standard error of prediction, a measure of the precision with which the actual value of the dependent variable, ln (BR), can be predicted by the regression line. Even the smaller of these figures indicates that 95% of the observations of ln (BR) should fall within an interval of plus or minus 1.38 logarithmic units from their values as predicted by the regression line. Evaluated at their sample means (ln (BR) = 0.452 for the unweighted sample and ln (BR) = 0.616 for the weighted sample) and after having been converted from log form into levels, these relatively large RMSEs establish a 95% confidence interval of prediction for BR ranging from 0.394 to 6.27 for the unweighted sample regression and between 0.446 and 7.68 for the weighted sample equation.

These wide ranges clearly indicate that the reference model cannot be used to provide a precise prediction of the bias ratio associated with any particular set of study characteristics. The reference model is thus unsuitable as a tool to offset the hypothetical bias that is inherent in all valuation exercises that attempt to value natural resources on the basis of survey respondents' answers to hypothetical questions.

Fixed Effects Regression

As a final robustness check, and to further explore the usefulness of the regression model in making predictions of the bias ratio associated with any particular survey, we re-estimated the reference model in a version that assigned study-specific fixed effect variables to 76 of the 77 studies from which we obtained our data. Table 4 provides results derived from the fixed effects specification alongside results from the reference model.

A fixed effects regression relies solely on variation within group effects in determining the coefficients to be placed on the other explanatory variables. This characteristic has several implications for our model. First, it means that studies that supply only one observation to the dataset are effectively ignored in estimating the other coefficients of our models. Second, we cannot estimate coefficients for variables that are held constant within each and every paper in which they appear. As a result, we cannot simultaneously estimate fixed effects coefficients and also estimate coefficients for the private, familiar good, and non-use variables.

The regression coefficients associated with five of the six indicator variables that are common to both the fixed effects and reference regressions are generally larger in magnitude and more likely to achieve statistical significance in the fixed effects specifications than is the case for their reference specification counterparts. This general observation is particularly evident when evaluating the coefficients on the potentially offsetting student and lab variables. The exception is the certainty correction variable, which drops in magnitude between the reference and fixed effects regressions, while remaining highly statistically significant.

Comparing the key regression statistics generated by the fixed effects specifications to those produced by the reference model, it is apparent that the fixed effects specifications do a better job than do their reference model counterparts in explaining the data. The fixed effects regressions generate

Table 4 Comparison between reference model and fixed effects regression coefficients

Variables	(1) ln (BR) Unweighted Non-use	(2) ln (BR) Weighted Non-use	(3) ln (BR) Unweighted Non-use F.E.	(4) ln (BR) Weighted Non-use F.E.
Certaintycorrection	−0.8907***	−0.8845***	−0.6332***	−0.6767***
	(0.10)	(0.15)	(0.10)	(0.10)
Cheaptalk	−0.3627**	−0.4547**	−0.5189***	−0.5160***
	(0.17)	(0.22)	(0.11)	(0.14)
Same	−0.1069	0.0175	0.1907*	0.2457
	(0.20)	(0.15)	(0.10)	(0.18)
Conjoint	−0.0331	−0.0748	0.0702	0.1387
	(0.11)	(0.19)	(0.04)	(0.10)
Student	0.1070	0.1879	0.2836*	0.3098*
	(0.23)	(0.21)	(0.17)	(0.17)
Lab	−0.1564	−0.3133*	−0.4132**	−0.4694**
	(0.21)	(0.19)	(0.19)	(0.22)
Private	0.5205***	0.6246***	NA	NA
	(0.14)	(0.16)		
Familiargood	−0.0871	−0.2716*	NA	NA
	(0.14)	(0.15)		
Non-use	0.3716*	0.4503**	NA	NA
	(0.19)	(0.18)		
Constant	0.3447*	0.4379**	0.6085***	0.7027***
	(0.20)	(0.19)	(0.02)	(0.02)
Observations	432	432	432	432
R-squared	0.2349	0.2329	0.6538	0.7532
RMSE	0.706	0.726	0.473	0.411
Degrees of freedom	422	422	347	347
Number of CV			78	78

Note: Robust standard errors in parentheses; *** $p < 0.01$, ** $p < 0.05$, * $p < 0.1$.

considerably higher R-squared statistics and lower RMSE statistics than those derived from the estimation of their corresponding reference model equations. This is to be expected, as incorporating a separate fixed effect for every study should improve the goodness of fit of a regression, but the extent of the improvements further illustrates how little of the underlying variation in the data can be attributed to readily observable study characteristics. Our results offer little hope for any efforts to develop "correction

CONCLUSIONS

This study considers whether economists have yet developed any practical and reliable ways to correct for or overcome the well-known phenomenon of hypothetical bias found in survey-based attempts to value environmental or other goods. It does so by updating and extending work done in prior meta-analyses of stated preference methods that has confirmed the widespread presence of hypothetical bias in stated preference studies and that has associated certain factors in survey design with higher or lesser degrees of observable bias. Our meta-analysis, like prior meta-analyses on the same topic, offers no definitive insights that can be used to eliminate or reduce hypothetical bias. While we find some, but generally weak, associations between the presence of a limited number of survey design characteristics and the degree of hypothetical bias likely to be exhibited in particular types of survey treatments, any insights provided by our analysis cannot reliably be used to control for or eliminate the degree of bias likely to be found in any particular survey as the regression coefficients produced by our analyses are typically associated with relatively wide standard errors and the equations can explain only a small fraction of the variance exhibited in the degree of hypothetical bias observed across various studies.

BIBLIOGRAPHY

Balistreri, E., G. McClelland, G. Poe, and W. Schulze (2001), "Can hypothetical questions reveal true values? A laboratory comparison of dichotomous choice and open-ended contingent values with auction values," *Environmental and Resource Economics*, **18**(3), 275–92.*

Barrage, L. and M.S. Lee (2010), "A penny for your thoughts: Inducing truth-telling in stated preference elicitation," *Economics Letters*, **106**(2), 140–42.*

Bishop, R.C. and T.A. Heberlein (1979), "Measuring values of extramarket goods: Are indirect measures biased?," *American Journal of Agricultural Economics*, **61**(5), 926–30.*

Blumenschein, K., M. Johannesson, K.K. Yokoyama, and P.R. Freeman (2001), "Hypothetical versus real willingness to pay in the health care sector: Results from a field experiment," *Journal of Health Economics*, **20**(3), 441–57.*

Blumenschein, K., G.C. Blomquist, M. Johannesson, N. Horn, and P. Freeman (2008), "Eliciting willingness to pay without bias: Evidence from a field experiment," *The Economic Journal*, **118**(525), 114–37.*

Blumenschein, K., M. Johannesson, G.C. Blomquist, B. Liljas, and R.M. O'Conor

(1997), "Hypothetical versus real payments in Vickrey auctions," *Economics Letters*, **56**(2), 177–80.*

Bohm, P. (1972), "Estimating demand for public goods: An experiment," *European Economic Review*, **3**(2), 111–30.*

Botelho, A. and L.C. Costa Pinto (2002), "Hypothetical, real, and predicted real willingness to pay in open-ended surveys: Experimental results," *Applied Economics Letters*, **9**(15), 993–6.*

Boyce, R.R., T.C. Brown, G.D. McClelland, G.L. Peterson, and W.D. Schulze (1989), "Experimental evidence of existence value in payment and compensation contexts," presented at the Joint Meeting of the Western Committee on the Benefits and Costs of Natural Resource Planning and the Western Regional Science Association, San Diego, CA.*

Broadbent, C.D. (2014), "Evaluating mitigation and calibration techniques for hypothetical bias in choice experiments," *Journal of Environmental Planning and Management*, **57**(12), 1831–48.*

Brookshire, D.S. and D.L. Coursey (1987), "Measuring the value of a public good: An empirical comparison of elicitation procedures," *American Journal of Agricultural Economics*, **77**(4), 544–66.*

Brown, K.M. and L.O. Taylor (2000), "Do as you say, say as you do: Evidence on gender differences in actual and stated contributions to public goods," *Journal of Economic Behavior & Organization*, **43**(1), 127–39.*

Brown, T.C., I. Ajzen, and D. Hrubes (2003), "Further tests of entreaties to avoid hypothetical bias in referendum contingent valuation," *Journal of Environmental Economics and Management*, **46**(2), 353–61.*

Brown, T.C., P.A. Champ, R.C. Bishop, and D.W. McCollum (1996), "Which response format reveals the truth about donations to a public good?," *Land Economics*, **72**(2), 152–66.*

Brynes, B., C. Jones, and S. Goodman (1999), "Contingent valuation and real economic commitments: Evidence from electric utility green pricing programmes," *Journal of Environmental Planning and Management*, **42**(2), 149–66.*

Camacho-Cuena, E., A. García-Gallego, H. Georgantzís, and G. Sabater-Grande (2003), "An experimental test of response consistency in contingent valuation," *Ecological Economics*, **47**(2–3), 167–82.*

Cameron, T.A., G.L. Poe, R.G. Ethier, and W.D. Schulze (2002), "Alternative non-market value-elicitation methods: Are the underlying preferences the same?," *Journal of Environmental Economics and Management*, **44**(3), 391–425.*

Carlson, J.L. (2000), "Hypothetical surveys versus real commitments: Further evidence," *Applied Economics Letters*, **7**(7), 447–50.*

Carlsson, F. and P. Martinsson (2001), "Willingness to pay for reduction in air pollution: A multilevel analysis," *Environmental Economics and Policy Studies*, **4**(1), 17–27.*

Carson, R.T. (2012), *Contingent Valuation: A Comprehensive Bibliography and History*, Cheltenham, UK and Northampton, MA, USA: Edward Elgar Publishing.

Champ, P.A. and T.C. Brown (1997), *A Comparison of Contingent and Actual Voting Behavior*, Rocky Mountain Research Station – USDA Forest Service.*

Champ, P.A. and R.C. Bishop (2001), "Donation payment mechanisms and contingent valuation: An empirical study of hypothetical bias," *Environmental and Resource Economics*, **19**(4), 383–402.*

Champ, P.A., R. Moore, and R.C. Bishop (2009), "A comparison of approaches to mitigate hypothetical bias," *Agricultural and Resource Economics Review*, **38**(2), 166–80.*

Champ, P.A., R.C. Bishop, T.C. Brown, and D.W. McCollum (1997), "Using donation mechanisms to value non-use benefits from public goods," *Journal of Environmental Economics and Management*, **33**(2), 151–62.*

Chang, J.B., J.L. Lusk, and F.B. Norwood (2009), "How closely do hypothetical surveys and laboratory experiments predict field behavior?," *American Journal of Agricultural Economics*, **91**(2), 518–34.*

Christie, M. (2007), "An examination of the disparity between hypothetical and actual willingness to pay using the contingent valuation methods: The case of red kite conservation in the United Kingdom," *Canadian Journal of Agricultural Economics*, **55**(2), 159–69.*

Cummings, R.G., G.W. Harrison, and E.E. Rutström (1995), "Homegrown values and hypothetical surveys: Is the dichotomous choice approach incentive-compatible?," *The American Economic Review*, **85**(1), 260–66.*

Cummings, R.G., S. Elliot, G.W. Harrison, and J. Murphy (1997), "Are hypothetical referenda incentive compatible?" *Journal of Political Economy*, **105**(3), 609–21.*

De Magistris, T., A. Gracia, and R.M. Nayga, Jr. (2011), "On the use of honesty priming task to mitigate hypothetical bias in choice experiments," *Centro de Investigación Y Tecnología Agroalimentaria De Aragón (CITA) Documento de Trabajo* No. 12/01.*

Duffield, J.W. and D.A. Patterson (1991), "Field testing existence values: An instream flow trust fund for Montana rivers," presented at the Association of Environmental and Resource Economics during the Valuing Environmental Goods with Contingent Valuation Session.*

Ehmke, M.D., J.L. Lusk, and J.A. List (2008), "Is hypothetical bias a universal phenomenon? A multinational investigation," *Land Economics*, **84**(3), 489–500.*

Ethier, R.G., G.L. Poe, W.D. Schulze, and J. Clark (2000), "A comparison of hypothetical phone and mail contingent valuation responses for green-pricing electricity programs," *Land Economics*, **76**(1), 54–67.*

Foster, V., I.J. Bateman, and D. Harley (1997), "Real and hypothetical willingness to pay for environmental preservation: A non-experimental comparison," *Journal of Agricultural Economics*, **48**(2), 123–38.*

Fox, J.A., J.F. Shogren, D.J. Hayes, and J.B. Kliebenstein (1998), "CVM-X: Calibrating contingent values with experimental auction market," *American Journal of Agricultural Economics*, **80**(3), 455–65.*

Frykblom, P. (1997), "Hypothetical question modes and real willingness to pay," *Journal of Environmental Economics and Management*, **34**(3), 275–87.*

Frykblom, P. (2000), "Willingness to pay and the choice of question format: Experimental results," *Applied Economics Letters*, **7**(10), 665–67.*

Getzner, M. (2000), "Hypothetical and real economic commitments, and social status, in valuing a species protection programme," *Journal of Environmental Planning and Management*, **43**(4), 541–59.*

Gregory, R. (1986), "Interpreting measures of economic loss: Evidence from contingent valuation and experimental studies," *Journal of Environmental Economics and Management*, **13**(4), 325–37.*

Griffin, C.C., J. Briscoe, B. Singh, R. Ramasubban, and R. Bhatia (1995), "Contingent valuation and actual behavior: Predicting connections to new

water systems in the State of Kerala, India," *World Bank Economic Review*, **9**(3), 373–95.*
Harrison, G.W. and E.E. Rutström (2008), "Experimental evidence on the existence of hypothetical bias in value elicitation methods," in C. Plott (ed.), *Handbook of Experimental Economics Results Volume 1*, Amsterdam: North-Holland, pp. 752–67.
Heberlein, T.A. and R.C. Bishop (1986), "Assessing the validity of contingent valuation," *The Science of the Total Environment*, **56**(1), 99–107.*
Hofler, R. and J.A. List (2004), "Valuation on the frontier: Calibrating actual and hypothetical statements of value," *American Journal of Agricultural Economics*, **86**(1), 213–21.*
Johannesson, M. (1997), "Some further experimental results on hypothetical versus real willingness to pay," *Applied Economic Letters*, **4**(3), 535–6.*
Johannesson, M., B. Liljas, and P. Johansson (1998), "An experimental comparison of dichotomous choice contingent valuation questions and real purchase decisions," *Applied Economics*, **30**(5), 643–7.*
Johansson-Stenman, O. and H. Svedsäter (2008), "Measuring hypothetical bias in choice experiments: The importance of cognitive consistency," *The B.E. Journal of Economic Analysis and Policy*, **8**(1), Article 41, 1–8.*
Johnston, J. (2006), "Is hypothetical bias universal? Validating contingent valuation responses using a binding public referendum," *Journal of Environmental Economics and Management*, **52**(1), 469–81.*
Kealy, M.J., J.F. Dovido, and M.L. Rockel (1988), "Accuracy in valuation is a matter of degree," *Land Economics*, **64**(2), 158–71.*
Landry, C.E. and J.A. List (2007), "Using ex ante approached to obtain credible signals for value in contingent markets: Evidence from the field," *American Journal of Agricultural Economics*, **89**(2), 420–29.*
List, J.A. (2003), "Using random nth price auctions to value non-market goods and services," *Journal of Regulatory Economics*, **23**(2), 193–205.*
List, J.A. and C.A. Gallet (2001), "What experimental protocol influence disparities between actual and hypothetical stated values?," *Environmental and Resource Economics*, **20**(3), 241–54.*
List, J.A. and J.F. Shogren (1998), "Calibration of the difference between actual and hypothetical valuations in a field experiment," *Journal of Economic Behavior and Organization*, **37**(2), 193–205.*
List, J., R.P. Berrens, A.K. Bohara, and J. Kerkvliet (2004), "Examining the role of social isolation on stated preferences," *American Economic Review*, **94**(3), 741–52.*
Little, J. and R. Berrens (2004), "Explaining disparities between actual and hypothetical stated values: Further investigation using meta-analysis," *Economics Bulletin*, **3**(6), 1–13.
Little, J., C.D. Broadbent, and R.P. Berrens (2012), "Meta-analysis of the probability of disparity between actual and hypothetical valuation responses: Extension and preliminary new results," *Western Economics Forum*, **11**(1).
Loomis, J., P. Bell, H. Cooney, and C. Asmus (2009), "A comparison of actual and hypothetical willingness to pay of parents and non-parents for protecting infant health: The case of nitrates in drinking water," *Journal of Agricultural and Applied Economics*, **41**(3), 697–712.*
Loomis, J., T. Brown, B. Lucero, and G. Peterson (1996), "Improving validity experiments of contingent valuation methods: Results of efforts to reduce the

disparity of hypothetical and actual willingness to pay," *Land Economics*, **72**(4), 450–61.*

Loomis, J., T. Brown, B. Lucero, and G. Peterson (1997), "Evaluating the validity of the dichotomous choice question format in contingent valuation," *Environmental and Resource Economics*, **10**(2), 109–23.*

Macmillan, D.C., T.S. Smart, and A.P. Thorburn (1999), "A field experiment involving cash and hypothetical charitable donations," *Environmental and Resource Economics*, **14**(3), 399–412.*

Miller, K.M., R. Hofstetter, H. Krohmer, and Z.H. Zhang (2011), "How should consumers' willingness to pay be measured? An empirical comparison of state-of-the-art approaches," *Journal of Marketing Research*, **48**(1), 172–84.*

Morrison, M. and T.C. Brown (2009), "Testing the effectiveness of certainty scales, cheap talk, and dissonance minimization in reducing hypothetical bias in contingent valuation studies," *Environmental Resource Economics*, **44**(3), 307–26.*

Moser, R., R. Raffaelli, and S. Notaro (2014), "Testing hypothetical bias with real choice experiment using respondents' own money," *European Review of Agricultural Economics*, **41**(1), 25–46.*

Murphy, J.J., T. Stevens, and D. Weatherhead (2002), "An empirical study of hypothetical bias in voluntary contribution contingent valuation: Does cheap talk matter?," Paper prepared for the World Congress of Environmental and Resource Economists, No. 789.000.*

Murphy, J.J., P.G. Allen, T.H. Stevens, and D. Weatherhead (2005), "A meta-analysis of hypothetical bias in stated preference valuation," *Environmental and Resource Economics*, **30**(3), 313–25.

Navrud, S. (1992), "Willingness to pay for preservation of species – an experiment with actual payments," in S. Navrud (ed.), *Pricing the European Environment*, Oslo: Scandinavian University Press, pp. 231–46.*

Neill, H.R., R.G. Cummings, P.T. Ganderton, G.W. Harrison, and T. McGuckin (1994), "Hypothetical surveys and real economic commitments," *Land Economics*, **70**(2), 145–54.*

Norwood, B.F. (2005), "Can calibration reconcile stated and observed preferences?," *Journal of Agricultural and Applied Economics*, **37**(1), 237–48.*

Paradiso, M. and A. Trisorio (2001), "The effect of knowledge on the disparity between hypothetical and real willingness to pay," *Applied Economics*, **33**(11), 1359–64.*

Park, J.H. and D.L. MacLachlan (2008), "Estimating willingness to pay with exaggeration bias – corrected contingent valuation method," *Marketing Science*, **27**(4), 691–8.*

Poe, G., J.E. Clark, D. Rondeau, and W.D. Schulze (2002), "Provision point mechanisms and field validity tests of contingent valuation," *Environmental and Resource Economics*, **23**, 105–31.*

Schläpfer, F. and B. Fischhoff (2010), "When are preferences consistent? The effects of task familiarity and contextual cues on revealed and stated preferences?," *Working Paper No. 1007*, Socioeconomic Institute, University of Zurich.

Seip, K. and J. Strand (1992), "Willingness to pay for environmental goods in Norway: A contingent valuation study with real payment," *Environmental and Resource Economics*, **2**(1), 91–106.*

Shechter, M., B. Reiser, and N. Zaitsev (1998), "Measuring passive use value:

Pledges, donations, and CV responses in connection with an important natural resource," *Environmental and Resource Economics*, **12**(4), 457–78.*

Silva, A., R.M. Nayaga, B.L. Campbell, and J.L. Park (2007), "On the use of valuation mechanisms to measure consumers' willingness to pay for novel products: A comparison of hypothetical and non-hypothetical values," *International Food and Agribusiness Management Review*, **10**(2), 165–80.*

Silva, A., R.M. Nayga, B.L. Campbell, and J. Park (2012), "Can perceived task complexity influence cheap talk's effectiveness in reducing hypothetical bias in stated choice studies?," *Applied Economics Letters*, **19**(17), 1711–44.*

Sinden, J.A. (1988), "Empirical tests of hypothetical bias in consumer surplus surveys," *Australian Journal of Agricultural Economics*, **32**(2–3), 98–112.*

Spencer, M.A., S.K. Swallow, and C.L. Miller (1998), "Valuing water quality monitoring: A contingent valuation experiment involving hypothetical and real payments," *Agricultural and Resource Economics Review*, **27**(1), 28–42.*

Taylor, L. (1998), "Incentive compatible referenda and the valuation of environmental goods," *Agriculture and Resource Economics Review*, **27**(2), 132–9.*

Veisten, K. and S. Navrud (2006), "Contingent valuation and actual payment for voluntarily provided passive-use values: Assessing the effect of an induced truth-telling mechanism and elicitation formats," *Applied Economics*, **38**(7), 735–56.*

Volinsky, D., W. Adamowicz, and M. Veeman (2011), "Predicting versus testing: A conditional cross-forecasting accuracy measure for hypothetical bias," *The Australian Journal of Agricultural and Resource Economics*, **55**(3), 429–50.*

Vossler, C.A. and J. Kerkvliet (2003), "A criterion validity test of the contingent valuation method: Comparing hypothetical and actual voting behavior for a public referendum," *Journal of Environmental Economics and Management*, **45**(3), 631–49.*

Vossler, C.A., R.G. Ethier, G.L. Poe, and M.P. Welsh (2003), "Payment certainty in discrete choice contingent valuation responses: Results from a field validity test," *Southern Economic Journal*, **69**(4), 886–902.*

Vossler, C.A., J. Kerkvliet, S. Polasky, and O. Gainutdinova (2003), "Externally validating contingent valuation: An open-space survey and referendum in Corvallis, Oregon," *Journal of Economic Behavior & Competition*, **51**(2), 261–77.*

Willis, K.G. and N.A. Powe (1998), "Contingent valuation and real economic commitments: A private good experiment," *Journal of Environmental Planning and Management*, **41**(5), 611–19.*

Wu, P. and C. Huang (2001), "Actual advertising expenditure versus stated willingness to pay," *Applied Economics*, **33**(4), 277–83.

11. Legal obstacles for contingent valuation methods in environmental litigation

Brian D. Israel, Jean Martin, Kelly Smith Fayne, and Lauren Daniel[1]

INTRODUCTION

Contingent valuation surveys, and other stated preference methods, are sometimes used by economists to solicit opinions from the public regarding the monetary value respondents place on the existence of natural resources, independent of the use of those resources. For example, economists may attempt to use surveys to measure how much the respondent values a particular natural resource, such as a bird species or habitat, even if he or she never uses or sees that resource.

For decades, economists, government officials, and others have debated whether such survey methods can accurately measure non-use values in natural resource damage ("NRD") cases. A central premise of this debate is the oft-repeated notion that contingent valuation and other similar methods are allowed by the NRD regulations and accepted by the courts.[2] As we demonstrate below, this premise is inaccurate for several reasons.

This chapter provides a brief overview of the regulatory context for NRD claims and the potential role for stated preference survey valuation methods for non-use damages. We then provide an overview of court decisions associated with contingent valuation methods (both in the

---

[1] Respectively, Partner, Arnold & Porter Kaye Scholer, LLP; Senior Counsel, BP America, Inc.; Associate, Latham & Watkins, LLP; Associate, Arnold & Porter Kaye Scholer, LLP.

[2] See, for example, *Ohio v. U.S. Dep't of the Interior*, 880 F.2d 432 (D.C. Cir. 1989); Montesinos, M. (1999), *It May Be Silly, but It's an Answer: The Need to Accept Contingent Valuation Methodology in Natural Resource Damage Assessments*, Ecology Law Quarterly, **26**(48), 57–60 accessed December 10, 2016 at http://scholarship.law.berkeley.edu/cgi/viewcontent.cgi?article=1601&context=elq; Unsworth, R.E. and T.B. Petersen (1997), "Primary methods for compensable value determination," Chapter 4 in *A Manual for Conducting Natural Resource Damage Assessment: The Role of Economics*, accessed December 10, 2016 at https://www.fws.gov/policy/NRDAManualFull.pdf.

292

NRD context and beyond), and clearly demonstrate that courts have not accepted contingent valuation methods nor are they likely to do so in the future. Next, we explain why the NRD regulations strongly disfavor these methods. Finally, we discuss the public policies that weigh against the use of stated preference surveys as a measure of non-use damages, and recommend that governmental agencies abandon these survey methods and instead focus their attention on determining the actual cost of activities necessary to restore and replace injured natural resources.

NRD REGULATORY FRAMEWORK AND THE BASIS FOR NON-USE DAMAGES

Pursuant to the Comprehensive Environmental Response, Compensation, and Liability Act of 1980 ("CERCLA") and the Oil Pollution Act of 1990 ("OPA"), federal, state and tribal governments (sometimes called "trustees") may seek compensation for natural resource damages resulting from the release of hazardous substances (covered by CERCLA) and petroleum (covered by OPA).[3] As a general rule, these claims are intended to restore the natural environment to its baseline condition and compensate the public for the interim losses from the time the damage occurs until the time that restoration is complete.

Regulations promulgated under both CERCLA and OPA provide for compensation for the total value of natural resource injuries, including non-use damages. For example, regulations promulgated under OPA define "the total value of a natural resource or service [to] include[] the value individuals derive from direct use of the natural resource, for example, swimming, boating, hunting, or birdwatching, as well as *the value individuals derive from knowing a natural resource will be available for future generations.*"[4] The second type of value is commonly referred to as the existence, bequest, or "non-use" value of the resource, and it may exist even for people who have never used, or even seen, the injured resource. For example, a person could place some value in the knowledge that a natural resource exists in its uninjured condition and will be available for use in the future.

Regulations promulgated under CERCLA provide for a similar calculation of damages. Specifically, the CERCLA regulations state that NRD

---

[3] 42 U.S.C. §9607 (a)(4)(C); 33 U.S.C. §2702(b)(2)(A).
[4] 15 C.F.R. §990.30 [emphasis added]. The OPA regulations further define "value" to include "the maximum amount of. . .money an individual is willing to give up [e.g., to pay] to obtain a specific good."

"may also include...the compensable value of all or a portion of the services lost to the public for the time period from the discharge or release until the attainment of the restoration, rehabilitation, replacement, and/or acquisition of equivalent of baseline."[5] Guidance issued with the regulations explains that "compensable value" may include compensation for non-use values.[6]

APPROACHES TO ESTIMATING NON-USE VALUE FOR NATURAL RESOURCE DAMAGES

There are multiple approaches to estimating the non-use value of lost or injured natural resources in NRD cases. These approaches generally fall into two categories: (1) the restoration-based approach, which determines the restoration projects necessary to provide services or resources of a similar type and quality lost by the pollution event; or (2) the economic valuation approach, which assigns a dollar value to the loss using economic tools, principally survey-based mechanisms.

Restoration-based Approach

A restoration-based approach compensates for natural resource damages through a determination of the type and scale of projects needed to provide services or resources of a similar type and quality as those lost. By restoring a resource to its baseline condition (the condition it would be in if the contamination never occurred), the non-use values associated with the resource will also be restored. Additional restoration can also be provided to compensate the public for the interim loss of a resource while it is in an injured state, including use and non-use values. So, for example, in the case of a contaminated river, in addition to restoring

---

[5] 43 C.F.R. §11.80. See also 15 C.F.R. §990.53 (regulation that ties NRD assessments under OPA to the costs of, among other things, "compensatory restoration" – compensation for the "interim loss of natural resources and services pending recovery").

[6] See, for example, Natural Resource Damage Assessments, 59 Fed. Reg. 23,098 (proposed May 4, 1994) (to be codified at 43 C.F.R. pt. 11) ("Under the March 25, 1994, final rule [for assessing NRD], the costs of restoring, rehabilitating, replacing, and/or acquiring the equivalent of the injured resources are the basic measure of damages; however, these costs are only one component of the damages that trustee officials may assess. Trustee officials also have the discretion to assess the value of the resource services that the public lost from the date of the release or discharge until completion of restoration, rehabilitation, replacement, and/or acquisition of equivalent resources. 59 FR 14283. The term 'compensable value' is used to encompass all of the lost public economic values, including both lost use values and lost nonuse values"), accessed December 10, 2016 at https://www.gpo.gov/fdsys/pkg/FR-1994-05-04/html/94-10636.htm.

the condition and stock level in the river to baseline, a responsible party might also be required to improve the ecological conditions in a nearby river or install new fishing access points to increase the number of future fishing trips beyond baseline. These above-baseline improvements, assuming they are properly calibrated, will compensate for both interim lost use and non-use values associated with the pollution event. Because it sometimes is not possible or feasible to provide identical resources and/or services as those lost, the restoration-based approach will allow for the replacement or acquisition of similar resources. When similar but not identical resources are used to compensate for the loss, it is important to consider the correct scale of those actions that will make the environment and public whole.

Contingent Valuation Methods

As an alternative to the restoration approach described above, the government could seek to calculate non-use damages by using stated preference, or survey, valuation methods. There are several types of survey methods used by economists to estimate non-use value. One of the most common methods is contingent valuation ("CV"), which estimates the value people place on a resource by asking a representative sample of the population how much their household would be willing to pay for changes in the condition of the resource. As part of the survey, the respondents are provided a description of the resource being valued, the improvement to be made or harm to be prevented, a planned program by which the improvements or prevention will be accomplished, and a payment mechanism by which the hypothetical program will be funded. Typically, the respondent will be asked whether he or she would be willing to pay a specified dollar amount for the program. Survey responses are used to calculate the average maximum amount each household says it is willing to pay, and this amount is then multiplied by the purported number of affected households to obtain the alleged total non-use value of the injured natural resource.[7]

---

[7] A related method used to estimate both use and non-use values of natural resources is the total value equivalency method ("TVE"). TVE is another type of survey-based assessment that derives from "conjoint" studies, which are common in marketing. Instead of asking respondents what they would be willing to pay for a resource in a single program, TVE presents multiple scenarios that describe programs of different size, scope, duration, and cost, and asks respondents what they would be willing to pay for each scenario. See Israel, B.D. (2008), "Natural resource damages," in M. Gerrard (ed.), *Environmental Law Practice Guide*, §§32B-1, 32B-71–32B-73 (discussing problems with CV and conjoint studies in NRD litigation).

NO COURT HAS EVER RELIED UPON A CONTINGENT VALUATION STUDY IN AN NRD CASE

As discussed below, both the OPA and CERCLA regulations provide the option (albeit as a last resort) of relying on CV and other stated preference survey methods to estimate non-use losses. And, in the abstract, courts have upheld these regulations, deferring to the agencies on the idea that stated preference methods should be among the tools available to trustees.[8] Similarly, courts have occasionally found that CV studies may be presented in court if they meet standard tests for the admission of expert evidence.[9] However, in no case has a court actually relied upon a CV or similar study in determining the value of damages in an NRD case. Furthermore, several courts have ruled that CV studies are so unreliable that they cannot even be admitted into evidence. Below are a few illustrative examples:

United States v. Montrose

United States v. *Montrose Chemical Corp. of California*[10] is perhaps the best-known case involving a CV study. There, the federal and state governments sued various companies for natural resource damages caused by the insecticide ingredient DDT and PCBs at the Palos Verdes Shelf near Los Angeles. NOAA commissioned a group of leading economists to conduct a CV study assessing the amount of NRD, including non-use values. The study is considered one of the most expensive CV studies ever conducted.[11] The *Montrose* survey presented respondents with a description of the injury to the natural resources (e.g., bald eagles, peregrine falcons, white croakers, and kelp bass) and then described two options for remediation. Respondents could choose a natural restoration process, which cost nothing and would take 50 years to restore the resources, or a remedial program to cap and contain the pollutants in place, and restore the resources around the capped area in five years. The survey assigned a per household tax cost for the program randomly among four values: $10, $30, $60, and $120. The conclusions based on

---

[8] See *Ohio*, 880 F.2d at 476 (CERCLA); *Gen. Elec. Co.* v. *U.S. Dep't of Commerce*, 128 F.3d 767 (D.C. Cir. 1997) (OPA).

[9] See, for example, Order denying ARCO's motion *in limine* regarding Montana's CV survey, *Montana* v. *Atl. Richfield Co.*, No. 6:83-cv-00317 (D. Mont. Mar. 3, 1997), ECF No. 856.

[10] No. 90-cv-3122 (C.D. Cal. 1990).

[11] See Thompson, D.B. (2002), "Valuing the environment: Courts' struggles with natural resource damages," *Environmental Law*, **32**(57), 78.

the CV survey were that the interim lost value, which included passive or non-use use, from the release of DDT and PCBs amounted to $575 million.

Defendants moved to exclude the CV study, arguing that the facts presented to respondents in the survey did not match the actual harms to natural resources at the Palos Verdes Shelf.[12] For example, whereas the survey told respondents that peregrine falcons had not been able to hatch any eggs and were having reproductive problems along the South Coast but not elsewhere, the government's experts admitted in deposition that there was no evidence of impaired reproduction and that the falcons were actually increasing along the South Coast. The defendants pointed to similar inconsistencies in the survey representations about bald eagles, white croakers, and kelp bass. The defendants argued that the expert testimony therefore did not "fit" the facts and did not accurately describe the injuries that Trustees were trying to value.

In opposition to this motion, the government plaintiffs argued that the basic facts in the survey – that DDT came from the Montrose plant and mixed with PCBs to cause injury to fish and birds, preventing certain recreational fishing over an extended period of time – matched the facts of the case. The government argued that the CV study could provide a yardstick for measuring and determining compensatory damages, notwithstanding the above factual differences. The government reasoned that any inconsistencies between the description of injury in the survey, and the injuries proven at trial, should go to the weight of the evidence before the trier of fact, not to admissibility of the survey. In addition, the government planned to conduct a supplemental CV study to focus on injuries to eagles and fishing of the white croaker, which could be used to further assess damages at trial.

The court granted the defendants' motion in a ruling from the bench, preventing the trustees from introducing the results of the CV study into evidence in their case.[13] The court similarly did not allow the government to submit its report regarding its supplemental CV study.[14] The court did not reject CV methods in all circumstances, but its refusal to admit the

---

[12] The defendants stated that they were not addressing all of the perceived problems with the CV study, which would have required a thorough review of the academic literature and deposition of the trustees' experts. See Memorandum of Points and Authori ies in Support of Defendants' Motion to Exclude Plaintiffs' Contingent Valuation Report and Testimony Based Thereon, *Montrose*, No. 90-cv-3122 (Mar. 6, 2000), ECF No. 1768. Accordingly, other potential problems with the CV study were not addressed by the parties or the court.
[13] Transcript of Hearing at 17:20–18:1, *Montrose*, No. 90-cv-3122 (Apr. 17, 2000).
[14] Id. at 18:3–9.

studies into evidence has far reaching implications that tie back to many of the underlying concerns with CV methods. As the court in *Montrose* concluded, the trustees will have to prove that the injuries described in a CV survey are a close "fit" to the injuries that trustees seek to prove at trial. Even if it is a well-designed survey, there will always be information that is omitted or simplified in the survey narrative. Furthermore, given that the conditions of resources are changing over time (and in many cases improving), it will be difficult, if not impossible, for trustees to design a survey that accurately describes the type and scope of harm that remains to be proven at trial.

Idaho v. Southern Refrigerated Transport Inc.

In *Idaho v. Southern Refrigerated Transport Inc.*,[15] the U.S. District Court for the District of Idaho determined that the CV study put forward by the Trustees as evidence of non-use damages was unreliable. Following a pesticide spill in the Little Salmon River, the State of Idaho brought claims against the distributor and trucking company for damages caused to the steelhead fish population. The state relied on a CV study to estimate non-use damages. However, the study had been prepared for a regional power planning council for purposes that were not related to the litigation, and it asked respondents how much they were willing to pay on their power bills to double the runs of steelhead and salmon in the Columbia River Basin. The government argued that the study provided a conservative and useful estimate of the dollar value of these fish species.

The court rejected the use of the study, concluding that it would be "conjecture and speculation" to determine damages in this case based on the study.[16] The court found that "the study fail[ed] to determine to any degree of certainty what value should be placed on these fish based on their existence value."[17] According to the court, the study looked at the value of doubling the number of steelhead in a large area (the entire Columbia River Basin), rather than at the value of losing a much smaller number of steelhead in a small part of the same area. Like the *Montrose* case, this decision indicates that it will be difficult, if not impossible, to develop a stated preference survey that accurately matches the type, location, and size of the injuries that trustees will ultimately seek to prove at trial.

---

[15] No. 88-1279, 1991 U.S. Dist. LEXIS 1869 (D. Idaho Jan. 24, 1991).
[16] Id. at *55.
[17] Id. at *56.

American Trader spill litigation

People v. *Attransco, Inc.*, the NRD case related to the American Trader oil spill, proceeded to trial under California law (not CERCLA or OPA) in California state court. Surveys of actual consumer behavior were relied on heavily at trial, but CV surveys were not relied upon as affirmative evidence by either the plaintiffs or the defendants. The defendants did rely on a CV survey in rebutting the plaintiffs' estimate that each lost beach trip should be valued at $13.19. In arguing that the plaintiffs' estimates were too high, the defendants relied upon a different survey that posed the following question: "Suppose the agency that manages this site started charging a *daily* admission fee of $X *per person*. The money from the admission fee will be used to maintain the site in the present condition, but there will be *no* improvements. Would you continue to use this site?"[18] The daily admission fee for each survey participant was one of ten randomly assigned amounts between $1 and $75. Most of those who responded said "no."

The jury was not persuaded by the CV survey. It assigned a daily beach trip value of $13.19, a number based on the plaintiffs' estimate, without any effort to rely on the CV survey results. While we have no information about the reasons behind the jury's decision, it shows that juries, as well as judges, may question the validity of CV and other similar stated preference survey values and may prefer to use other methods to calculate damage to natural resources.

CONTINGENT VALUATION METHODS HAVE ALSO NOT BEEN RELIED UPON IN NON-NRD CONTEXTS

Similar to the NRD cases described above, CV methods have a poor record in other contexts as well. In the false advertising arena, for example, plaintiffs have tried to use CV methods to support alleged false advertising of the health benefits of "light" branded cigarettes. One such case is instructive. In *Price* v. *Philip Morris, Inc.*, CV was used as the basis for the largest jury award in Illinois history, and, on appeal, the Illinois Supreme Court considered whether the jury's reliance on the CV was proper.[19] A majority

---

[18] Heyes, A. (2001), *The Law and Economics of the Environment*, Cheltenham, UK and Northampton, MA, USA: Edward Elgar Publishing, p. 340; original emphasis.

[19] 848 N.E. 2d 1 (Ill. 2005), cert. denied, 549 U.S. 1054 (2006). The plaintiffs' expert used the results of an Internet survey conducted by Knowledge Networks to calculate damages based on the CV method. The respondents were asked to assume that Marlboro Lights were more hazardous than full-flavor cigarettes and to imagine the existence of a Marlboro Light that was identical in all other respects to the current product, except that it was truly safer to smoke. The respondents were then asked to state how much of a discount would be required to cause them to purchase the more hazardous product if the safer version were actually

of the Illinois Supreme Court voted to vacate the jury verdict and dismiss the plaintiffs' claims for reasons unrelated to CV.[20] However, a concurring opinion discussed the reliability of the CV in detail and found several problems. For example, according to the concurring opinion, the survey did not look at actual customer behavior in the marketplace and "did not measure or purport to measure how consumers would actually behave if, as is really the case, there is no truly healthier version."[21]

Another arena in which plaintiffs have attempted to use CV to value their damages has been in cases involving the diminution of real property values. One such case was in the Western District of Louisiana arising from an oil spill in the Calcasieu Ship Channel in June 2006.[22] There, Dr. Robert Simons conducted a CV survey to assess the drop in property values following a hypothetical oil spill to determine damages from the Calcasieu Ship Channel spill to property owners. In its motion to exclude Dr. Simons' testimony, the defendant Citgo criticized Dr. Simons for ignoring actual market data that showed no drop in property values. While the court allowed Dr. Simons to testify at trial, the jury returned a verdict in favor of Citgo.

A final example comes from Dr. Jerry Hausman's article "Contingent valuation: From dubious to hopeless,"[23] in which he reports on a CV survey utilized by plaintiffs in a copyright infringement case brought in the Australian Copyright Tribunal. In 2001, a change in Australian law defined retransmission of television programs as an infringement of copyright, requiring the cable TV companies to pay "equitable remuneration" to the copyright owners. The case was brought to determine the definition of "equitable remuneration," and the copyright owners' primary evidence was a CV study involving two parts.

The defendant cable TV companies, with the assistance of Dr. Hausman

---

available. Based on the answers to this question, the plaintiffs' expert calculated that class members, on average, would demand a 92.3% discount from the market price if they were to continue to purchase Marlboro Lights. Applying this discount to all purchases of Marlboro and Cambridge Lights during the relevant class periods, and calculating prejudgment interest at 5%, non-compounded, the plaintiffs' expert concluded that the 1.14 million members of the class had suffered $7.1005 billion in economic damages. Id. at 29.

[20] Id. at 50–51.

[21] Id. at 59.

[22] See Citgo Petroleum Corporation's Motion to Exclude Opinion Testimony of Plaintiffs' Expert Robert Simons, *Naquin* v. *Citgo Petroleum Corp.*, No. 2:09-cv-543, 2009 WL 2417500 (W.D. La. June 6, 2009) and Opposition to Defendant's Motion to Exclude Testimony of Robert Simons, *Naquin*, No. 2:09-cv-543, 2009 WL 2417506 (W.D. La. June 15, 2009) and *Naquin*'s sister cases, *Dartez* v. *Citgo Petroleum Corp.*, No. 2:09-cv-525, and *Boullion* v. *Citgo Petroleum Corp.*, No. 2:09-cv-518.

[23] Hausman, J. (2012), "Contingent valuation: From dubious to hopeless," *Journal of Economic Perspectives*, **26**(4), 43.

and others, brought various challenges to the study, including that preferences in the study appeared to be irrationally unstable and that the willingness to pay for the bundle of goods did not add up to the sum of the willingness to pay for the component part of the bundle. These challenges proved effective, and the Tribunal explicitly disregarded the results of the CV survey, stating that "[c]ourts and tribunals must proceed on the basis of probative evidence, not speculation... We have such a level of doubt about the Survey that we attach no weight to it."[24]

CONTINGENT VALUATION METHODS ARE HIGHLY DISFAVORED BY THE NRD REGULATIONS

Both the OPA and CERCLA regulations strongly favor use of the restoration-based approach to valuation of all NRD. The OPA regulations, for example, plainly require that the governmental trustees may proceed with an economic valuation approach (such as CV) only after a restoration approach has *twice* been determined to be inappropriate.

Under the OPA regulations, trustees are required to first consider a resource-to-resource approach or a service-to-service approach that will provide natural resources and/or services equal in quantity to those lost. Only if they make an affirmative determination that this approach is inappropriate – presumably because an equal quantity of resources or services is not available and cannot be developed – can the trustees consider compensating the loss through a scaling approach.[25] Under a scaling approach, the trustees must measure the value of the loss, and identify the amount of replacement resources needed to provide the same value to the public. Damages are still measured by the cost of providing the public with the correct amount of resources and services.[26] Finally, only if the trustees also find that work to value replacement resources and/or services cannot be performed in a reasonable time frame or at a reasonable cost (a second affirmative determination), can the trustees turn to a non-restoration approach such as contingent valuation.[27]

In short, a trustee assessing damages under OPA can estimate the total

---

[24] Id. at 53.
[25] 15 C.F.R. § 990.53(d)(3)(i) ("Where trustees have determined that neither resource-to-resource nor service-to-service scaling is appropriate, trustees may use the valuation scaling approach").
[26] Id. ("Under the valuation scaling approach, trustees determine the amount of natural resources and/or services that must be provided to produce the same value lost to the public").
[27] 15 C.F.R. §990.53(d)(3)(ii) ("If, in the judgment of the trustees, valuation of the lost services is practicable, but valuation of the replacement natural resources and/or services cannot be performed within a reasonable time frame or at a reasonable cost, as determined

value of an injured animal or an injured acre of habitat, and use that as the measure of damages *only if* the trustee finds that those resources cannot be restored or replaced with similar substitutes, *and* an alternative restoration scaling approach would be inefficient. The trustees must make each of these affirmative determinations before they can even commission a stated preference survey to measure non-use damages.[28] If these two determinations have not been made, the NRD defendants will have a strong legal basis to reject not only the use of such studies in assessing damages but also claims to reimburse the trustees for the cost of implementing the studies as part of the reasonable costs of a damages assessment.[29]

The approach to valuation in the CERCLA regulations has a more complex history. The initial regulations have seen various court challenges and amendments since they were first promulgated by the Department of the Interior (DOI) in 1986. In all versions of these rules, economic valuation techniques like CV and TVE are only available to measure interim losses, that is, those losses occurring during the time it takes to restore the resources and/or services lost to baseline (sometimes called "compensatory damages"). Unlike the OPA rules, however, some prior versions of the CERCLA rules arguably required trustees to ascertain a dollar value of interim loss damages through the use of economic tools.[30]

Following the promulgation of the OPA rules in 1996, the lack of a focus on restoration-based approaches to valuation of interim losses under CERCLA emerged as a concern within the NRD community, and in December 2005, DOI convened a federal advisory committee, comprised of a diverse group of interested stakeholders, to consider the

by §990.27(a)(2) of this part, trustees may estimate the dollar value of the lost services and select the scale of the restoration action that has a cost equivalent to the lost value").

[28] These regulatory obstacles to the trustees' reliance on stated-preference methods may also apply to NRD categories beyond "non-use" including recreational losses.

[29] See, for example, Letter from Brian D. Israel to Craig O'Connor, dated February 8, 2012 ("Only after determining that such scaling methods are inappropriate may the Trustees turn to valuation methods. To our knowledge, the Trustees have not made any of the determinations necessary to justify their current assessment proposal. Accordingly, the regulatory conditions precedent have not been satisfied, and the Trustees are not properly following their own legal framework").

[30] Note also that there is some case law regarding prior versions of the CERCLA rules that treats economic valuation of interim damages and compensation of non-use values favorably. In *Ohio*, 880 F.2d 432, which was a challenge to the rules promulgated in 1986 and amended in 1988, the court upheld DOI's inclusion of CV as a method that could be used to estimate use and non-use values. It also struck down DOI's rule that option and existence values be estimated in lieu of use values only when use values cannot be determined, finding instead that "[o]ption and existence values may represent 'passive' use, but they nonetheless reflect utility derived by humans from a resource, and thus, *prima facie*, ought to be included in a damage assessment." Id. at 464 (citing Cross, F.B., 1989, "Natural resource damage valuation," *Vanderbilt Law Review*, **42**(269), 285–9).

issue. A key recommendation of this advisory committee was that DOI should seek to conform the CERCLA regulations with the OPA regulations and undertake, without delay, a targeted revision to emphasize restoration over monetary damages. DOI undertook to implement this recommendation and in 2008 promulgated amendments to the rules. The new regulations, which are the version currently in effect, provide the option for a restoration-based approach to all damages, including use and non-use interim losses. The Federal Register notice issued by DOI in connection with the revisions expresses a clear preference for this approach: "Methodologies that compare losses arising from resource injury to gains expected from restoration actions are frequently simpler and more transparent than methodologies used to measure the economic value of losses."[31]

THE TRUSTEES THEMSELVES PREFER TO AVOID CONTINGENT VALUATION METHODS

While economists and others have debated the validity and reliability of survey valuation methods, the government itself rarely relies upon such studies in NRD cases. To our knowledge, NOAA, for example, has never used survey methods to measure non-use damages under OPA.

Perhaps the most instructive example of the government's reluctance to rely on CV methods involved the *Deepwater Horizon* oil spill that occurred in the Gulf of Mexico in 2010. Injury from that incident was eventually assessed in a document called the *Deepwater Horizon Oil Spill: Final Programmatic Damage Assessment and Restoration Plan and Final Programmatic Environmental Impact Statement* ("Deepwater PDARP"), prepared on behalf of multiple federal agencies as well as agencies of the states of Texas, Louisiana, Mississippi, Alabama, and Florida (the "*Deepwater Horizon* Trustees").[32] Initially, the *Deepwater Horizon* Trustees had commissioned multiple in-depth surveys designed to estimate the lost use and non-use values resulting from the spill. BP Exploration & Production Inc. ("BP"), one of the responsible parties for the incident, challenged the Trustees' decision to undertake these studies and, despite agreeing to perform a cooperative assessment and fund much of the *Deepwater Horizon* Trustees' investigation, refused to fund the non-use

---

[31] Natural Resource Damages for Hazardous Substances, 73 Fed. Reg. 57, 259 (Oct. 2, 2008) (to be codified at 43 C.F.R. pt. 11), accessed December 10, 2016 at https://www.gpo.gov/fdsys/pkg/FR-2008-10-02/html/E8-23225.htm.
[32] Accessed December 10, 2016 at http://www.gulfspillrestoration.noaa.gov/restoration-planning/gulf-plan/.

surveys before the Trustees had made a formal determination, as required by the OPA regulations, that in-kind restoration or scaled restoration was inappropriate.[33] Ultimately, the damage assessment set forth in the *Deepwater Horizon* PDARP relied on none of the stated preference surveys regarding the dollar value of injured habitat and wildlife. Instead, the Trustees used a restoration approach, setting forth a comprehensive restoration plan for both use and non-use alleged damages.

During the public comment period after the release of the Draft *Deepwater Horizon* PDARP, multiple commenters asserted that the PDARP was incomplete because it failed to value ecosystem services through CV surveys. The Trustees responded by stating that:

> The commenter is correct that the Trustees did not use a CV approach to value ecosystem services here, but the commenter's proposed approach is not required by law or regulations. In fact, *the Oil Pollution Act regulations contain a clear preference for basing the amount of natural resource damages sought from the responsible parties on the costs of implementing a restoration plan* that would repair or replace injured natural resources where practicable and compensate the public for interim losses of natural resource and ecosystem services until the ecosystem has fully recovered. That is the primary approach to damage assessment that the Trustees adopted in response to the *Deepwater Horizon* spill and the basis for the preparation of this PDARP/PEIS... The Trustees performed a CV total value study for the *Deepwater Horizon* incident. However, because the Trustees concluded that natural resource injuries and ecosystem service losses in this case can be addressed by the preferred ecosystem-wide restoration alternative described in the Final PDARP/PEIS, the Trustees did not complete that study and did not rely on it.[34]

The fact that CV surveys were considered and rejected for the *Deepwater Horizon* incident is particularly significant in light of the diverse and sensitive resources that the Trustees asserted had been injured. According to the Trustees, the incident was "the largest offshore oil spill in the history of the United States," which "injured natural resources as diverse as deep-sea coral, fish and shellfish, productive wetland habitats, sandy beaches, birds, endangered sea turtles, and protected marine life."[35] The Trustees also concluded that "[t]he oil spill prevented people from fishing, going to

---

[33] See document in Footnote 32.

[34] *Deepwater Horizon* Trustees (2016), "8. Trustee responses to public comments on the draft PDARP/PEIS," *Deepwater PDARP*, pp. 8–21 to 8–22, accessed December 10, 2016 at http://www.gulfspillrestoration.noaa.gov/wp-content/uploads/Chapter-8_Trustee-Responses-to-Public-Comments_508.pdf [emphasis added].

[35] *Deepwater Horizon* Trustees (2016), "1: Introduction and Executive Summary," *Deepwater PDARP*, pp. 1–3, accessed December 10, 2016 at http://www.gulfspillrestoration.noaa.gov/wp-content/uploads/Front-Matter-and-Chapter-1_Introduction-and-Executive-Summary_508.pdf.

the beach, and enjoying their typical recreational activities along the Gulf of Mexico."[36] Given that a restoration-based approach can effectively be applied to this varied range of injuries, including resources as unique as endangered and protected species, and resources as difficult to restore as deep-sea coral, it is difficult to identify any scenario where a CV approach would be appropriate.

TRUSTEES SHOULD ABANDON CONTINGENT VALUATION AND SIMILAR METHODS AS A MATTER OF POLICY

As we have demonstrated above, there are enormous – possibly insurmountable – legal obstacles to the use of survey valuation methods for measuring non-use damages in environmental litigation. These methods are highly disfavored by the relevant regulatory structures. These methods have been rejected or disregarded by the courts. And, since the *Montrose* decision nearly two decades ago, these methods are generally shunned by the very government trustees responsible for implementing the NRD program in our country.

Despite this legal landscape, and despite the extensive econometric hurdles presented in this book, some economists continue to advocate for the use of CV as a viable method for capturing non-use value.

There are at least two additional policy reasons why trustee agencies should abandon CV methods and focus instead on capturing non-use values through restoration. First, CV methods are extraordinarily expensive. The CV studies conducted in *Montrose*, *Exxon Valdez* and *Deepwater Horizon* cost tens of millions of dollars. Given that in no case have these studies actually worked, it is hard to justify the cost.[37] In *Deepwater Horizon* – perhaps the most complicated, wide-ranging NRD assessment ever undertaken – the trustees spent millions of dollars on a CV study and, in the end, concluded it was not necessary or appropriate to rely upon that study. If a restoration-based assessment approach is viable in the case of alleged impacts across the entire northern Gulf of Mexico, it is hard to imagine any plausible scenario where a restoration-based approach would be inappropriate.

---

[36] Id.
[37] Indeed, under the CERCLA regulations, NRD assessment costs are not considered reasonable, and thus are not recoverable, if "the anticipated increment of extra benefits in terms of the precision or accuracy of estimates obtained by using a more costly...methodology are greater than the anticipated increment of extra costs of that methodology," 43 CFR §11.14.

Finally, CV and other survey methods rest upon a flawed premise. The governmental agencies charged with assessing and restoring damages (i.e., natural resource trustees) have extensive information about the real cost of protecting and restoring natural resources, gained through their work on other NRD cases and their work to manage natural resources in national and state parks, forests, seashores, fisheries, and other public lands and waters. Agencies rely on that information and their experience to identify the actual cost of work to protect, restore, and expand these resources on a daily basis. But when they instead rely on the results of stated preference surveys in assessing damages, the trustees willingly step aside and instead rely upon a randomly selected sample of the public to assign a dollar value to these resources.

The supposed rationale for relying upon a public survey is that the public has suffered a loss and, as such, only the public can measure the value of that loss. But that rationale does not apply in other environmental contexts. For comparison, in the case of environmental risk from industrial activities, no one would ever think to use a survey of randomly selected members of the public to determine the levels of contaminants that present a risk to human health and the environment. Instead, we routinely rely upon scientists, economists, and other experts to make those judgments based on data and analysis. Likewise, with the valuation of damages resulting from a pollution event, the better approach for measuring such damages is for experts (not a group of randomly selected members of the public) to determine how much restoration is required to return natural resources to baseline conditions and to compensate for the interim losses. Fortunately, the NRD jurisprudence, regulations, and precedent all point to exactly that outcome.

Index

ABERS
  approach 196
  estimate for lower bound 200, 204, 206–7, 218
  non-parametric estimator 74
adding-up test
  adaptation for 70–73
  "adding-up condition"
    applying only to goods obtained incrementally 60
    consumer preferences not adhering to 67–8
    definition 59
    description 61–3
    deviations from 68
    findings 61, 78
    implementation of 59
    in previous studies 60
    testing 60–61
  and adequate response to differences in scope 59, 66, 78
  applied to restoration program for river system and lake 60–61, 69–75
  elicitation method 63, 67–8, 78
  explanation 61–3
  findings 61, 78
  income effects 64–5, 75–7
  incremental parts
    for accelerated restoration 71
    and cognitive burden 64
    findings 61, 78
    lack of studies on 59–60
    meaning 59
    in original study's design 70
    past studies review 66–8
    use to test adding-up condition 60–61
  limitations of scope tests 58–9
  original study 68–70
  potential difficulties in implementing
    cognitive burden 64
    cost 66
    income effects 64–5
    provision mechanism 65
  for reliability of CV 88–90
  results 73–5
  study discussion and conclusions 78
  and truthfulness 60–61, 69, 78
adequate
  sensitivity to scope 129–37, 140
  use of term 88, 140
algae 60, 69, 100, 117, 257, 259
alum 60, 69–70, 72, 74, 100, 117
American Trader spill litigation 299
anchoring
  biases 178
  cost 2, 5, 10, 84
  effects 2, 5, 84, 114, 160, 163, 215, 277
  as issue surrounding CV 30, 36
  in red knot study 55–6
  response distortions in 165

behavior
  choice 14, 176–9, 237–8
  deterministic heuristic rule predicting 239–40
  ideal, for validity of WTP estimates 224–5
  irrational 48
  market 153–4, 156–7
  protest 232
  purchase 172, 277
  randomizer 234
  surveys of consumer, in court cases 299–300
  use of conjoint methods for predicting 162, 168–70, 173, 176
  of utility maximizing 231, 255
behavioral anomalies 36, 112, 154
behavioral economics 155, 157, 159

behavioral response
  to high bids 17–18, 36
  questions to explore 34–5
  true 23
behavioral theories 78, 154–5, 157, 159, 252
belief in bid values 32–5
bias ratio (BR) 271–4, 277–85
bids
  "composite good" approach
    bid levels
      cognition difficulties with part-whole relationships 214–15
      comparison between composite good and V1 COS 207
      non-monotonicity 200
      propensity to shift votes 204–6
  marine species preservation case 3
  percentage of respondents voting for alum treatments 73–4
  red knot studies
    belief in bid values 32–5
    bid amount
      non-parametric estimates by 27, 32, 35
      percentage of respondents who believed they would pay more or pay less than offered 34
      percentage of yes responses at highest 19–21
      percentage of yes responses by 27
      yes response irrespective of 30
      yes responses v. responses adjusted for "believed" 33
      yes responses v. responses adjusted for certainty 31
    bid design 22, 24–5
    bid levels
      highest 17–23, 25, 28–36
      low-end 22–3, 30
      share of "yes" votes 50, 52
    bid range 18
    non-monotonicity 26
    truncated 17–18, 23, 25, 27–9, 36
    willingness to pay estimates 28–30, 36
    and yes-response function 26–7

single-focus approach bid levels 194–6
  and WTP for meal vouchers 67–8
"bounded substitution" 84–5, 88–9, 131
brain activity 178–9
budget awareness
  adoption in survey 192
  in CVM studies 188
  findings 219
  three related enhancements 193
  "wording additions" intended to enhance 216–19
budget constraint
  affecting responses to valuation questions 189
  findings 219
  in single-focus valuation method 190
  in WTP survey methods 189

California Environmental Improvement Program 193–4, 199–202, 205–8, 213, 215
California oil spill (COS) study *see* "composite good" approach
Carson, R.T. 17, 19, 58, 60–61, 69, 78, 85–8, 91–8, 100, 112–14, 117, 123, 132, 135, 140, 155, 159, 179, 192, 196, 209, 252–3, 255, 257, 271
CBC *see* choice-based conjoint (CBC)
census weights 54–5
certainty
  adjustment 31–2
  correction 138–40, 273–6, 279–81, 283–5
  elimination of uncertainty 54–5
  levels 30–31
  questions 30–31
  of response 255–6, 262, 266
  weights 54–5
cervical screening study 3–4
"cheap talk"
  in "composite good" approach 193, 215–16, 218–20
  in hypothetical bias study 272, 274, 277, 279–81
  in marine species preservation study 6, 228
  in scope studies 137–8

Index

choice-based conjoint (CBC)
  behavioral effects 154
  comparison to CVM 154, 160
  elicitations directly mimicking market choice tasks 158
  example of typical menu 158
  as leading SP method 153
  lessons for 179–80
  method and applicability 160–62
  study design
    data analysis 176–7
    experimental design 166–8
    failures 177–9
    important issues 162–5
    incentive alignment 170–71
    making menus realistic 173–6
    reconciliation and validation 171–3
    sampling and recruitment 165–6
    subject training 168–70
  as variable in hypothetical bias study 278, 280–81, 283, 285
choice experiment (CE)
  choice
    based on absolute costs 5, 11, 14
    based on relative costs 5, 11, 14
    behavior 14
    corner 10–11
    in higher cost scale 8–11, 14
    in lower cost scale 8–11
    pattern for do-something 2, 5, 8, 10
    pattern for status quo 8, 10–11, 14
    proportions 4–5
    tasks, performing 2
  choice questions
    answering 6
    sample 7, 229
  components 1
  definition 82
  fat tails equivalent for 36
  in hypothetical bias study 272, 278
  implications for choice behavior 14
  method 1–2
  NOAA sponsored online study 202, 216
  popular use of 1
  in previous scope test studies 105–6
  see also choice-based conjoint (CBC); dichotomous choice surveys

choke price 18, 28
cognition difficulties
  with part-whole relationships 214–16
  sizeable proportion in responses 209–13
cognitive burden 64, 258
"composite good" approach
  "cheap talk" 193, 215–16, 218–20
  composite good version
    priority allocations for components 201–4
    standalone COS
      reactions to scenario 204–5
      values for program 205–6
    valuing Version 2 199–200
  context and rationale
    foci 188–9
    and single-focus approach 189–91
    study design 192–4
  not-for votes 196–7, 200, 206–8, 214, 218, 220
  and single-focus approach 189–91, 199, 205, 208–9, 211, 213–15
  single-good version
    1995 test-bed study
      comparisons 196–8
      similarities and differences 194–6
  study findings
    budget exercise and COS 213–14
    cognition difficulties
      with part-whole relationships 214–16
      sizeable proportion in responses 209–13
    lack of sensitivity to huge scope difference 206–8
    plausible rationalization 219–21
    within-questionnaire "wording additions" 216–19
  single-good v. composite good WTP estimates 208–9
Comprehensive Environmental Response, Compensation, and Liability Act (CERCLA) 293–4, 296, 299, 301–3, 305
consequentiality 18, 23, 35–6, 189, 191, 219
consumer choice behavior 14, 176–9, 237–8

consumer utility theory 83–4, 140, 157, 177
consumer well-being 154, 156, 160, 168, 177–8, 180
contingent valuation (CV)
   concepts examined
      difficulty answering questions *xiii–xv*
      inadequate response to cost *x–xi*
      inadequate response to number of payments *xii*
      inadequate response to scope *xii–xiii, xvii*
      legal issues *xvi*
      restoration programs *xvi–xvii*
      restricted samples *xv*
   consequentiality as important issue in 35–6
   definition 58
   estimates of WTP for non-use environmental goods *see* scope tests
   hypothetical bias presence in 29–30, 36
   prominent concern about 58
   reliability
      adding-up test 88–90
      examination of criteria 86–8
      gradient 154, 179
      as ignored issue 91
      question of x, 58
      recognizing unreliability *xvii*
      survey problems 300
   use of term x
   use values 82–3
   "warm glow" that can arise in 68
   see also "composite good" approach; referendum-style CV
contingent valuation method (CVM)
   applicability 153
   assumptions of 191
   comparison to CBC 154, 160
   in "composite good" approach 188–9
   as controversial in economics community 160
   criteria of reliability of 86–7
   development of 159–60
   hypothetical bias observed with 220

   incentive compatibility as issue for 171
   as leading SP method 153
   legal obstacles
      approaches to estimating non-use value for NRD 295
      as highly disfavoured by NRD regulations 301–3
      for non-use damages 292–3
      as not relied on in non-NRD contexts 299–301
      as not relied upon in NRD cases 296–9
      trustees abandoning as matter of policy 305–6
      trustees avoiding 303–5
   as mimicking direct democracy by referendum 170
   possible reasons for lack of development 154–5
   and "protest no" votes 212
   recreational use value of birdwatching 179–80
   as sensitive to context and survey design considerations 199
   tendency to pass scope tests 112–13, 128
   typical referendum elicitations 159
   valuation of lost use 162, 179
   value of experience of SP methods 154
   as widely used to value environmental goods and services 1
COS (California oil spill) *see* "composite good" approach
cost
   adding up v. scope test 66, 90
   anchoring 2, 5, 10, 84
   annual v. one-time payments *xii*, 43–56
   application to endangered shorebird species *xi*, 17–36
   in CBC studies 167, 177
   in choice experiments 1–2
   household 24–5, 30, 32, 212, 216–17
   in logit model of yes/no vote 76–7
   in SP valuation of environmental goods *x–xi*, 1–14

cost-benefit trade offs *see* trade-offs
cost prompts *see* bids
cost scales
    effect of quadrupling costs on mean WTP estimates 8–11, 13–14, 108, 207
    effect on consumer goods 14
    effect on estimated WTPs 108–12
    effect on use and non-use amenities 5, 14
    effects on "T&E" species status 11, 14, 207
    estimation results for conditional logit model by 12
    in four survey versions 6, 8–11
    frequency of choosing improvement option by 9
    as having strong positive correlation with WTP 108
    impact on utility function 11, 14
    influence on WTP 2–5
    and scope effects 109–12
    status quo and corner choices by 10–11, 14
    summary of studies 4
cumulative distribution function (CDF) 30
CV *see* contingent valuation (CV)
CVM see contingent valuation method (CVM)

DDT and PCBs case 296–8, 305
debriefing questions *see* follow-up questions
Deepwater Horizon oil spill *xvii*, 121, 303–5
Desvousges, W., Mathews, K. and Train, K. (DMT) 17, 19, 22, 58, 69, 87, 90–92, 98–104, 112–13, 117, 126, 140
dichotomous choice surveys 2, 21–3, 82, 124, 126, 137, 192, 218, 271
disbelief of cost, elimination 54–5
DMT *see* Desvousges, W., Mathews, K. and Train, K. (DMT)

economic valuation approach 294–5
emotional intensity scales 85
endangered shorebird *see* red knot studies

Endangered Species Act (ESA) 5–7, 13, 228–9
environmental litigation *see* legal issues
Exxon Valdez oil spill 86, 305

familiarity 162–3, 168–9, 279
fat tails
    and consequentiality 35–6
    extent in response data 18
    in follow-up question responses 35
    as manifestation of hypothetical bias 29–30, 36
    as manifestation of yea-saying 30, 36
    for non-parametric estimators 17, 27
    for parametric estimators 17
    paths for future research 36
    phenomenon *xi*, 17
    sensitivity of WTP to response data with 23, 36
    truncating high-end bids in response to 36
follow-up questions
    to assess validity of SP data
        earliest examples 253
    in fourth section of survey 258
    invalid responses 267
    lack of consistency in use of 253
    literature review 255–7
    method and results 259–66
    as used to identify problem responses 254
    in hypothetical bias study 276
    and identification of protestors 227, 232, 243
    as inducing "bargaining" mind-set 162
    in red knot study 34–6
    yea-saying as result of 124–5

GfK Custom Research 25, 194
Groves, T. 60–61, 69, 78, 171, 252

Hanemann, W.M. 58, 65, 101, 112, 118, 123, 126, 133, 136, 162
Hicksian welfare measures 252
hypothetical bias
    adjusting for 30–32
    effect of "wording additions" 189
    fat tails as manifestation of 29–30, 36

meta-analysis
  current v. prior studies on 270
  data
    bias ratio 271–4
    certainty correction 273–6
    cheap talk 277
    conjoint/choice experiment 278
    familiar good 279
    lab experiment 278
    non-use 279
    private good/public good 278–9
    same respondents v. different respondents 277
    student 278
  regression analysis
    base model 279–81
    fixed effects regression 284–6
    functional form 281–2
    time trend 282–4
  study conclusions 286
  method of detecting 29
  observed with CVM surveys 220

Idaho v. Southern Refrigerated Transport Inc. 298
"inadequate", use of term 88
incentive alignment 170–71, 175–6, 179
incentive compatibility 163–4, 170–71
income effects 64–5, 75–7

Kahneman, D. 44–5, 86–7, 92–4, 101–2, 119, 154, 157, 160, 178, 191
Knetsch, J.L. 44–5, 86–7, 93, 102, 119, 191
Knowledge Networks 6–7, 25–6, 194, 228–9, 299

lab experiment variable 273–4, 278–85
latent class models 226–7, 230–34
legal issues
  approaches to estimating non-use value for NRD
    contingent valuation methods 295
    restoration-based approach 294–5
  contingent valuation methods
    approach to estimating non-use value for NRD 295
    as highly disfavoured by NRD regulations 301–3

  for non-use damages 292–3
  as not relied upon in non-NRD contexts 299–301
  as not relied upon in NRD cases 296–9
  trustees abandoning as matter of policy 305–6
  trustees avoiding 303–5
court cases
  American Trader spill litigation 299
  Idaho v. Southern Refrigerated Transport Inc. 298
  People v. Attransco, Inc., 299
  Price v. Philip Morris, Inc 299–300
  United States v. Montrose 296–8
NRD regulatory framework and basis for non-use damages 293–4
logit
  model
    binary 266
    estimates for low-cost and high-cost data samples 11–13
    mixed form
      v. model with heuristics 235–7, 244–9
      multinomial 176–7, 226
      of trade-off respondents 238, 240–45
      traditional 225–6, 231, 242–6, 248
    of yes/no vote 76
  parametric estimator 17
  of random utility model 1–2
  regression 264–6
Loureiro, M.L. 98, 105–9, 112
Louviere, J. 6, 157–8, 164, 172, 252–3, 257

mandatory payment
  mechanism 191
  survey mode 138
marginal utility
  diminishing 60, 62, 83–5, 88–9, 112, 129–31
  of income 231
  levels for species improvement 231

marine species preservation case
  inferences from stated preference surveys 225–49
  response to cost prompts *xi*, 5–14
Mathews, K. *see* Desvousges, W., Mathews, K. and Train, K. (DMT)
menus *see* choice-based conjoint (CBC)
migratory bird studies *see* red knot studies
minced pork study 3–4, 14
Mitchell, R.C. 85–6, 94, 117, 155, 252

natural resource damage (NRD)
  ability of survey methods to measure non-use values in 292
  approaches to estimating non-use value for
    contingent valuation methods 295
    restoration-based approach 294–5
  assessment (NRDA) 253, 305
  better approach for valuation of 306
  contingent valuation methods as disfavoured by regulations of 301–3
  court decisions associated with 296–9
  Deepwater Horizon oil spill *xvii*, 303–5
  regulatory framework and basis for non-use damages 293–4
"no purchase" option 163, 176
NOAA (National Oceanic and Atmospheric Administration)
  adding up test addressing concerns of 59, 63, 78
  clarification of term "inadequate" 88
  commissioning study of NRD 296
  concern over scope 129, 140
  conclusion on respondents' WTP 114
  and consequentiality 189
  marine species survey
    application of 225–7
    data 5–11, 228–9, 243
    mixed logit analysis of 248
    model 230–4, 237
  purpose of 58, 86
  recommendation of referendum format question 195
  recommendation of "Yes/No" follow-up questions 253
  reliability of CV 86–8, 91, 140
  scope studies 91
non-parametric estimators
  in red knot study
    estimates by bid amount 27
    adjusted for believed bid 35
    adjusted for hypothetical bias 32
    estimates of WTP 28–9
    WTP and truncation of bids 23, 36
  relation to fat tails 17
  in river and lake quality study 73–5
non-use amenities 3, 5, 14, 83, 107, 141
  see also scope tests: and CV estimates of WTP for non-use environmental goods
non-use damages
  in court case 298
  NRD regulatory framework and basis for 293–4
  role of trustees 302
  survey valuation methods
    legal obstacles to use 305
    non-use by trustees 303–4
non-use, in hypothetical bias study
  considerations 270, 273, 275, 279–80
  variable 279–81, 283–5
non-use values
  approaches to estimating for NRD
    CV methods 82–3, 253, 292, 295, 302, 305
    restoration-based approach 294–5, 303–4
  as at bad end of reliability gradient 154
  and brain activity 179–80
  in California 192–3
  compensation for 294
  in court cases 296, 303–4
  CV and CE as designed to infer WTP for 108
  CVM eliciting from consumers 154–5
  effects of training and context 170
  greatest need for SP data in application to environmental 180

lack of data to support WTP
    estimates 252
lack of success stories 180
relation to market benchmarks 162
SP discrete choice experiment for
    estimating 1
SP methods applicable to 180
NRD *see* natural resource damage
    (NRD)

Oil Pollution Act (OPA) 192, 293–4,
    296, 299, 301–4
Ojea, E. 98, 105–9, 112
one-time tax 24, 199, 216–17
ordering problem *xiv*, 164

parametric estimators 17, 22–3, 43–4,
    46, 53, 55, 126–7
payments, frequency of, inadequate
    response to
  analysis 50–55
  annual payments
    comparison of split samples 52
    implicit discount rates 44–9
    lower-bound estimates 53
    probit estimates 54
    referendum question 50–51
    relation to WTP 55–6
    sensitivity results 55
    share of "yes" vote by bid amount
      52
    in split-sample survey 43–4, 50
    version B of survey instrument 50
  literature review 44–9
  one-time payments
    comparison of split samples 52
    implicit discount rates 44–9
    lower-bound estimates 53
    probit estimates 54
    referendum question 50–51
    relation to WTP 55–6
    sensitivity results 55
    share of "yes" vote by bid amount
      52
    in split-sample survey 43–4, 50
    version A of survey instrument 50
  purpose and method 43–4
  relation to WTP 55–6
  study conclusions 55–6
  survey 49–50

People v. *Attransco, Inc.*, 299
power outages study 3–4
present value willingness to pay (PV
    WTP)
  analysis 50–55
  conclusion 55
  literature review 44–9
  survey 49–50
Price v. *Philip Morris, Inc* 299–300
private good/public good variable
    273–4, 278–81, 283–5
probit
  estimates 54
  model of yes/no vote 53
  multivariate regressions 138–40
  parametric estimator 17, 43
protestors
  common practice of excluding 7, 9,
    124, 225, 240
  definition 7, 9
  and sensitivity of lower-bound mean
    WTP 211–12
  in stated preference assessing validity
    study 253, 255–6, 260
  in stated preference inferences study
    and estimated population share
      239–40
    model with three heuristics to
      identify 225
    in sensitivity analysis 242–5
    status quo only respondents 232
    study conclusion on 249
    use of latent class models to
      identify 227
PV WTP *see* present value willingness
    to pay (PV WTP)

Qualtrics sample 25–6

random utility model (RUM) 1–2, 8
rational choice model (RCM) 252
red knot studies
  fat tails and truncated bids
    purpose and method 17–18
    related literature 19–23
    results
      adjusting for hypothetical bias
        30–32
      belief in bid values 32–4
      follow up questions 34–5

willingness to pay estimates
28–30
yes-response function 26–7
study discussion 35–6
survey 24–6
response to frequency of payments
analysis 50–55
literature review 44–9
purpose and method 43–4
study conclusions 55–6
survey 49–50
referendum-style CV
in hypothetical bias study 271
red knot studies 18–21, 24–5, 43, 50–51, 55–6
in river and lake quality study 69, 76
in single-focus and "composite good" approaches 190, 192–7, 199–206, 208, 210–13, 218, 220
in stated preference methods study 159–60, 163, 170–71
responsible parties (RPs) 303–4
restoration-based approach 294–5, 301–3, 305
restoration programs
and contingent valuation xvi–xvii
oyster reef 44, 46
pros and cons of voting for 258
for river and lake 60–61, 69–75, 78
wetland 254–67
revealed preference (RP) 82–3, 153–4, 156, 172, 178–9, 219
river and lake quality study *see* adding-up test
river health improvements study 3–5

sample allocation 3
scope effects 63, 84, 88, 91, 98, 108, 112–13, 123, 128
scope elasticities 112, 129–37, 141
scope insensitivity
categorical 84
demand for environmental amenity 83
evidence for 126
factors leading to 85–6
as often attributed to diminishing marginal utility and satiation 84–5
quantitative 84

regressions examining factors affecting 139–40
rejection of hypothesis 91, 97
"warm glow" as explanation for 86
for wolves 83
scope tests
and adding-up test study
adding-up test extending 62
cost 66
examining estimated WTP increases 58–9, 63
issue of adequate response 59, 66, 78
non-negative scope effects 63
restoration program
discussion 78
results 73–4
of river and lake 69–70
and CV estimates of WTP for non-use environmental goods
diminishing marginal utility 83–5, 88–9, 112, 129–31
inconsistent statistical significance results 127–9
pass and fail results affected by measureable survey characteristics 137–40
reliability of CVM 86–90
scope effects 84, 88, 91, 98, 108, 112–13, 123, 128
scope elasticities 112, 129–37, 141
scope insensitivity 83–6, 91, 97, 126, 139–40
scope literature
Carson's review 91–7, 112–14
DMT's review 91, 98–104
effect of cost scale on estimated WTPs 108–12
flaws in 107–8, 140–41
frequency of CV studies passing scope test 128–9
Ojea and Loureiro 98, 105–9
review of scope results reported in 113–24
scope sensitivity in 83, 87, 96–8, 107–8, 112, 123, 126
summary of state of 112–13
on use amenities 107

scope sensitivity
  demonstration of adequate 129–37
  in scope literature 83, 87, 96–8, 107–8, 112, 123, 126
  study conclusions 140–41
  use of external 84, 91–104, 112–15, 123–4, 129
  use values 82–3
  variations
    in analytical models and statistical procedures 126–7
    in data included in analysis 124–5
    in survey design 125–6
sensitivity analysis 209–13, 242–8
single-focus approach 189–91, 199, 205, 208–9, 211, 213–15
SP *see* stated preference (SP)
stated preference (SP) evaluation of environmental goods
  assessing validity of data using follow-up questions
    consistency of questions 253
    criteria for 252–3, 266–7
    literature review 255–7
    methods and results
      cumulative assessment of validity of responses 261–4
      descriptive statistics 260–61
      regression analysis 264–6
      three basic components 259–60
    "problematic responses" 253–4
    study design and data 257–9
    study discussion and conclusions 266–7
    survey subject 254
  inferences from surveys when costs and benefits are not compared
    application of methodology to data 225
    estimation 235–8
    heuristic decision rules
      attentive to environmental costs only 233–4
      attentive to environmental improvements only 232–3
      environmental improvements ignoring costs and benefits 234
      randomizers ignoring costs and benefits 234
      status quo only 232
    model
      alternative to benefit-cost trade-offs 231–4
      trade-off respondents 230–31
    related literature 226–7
    results
      estimated population shares of choice rules 238–40
      estimated WTP for species status improvement 240–42
      sensitivity analysis 242–8
      study conclusions 248–9
      survey data 228–9
    WTP estimate
      features determining 224
      ideal behavior for validity 224–5
      for species status improvement 240–42
  methods and applicability
    choice-based conjoint study design 160–79
    history of 155–61
    importance of 153–4
    lessons for 179–80
    possible reasons for lack of development 154–5
  response to cost prompts
    choice experiment method 1–2
    cost scale studies 2–5
    study conclusion 11–14
    survey data 5–11
status quo
  in CBC studies 165, 177–8
  in marine species preservation study 6–11, 14
  in non-use amenities study 3–5
  in stated preference inferences study 224, 227–8, 232, 235–40, 243–9
  in stated preference validity study 258, 264, 266
steelhead fish population damage case 298
student variable 273–4, 278–81, 283–5
subject training 168–70
"subjective well-being" methods 160

threatened and endangered ("T&E") species
  marine
    choice experiment
      effects of cost scales on status 11, 14, 207
      NOAA survey data 5–11
      study conclusions 11–14
    stated preference survey
      estimation 235–8
      model 230–34
      NOAA survey data 228–9
      related literature 226–7
      results 238–48
      study conclusions 248–9
  scope tests 105, 130
total value equivalency method (TVE) 295, 302
trade-offs
  in CBC studies 175, 178
  criterion in assessment of SP 255
  and familiarity 163
  in red knot study 35–6
  in stated preference inferences study
    alternatives to benefit-cost trade-offs
      attentive to environmental costs only 233–4
      attentive to environmental improvements only 232–3
      environmental improvements ignoring costs and benefits 234
      randomizers ignoring costs and benefits 234
      status quo only 232
    estimation 235–8
    need for heuristics 225
    and respondent behavior 224–5
    respondents 230–31
    results 238–49
  between status quo and do-something options 8–11, 14
Train, K. *see* Desvousges, W., Mathews, K. and Train, K. (DMT)
truncated bids
  as common practice 18
  effect on WTP 27–9
  explanation 17
  implications 25
  intentional 23
  as tempting response to fat tails 36
truthfulness 60–61, 69, 78, 161, 163–4, 169, 171, 176, 195
Turnbull, B.W. 17, 43, 50, 53, 109, 196, 219

United States v. Montrose 296–8, 305
use amenities 3, 5, 14, 83, 107
use values
  applications of SP methods to environmental 179
  and brain activity 179
  CBC elicitations of 179–80
  and contingent valuation 82–3
  passive 1, 11, 86, 94, 121
  from SP studies 154
utility function 1–2, 8, 11, 107, 155–6, 158, 233–4, 237

valuation of lost use 162, 179
"vignette analysis" 160
voluntary contributions 124, 191
voting question example 25, 51

"warm glow" concept 60, 68, 83–4, 86–7, 89–90, 115, 125, 131, 208, 216, 220
water quality studies
  annual v. one-time payments 46–7
  cost scale study 3–4
  measuring yes-response rates 19–21, 23
  scope tests
    Carson 91–8
    DMT 98–104
    summary 117–24
  use of debriefing questions 256
wetland restoration project study *see* stated preference (SP) assessing validity study
willingness to accept (WTA) 63, 67, 190
willingness to pay (WTP)
  in adding-up test
    addressing adequate response 59–60
    description 62–3
    findings 61, 78

income effects 64–5, 75–7
   in original study 69
   in previous studies 59–60
   provision mechanism 65
   questionnaire versions 71
   relation to adding-up condition 59–60
   in restoration program 60–61, 69, 71, 74–5
   results 74–5
   review of past studies 66–8
   and willingness to accept (WTA) discrepancy 63
in CBC studies 165
in "composite good" approach
   in aggregate for large basket of alternative public goods 190
   effect if valuation question delayed 199
   effect of propensity to shift votes 204
   embodying budget constraint 189
   estimates
      effect of "wording additions" 216–19
      sensitivity to cognitive difficulties 209–13
      single-focus v. composite good 208–9
   exploration of, using split-sample design 188
   impact of budget exercise 214
   lower-bound mean 196–7, 200, 203–4, 206–7, 210–11, 213, 218
   lowering of statistics 198
   respondents expressing value for first environmental good 215–16
   and scope failure 207
   similarities with average charitable donations 220
   v. single-focus survey 190–91
   statistics for long and short forms 198
and consumer well-being 178–9, 180
hurdles faced by CBC or CVM elicitation of 179
in hypothetical bias study 271, 276–8

marine species preservation case
   impact of fourfold increase in costs 8–11, 13–14, 108, 207
   influence of cost scales on 2–5, 14
modeling consumer utility in "money metric" form 177
for non-use amenities 3, 5, 14
in red knot studies
   adjusting for hypothetical bias 31–2
   belief in bid values 34
   effect of bid truncation on 27–8
   estimates 18, 28–30
   fat tails of yes-response function 24–5, 30
   importance of maximum bid selection 28–9
   lower-bound mean 27–9, 31–2, 35–6, 50–51, 53, 55
   present value (PV WTP) 44–55
   problem of negative estimates 17
   related literature 22–3
   sensitivity
      to frequency of payments 43–4, 49, 55–6
      of mean, to largest bid 36
   results 55
   size of mean bids 29
scope tests
   and CV estimates of WTP for non-use environmental goods 82–141
   effect of cost scale on estimated WTPs 108–12
   and increase in environmental benefits 58–9
   and prominent concern of CV 58
in stated preference inferences study estimates
   features determining 224
   fragility of 242–8
   ideal behavior for validity 224–5
   for maximization of utility 249
   for species status improvement 240–42, 248
   estimation 235–8
   for landscape improvements 227
   and trade-off respondents 231
for use amenities 3, 5, 14

wine scent wheel 174
"wording additions" 216–19

yea-saying 30, 36, 253, 255–6
yes-response function
   adjusting for hypothetical bias 30–31
   fat tails of 17–18, 34–5
   many studies with truncated 18–21, 35
   pinning down tails of 24–5, 35
   results in red knot study 26–7
   WTP captured in high-end tail of 36
yes-response rates
   bid design for 25
   in binary choice models 23
   expectations in valid surveys 30
   at higher bid prices
      effect of high 29
      explanation for high 35
   to highest bid in referendum-style CV studies 18–21
   in non-parametric estimates by bid amount 27
   to question about tax amount 33
   relation to fat tails 17
   share by bid amount 50, 52
   in study of migratory birds 22
   in WTP estimates 28